Developmental Variations in Learning

Applications to Social, Executive Function, Language, and Reading Skills

T0348085

Developmental Variations in Learning

Applications to Social, Executive Function, Language, and Reading Skills

Edited by

Dennis L. Molfese
Victoria J. Molfese
University of Louisville

Psychology Press
Taylor & Francis Group

New York   London

First published by Lawrence Erlbaum Associates, Inc., Publishers
10 Industrial Avenue
Mahwah, New Jersey 07430

Reprinted 2008 by Psychology Press

First issued in paperback 2013

Psychology Press
Taylor & Francis Group
711 Third Avenue
New York, NY 10017

Psychology Press
Taylor & Francis Group
27 Church Road
Hove, East Sussex BN3 2FA

Psychology Press is an imprint of the Taylor & Francis Group, an informa business

Cover design by Kathryn Houghtaling Lacey

Library of Congress Cataloging-in-Publication Data

Developmental variations in learning : applications to social, executive function, language, and reading skills / [edited by] Dennis L. Molfese and Victoria J. Molfese.
      p. cm.
      Includes bibliographical references and index.
ISBN 0-8058-2229-1 (cloth : alk. paper)
ISBN 978-0-415-64906-3 (Paperback)
1. Cognition in children. 2. Individual differences in children.
    3. Child development. I. Molfese, Dennis L. II. Molfese, Victoria J.
BF723.C5 D477 2001
155.4'13—dc21   00-061863
                                                   CIP

Contents

Preface   ix

1   Intelligence and Achievement: Measurement   1
and Prediction of Developmental Variations
Victoria J. Molfese
Tina B. Martin

2   Developmental Trends in Teacher Perceptions of   23
Student Cognitive and Behavioral Status as Measured
by the Multigrade Inventory for Teachers: Evidence
From a Longitudinal Study
John M. Holahan
Bennett A. Shaywitz
Vinita Chhabra
Abigail Shneider
Karen Marchione
Sally E. Shaywitz
Jack M. Fletcher

3   Social Interaction Impairments   57
Lynn Waterhouse

4   Individual Difference in the Development of Social   81
    Communication Competency in Very Low Birthweight
    Children
      Susan H. Landry
      Cynthia L. Miller-Loncar
      Karen E. Smith

5   Individual Differences in the Development   113
    of Executive Function in Children: Lessons
    From the Delayed Response and A-not-B Tasks
      Kimberly Andrews Espy
      Paul M. Kaufmann

6   Developmental and Clinical Variations in Executive   139
    Functions
      Marilyn C. Welsh

7   The Relation Between Language Development   187
    and Brain Activity
      Dennis L. Molfese
      Dana B. Narter
      Arlene Modglin

8   Naming Abilities in Children With Brain Tumors   225
      Robin D. Morris
      Lorna Lazarus-Benbenisty
      Nicholas Krawiecki
      Maryanne Wolf

9   Patterns of Language Development Through   257
    Augmented Means in Youth With Mental Retardation
      Mary Ann Romski
      Rose A. Sevcik

10 Modeling Developmental and Individual Variability   275
    in Reading and Writing Acquisition: A Developmental
    Neuropsychological Perspective
      Virginia W. Berninger
      Robert D. Abbott

11   The Search for Individual and Subtype Differences   309
in Reading Disabled Children's Response to
Remediation
Maureen W. Lovett
Roderick W. Barron

Author Index   339

Subject Index   355

Preface

Developmental changes in cognitive abilities in childhood have long been of interest to researchers across many fields, including behavioral sciences, communications, education, and medicine. With the publication of research findings showing individual differences in the development of children's learning skills has come the realization that models, methodologies, and analysis approaches that include consideration of individual differences are needed. So too has come an increase in research collaborations among experts in different fields who bring different approaches that include consideration of individual differences are needed. So too has come an increase in research collaborations among experts in different fields who bring different approaches together in studies of cognitive abilities. This work has yielded a growing body of knowledge about how children with normal abilities and children with developmental disorders learn, gain skills in social competency, develop decision-making and planning abilities, and acquire language skills and the skills needed for reading and writing. More recently, researchers have sought to use this body of knowledge as a basis for the early identification of children at risk for cognitive delays and for the development and evaluation of intervention approaches. This book reviews literature in five areas of cognition and provides theory- and research-based information on the applications of research findings and intervention approaches to normally developing children and children with developmental disorders. Running throughout is information on the interactions of different cognitive abilities and the role of individual differences in development that influences development assessments.

The first two chapters discuss the assessment of achievement skills in children. In chapter 1, Intelligence and Achievement: Measurement and Prediction of Developmental Variations by Molfese and Martin, the development of both intelligence and achievement are the focus. Measures of intelligence and achievement are used to make important decisions concerning children's abilities, placement in special education programs, and both have been used to identify children needing intervention of learning, math, reading, and other educational handicaps. Research on predictors of performance on achievement and intelligence tests is discussed. Chapter 2, Developmental Trends in Teacher Perceptions of Student Cognitive and Behavioral Status as Measured by Multigrade Inventory for Teachers: Evidence From a Longitudinal Study, Holahan et al. describes newly developed inventories for use by teachers to quantify their perceptions of academic, attentional, and behavioral status for children from kindergarten through Grade 11. The purpose of these inventories is to enable an evaluation of teacher expectations and student developmental changes so that problems affecting school performance can be identified. The use of these inventories by clinicians and educators is described.

The next two chapters describe developmental changes in social skills. Chapter 3, Social Interaction Impairments by Waterhouse, traces the evolutionary and genetic bases for the development of social interaction behavior and provides a model of the skills involved in affiliative and individually strategic social behaviors. Variations in social skills systems, as well as the influence of developmental disorders (i.e., Downs syndrome, special language impairment, and autism) on the development of individual variation in these skills, are discussed. Chapter 4, Indvidual Differences in the Development of Social Communication Competency in Very Low Birthweight Children by Landry, Miller-Loncar, and Smith, continues the presentation of information on the development of social skills. The behaviors needed to initiate social interactions depend on executive function or planning skills that seem to be more difficult for children with central nervous system deficits, such as those in medically compromised children. It describes their research with very low birth weight children which links skills in initiation of social communication with parenting behaviors and the demands of the social context, to illustrate the complex cognitive skills needed for development of social communication.

The importance of executive function skills in the development of cognitive abilities is the focus of the next chapters. Executive function skills include behaviors such as planning, inhibition, monitoring, flexibility, and working memory. Chapter 5, Individual Differences in the Development of Executive Function in Children: Lessons From the Delayed Response and A-not-B Tasks, continues the discussion of the development of executive function skills in childhood. Espy and Kaufmann describe research on development of executive function skills in infants and young children and evaluate individual differences in development. Chapter 6, Developmental and Clinical Variations in Executive Functions by Welsh, discusses both normal development during early childhood through the school-age years and clinical variations in development as seen in children with phenylketonuria, autism, attention deficit hyperactivity disorder, learning disabilities, epilepsy, and Down syndrome. Both chapters include coverage of the measurement of executive function skills and the neuropsychological implications of the behaviors assessed.

The development of language and communication skills impact the development of a variety of cognitive abilities. Chapters 7 through 9 discuss the development of language skills, how these skills are influenced by brain development and pathology, and how the language skills of children with mental retardation can be improved. Chapter 7, The Relation Between Language Development and Brain Activity, presents information on how neuroelectrophysiological measures have been used to assess the language and cognitive abilities of infants and children, and their usefulness for the early identification of cognitive disabilities. Molfese, Narder, and Modglin review studies using event-related potentials (ERP) in studies of intellectual abilities, including language and specific speech perception skills. The development and usefulness of predictive models involving ERP's, medical complications, and cognitive behaviors is described. Chapter 8, Naming Abilities in Children With Brain Tumors, describes the nature of naming disorders in childhood compared to adulthood and presents research on the assessment of naming abilities in children with brain lesions in contrast to children without lesions. Morris et al. also discuss issues related to selection of assessment batteries, implications for lexical access patterns, and effects of lesion site on performance. Chapter 9, Patterns of Language Development Through Augmented Means in Youth With Mental Retardation, describes the challenges facing children and youth with moderate and severe mental retardation.

Finally, the development of reading abilities involves multiple cognitive skills, each of which can show individual differences in acquisition. Efforts to identify remediation strategies for children with reading disabilities are increasingly focusing on group level and individual levels of skills development. Chapter 10, Modeling Development and Individual Variability in Reading and Writing Acquisition: A Developmental Neuropsychological Perspective, describes and critiques developmental models and research designs used in studying reading and writing. Berninger and Abbott also describe their research program investigating intraindividual, interindividual, and group differences in the development of reading and writing skills. Chapter 11, The Search for Individual and Subtype Differences in Reading Disabled Children's Response to Remediation by Lovett and Barron, continues the discussion of group and individual differences in the development of reading skills. It's focus is on the role of nonreading skills in the development of reading and in the response to remediation by reading disabled children.

Together, the chapters form an important volume combining extensive reviews of the works of other researchers with original research by the authors. The chapters address important issues in the development of cognitive abilities in children, and specifically, seek to understand individual variations in development that arise from both normal and pathological sources. It is through such comparisons that insights into the development of predictive models useful for the early identification of children at risk for developmental delays and the development of intervention techniques can be formulated.

—Dennis L. Molfese
—Victoria J. Molfese

Intelligence and Achievement: Measurement and Prediction of Developmental Variations

Victoria J. Molfese
University of Louisville
Tina B. Martin
Southern Illinois University at Carbondale

Achievement tests are used by the schools to make important decisions, including preliminary decisions about placement of children into gifted programs, and referral for assessments of learning, math, reading, and other educational handicaps. Indeed, based on a survey of school psychologists, Hutton, Dubes, and Muir (1992) reported that whereas the use of achievement tests in assessment has increased since the early 1990s, the use of intelligence tests has decreased. Yet, developmental and cognitive researchers have focused little on achievement tests as criterion measures in their efforts to identify factors correlated with developmental variabilities in children. The most extensive work to date has focused almost exclusively on intelligence tests and researchers have reported considerable success in identifying a set of early predictors, obtained from infant and early childhood measures, that can successfully predict early childhood intelligence and cognitive test scores.

One purpose of these research efforts with intelligence tests has been to identify a set of predictor variables that can be used with children as an early screening battery for detection of later learning and other cognitive disabilities. It is hoped that early detection will lead to early remediation, and such early remediation efforts will show greater success in effecting positive change than is shown when remediation efforts are started at later ages. Research reports have noted considerable success in developing predictive models using intelligence tests as the criterion measure. Particularly successful have been models using measures of biomedical risk conditions associated with pregnancy, labor, delivery and neonatal status, socioeconomic status (SES), and evaluation of the quality of the home environment and parenting skills as the predictor variables. These measures have been found to account for up to 50% of the variance when used to predict intelligence scores as outcomes.

The following sections briefly review the literature reporting the results of models involving combinations of biomedical, SES, home environment, and other measures as predictors of intelligence. Following this review, a rationale for extending these models to predict performance on achievement tests and for considering three additional predictor variables— length of time in school, chronological age when the tests are administered, and verbal scores—is presented. Finally, the results of this research are discussed. In this research, the variables already described are used to predict performance on intelligence tests and on achievement tests using a longitudinal sample of children who have been studied from birth through age 8.

PREDICTING PERFORMANCE
ON INTELLIGENCE TESTS

A number of studies have examined the effectiveness of biomedical risk conditions, SES index measures, and measures of the quality of the home environment as predictors of performance on cognitive and intelligence tests. Many studies have focused on children characterized by very low birthweight, perinatal compromise, and/or preterm births. A variety of predictor variables have been used to predict performance on intelligence tests using scores obtained from normal and "at risk" children. Crisafi, Driscoll, Rey, and Adler (1987) studied 144 children characterized by very low birthweight (< 1,500 grams). They found that asphyxia at birth, SES, and sex of infant (male infants are at greater risk) combined to account for 32% of the variance in predicting 2-year Bayley Mental Development Index (MDI) scores. Siegel (1982a) reported results of a study with 42 children who had been characterized as preterm and very low birthweight (< 1,501 grams). She found a variety of biomedical and social risk conditions (e.g., birth order, maternal smoking, respiratory distress, birthweight, SES) to be predictive of 3-year Stanford–Binet and Reynell language scores, accounting for from 22% to 35% of the variance. H. Johnson, Glassman, Fiks, and Rosen (1987) predicted scores of 3-year-olds on the Merrill Palmer Test. The scores of 39 children who had been exposed to methadone as infants were predicted by a combination of neonatal complications and family social organization, with 32% of the variance accounted for. Hack and Breslau (1986) found that neonatal risk conditions, birthweight, head circumference, measures of neurologic impairment obtained at 20 and 33 months, race, and SES accounted for 43% of the variance in 3-year Stanford–Binet scores of 139 children characterized as very low birthweight at birth.

Studies with older "at risk" children have reported somewhat different contributions of biomedical risk conditions, SES, and home environment measures to predictive models. Low et al. (1985) found that the performance on McCarthy and the Reynell Language tests by 300 children who were characterized as high risk at birth could be predicted by severe neonatal respiratory complications, neonatal infections, and SES at age 4. However, children who were found to be normal at age 1, but developmentally delayed at age 4, were predicted only by SES and quality of home environment (as measured by Home Observation for Measurement of the Environment, HOME) scores. O'Connor, Cohen, and Parmelee (1984) found that performance of preterm and full-term children at age 5 on the Stanford–Binet were correlated with gestational age, maternal education, and a visual response score, but strongest correlations were with Bayley MDI at 18 months. Siegel (1982b) found similar results. She examined the usefulness of biomedical and social factors in predicting 5-year scores on the McCarthy General Cognitive Index (GCI) of 42 children who had been preterm at birth. A combination of perinatal risk items, SES, and maternal education accounted for 26% of the variance. The addition of Bayley motor scores increase the variance accounted for to 46%. Wilson (1985) found that the performance of twins on the Stanford–Binet at ages 3 and 6 were correlated with gestational age and birthweight. However, the strength of these correlations declined after age 18 months, while the influence of maternal education and SES increased. Thus, the strong influence of biomedical risk scores on developmental status and intelligence tests noted in infancy appears to decline in early childhood as social-environmental variables become increasingly stronger influences.

Interestingly, the predictive success achieved with these at risk children is typically poorer than that achieved with children characterized by normal birth status using similar predictors as measures. Although it may seem unusual that children with normal birth status would have measurable biomedical risk conditions, studies of large samples of newborns (Molfese, 1992) have shown that these children are still characterized by a variety of biomedical risk conditions at birth, although the risk conditions are less severe (e.g., maternal smoking, length of labor, hyperbilirubinaemia). As shown by the studies described later, these biomedical risk conditions are predictive of performance on intelligence tests. Indeed, several studies have shown that the amount of variance accounted for and the predictive accuracy achieved are somewhat better when scores from children with normal birth status are used. For example, Siegel (1982b) reported that 40% of the variance was accounted for in predicting 5-year Mc-

Carthy GCI scores of 44 of normal children using biomedical risks, SES, and maternal education. The variance accounted for increased to 46% when 12-month Bayley motor scores were added. The comparable figure for preterm children was 26%. In addition, classification accuracy for normal children (92%) was higher than for preterm children (71%). Similar results showing a greater predictive accuracy with normal than at risk children were reported for 6-year scores on the Wechsler Intelligence Scale for Children–Revised (WISC–R; Siegel, 1985). Bee et al. (1982) reported that biomedical, SES, measures of home environment, and 2-year MDI measures were predictive of 3-year language scores in a sample of normal children, and infant sex (boys receiving higher risk scores) and a variety of social measures were predictive of 4-year Stanford–Binet scores. Molfese and DiLalla (1995) studied variables affecting Stanford–Binet scores of children ages 4 through 6 and WISC–III scores of 7-year-olds participating in a longitudinal study. A combination of biomedical risk scores and HOME scores was able to classify from 84% to 91% of the children as developmentally delayed or normal. Together these studies support the notion that biomedical risk conditions, SES index measures, and measures of the quality of the home environment are useful predictors of intelligence test performance in children characterized by at risk status at birth as well as normal children.

PERFORMANCE ON INTELLIGENCE
AND ACHIEVEMENT TESTS

The successful efforts described earlier all used intelligence scores or scores on other tests of cognitive abilities as the criterion measures. The variables found to be predictive of performance on intelligence and cognitive tests with at risk and normal children may by extension be applicable to the prediction of achievement scores that are derived from cognitive tests. However, there is some uncertainty as to the success of such an extension because the magnitudes of the correlations between intelligence scores with achievement scores have not been strong. Whether used with gifted or normal children, or children referred for academic problems, the correlations between intelligence and achievement scores are generally low to moderate in children ranging from age 6 to 17. The correlations of WISC–R Full Scale IQ scores were .16 to .64 with Kaufman Achievement scores; –.06 to .67 with Wide Range Achievement Test (WRAT) Reading, Spelling, Arithmetic scores; and .11 to .49 with California Achievement Test (CAT) scores (Drudge, Reilly, Rosen, Fischer & Loew, 1981; Grossman & K. Johnson, 1982; Karnes, Edwards, & McCallum, 1986; Prewett & Fowler, 1992; Svanum & Bringle, 1982; Vacc, 1988). Similar magnitudes of correlations were found between Stanford–Binet scores and CAT scores (range: .01–.26), Kaufman Achievement scores (range: .22–.59), and

WRAT scores (range: .24–.30) reported by Carvajal, Weaver, and McKnab (1989), Karnes et al. (1986), Prewett and Giannuli (1991), and Whorton and Karnes (1987). Somewhat better ranges of correlation magnitudes are reported between WISC or Stanford–Binet scores and Woodcock Johnson scores (range: .22–.88) by Beck, Spurlock, and Lindsey (1988), Carvajal et al. (1989), Prewett and Giannuli (1991), and Rothlisberg (1990). Overall, the low to moderate correlations have been interpreted as indicating that the types of abilities and performance assessed by intelligence tests do not completely overlap those assessed by achievement tests. This low to moderate overlap is one reason why a mix of intelligence and achievement tests is recommended for student assessments (Carvajal et al., 1989; Klausmeier, Mishra, & Maker, 1987).

Despite the modest correlations between intelligence and achievement scores, there is some evidence that the types of variables that are predictive of performance on intelligence tests are predictive of achievement test performance. For example, Antonak, King, and Lowy (1982) reported that IQ (which was the single best predictor) and two child characteristics (sex of child and years spent in a specific school district) were predictive of achievement scores in second- and fourth-grade children. Rubin and Balow (1979) found that SES and 8-month Bayley MDI scores were predictive of intelligence scores at ages 4 and 7, as well as being predictive of achievement scores at ages 7 and 9. An ambitious study by Smith, Flick, Ferriss, and Sellmann (1972) sought to predict the scores of 6- and 7-year-olds using scores on a battery of intelligence, achievement, and psychological tests. A single criterion variable was created from a combination of intelligence, achievement, and psychological scores. Predictor measures included biomedical risk conditions, maternal IQ, 8-month Bayley MDI scores, 4-year motor skills scores, and SES measures. Grouping the children as abnormal and normal based on their performance at age 7, 82% of the children could be correctly classified at 1 year and 98% correctly classified at 4 years. Although achievement scores were reported to have played a weaker role than did IQ in the variance of the 7-year criterion scores, the Smith et al. study suggests that the types of variables that influence performance on intelligence tests also may influence performance on achievement tests. However, there are only a few predictive studies using infant and child characteristics to determine their influence on achievement test performance and further study is clearly needed.

PERFORMANCE ON ACHIEVEMENT TESTS

As a starting point for comparing the results of predictive models obtained with intelligence scores and with that obtained with achievement scores, the predictor variables should include the measures most frequently used in prior research. Thus, biomedical risks, SES, and measures of the quality of the home environment are the basic measures to use. There are other predictor variables that could be added. For example, Ceci (1991) presented evidence that the amount of time a child spends in school influences performance on both intelligence and achievement tests. He argued that performance gains made during the school year are at least partly reversed during summer vacations, with both gradually recovering in the months following the resumption of school in the fall. It might be reasonable to assume that the gains made due to length of time in school are reflected in the scores of children tested at different times during the school year. Some schools administer achievement tests in the fall and others do it in the spring. One factor that should be included in predictive models for achievement scores is time of year at which test administration occurred. Although many achievement tests are normed for fall, midyear, and spring administrations, it appears from Ceci's arguments that the norms are not completely effective.

It seems reasonable to extend this model to intelligence tests by determining whether intelligence tests also are influenced by environmental events, including the time in the school year when they are administered to children. In this respect, considering environmental influences on intelligence test scores is interesting because a common view is that intelligence is fixed (Sternberg & Kaufman, 1998), either by genetic factors or psychometric manipulations by scale developers. However, this view has been questioned by findings showing that changes in IQ have been found over generations, with each successive generation obtaining higher scores (the "Flynn effect"; Flynn, 1987). These changes are thought to be due to environmental factors and have been cited as reasons for revisions of standard intelligence tests (e.g., Wechsler, 1991). Espy, Molfese and DiLalla (2001) found evidence of the influence of other environmental factors (HOME and SES) on the intelligence scores of children aged 3 and 6 years. The home environment as measured by the HOME was a stable predictor of early performance on the Stanford–Binet Intelligence scale but HOME did not predict changes in performance over time. SES, which is more commonly used as a measure of home environment but which is a less direct measure of the environment, was found to have an on-going influence on intelligence test performance across the age span. It seems reasonable that other factors such as age at school entrance and time in the school year when tests are administered would affect test scores. Some researcher have reported just such effects for age at school entrance and season of birth and reading achievement scores (Flynn & Rahbar, 1993; Flynn, Rahbar, & Bernstein, 1996).

Ceci (1991) also argued that amount of time in school is not a simple maturity issue. Indeed, maturity and time in the school year when tests are administered yield different effects, with length of schooling having a greater influence on scores than maturation. This difference can be tested by examining data from children who are grouped according to grade in school (e.g., first grade, second grade). Those children whose birthdates are just before the cutoff date for school entry are younger when they enter each grade than children who just miss the cutoff date and who must enter school the following year. For example, first grade is composed of children who have reached age 6 by a specific cutoff date (e.g., a common cutoff date is September 1), children who have birthdates after the cutoff date who enter first grade when they have reached age 7, and by children whose school entrance is delayed due to parent/teacher decisions. Thus, first-grade classes are composed of children who range from age 6 to 7 or older. By comparing predictive models in which children are grouped by grade, it is possible to examine performance scores for the effects of maturity (chronological age in months) at the time when the tests are administered. By including children who have been administered intelligence and achievement tests at different times in the school year, it is possible to examine the separate effects of length of time in school on performance.

PREDICTING PERFORMANCE ON INTELLIGENCE AND ACHIEVEMENT TESTS

To examine the effects of the variables already described, a study of variables affecting the prediction of children's performance on intelligence and achievement tests was conducted. The study used measures of biomedical risk conditions, SES, quality of the home environment, time in the school year when the tests were administered, and chronological age at the time the tests were administered as predictor variables. Scores on intelligence and achievement tests were used as criterion variables. Data used in the study were obtained from children participating in a longitudinal study. For these children, intelligence tests were administered at their yearly test session, which occurred within a month of their birth dates and achievement tests were administered by schools according to the schools' preferred times in the school year.

The purposes of the study were threefold: to investigate the extent to which the variables used to predict intelligence scores can also be used to predict achievement scores; to determine how the results are influenced by the addition of two variables hypothesized to influence test performance: maturation (chronological age) and length of time in school when tests were administered; and to investigate the effectiveness of the variables to identify children when they are divided into two groups using a mean split to create groups in which children are divided into those scoring one standard deviation below the mean and those scoring above that score.

The sample consisted of children participating in a longitudinal study of cognitive development conducted in a rural, midwestern community. The children in the study were recruited at birth from families willing to participate and who expected to be available for follow-up testing sessions. The children were tested at yearly intervals from birth through age 8. Data were available for 68 (26 males, 42 females) of the children at first grade and for 64 (30 males, 34 females) of the children at second grade. There were no significant differences in intelligence or in achievement test scores between children for whom scores were available at first and second grade, as compared with children for whom scores were only available at first or second grade (see Table 1.1).

At birth, the children had few severe biomedical risk conditions, but were characterized by a variety of biomedical risk conditions that have been found to be related to performance on intelligence and achievement tests. These biomedical medical risk conditions were scored from medical rec-

TABLE 1.1
Descriptive Statistics for Subject Sample

	First-Grade Children (N = 68)		Second-Grade Children (N = 64)	
	Mean	SD	Mean	SD
Predictors				
Biomedical Risk[1]	5.26	1.78	5.32	2.27
HOME Total Score	45.41	4.19	46.41	3.97
SES Index[2]	4.90	1.19	5.06	1.24
Test Time[3]				
Intelligence Tests	5.75	3.39	5.45	3.24
Achievement Tests	7.08	2.88	7.13	3.05
Age at Test[4]				
Intelligence Tests	83.75	.61	95.98	.51
Achievement Tests	84.21	5.59	96.15	5.16
Criterion Measures				
Intelligence (standard scores)	104.72	12.92	108.61	10.56
Achievement Composite (t scores)	72.72	19.96	71.65	24.12

[1]Scores are calculated using infant sex [male], parity, 5-minute Apgar, maternal smoking, number of prior abortions, and birthweight. See text for scoring.

[2]Scores reflect the sum of parental education and occupation and family income. Education: 1 = some high school; 2 = completed high school; 3 = some college; 4 = completed college. Occupation used Hollingshead's scheme of occupational categories (Bonjean, Hill, & McLemore, 1967) from 1 to 7; high scores "best." Income: 0 = < $5,000; 1 = $5,000–10,000; 2 = $10,000–15,000; 3 = $15,000–20,000; 4 = $20 000–25,000; 5 = $25,000–30,000; 6 = $30,000–35,000; 7 = > $35,000.

[3]Time in the school year when tests were administered. Months were score from August (1) to July (12).

[4]Score reflect the children's chronological ages in months at the time the tests were administered.

ords using Siegel's Risk Index (1982a, 1982b). The risk index was selected because it has been used across a broad age range of children characterized by preterm, low birthweight, and normal birth histories in studies examining the development of intelligence and achievement abilities. Six risk items (infant sex [male], parity, 5-minute Apgar, maternal smoking, number of prior abortions, and birthweight) were used. These items were scored as present or absent, except Apgar scores for which actual scores were used, parity that was scored as normal (1–3 births) and at risk (no or > 4 previous births), and birthweight that was scored as normal (within one standard deviation around the sample mean) or abnormal (greater than one standard deviation around the mean). Absent and normal conditions received a score of 0. Abnormal/risk and present conditions received a score of 1.

Intelligence tests were administered to the children within 4 weeks of the child's birthdate. The Stanford–Binet Intelligence Scale (4th ed.; Thorndike, Hagen, & Sattler, 1986) was administered to children at ages 3 through 6. The Wechsler Intelligence Test for Children–III (Wechsler, 1991) was used to measure intelligence at age 7 onward. The WISC–III was used rather than the Stanford–Binet at older ages to avoid test familiarity due to repeated administration at the yearly testing sessions.

The results of school-administered achievement tests were provided by the schools attended by the children. The schools administered a wide variety of different achievement tests. The most common achievement tests were: the California Achievement Test (CAT; 1985, McGraw-Hill, Inc.), the IOWA Tests of Basic Skills (ITBS; 1993, Riverside Publishing Co.), and the Stanford Achievement Test Series (SAT; 1989, Harcourt Brace Jovanovich, Inc.). Only achievement tests that yielded national percentile rankings were used as achievement test scores in the present study. For all achievement tests, standard scores were used.

Two types of social-environmental measures were obtained: A socioeconomic status (SES) index was calculated for each child using parental education, parental occupation (using the Hollingshead scheme of occupational categories; Bonjean, Hill, & McLemore, 1967), and family income. The second social-environmental measure was the preschool version (age 3–6) of the Home Observation for Measurement of the Environment (HOME) Inventory (Caldwell & Bradley, 1978). The HOME was administered during the home visit that was scheduled within 1 week of the testing session at age 3. The two social-environmental measures were used as separate scores on the analyses.

FINDINGS

Shown in Table 1.1 are the descriptive statistics for the first- and second-grade children. The number of children included in each analysis varied slightly due to occasional missing scores. Pearson Correlations were obtained to determine the relation between achievement and intelligence scores. In first grade the correlation was .41 ($p < .001$), and in second grade the correlation was .64 ($p < .001$).

Three models were tested to determine their effectiveness in discriminating between the children based on their test scores. The first model used the scores from the Risk Index (BioRisk), SES, and Total HOME scores as discriminant variables. The second model used five discriminant variables: BioRisk, SES and Total HOME, age when tests were administered (Age at Test), and time in the school year when tests were administered (Test Time). The third model used only Age at Test and Test Time as variables. The three discriminant models were tested with the children grouped in two ways—in one set of analyses, the children were divided into two groups at the mean score obtained from the sample (mean split), and in the second set of analyses, the children were divided into two groups with one group scoring one standard deviation or more below the mean (Low) obtained for the sample and the other group scoring above the LOW group (Average/high). Whereas the Low group tended to have few children (4–12) as compared to the Average/High group (51–58), it was important to examine the effectiveness of the predictors when the discriminant analyses included the identification of the lowest scoring children.

The results of the discriminant analyses are shown in Tables 1.2 and 1.3. Results are presented separately by grade and by type of test (intelligence and achievement). Separate results are also presented for the two groupings of the children. When the children were divided using a mean split, all but one of the models resulted in significant discriminant functions. A consistent superiority for Model 2 (BioRisk, SES, Total HOME, Test Time, Age at Test) over the other models was shown in the Wilks's lambda and chi square results for both intelligence and achievement. Model 1 (BioRisk, SES, Total HOME) was a close second in Wilks's lambda and chi square statistics and yielded classification accuracies that were nearly identical to those of Model 2. Model 3 (Test Time, Age at Test) resulted in nonsignificant discriminant functions except for intelligence scores in second grade.

When the children were divided by standard deviation into Low and Average/High groups (Table 1.3), the results were nearly the same. Models 1 and 2 resulted in significant discriminant functions in all but one case for both intelligence and achievement, with Model 1 for second-grade intelligence scores being the nonsignificant exception. Although Model 3 did not result in significant discriminant functions for first-grade intelligence and achievement scores, the model did result in a significant discriminant function for second-grade scores, but the model was weaker and achieved poor classification accuracy than Models 1 and 2.

TABLE 1.4
Discriminant Function Results for First- and Second-Grade Students Grouped by Mean Split

Models	Canonical Correlation	Number Classified	Wilks's Lambda and Chi Square	Classification Accuracy	Discriminant Function Coefficients
First Grade					
			Intelligence		
1. SES, HOME, BioRisk	.39	1 2 / 1 22 9 / 2 11 17	.88 / 9.14*	66%	SES .90 / HOME .63 / BioRisk .05
2. SES, HOME, BioRisk, Test Time, Age at Test	.45	1 2 / 1 21 7 / 2 9 17	.80 / 10.97*	70%	SES .78 / HOME .49 / Test Time .49 / Age at Test .23 / BioRisk .02
3. Test Time, Age at Test	.29	1 2 / 1 22 9 / 2 12 20	.92 / 5.07	66%	Test Time .99 / Age at Test -.04
			Achievement		
1. SES, HOME, BioRisk	.41	1 2 / 1 26 13 / 2 11 13	.83 / 11.08*	62%	HOME .80 / BioRisk -.62 / SES .23
2. SES, HOME, BioRisk, Test Time, Age at Test	.44	1 2 / 1 25 14 / 2 8 16	.81 / 12.28*	65%	HOME -.87 / BioRisk .50 / Age at Test .43 / SES .20 / Test Time -.18
3. Test Time, Age at Test	.07	1 2 / 1 18 20 / 2 11 18	.99 / .36	54%	Test Time .82 / Age at Test -.05

(Continued)

TABLE 1.2
(Continued)

Models	Canonical Correlation	Number Classified			Wilks's Lambda and Chi Square	Classification Accuracy	Discriminant Function Coefficients
Second Grade					*Intelligence*		
1. SES, HOME, BioRisk	.53		1	2	.72	76%	HOME .94
		1	22	5	16.61**		SES .40
		2	8	19			BioRisk −.09
2. SES, HOME, BioRisk, Test Time, Age at Test	.58		1	2	.66	75%	HOME .79
		1	20	6	19.32**		Test Time .47
		2	7	18			SES .33
							Age at test .10
							BioRisk −.09
3. Test Time, Age at Test	.33		1	2	.89	60%	Test Time .99
		1	16	14	3.97*		Age at Test .09
		2	10	20			
					Achievement		
1. SES, HOME, BioRisk	.53		1	2	.72	73%	HOME .71
		1	25	8	16.78**		SES .51
		2	7	15			BioRisk −.42
2. SES, HOME, BioRisk, Test Time, Age at Test	.55		1	2	.70	75%	HOME .69
		1	22	9	17.54**		SES .44
		2	4	18			BioRisk −.37
							Age at Test .37
							Test Time .28
3. Test Time, Age at Test	.26		1	2	.93	65%	Test Time .99
		1	25	9	4.23		Age Grade .67
		2	13	15			

*p < .05. **p < .01.

Discriminant Function Results for First- and Second-Grade Students Grouped by Standard Deviation

Models	Canonical Correlation	Number Classified		Wilks's Lambda and Chi Square	Classification Accuracy	Discriminant Function Coefficients
		1	2			
First Grade						
				Intelligence		
1. SES, HOME, BioRisk	.44	1 45 10 2 1 3		.81 11.72**	81%	HOME .86 SES .68 BioRisk −.54
2. SES, HOME, BioRisk, Test Time, Age at Test	.47	1 41 9 2 1 3		.77 12.42*	81%	HOME .82 SES .63 BioRisk −.48 Age at Test .24 Test Time −.12
3. Test Time, Age at Test	.13	1 31 23 2 3 5		.98 1.13	58%	Test Time .98 Age at Test .11
				Achievement		
1. SES, HOME, BioRisk	.46	1 40 13 2 4 6		.79 14.12**	73%	HOME .78 BioRisk −.60 SES .49
2. SES, HOME, BioRisk, Test Time, Age at Test	.47	1 41 12 2 4 6		.78 14.70*	75%	HOME .75 BioRisk −.58 SES .48 Age at Test .35 Test Time .19
3. Test Time, Age at Test	.14	1 32 22 2 6 7		.98 1.23	58%	Age at Test .99 Test Time .43

(Continued)

13

TABLE 1.3
(Continued)

Models	Canonical Correlation	Number Classified			Wilks's Lambda and Chi Square	Classification Accuracy	Discriminant Function Coefficients
			1	2			
Second Grade					Intelligence		
1. SES, HOME, BioRisk	.34	1	31	13	.88	76%	SES .86
		2	3	7	6.31		HOME .65
							BioRisk −.08
2. SES, HOME, BioRisk, Test Time, Age at Test	.55	1	34	7	.69	84%	Test Time .81
		2	1	9	17.03**		SES .49
							HOME .42
							BioRisk −.03
							Age at Test .00
3. Test Time, Age at Test	.45	1	31	17	.79	72%	Test Time .99
		2	0	12	13.46**		Age at Test −.03
					Achievement		
1. SES, HOME, BioRisk	.42	1	38	9	.83	80%	SES .84
		2	2	6	9.88*		HOME .37
							BioRisk .37
2. SES, HOME, BioRisk, Test Time, Age at Test	.48	1	36	9	.77	77%	HOME .77
		2	3	5	12.95*		Age at Test .56
							SES .49
							Test Time .46
							BioRisk −.06
3. Test Time, Age at Test	.43	1	37	13	.81	75%	Test Time .99
		2	2	9	11.92**		Age at Test .66

*$p < .05$. **$p < .01$

14

The contribution of the variables in the discriminant function analyses differed for intelligence and achievement. Taking the results for intelligence first, SES and HOME contributed most strongly to the discriminant functions in Models 1 and 2 at first and second grades when groups are created using mean splits. The time of year when the test were administered (Test Time) also contributed to Model 2 in both first and second grades. Test Time was also the strongest discriminant variable in Model 3 at both grades, but the model was not significant. When groups were created using standard deviations, HOME and SES again contributed most strongly to the discriminant functions in Models 1 and 2 at both grades. However, BioRisk was also an important contributor to the discriminant functions for Models 1 and 2 in first grade, but not at second grade. Test Time was an important contributor to Model 2 in second grade but not at first grade. Test Time was again the strongest discriminant variable in Model 3, but again the model was not significant. Chronological age at the time the tests were administered (Age at Test) contributed only to the discrimination of intelligence scores in Model 2 at first grade.

For achievement, HOME, BioRisk, and SES all contributed most strongly to the discriminant functions in Model 1 at first and second grade to discriminate group membership using mean split. These variables combined with Age at Test in Model 2 in first grade and with Test Time in second grade to discriminate achievement scores in Model 2. Test Time was a strong discriminant variable in Model 3 in first grade and both Age at Test and Test Time were strong discriminant variables in second grade, but the models were not significant. When groups were created using standard deviations, HOME, BioRisk, and SES again contributed most strongly to the discriminant functions in Model 1 at both grades. These variables combined with Age at Test in Model 2 to predict first-grade achievement scores. For second grade, a combination of HOME, Age at Test, SES, and Test Time were important predictors in Model 2. Both Age at Test and Test Time were strong predictors in Model 3, but the models were not significant.

IMPLICATIONS

Although the correlations between intelligence and achievement scores were modest, which is consistent with previously published reports, the results of the discriminant analyses are quite similar. Model 1, which included BioRisk, SES, and HOME scores, and Model 2, which included those measures plus Age at Test and Test Time, yielded the best results of the four models and did so for both intelligence and achievement. The results obtained with Model 3, which included only Age at Test and Test

Time, were consistently weaker than the other two models. The effectiveness of Models 1 and 2 were the same when the children were divided using mean split and when standard deviation was used to create a Low group and an Average/High group.

The differential effectiveness of the models is due to the contribution of the individual predictors to the discriminant functions. The influence of three variables, HOME, SES, and biomedical risks conditions, which have traditionally been found to be predictive of preschool performance on intelligence tests, were specifically tested here. The findings confirmed the effectiveness of these variables in discriminating intelligence scores and also showed that their effectiveness could be extended to discrimination of achievement scores. Both HOME scores and SES consistently contributed to the significant discriminant functions for intelligence. Although BioRisks also discriminated intelligence scores, it did so only when the children were divided into Low and Average/High groups and only in first grade. For achievement scores, HOME and BioRisk were the strongest predictors in first grade regardless of how the children were divided into groups, with SES a weak third or fourth discriminant variable. By second grade, however, the strongest discriminant variable was SES and/or HOME in all cases, with BioRisk either tied with HOME or a weaker contributor to the discriminant function.

Several researchers (Cohen & Parmelee, 1983; Molfese, DiLalla, & Bunce, 1997; Molfese, Holcomb, & Helwig, 1994; Sameroff & Chandler, 1975; Siegel, 1985) have reported that the influence of biomedical and social-environmental variables changes during the preschool years, with biomedical conditions having their greatest influence on cognitive performance during the infancy and early childhood years, and social-environmental variables having increasingly greater influence as childhood progresses. The results of the present study appear to confirm these findings by showing that biomedical risk conditions and social-environmental variables do play important roles in both intelligence and achievement performance in first grade. By second grade, however, the role of biomedical risk conditions has weakened, with the social-environmental measures more consistently involved in discriminating the groups. These results are important because the children participating in the study were largely characterized by normal birth conditions. Yet, the relatively common biomedical risk conditions that have been identified by Siegel (1982a, 1982b) as effective predictors of performance on intelligence and achievement tests in 5-year-old children have been confirmed as effective for predicting performance of older children (6- to 8-year-olds) in the present study. These findings point to the importance of including biomedical risk conditions in assessing both normal and at risk children for normal and low performance on intelligence and achievement tests.

In addition to these traditional variables, the effects of two other variables (Age at Test and Test Time) were tested. Test Time was found to contribute to the discrimination of first- and second-grade intelligence scores, with much less contributed by Age at Test. For achievement scores, Age at Test contributed more strongly to the discriminant functions than Test Time. Although the use of these two variables alone (Model 3) did not generally yield significant discriminant functions, Ceci's (1991) assertion that the time in the school year when tests are administered and chronological age influence performance appears to be confirmed by the results achieved with Model 2. These findings are important because the time at which tests are administered is based either on testing protocol (e.g., in the current study, all intelligence testing occurred within a month of the child's birthdate), on tradition within a school district, or on state mandates. In the present study, Test Time for intelligence testing varied broadly across children because it was based on birthdate, but for achievement tests, Test Time tended to occur in late fall and late spring. Age at Test varied little for intelligence tests because all children were within 1 month of their birthdates, but Age at Test varied broadly for achievement tests, which were given at times determined by each school.

Whereas the discriminant results appear to reflect the differential amounts of variability of Test Time compared to Age at Test, there are further implications. The creators of achievement tests control for time in the school year when the tests are administered by providing separate norms for fall versus spring administration. The results of the present study appear to show that the controls may not be adequate because Test Time did influence achievement test performance. The effects due to chronological age are also interesting. Because chronological age varied little across children when the intelligence tests were administered, it is not surprising that the chronological age was not a strong discriminant variable for intelligence test performance. In contrast, the chronological ages of the children varied more at the time achievement tests were administered and Age at Test was shown to be a stronger discriminant variable with achievement scores. These results suggest that Ceci's contention that both variables be considered in evaluating test performance is correct.

Language Measures As Predictors

One additional measure that has the potential of adding predictive power to the biomedical risk and social-environmental models already described is verbal abilities. A number of studies have reported that the same variables found to be predictive of intelligence are also useful for predicting early verbal abilities. For example, researchers have found measures of biomedical risk conditions, maternal characteristics (e.g., IQ, education, age at first birth), and social measures (e.g., HOME scores, SES, marital status) are predictive of preschool verbal abilities (Bee et al., 1982; Sameroff, Siefer, Barocas, Zax, & Greenspan, 1987; Schaimberg, 1991; Siegel, 1985). Preschool verbal abilities have also been found to play an important role in predicting performance on intelligence tests in school-age children. One reason for this success is the moderate to high correlations reported between measures of verbal abilities and intelligence scores ($r = $ .21–.62) that have been found in studies comparing the verbal abilities of children measured as early as age 1 with intelligence measured at ages 4 to 6 (Bee et al., 1982; Siegel, 1985).

Other researchers have examined the relation between verbal abilities and performance on achievement tests. Correlations between concurrently measured performance on intelligence and achievement tests are slightly stronger between verbal intelligence scores ($r = $ .25–.70) than performance scores ($r = $ .09–.68) with WRAT subscale scores (Grossman & K. Johnson, 1982; Prewett & Fowler, 1992; Spruill & Beck, 1986). There is also evidence that one of the variables proposed by Ceci (1991) as strongly influencing school achievement is differentially related to verbal intelligence. Ceci reported that stronger correlations have been found between length of schooling and verbal intelligence as compared with nonverbal intelligence.

Together these data appear to show that adding a measure of verbal intelligence to the models designed to predict intelligence and achievement performance might be useful. The models presented previously were designed to permit the identification of a set of predictor variables that can be used with children as an early screening battery for detection of later disabilities. Consistent with this design, the verbal measure proposed is from the McCarthy Scales of Children's Abilities (McCarthy, 1972), which can be administered to children from age 2 to 8. The preschool period, particularly from age 2 onward, increasingly is being seen as the beginning of the time at which valid assessments of cognitive functioning can be made (Bracken, 1987). In the present study, verbal scores on the McCarthy scales were obtained at age 3. These scores, together with biomedical risk conditions and social-environmental scores, were used to classify children grouped according to the same scheme already described. Of particular interest here was the question of whether the language scores might add additional power to the predictive models used with intelligence and achievement scores.

Scores on all predictor and outcome measures were available on 55 first-grade children and 51 second-grade children within the longitudinal sample. The mean McCarthy Verbal Scale Index scores at age 3 was 54.77 ($SD = 8.14$). The correlations between McCarthy scores and intelligence in first grade and second grade were .38 and .46, respectively, and for the achievement scores in first grade and second grade were .33 and .37, respectively. Shown in Table 1.4 are the results of the discriminant function analyses for the first- and second-grade children divided at the mean. Only one model (BioRisk, SES, HOME, Test Time, Age at Test, and McCarthy VSI) was tested, with number of cases per parameter in each analyses exceeding the suggested minimum of five cases per parameter (Bentler & Chou, 1987). The addition of the McCarthy VSI increased the classification accuracy by 9 to 15 points for intelligence, although the improvement was not as impressive for achievement. Dividing the children into groups using standard deviations did not produce appreciably different results.

TABLE 1.4
Discriminant Function Results for Intelligence and Achievement

	Canonical Correlation	Number Classified		Wilks's Lambda and Chi Square	Classification Accuracy	Discriminant Function Coefficients
		Intelligence				
·st Grade						
S	.62	1	2	.61	.85	SES .61
)ME		1 22	4			Test Time .52
ɔRisk		2 3	18	20.61**		McCarthy VSI .40
st Time						HOME .29
e at Test						Age at Test .21
:Carthy VSI						BioRisk .11
ːond Grade						
S	.68	1	2	.54	.84	HOME .62
)ME		1 21	5			McCarthy VSI .53
ɔRisk		2 3	20	26.84**		Test Time .50
st Time						SES .31
e at Test						BioRisk −.06
:Carthy VSI						Age at Test .04
		Achievement				
·st Grade						
S	.36	1	2	.86	.58	HOME .72
)ME .		1 22	15			BioRisk −.61
ɔRisk		2 8	10	7.17		McCarthy VSI .58
st Time						Age at Test .18
e at Test						Test Time −.17
:Carthy VSI						SES .14
ːond Grade						
S	.58	1	2	.66	.78	McCarthy VSI .65
)ME		1 24	7			HOME .64
ɔRisk		2 4	16	18.95**		SES .50
st Time						Test Time .34
e at Test						Age at Test .34
:Carthy VSI						BioRisk −.32

**$p < .01$.

Overall, the results of adding verbal scores to a mix of variables to predict intelligence scores produced a clear improvement in classification accuracy. This finding may reflect the generally strong relation between verbal abilities and intelligence scores. That a similar improvement in classification of achievement scores was not obtained is perplexing. The effect of the verbal scores on the order of the discriminant function coefficients is interesting. As can be seen from a comparison of Tables 1.2 and 1.3 (Model 3) with Table 1.4, the McCarthy VSI appeared in either second or third position in the listing, and most frequently the McCarthy VSI affected all the other variables by slightly reducing their magnitudes, rather than weakening only specific variables. This was true for the discriminant functions for both intelligence and achievement, yet the overall effect was additional classification accuracy for intelligence scores but not for achievement scores. It may be that the types of verbal abilities assessed on the McCarthy scales are different from those affecting performance on achievement tests. There is more work to do in identifying the types of measures that can be obtained early in the preschool period and that are effective for discriminating children who will show normal or below normal performance. Whereas the accuracy by which intelligence performance can be predicted is improving, greater improvement in predicting both intelligence and achievement scores is still needed as better methods are developed for the early identification of children at risk for poor future performance.

REFERENCES

Antonak, R., King, S., & Lowy, J. (1982). Otis–Lennon mental ability test, Stanford achievement test, and three demographic variables as predictors of achievement in Grades 2 and 4. *Journal of Educational Research, 75*, 366–373.

Beck, F., Spurlock, D., & Lindsey, J. (1988). The WISC–R and the Woodcock–Johnson tests of achievement: Correlations for exceptional children. *Perceptual and Motor Skills, 67*, 587–590.

Bee, H., Barnard, K., Eyres, S., Gray, C., Hammond, M., Spietz, A., Snyder, C., & Clark, B. (1982). Prediction of IQ and language skill from perinatal status, child performance, family characteristics, and mother-infant interaction. *Child Development, 53*, 1134–1156.

Bentler, P., & Chou, C. (1987). Practical issues in structural modeling. *Sociological Methods and Research, 16*, 78–117.

Bonjean, C., Hill, R., & McLemore, S. (1967). *Sociological measures: An inventory of scales and indices.* San Francisco: Chandler Publishing.

Bracken, B. (1987). Limitations of preschool instruments and standards for minimal levels of technical adequacy. *Journal of Psychoeducational Assessment, 4*, 313–326.

Caldwell, B., & Bradley, R. (1978). *Manual for the Home Observation Measurement of the Environment.* Little Rock: University of Arkansas.

Carvajal, H., Weaver, K., & McKnab, P. (1989). Relationships between scores of gifted children on the Stanford–Binet IV and Woodcock–Johnson Tests of Achievement. *Diagnostique, 14*, 241–246.

Ceci, S. (1991). How much does schooling influence general intelligence and its cognitive components? A reassessment of the evidence. *Developmental Psychology, 27*, 703–722.

Cohen, S., & Parmelee, A. (1983). Prediction of the 5-year Stanford–Binet scores in preterm infants. *Child Development, 54*, 1242–1253.

Crisafi, M., Driscoll, J., Rey, H., & Adler, A. (1987, March). *A longitudinal study of intellectual performance of very low birthweight infants in the preschool years.* Paper presented at the Society for Research in Child Development, Baltimore.

Drudge, O., Reilly, T., Rosen, J., Fischer, M., & Loew, D. (1981). *A comparison of the WISC–R, McCarthy scales, Woodcock-Johnson, and academic achievement: Concurrent and predictive validity.* Technical Report available from Educational Resources Information Center (ERIC).

Espy, K. A., Molfese, V. J., & DiLalla, L. F. (2001). Effects of environment on intelligence in children: Growth curve modeling of longitudinal data. *Merrill Palmer Quarterly, 47,* 42–72.

Flynn, J. (1987). Massive IQ gains in 14 nations: What IQ tests really measure. *Psychological Bulletin, 95,* 29–51.

Flynn, J., & Rahbar, M. (1993). The effects of age and gender on reading achievement: Implications for pediatric counseling. *Developmental and Behavioral Pediatrics, 14,* 304–307.

Flynn, J., Rahbar, M., & Bernstein, A. (1996). Is there an association between season of birth and reading disability? *Developmental and Behavioral Pediatrics, 17,* 22–26.

Grossman, F., & Johnson, K. (1982). WISC–R factor scores as predictors of WRAT performance: A multivariate analysis. *Psychology in the Schools, 19,* 465–468.

Hack, M., & Breslau, N. (1986). Very low birthweight infants: Effects of brain growth during infancy on intelligence quotients at 3 years of age. *Pediatrics, 77,* 196–202.

Hutton, J., Dubes, R., & Muir, S. (1992). Assessment practices of school psychologists: Ten years later. *School Psychology Review, 21,* 271–284.

Johnson, H., Glassman, M., Fiks, K., & Rosen, T. (1987). Path analysis of variables affecting 36-month outcome in a population of multi-risk children. *Infant Behavior and Development, 10,* 451–465.

Karnes, F., Edwards, R., & McCallum, S. (1986). Normative achievement assessment of gifted children: Comparing the K–ABC, WRAT, and CAT. *Psychology in the Schools, 23,* 346–352.

Klausmeier, K., Mishra, S., & Maker, J. (1987). Identification of gifted learners: A national survey of assessment practices and training needs of school psychologists. *Gifted Child Quarterly, 31,* 135–137.

Low, J., Galbraith, R., Muir, D., Broekhoven, L., Wilkinson, J., & Karchmar, E. (1985). The contribution of fetal-newborn complications to motor and cognitive deficits. *Developmental Medicine and Child Neurology, 27,* 578–587.

McCarthy, D. (1972). *Manual for the McCarthy Scales of Children's Abilities.* New York: Psychological Corporation.

Molfese, V. (1992). *Perinatal risk and infant development.* New York: Guilford.

Molfese, V., & DiLalla, L. (1995). Cost effective approaches to identifying developmental delay in 4- to 7-year-old children. *Early Education and Development, 6,* 265–277.

Molfese, V., Holcomb, L., & Helwig, S. (1994). Biomedical and social environmental influences on cognitive and verbal abilities in children 1 to 3 years of age. *International Journal of Behavioral Development, 17,* 271–287.

O'Connor, M., Cohen, S., & Parmelee, A. (1984). Infant auditory discrimination in preterm and full-term infants as a predictor of 5-year intelligence. *Developmental Psychology, 20,* 159–165.

Prewett, P., & Fowler, D. (1992). Predictive validity of the Slosson Intelligence Test with the WISC–R and the WRAT–R Level 1. *Psychology in the Schools, 29,* 17–21.

Prewett, P., & Giannuli, M. (1991). Correlations of the WISC–R, Stanford–Binet Intelligence Scale: Fourth Edition, and the reading subtests of three popular achievement tests. *Psychological Reports, 69,* 1232–1234.

Rothlisberg, B. (1990). The relation of the Stanford–Binet: Fourth Edition to measures of achievement: A concurrent validity study. *Psychology in the Schools, 27,* 120–125.

Rubin, R., & Balow, B. (1979). Measures of infant development and socioeconomic status as predictors of later intelligence and school achievement. *Developmental Psychology, 15,* 225–227.

Sameroff, A., & Chandler, M. (1975). Reproductive risk and the continuum of caretaking casualty. In F. Horowitz, S. Hetherington, S. Scarr-Salapatek, & G. Siegel (Eds.), *Review of child development research* (Vol. 4, pp. 187–244). Chicago: University of Chicago Press.

Sameroff, A., Seifer, R., Barocas, R., Zax, M., & Greenspan, S. (1987). Intelligence quotient scores of 4-year-old children: Social-environmental risk factors. *Pediatrics, 79,* 343–350.

Schiamberg, L. (1991, April). *Predictors of verbal intelligence and behavior problems among four-year-old children.* Paper presented at the biennial meeting of Society for Research in Child Development, Seattle.

Siegel, L. (1982a). Reproductive, perinatal, and environmental factors as predictors of the cognitive and language development of preterm and fullterm infants. *Child Development, 53,* 963–973.

Siegel, L. (1982b). Reproductive, perinatal, and environmental variables as predictors of development of preterm (< 1501 grams) and fullterm children at 5 years. *Seminars in Perinatology, 6,* 274–279.

Siegel, L. (1985). Biological and environmental variables as predictors of intellectual functioning at 6 years of age. In S. Harel & N. Anastasjow (Eds.), *The at risk infant: Psychosocial medical aspects* (pp. 65–73). Baltimore: Brookes Publishing.

Smith, A., Flick, G., Ferriss, G., & Sellmann, A. (1972). Prediction of developmental outcome at seven years from prenatal, perinatal and postnatal events. *Child Development, 43,* 495–507.

Spruill, J., & Beck, B. (1986). Relationship between the WAIS–R and wide range achievement test-revised. *Educational and Psychological Measurement, 46,* 1037–1040.

Sternberg, R., & Kaufman, J. (1998). Human abilities. *Annual Review of Psychology.* Palo Alto, CA: Annual Reviews.

Svanum, S., & Bringle, R. (1982). Race, social class, and predictive bias: An evaluation using the WISC, WRAT, and teacher ratings. *Intelligence, 6,* 275–286.

Thorndike, R., Hagen, E., & Sattler, J. (1986). *Guide for administering and scoring the fourth edition Stanford-Binet Intelligence Scale.* Chicago: Riverside.

Vacc, N. (1988). Early adolescents' performance on the WRAT compared to their WISC–R IQs, reading achievement scores and selected demographic variables. *Journal of Early Adolescence, 8,* 195–205.

Wechsler, D. (1991). *Wechsler Intelligence Scale for Children* (3rd ed.). New York: Psychological Corporation.

Whorton, J., & Karnes, F. (1987). Correlation of Stanford–Binet Intelligence Scale scores with various other measures used to screen and identify intellectually gifted students. *Perceptual and Motor Skills, 64,* 461–462.

Wilson, R. (1985). Risk and resilience in early mental development. *Developmental Psychology, 21,* 795–805.

## CHAPTER TWO

Developmental Trends in Teacher Perceptions of Student Cognitive and Behavioral Status as Measured by the Multigrade Inventory for Teachers: Evidence From a Longitudinal Study

John M. Holahan
Bennett A. Shaywitz
Vinita Chhabra
Abigail Shneider
Karen Marchione
Sally E. Shaywitz
Yale University School of Medicine

Jack M. Fletcher
University of Texas Medical School, Houston

Teachers are in an optimal position to observe and provide feedback on the academic and behavioral status of their students. Teachers spend a substantial amount of time with students (Atkins & Pelham, 1991), they can place the student's behavior in a broad context, and they may be less susceptible to bias than are parents (Ulmann, Sleator, & Sprague, 1984). Teachers can provide observations pivotal to the disentangling of learning and behavioral difficulties (Shaywitz et al., 1995); furthermore, the incorporation of the teacher's perspective allows the child to be assessed in a naturalistic setting within the confines of the classroom (Keogh, 1977). Clearly, it would be extremely helpful to have a systematic, standardized method that would allow teachers to record their observation of students over time. Such information would provide the empiric database necessary to describe the ontogeny of cognitive, linguistic, and behavioral domains over the critical school years; moreover, these data could indicate the relation between teacher observations and other measures (e.g., individual tests of academic achievement) over time.

The Multigrade Inventory for Teachers (MIT; Shaywitz, 1987), a teacher-based instrument designed to evaluate a teacher's perceptions of a school-age child's academic status, as well as attentional and behavioral status, was developed to assist the classroom teacher in providing an assessment of academic, attentional, and behavioral problems affecting the school-age child. The MIT provides teachers with the opportunity to record their observations on a full range of specific behavioral and learning styles in a consistent and systematic manner; its format is user friendly, requiring only from 5 to 10 minutes to complete. In addition to specific items, there are global items to assess overall problems in school and items to evaluate specific areas of academic performance.

This report provides a more extensive description of the properties of the MIT based on data obtained on a survey sample of over 400 boys and girls followed longitudinally from kindergarten through grade 11; these students were participants in the Connecticut Longitudinal Study (CLS) described later. More specifically, evidence is presented of the reliability and validity of the MIT scales in grades 6 to 11. In addition, the scale developments, reliability, and validity of a revised and expanded instrument for use in grades 9 through 11, the Adolescent MIT (ADMIT), is described. Furthermore, the ontogeny of students' learning and behavioral characteristics from kindergarten through grade 11 is described with systematic evidence of gender differences and developmental trends in teacher ratings of students' cognitive and behavioral status.

CONTENT AND DESIGN OF THE MIT

The MIT consists of 56 items representing various dimensions of cognitive and behavioral domains. Specific characteristics are listed under headings relating to categories of school behavior: Activity, Attention, Adaptability, Social, Language, and Academic. Teachers evaluate the child on a 6-point Likert scale: 0 = *never* to 5 = *always*. Each category includes items that focus on a student's academic experiences in the classroom, including overall learning and academic performance. Attentional difficulties, in particular, can hinder the learning process and may be highly visible in the academic environment. Attention deficit hyperactivity disorder (ADHD) characteristics are incorporated into items as part of the MIT to help teachers identify their students' academic difficulties. Specifically, items pertaining to attention and activity indicative of ADHD are based on what were then current *Diagnostic and Statistical Manual of Mental Disorders* (3rd ed.; *DSM–III*) criteria. Furthermore, there are four global items to assess overall problems in school. The teacher rates whether the child has a problem with learning, behavior, getting along with others, and whether the child will be ready to go on to the next grade. These items are scored from 0 = *definitely* to 5 = *not at all*. Finally, there are seven items that evaluate specific areas of academic performance. Teachers rate their student's reading level, decoding, comprehension, arithmetic processes, arithmetic reasoning, written expression, and handwriting. These items are scored on a 5-point Likert scale from *superior* or *highest* (1) to *poorest* or *lowest* one or two in class (5). The item content of the MIT is presented in Table 2.1. This table reports the development and properties of the MIT, from kindergarten through high school.

TABLE 2.1
Items of the Multigrade Inventory for Teachers (MIT)
and the Adolescent MIT (ADMIT)

MIT	ADMIT
Activity	
1 Out of chair when supposed to be doing his work—sharpens pencils, walks around	
2 In constant motion—always on the go	
3 Restless, can't sit still—taps pencils, claps, taps feet	Restless, can't sit still—taps pencils, claps, taps feet, clicks pen
4 Flits from one activity to another	Shifts from one activity to another
5 Distractible—notices and distracted by slightest noise or movement	
	Acts before thinking
	Does things in a loud and noisy way
	Fidgets
	Acts as if driven by a motor
Attention	
6 Needs reminders to listen carefully	
7 Gets to work immediately, without hesitation	
8 Slow to complete academic tasks—requires extra time	
9 Requires constant supervision or reminders to finish a task	
10 Loses interest before completing most tasks	
11 On a difficult task will keep trying, persist	
12 Doesn't finish what he/she starts (a book, a worksheet)	
13 Needs to have instructions repeated several times	
14 Needs individual help (1:1) in order to complete a task	

(Continued)

TABLE 2.1
(Continued)

MIT	ADMIT
15 Side-tracked from task at hand	
16 Disorganized—loses pencils, papers, work area messy	
	Attention II
	Ignores or overlooks details
	Makes careless mistakes
	Forgets assignments
	Appears low energy, sluggish
	Appears apathetic, low motivation
	Seems to daydream during class
	Requires quiet atmosphere in order to work
	Works independently
	Assignments handed in on time
Adaptability	
17 Gets upset by and can't tolerate changes in routine/schedule	
18 Problems during transitions—waiting, lining up for bus	Problems during transitions—waiting, changing classes
19 Takes challenges eagerly—adapts to new tasks	
20 Takes a long time to settle down to a new activity	
Social	
21 Interested participant in most class activities	
22 Wanders aimlessly around classroom	
23 Immature	
24 Calls out in class	
25 Easily frustrated	
26 Able to wait turn	
27 Inhibited—needs to be coaxed in order to participate	
	Interrupts or intrudes on others
	Seeks out assistance when needed
	Respected by peers
Language	
28 Retells a story in a logical sequence	
29 Ideas come out jumbled, incomplete, in bits and pieces	
30 Trouble expressing his/her thoughts in words	
31 Trouble identifying letters/numbers	Trouble decoding or reading words
32 Difficult to understand	
33 Expresses self physically or through gestures rather than verbally	
34 Requires extra help—gestures, repetition to follow verbal directions	

(Continued)

26

TABLE 2.1
(Continued)

MIT	ADMIT
	Language II
	Mispronounces words or phrases
	Trouble finding correct word, talks around a topic, imprecise
	Speech is smooth, fluent
	Problems in oral reading
	Speech interrupted by pauses, hesitations, repetitions
	Uses imprecise words: "stuff," "thing," "you know"
	Confuses words that sound alike: says tornado for volcano
	Uses mature vocabulary

Academic

MIT	ADMIT
35 In general, does his/her work well	
36 Interest in books/reading	
37 Gets the concept being presented	
38 Retains information learned	
39 Trouble forming letters, numbers (mirrors/reverses/illegible)	Handwriting hard to read
40 Seems to understand rules, but confuses application	
41 Trouble learning new tasks	Trouble learning new material
42 Writing slow and laborious	
43 Difficulty in manipulating pencil, scissors	Difficulty in manipulating pencil or pen
44 Trouble following directions	
45 Associates sound with letter	Trouble sounding out words
	Curious and interested in learning
	Behavior
	In general, follows school rules
	Loses temper
	Argumentative
	Tends to refuse adult's requests or rules
	Tends to do annoying things
	Blames others for his or her mistakes/misbehavior
	Tends to be touchy
	Seems to be angry
	Respectful of other's property
	Swears
	Tells the truth
	Tends to be bossy or bully others
	Gets into fights

(Continued)

TABLE 2.1
(Continued)

MIT	ADMIT

Overall, do you think this student:
46 Has a problem learning
(47–49, and 53 deleted)
50 Has a problem in behavior
51 Has a problem getting along with others
52 This child will be ready to go on to the
     next grade in September
54 Within the class, this child's reading is
     (lowest–highest)
For this student's grade, what is his or her
Mastery Level for the following academic
skills:
55 Decoding
56 Comprehension
57 Arithmetic Processes
58 Arithmetic Reasoning
59 Written Expression
60 Handwriting

PREVIOUS RESEARCH ON THE MIT

The scale development, reliability, and validity of the MIT have been reported previously for kindergarten through grade 5 (Agronin, Holahan, B. A. Shaywitz, & S. E. Shaywitz, 1992). Six scales emerged from this initial study: Attention, Academic, Language, Activity, Dexterity, and Behavior. In second-order factor analyses, the MIT scales formed two broadband factors: Behavioral and Cognitive. The Behavioral broadband scale group consisted of Activity, Behavior, and Attention scales. The Cognitive broadband scale group consisted of Academic, Dexterity, and Attention. Thus, the Attention scale loaded substantially on both broadband scale groups in grades 1, 2, 3, and 5. Systematic gender differences in the teacher ratings of students cognitive and behavioral status were also reported by Agronin et al. (1992). Boys were rated by their teachers as having higher levels of problems in the six domains than were the girls. Statistically significant main effects for grade were found in five of the six scales, with the Activity scale being the exception. Finally, significant grade by gender interactions were detected for the Attention and Behavior scales. Over time, boys are rated as more inattentive, but for girls attention remains fairly constant. Similarly, the Behavior scale means for boys generally increase (get worse), and the mean scores for girls generally decrease (improve) or remain stable.

ADOLESCENT MIT (ADMIT)

In order to accommodate the breadth and depth of behavior and learning styles that adolescent boys and girls demonstrate in the classroom as they progress through high school, the MIT was revised and expanded in 1993, when the participants in the CLS were in the ninth grade. The Adolescent MIT (ADMIT) consists of 93 items and was designed to reflect both changes in the children and in the school environment as they progress through school into higher grade levels. Specifically, items related to ADHD were revised and expanded to be consistent with *DSM–IV* criteria and items related to Oppositional-Defiant Disorder (ODD) consistent with *DSM–IV* criteria were added to the ADMIT.

Four new items relevant to ADHD were introduced into the Activity category of the ADMIT; three items were added to the Social category to reflect age-appropriate behavior. In the Academic category, some items were changed in wording, and new items were added to reflect age-appropriate academic and behavioral demands in the classroom. Additional Attention and Language categories (Attention II and Language II) were added to supplement the original categories and provide more detailed questions in those domains. The global items of the ADMIT dealing with overall learning, behavior, and readiness for academic advancement and the items that assess the child's current academic function in reading and mathematics remain consistent with the MIT. The revised and new items of the ADMIT are presented in Table 2.1.

METHOD

Sample

Data gathered regarding the scale development, reliability, and validity of the MIT came from the ongoing Connecticut Longitudinal Study (CLS). This population has been described in a number of previous reports (B. A. Shaywitz, Fletcher, Holahan, & S. E. Shaywitz, 1992; S. E. Shaywitz, Escobar, B. A. Shaywitz, Fletcher, & Makuch, 1992; S. E. Shaywitz, B. A. Shaywitz, Fletcher, & Escobar, 1990). The sample continues to be followed to provide normative data regarding the developmental course of learning and behavior. The target population for the CLS was Connecticut children attending public kindergarten during the 1983–1984 school year. The children included in the study were selected by a two-stage probability sampling procedure. Administratively, the state is stratified into six regional educational areas comprising 146 towns and 9 rural districts, or 155 primary sampling units. Within each regional area, a systematic sample of a pair of towns was selected with probability proportional to size based on 1981 kindergarten enrollments. The second stage of sampling consisted of selection of two kindergarten classes within the school system of each of the 12 towns. The decision to select two classes within each town was based primarily on the need for an adequate sample size. Each class within a given town had equal probability of selection. For each town, two random numbers selected the two classes, with a total of 24 classes selected.

Subjects

All children entering public kindergarten in each of the towns were invited to participate in the study. Exclusionary criteria were limited to significant sensory impairment, serious psychiatric problems, or to English not being the primary language. These criteria resulted in the exclusion of one blind child. Four hundred forty-five children participated, representing an acceptance rate of 96.5%, including 235 girls (53%) and 210 boys (47%). The sample included 375 White (84.3%), 50 Black (11.2%), 4 Asian (0.9%), and 9 Hispanic (2.0%) children, and 7 children whose race was unknown (1.6%).

Procedure

The CLS sample has been carefully followed since entry into kindergarten and had completed 11th grade in spring 1995. In the spring of each school year, the Woodcock–Johnson Psychoeducational Battery (achievement sections) (Woodcock & Johnson, 1977) was administered to each child. Teachers completed the MIT (kindergarten–grade 8), or the ADMIT (grades 9–11) each year for each participant. MIT scale data are available for kindergarten through grade 11, and ADMIT scale data are available for grades 9 through 11, so there is an overlap of three grades for which both the MIT and the ADMIT data are available. School personnel recorded any special educational services received by the child (e.g., self-contained class, resource room) for each possible academic domain (e.g., reading, math, writing, etc.) on the End of Year Evaluation Form. On alternate odd-numbered years (grades 1, 3, 5, 7, 9), the Wechsler Intelligence Scale for Children–Revised (Wechsler, 1974) was administered to each child. Parents completed a symptom checklist of *DSM–IV* criteria for ADHD in grade 9; this allowed scoring for both categorical and dimensional diagnoses of ADHD.

RESULTS

Scale Development

ADMIT items were examined with two series of exploratory principal component analyses using varimax orthogonal rotation. The first series of analyses was undertaken to reduce the item pool and to estimate the number of factors to be extracted. At the beginning of the first series, 93 items were analyzed. Three to 10 factors were extracted for the data, with 4 to 6 factors yielding reasonable factor structures. Items with substantial factor loadings (< ±.50) on more than one factor, or items without substantial loadings on any factor, were removed and the subsequent reduced item pool was reanalyzed. Throughout the series of analyses, items consider for elimination were reviewed for their content and construct validity. Particular attention was given to items designed to assess *DSM–IV* criteria for AD and ODD. Through the first series of analyses, the pool was reduced to 66 items. The 66-item pool was then subjected to a second series of exploratory principal component analyses. In this series, 3 to 6 factors were extracted in each analysis. During the second series of analyses, it became apparent that the items related to behavior problems (the two items from the MIT Behavior scale; Agronin et al., 1992) and some of the ADMIT items related to ODD criteria were consistently factorially ambiguous. Those items were removed from subsequent analyses and two a priori scales were created: Behavior and Oppositional Defiant Disorder. After removal of those items, the 54-item pool was reanalyzed. The three-factor solution achieved an adequate orthogonal simple structure and accounted for 65% of the variance in the 54-item pool. The final rotated factor matrix is presented in Table 2.2. Thus, the ADMIT consists of 67 items in five scales: Three were factor-based scales and two were designated on the basis of construct and content validity. The three factor-based scales were Academic (20 items, including four items from the MIT Academic scale, three items from the MIT Language scale, and one item from the MIT Dexterity scale); Activity/Impulsivity (18 items; including all nine items from the MIT Activity scale); and Attention (16 items; including two items from the MIT Attention scale and two items from the MIT Academic scale). Two a priori scales were designated: Behavior (2 items; the same as the MIT Behavior scale) and Oppositional Defiant Disorder (11 items; none from the MIT, corresponding to *DSM–IV* criteria for ODD).

Scale scores for the ADMIT scales were calculated by averaging the scores of the constituent items. Items indicative of positive characteristics were reflected so that higher scores were indicative of poorer performance.

Reliability of MIT and ADMIT Scales

Internal consistency reliability estimates for the MIT scales in grades 6 to 11 and the ADMIT scales in grades 9 to 11 were estimated with alpha coefficients. Reliability coefficients of the MIT scales are substantial (Table 2.3). Activity, Attention, and Academic scales demonstrate systematically higher reliability coefficients compared to those of the Behavior, Lan-

TABLE 2.2
Final Rotated Factor Loadings for the ADMIT Items in Grade 9

Academic	Factors		
	I	II	III
Trouble decoding or reading words	.81	.12	.16
Problems in oral reading	.78	.17	.19
Trouble expressing his or her thoughts in words [30] (Language)	.77	.02	.23
Trouble sounding out words	.77	.20	.16
Trouble finding correct word, talks around a topic, imprecise	.76	.08	.15
Trouble learning new material [41] (Academic)	.73	.15	.37
Speech interrupted by pauses, hesitations, repetitions	.73	.11	.23
Difficult to understand [32] (Language)	.73	.16	.15
Ideas come out jumbled, incomplete, in bits and pieces [29] (Language)	.71	.20	.27
Has a problem learning [46] (Academic)	-.70	-.19	-.28
Mispronounces words or phrases	.68	.19	.13
Gets the concept being presented [37] (Academic)	-.65	-.22	-.52
Retells a story in a logical sequence	-.64	-.16	-.47
Writing slow and laborious [42] (Dexterity)	.64	.16	.27
Confuses words that sound alike: says tornado for volcano	.62	.25	.13
Retains information learned [38] (Academic)	-.62	-.17	-.55
Uses mature vocabulary	-.62	-.16	-.36
Speech is smooth, fluent	-.61	-.16	-.22
Uses imprecise words: "stuff", "thing", "you know"	.57	.26	.31
Seems to understand rules, but confuses application	.54	.34	.30
Activity/Impulsivity			
Does things in a loud and noisy way	.13	.88	.10
Fidgets	.18	.87	.15
In constant motion—always on the go [2] (Activity)	.08	.86	.02
Restless, can't sit still—taps pencils, claps, taps feet, clicks pen [3] (Activity)	.11	.86	.11
Interrupts or intrudes on others	.13	.85	.15
Acts as if driven by a motor	.14	.85	.03
Calls out in class [24] (Activity)	.15	.85	.12
Out of chair when supposed to be doing his or her work—sharpens pencils, walks around [1] (Activity)	.09	.82	.21
Distractible—notices and distracted by slightest noise or movement	.25	.78	.29
Shifts from one activity to another [4] (Activity)	.16	.75	.19
Wanders aimlessly around classroom [22] (Activity)	.17	.73	.19
Takes a long time to settle down to a new activity [20] (Activity)	.24	.71	.45
Problems during transitions—waiting, changing classes [18] (Activity)	.25	.69	.28
Immature	.20	.68	.35
Acts before thinking	.21	.66	.17
Needs reminders to listen carefully	.26	.65	.47
Able to wait turn [26] (Activity)	-.19	-.64	-.24
Easily frustrated	.38	.58	.34

(Continued)

TABLE 2.2
(Continued)

	Factors		
Academic	*I*	*II*	*III*
Attention			
Loses interest before completing most tasks [10] (Attention)	.29	.51	.66
Appears apathetic, low motivation	.26	.15	.81
Seems to daydream during class	.19	.11	.78
Interested participant in most class activities	-.32	-.12	-.76
Curious and interested in learning	-.44	-.20	-.72
In general, does his or her work well [35] (Academic)	-.43	-.35	-.72
Appears low energy, sluggish	.25	-.13	.70
Assignments handed in on time	-.23	-.42	-.69
On a difficult task will keep trying, persist	-.25	-.39	-.68
Takes challenges eagerly—adapts to new tasks	-.39	-.30	-.68
Doesn't finish what he/she starts (a book, a worksheet) [12] (Attention)	.26	.41	.67
Forgets assignments	.26	.44	.67
Interested in books/reading [36] (Academic)	-.50	-.23	-.61
Ignores or overlooks the details	.36	.44	.60
Works independently	-.33	-.44	-.58
Makes careless mistakes	.35	.34	.56
A Priori Scales			
ODD			
In general, follows school rules			
Loses temper			
Argumentative			
Tends to refuse adult's requests or rules			
Tends to do annoying things			
Blames others for his or her mistakes/misbehavior			
Tends to be touchy			
Seems to be angry			
Swears			
Tends to be bossy or bully others			
Gets into fights			
Behavior			
Has a problem in behavior [50] (MIT Behavior)			
Has a problem getting along with others [51] (MIT Behavior)			

guage, and Dexterity scales, a finding in general agreement with Agronin et al. (1992). The reliability estimates for the ADMIT scales are consistently very high; the Behavior scale (from Agronin et al., 1992) reliability estimates are substantial, particularly because the scale consists of two global questions: (a) Does this child have a problem with behavior, and (b) does this child have a problem getting along with others? Nonetheless, teachers demonstrate a high degree of consistency in answering those questions.

TABLE 2.3
Cronbach's Alpha Reliability Coefficients for MIT and ADMIT Scales

MIT

Grade	Academic	Language	Dexterity	Attention	Activity	Behavior
6	.91	.81	.77	.92	.94	.82
7	.91	.83	.81	.93	.94	.86
8	.93	.82	.76	.93	.94	.81
9	.93	.78	.75	.92	.94	.89
10	.93	.80	.72	.91	.92	.88
11	.93	.78	.75	.92	.94	.89

ADMIT

Grade	Academic	Activity/ Impulsivity	Attention	Behavior	Oppositional/ Defiant Disorder
9	.96	.97	.96	.89	.96
10	.96	.96	.96	.88	.95
11	.95	.95	.96	.89	.95

Second-Order Factor Analyses (Grades 9–11)

Correlations among the five ADMIT scales within each grade are presented in Table 2.4. Across grades 9 to 11, consistently high pairwise correlations were found for the Academic and Attention scales, representing
the cognitive domain and among the Activity/Impulsivity, Behavior, and
the Oppositional Defiant Disorder scales representing the behavioral domain. Conversely, correlations between scales from the separate domains
(e.g., Academic and Behavior, or Attention and Activity/Impulsivity) are
systematically lower than those for scales from the same domain. The five
ADMIT scales were subjected to three separate second-order principal
component analyses for data collected in grades 9, 10, and 11. As was the
case with the MIT scales (Agronin et al., 1992), two factors accounted for a
minimum of 86.5% of the variance in the scales. The factor loadings for the
varimax rotated solutions are presented in Table 2.5; the factor solutions
are consistent with the correlation matrices.

Descriptive Statistics for the MIT and ADMIT Scales

The means for the overall sample, males and females, for each MIT scale
are plotted in Fig. 2.1, and the means for the overall sample, males and females, for each ADMIT scale are plotted in Fig. 2.2. Means and standard
deviations of the MIT scales in grades 6 through 11 and ADMIT scales in

TABLE 2.4
Pearson Correlations Among the ADMIT Scales

		Scales		
	Academic	Activity/ Impulsivity	Attention	Behavior
Grade 9				
Activity/Impulsivity	.53			
Attention	.76	.64		
Behavior	.46	.73	.60	
Opp/Def Disorder	.50	.82	.67	.82
Grade 10				
Activity/Impulsivity	.60			
Attention	.76	.62		
Behavior	.48	.72	.57	
Opp/Def Disorder	.51	.81	.62	.81
Grade 11				
Activity/Impulsivity	.62			
Attention	.78	.64		
Behavior	.53	.69	.60	
Opp/Def Disorder	.53	.81	.59	.80

grades 9 through 11 for the whole sample are presented in Appendix A. Similarly, means and standard deviations of the MIT and ADMIT scales for males and females are reported in Appendix B.

Data for each of the six MIT scales were organized into a 2 × 6 (Gender × Grade) design, with repeated measures on Grade. Results of the six two-way analysis of variance (ANOVAs) are presented in Table 2.6. Consistent with Agronin et al. (1992), the gender main effect is statistically significant ($p < .001$) for all six scales, in each case girls were rated as demonstrating significantly better behavior than boys. The main effect for grade is statistically significant ($p \leq .02$) for all six scales. Only one scale, Activity, was found to yield a statistically significant ($p < .002$) gender by grade interaction. As can be seen in Fig. 2.1, the means for the MIT Activity scale generally decline (improve) from grades 7 to 11. The significant interaction can be attributed to relatively small variation in the differences between boys and girls—tending to be smaller in grades 10 and 11 relative to grades 6 and 7, rather than a systematic difference in profiles for boys and girls. Finally, observed, but not significant, interactions were found for the MIT Dexterity scale ($p = .063$) and for the MIT Behavior scale ($p = .07$). Statistically significant trend components associated with the main effects for Grade are noted in Table 2.6. There is substantial fluctuation in the mean ratings from grade to grade across each of the scales. In general, however, it may be noted that means for the Academic, Language, and

TABLE 2.5
Rotated Loadings for Second-Order Factor Analyses
of the ADMIT and MIT Scales

ADMIT					
	Grade				
	9		10		11
	Factors				
Scale	I	II	I	II	I	II
Oppositional Defiant Disorder	.89	.32	.90	.31	.91	.28
Behavior	.89	.25	.89	.25	.86	.31
Activity/Impulsivity	.84	.36	.80	.43	.79	.44
Academic	.23	.93	.26	.92	.29	.91
Attention	.46	.82	.39	.84	.38	.86

MIT											
	Grade										
	6		7		8		9		10		11
	Factors										
Scale	I	II	I	II	I	II	I	II	I	II	I	II
Academic	77	43	51	73	52	73	83	36	80	39	53	69
Dexterity	84	04	08	89	05	89	80	21	85	17	06	87
Language	76	33	40	76	38	77	86	23	82	31	47	67
Attention	66	56	70	55	66	60	61	65	62	60	56	64
Behavior	19	89	86	22	88	21	23	88	21	89	88	17
Activity	27	89	89	20	88	20	26	87	33	84	83	29

Dexterity scales tend to be higher in grades 9, 10, and 11 than the corresponding means in grades 7, 8, and 9. In contrast, Attention and Behavior scale means are only slightly higher in grades 9, 10, and 11 than the corresponding means in grades 7, 8, and 9.

Similarly, data for each of the five ADMIT scales were organized into a 2 × 3 (Gender × Grade) design with repeated measures on Grade, and results of the five two-way ANOVAs are presented in Table 2.6. The main effect for gender is statistically significant ($p < .001$) for all five scales, consistent with Agronin et al. (1992), that is, boys are scored in showing poorer performance in each of the scale areas rated. The main effect for grade is statistically significant ($p \leq .02$) for two of the five scales (Attention and Behavior). Statistically significant trend components associated with the main effects for grade are noted in Table 2.6. Trend analyses identify slight

MIT Academic Scale

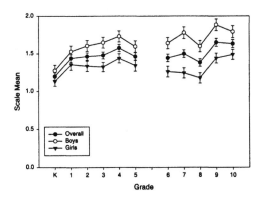

MIT Language

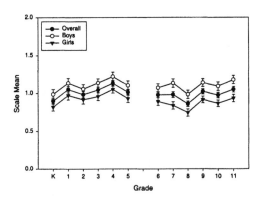

MIT Dexterity Scale

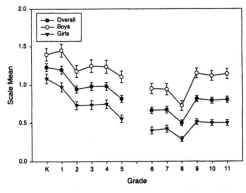

FIG. 2.1. *(Continued)*

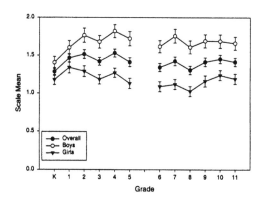

MIT Attention Scale

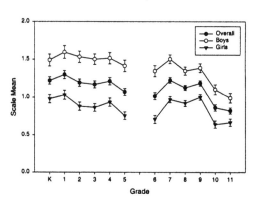

MIT Activity Scale

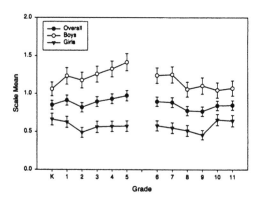

MIT Behavior Scale

FIG. 2.1. Means for the overall sample, males, and females for the MIT Scales.

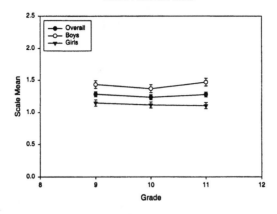

ADMIT Academic Scale

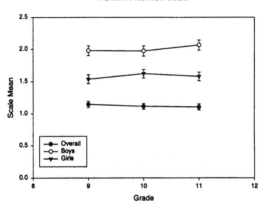

ADMIIT Attention Scale

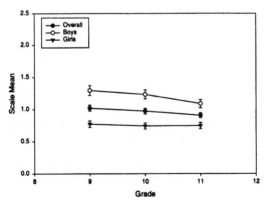

ADMIT Activity/Impulsivity Scale

FIG. 2.2. *(Continued)*

39

ADMIT Behavior Scale

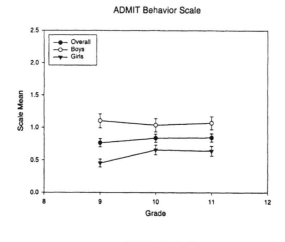

ADMIT ODD Scale

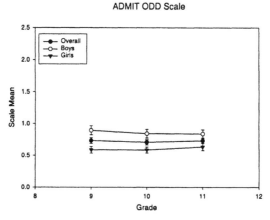

FIG. 2.2.   Means for the overall sample, males, and females for the ADMIT
Scales.

linear increases in the means for the Attention and Behavior scales from
grade 9 to grade 11, indicating that teachers are identifying increasing levels of problems in attention and behavior as the students progress
through those grades. Interestingly, the Activity scales remain relatively
stable from grades 9 to 11. It should be noted that the MIT Activity scale
consists of motorically related items based on *DSM–III* criteria. In contrast,
the ADMIT scale reflects *DSM–IV* criteria that include both activity and
impulsivity so that the scale is then labeled Activity/Impulsivity. Therefore,
this is interpreted to indicate that whereas activity levels do decrease with
age, impulsivity remains stable. The implications of these findings are that
it may be more appropriate to consider activity and impulsivity as separate
constructs, even as children mature.

TABLE 2.6
ANOVA Summary for MIT and ADMIT Scales in Grades 6–11

Scale	MSE Between	F Gender	p	MSE Within	F Grade	p	F Grade × Gender	p	N
				MIT					
Academic	3.75	24.77	< .001	.483	14.81	< .001[a,e]	1.17	NS	366
Language	1.24	21.06	< .001	.354	5.021	< .001[a,b,e]	.20	NS	366
Dexterity	1.48	111.69	< .001	.388	16.23	< .001[a,b,c,e]	2.10	.063	365
Attention	3.63	41.73	< .001	.605	2.96	< .013[d]	1.16	NS	368
Activity	1.55	79.53	< .001	.321	9.52	< .001[a,b,c,e]	3.93	< .002	368
Behavior	3.95	40.44	< .001	.786	2.75	.02[b,d]	1.61	.07	365
				ADMIT Scales in Grades 9–11					
Academic	1.10	21.98	< .001	.290	.74	NS	.623	NS	370
Activity/Impulsivity	1.33	39.22	< .001	.327	1.55	NS	2.57	.078	371
Attention	1.97	23.33	< .001	.488	4.40	.013[a]	.646	NS	371
Behavior	2.53	19.53	< .001	.723	5.66	.004[a]	1.41	NS	369
ODD	1.22	14.58	< .001	.337	1.04	NS	1.27	NS	369

[a]Significant ($p < .05$) linear trend for the grade main effect.
[b]Significant ($p < .05$) quadratic trend for the grade main effect.
[c]Significant ($p < .05$) cubic trend for the grade main effect.
[d]Significant ($p < .05$) quartic trend for the grade main effect.
[e]Significant ($p < .05$) quintic trend for the grade main effect.

41

Validity

External validity for the ADMIT scales was investigated using measures of ability (WISC–R IQ in grades 6 and 9), academic achievement (Woodcock–Johnson Reading, in grades 6, 9, 10, and 11, and Mathematics, in grades 9 and 10), and educational services received (receipt of special education services for reading in grades 6, 9, and 11 from the End of Year Evaluation, EYE, form). Reading disability status in grades 6 and 9 was based on WISC–R Full Scale IQ and Woodcock–Johnson Reading Cluster scores in these grades. Students were defined as reading disabled if they met either a low achievement criterion (WJ age-adjusted Reading Cluster score below the 25th percentile) or by a discrepancy (defined as attaining a WJ age-adjusted Reading Cluster score that is 1.5 standard errors below the score predicted by the child's WISC–R Full Scale IQ).

Further evidence of the validity of the ADMIT scales was sought by constructing an additional a priori scale consisting of the items listed under the Language II heading. Those items are designed to measure components of language that have been implicated in reading disability, particularly phonologic processing and fluency. Two individual items (from the ADMIT Academic Scale) were also selected for validation: "Trouble decoding or reading words" and "Trouble sounding out words." Finally, the "evaluative" items related to reading, for which the teacher assesses the student's current level of academic achievement, were correlated with IQ and achievement.

Concurrent validity coefficients for the MIT and ADMIT scales with IQ and achievement criteria are presented in Table 2.7. Scales excluded from this table and the following tables failed to correlate > ±.30 with any of the criteria. Coefficients less than ±.30 are omitted from the tables in order to simplify the presentation. The MIT Academic, Attention, and Activity scales each have validity coefficients ±.40 and higher in grade 9. Similarly, the ADMIT Academic and Attention scales each have validity coefficients exceeding ±.40 and higher in grade 9. The MIT and ADMIT Academic Scales are the only scales to have validity coefficients exceeding ±.40 with achievement criteria in grades 10 and 11.

Concurrent and predictive validity coefficients for the Language II a priori scale, the "Trouble decoding" and "Trouble sounding out words" items, and the evaluative items related to reading using WJ reading and WISC–R measures as criteria are presented in Table 2.8. The validity coefficients for the Language II scale, "Trouble decoding," and "Trouble sounding out words" items had consistent correlations with the WJ Reading Cluster scores in each grade ranging from −.36 to −.52. Similarly, the validity coefficients using WISC–R Verbal Intelligence Quotient (VIQ), Perform-

TABLE 2.7
ADMIT Concurrent Validity Coefficients
with Measures of Ability and Achievement

Scale	Woodcock–Johnson		WISC–R		
	Reading	Math	VIQ	PIQ	FSIQ
Grade 10					
Academic	−.49	−.51	−.54	−.39	−.52
Activity/Impulsivity	−.30	−.32	−.32		−.30
Attention	−.37	−.43	−.45		−.41
ODD	−.30	−.34	−.34		−.31
Grade 10					
Academic	−.42	−.41			
Activity		−.32			
Attention	−.31	−.38			
ODD		−.34			
Grade 11					
Academic	−.48				
Attention	−.35				

Note: The WISC–R was not administered after 9th grade and the Woodcock–Johnson Math subtests were not administered after 10th grade.

ance Intelligence Quotient (PIQ), and Full Scale Intelligence Quotient (FSIQ) in grade 9 as criteria were in the same range. As would be expected, those items had fewer coefficients exceeding ±.30 with PIQ than with VIQ and FSIQ. The evaluative items for reading level, decoding, and comprehension have systematically higher validity coefficients with reading achievement and IQ. The teachers' evaluation of handwriting in grade 9 achieved coefficients exceeding ±.30 with reading; the teachers' evaluation of handwriting in grades 10 and 11 failed to achieve coefficients exceeding ±.30 with either reading achievement or IQ.

Because teachers can provide reliable ratings of student status, it is reasonable to determine the relations between the discriminant variables (Teacher ratings) and the student's reading status (reading disability or not) or behavioral status (ADHD or not). It is also important in assessing the validity of the predictor measures to determine which, if any, constructs are highly related to classification of subjects into their diagnostic groups.

The CLS study design provides for school-based and research-based criteria for identification of reading disability (S. E. Shaywitz et al., 1990). School-based identification (SI) is determined from school records of subjects who have received special education services in reading each year. Research-based criteria for identification as reading disabled (RI) uses test-based empirical criteria for low achievement and discrepancy status in each year. The validity of teacher ratings on the MIT and ADMIT in determining

TABLE 2.8
Concurrent and Predictive Validity Coefficients for
Measures Related to Reading and Evaluative Items

| | WJ Reading | | | WISC–R Grade 9 | | |
| | Grade | | | IQ Score | | |
ADMIT Item/Scale	9	10	11	Verbal	Performance	Full Scale
Language II 9	−.46	−.51	−.48	−.51	−.38	−.49
Language II 10	−.36	−.39	−.39	−.42		−.39
Language II 11	−.43	−.46	−.48	−.48		−.43
Trouble decoding 9	−.48	−.51	−.47	−.51	−.41	−.51
Trouble decoding 10	−.42	−.43	−.43	−.46		−.41
Trouble decoding 11	−.42	−.45	−.47	−.43	−.31	−.42
Trouble sounding out 9	−.48	−.52	−.49	−.46	−.34	−.45
Trouble sounding out 10	−.38	−.39	−.40	−.39		−.37
Trouble sounding out 11	−.36	−.37	−.38	−.39	−.30	−.38
Evaluative Items						
Reading Level 9	−.46	−.52	−.49	−.47	−.37	−.47
Reading Level 10	−.35	−.39	−.40	−.41	−.32	−.41
Reading Level 11	−.39	−.41	−.41	−.39		−.36
Decoding Level 9	−.56	−.60	−.56	−.60	−.46	−.59
Decoding Level 10	−.43	−.47	−.48	−.49	−.33	−.46
Decoding Level 11	−.50	−.55	−.54	−.51	−.32	−.47
Comprehension 9	−.51	−.56	−.51	−.56	−.45	−.56
Comprehension 10	−.41	−.45	−.45	−.49	−.34	−.47
Comprehension 11	−.45	−.50	−.50	−.51	−.38	−.50
Written Expression 9	−.51	−.54	−.51	−.53	−.40	−.52
Written Expression 10	−.36	−.41	−.41	−.42	−.31	−.41
Written Expression 11	−.43	−.49	−.46	−.47	−.33	−.45
Handwriting 9	−.31	−.32	−.31			

ADHD was assessed by the parent symptom checklist for ADHD completed in grade 9. This instrument permits a categorical diagnosis of ADHD using *DSM–IV* criteria and a dimensional diagnosis using inattention, hyperactivity, and impulsivity on scales from this same symptom checklist.

Four discriminant analyses were performed using ADMIT scales and items and gender as discriminant variables. The four models predicted to SI, RI, ADHD (Dimensional), and ADHD (Categorical) criteria, respectively.

Summaries of the canonical correlations and canonical variate loadings for the four ADMIT models are presented in Table 2.9. The highest canonical correlation is for the model predicting SI, followed by RI, ADHD (Categorical), and ADHD (Dimensional). Most important, for predicting to SI and RI criteria, it may be seen that the loadings for the scales and items from the cognitive domain (e.g., Academic scale, Trouble decoding) have

TABLE 2.9
Canonical Variate Loadings for Discriminant Functions
for the ADMIT Scales and Items

	Receipt of Special Ed Services	RD Status	ADHD (Dimensional)	ADHD (Categorical)
ADMIT Academic 9	.88	.69	.54	.31
Trouble Decoding 9	.83	.80	.23	.11
Language II Scale 9	.76	.63	.43	.23
Trouble Sounding Out Words 9	.76	.82	.35	.18
ADMIT Attention 9	.64	.51	.74	.56
ADMIT ODD 9	.54	.59	.94	.85
ADMIT Behavior 9	.49	.49	.76	.75
ADMIT Activity 9	.48	.56	.82	.90
Gender	−.29	−.09	.27	.41
Canonical Correlation	.54	.42	.30	.31

higher loadings than the scales representing the behavioral domain, whereas the scales from the behavioral domain have higher canonical variate loadings in both models predicting ADHD status. Note that the loading for gender in the SI model is greater than ±.25 in the SI model but near 0 in the RI model. The canonical variate loadings (absolute values) for the RI, ADHD (Dimensional), and ADHD (Categorical) models are plotted in Figs. 2.3, 2.4, and 2.5, respectively.

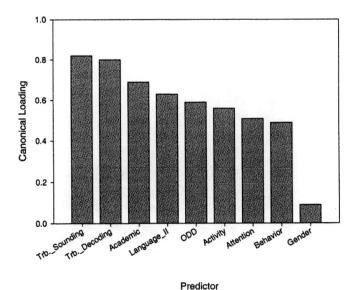

FIG. 2.3.   Prediction of reading disability.

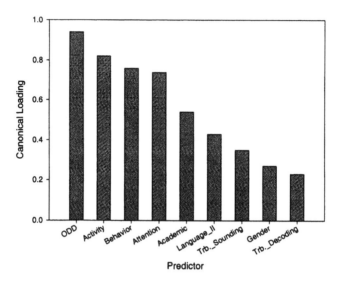

FIG. 2.4.   Prediction of ADHD (dimensional).

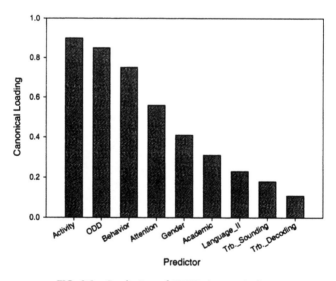

FIG. 2.5.   Prediction of ADHD (categorical).

CONCLUSIONS

These data are unique in providing a systematic description of the cognitive and behavioral characteristics of a randomly selected group of boys and girls monitored from kindergarten through high school. They demonstrate, for the most part, relative stability from year to year for constructs of academic function, language, and attention; activity and behavioral difficulties tended to show minimal reduction over time. At the same time, these data suggest that, over longer time intervals, there are systematic changes in teachers' expectations of the children, reflected primarily in the teachers' perception of attention. An earlier report (Agronin et al., 1992) found that the MIT Attention scale tended to straddle both the cognitive and behavioral domains, that is, Attention loaded on both the cognitive and behavioral broadband groupings of MIT scales. In contrast, the current data indicate that the ADMIT Attention scale loads only on the cognitive broadband scale—there is no overlap with the behavioral broadband scale. By 9th grade, Attention and Academic scales are clearly differentiated from the Activity/Impulsivity, Behavior, and Oppositional Defiant Disorder scales (Table 2.5). Thus, the relations between the construct of attention and the other cognitive and behavioral domains change from the elementary school years (kindergarten–grade 5) to the middle and high school years. Whether this reflects an underlying change in the underlying construct of attention in the children themselves or in the expectations of their teachers is not clear. As we have noted previously (S. E. Shaywitz, Fletcher, & B. A. Shaywitz, 1994), the concept of attention has intrigued psychologists for almost a century, and whereas numerous conceptual models of attention have been elaborated (Barkley, 1994, 1996; Cooley & Morris, 1990; Kinchla, 1992; Mirsky, Anthony, Duncan, Ahearn, & Kellam, 1991; Posner, 1988; Posner & Petersen, 1990), their relation to what clinicians mean by "attentional problems" or ADHD remains unclear. It is also possible that the change in attention over time reflects the teachers' changing concepts of attention as the children mature. From this perspective, it is reasonable to suggest that middle school and high school teachers view poor academic performance more as a product of inattention than as an explicit cognitive deficit.

A striking finding was the persistent differences between boys and girls. Boys were consistently rated as having higher levels of cognitive and behavior problems from kindergarten through 11th grade, confirming and extending previously reported results throughout the school years (Table 2.6). These findings are consonant with earlier reports from the Dunedin longitudinal study in New Zealand of gender differences as children mature. Thus, McGee, Williams, and Silva (1987) found that, at ages 9 and 11, teachers rated boys as having significantly more problems with attention than girls and ratings of hyperactivity and antisocial behavior were more stable for boys. Moreover, they found that the inattentive boys were more often rated as having poor concentration at age 5 than were the inattentive girls, even though the inattentive boys and girls had similar histories of behavior problems at age 5. Jorm, Share, Matthews, and Maclean (1986) reported that attentiveness had low, but statistically significant, correlations with gender (i.e., boys were rated as having significantly higher levels of attention problems than girls) during the first 3 years in school. The data also indicate how the significant differences in behavior between boys and girls influence teacher perceptions of academic performance and identification of school difficulties. For example, in the ADMIT, gender correlated with SI designation significantly, whereas, in contrast, the relation between RI and gender was near zero. The implications of these findings were demonstrated in an earlier report (S. E. Shaywitz et al., 1990) in which there was a four to one prevalence of boys to girls identified by their schools (SI) as reading disabled compared to similar numbers of boys and girls identified by research criteria (RI) based on ability and achievement testing. Together these data suggest that teachers may internalize and apply a norm of behavior that is more appropriate for girls than it is for their male classmates. Furthermore, the findings indicate that any rating instruments of school-age children must include separate normed scales for boys and for girls. Otherwise, what may be on the higher end of a continuum of a "normal" behavior for boys may be misinterpreted as excessive and deviant.

Teacher ratings, reflected in the MIT and ADMIT, were useful in helping to identify learning and attention problems. For example, at 9th grade, teachers' responses to the evaluative items "Trouble sounding out words" and "Trouble decoding words" and scores on the Academic and Language II scales were predictive of reading disability (based on research criteria). A large body of evidence has now accumulated, indicating that reading difficulties reflect an impairment in a specific component of language, phonology (I. Y. Liberman, Shankweiler, & A. M. Liberman, 1989; Stanovich, 1988; reviewed by S. E. Shaywitz, 1996). Children with reading disability do not easily apprehend the basic underlying sound structure of the written word; these data are important because they indicate that even as children mature and enter high school, difficulties at the phonologic level (decoding words) are still evident and are significantly related to poor performance on tests of reading. Teachers' notions of whether children required special education services were strongly related to the Academic scale scores and to the items, Decoding and Sounding out words. This may indicate that teachers take phonologic processing into consideration when recommending children for special education or may simply reflect that the teachers knew whether the children were receiving special services when they completed the MIT and ADMIT. Teacher ratings on the ODD, Activity, Behavior, and Attention scales were highly correlated with parents' identification of the child as having ADHD (Figs. 2.4 and 2.5).

These findings in the 9th grade are somewhat different from those noted in previous reports in younger children. McGee, Williams, Share, Anderson, and Silva (1986) examined longitudinal parent and teacher ratings for boys from ages 5 to 11 using the Rutter (Rutter, Tizzard, & Whitmore, 1970) scales for behavior and the Burt Wording Reading Test (Scottish Council for Research in Education, 1976) and the WISC–R (Wechsler, 1974) to establish reading disability. The analysis of the association between reading disability and problem behavior was restricted to boys because of the small number of girls in the two reading disabled groups. Results indicated a significant longitudinal association between reading disability and problem behaviors, noted by teacher report. Jorm et al. (1986) examined the relation between longitudinal teacher ratings using Rutter's Children's Behavior Questionnaire (Rutter, 1967), reading disability using the Columbia Mental Maturity Scale (Burgemeister, Blum, & Lorge, 1972) to assess intelligence, and the Neale Analysis of Reading Ability (Neale, 1966) to assess achievement for boys from age 5 to 11. Their findings indicated that boys with specific reading retardation did not demonstrate behavior problems, whereas the boys with general reading backwardness had significantly higher levels of behavior problems at entry and throughout the first 3 years of school.

Finally, the decline of MIT Activity level over time, particularly in grades 7 to 11, is consistent with a large body of data indicating that, in ADHD, activity levels are highest in the early school years then abate as the child matures. The data also suggest that although activity levels may decline with time, levels of impulsivity remain stable. Because the ontogeny of these two behaviors may be distinct, it may be most appropriate to consider them as separate constructs, rather than as a combined Activity/Impulsivity scale as on the current *DSM–IV*.

In summary, these data obtained longitudinally and on a representative sample of Connecticut schoolchildren indicate that, for the most part, children's behaviors are fairly stable over the school years. An exception is the level of activity that tends to decline as children mature. This decrease in activity levels may be obscured if activity and impulsivity are conflated on the same scale. The data clearly indicate, too, that the normative levels of the range of behaviors assessed by the MIT and ADMIT scales are significantly different for boys and girls over the full course of schooling; these findings have significant implications for how children are identified as reading disabled in schools and classrooms. These data indicate how, for many years, based on school identification, reading disability was considered to be more prevalent in boys than in girls. These results also indicate that the basic phonologic difficulties characterizing reading disability are not restricted to young children, but rather remain evident through adolescence at least.

The data presented in this chapter provide strong evidence for the utility of the MIT and ADMIT: The constructs measured by the MIT and ADMIT are robust and the factor structures from one grade level to the next are remarkably consistent, particularly because the MIT and ADMIT reflect observations by different teachers in different schools in virtually all geographic areas of the country of the same child. These data add to and extend a growing body of literature that supports the notion that teacher ratings are accurate and reliable in assessing behavior and cognitive performance (Gresham, MacMillan, & Bocian, 1997; Keogh & Smith, 1970; Morine-Dershimer, 1978–1979). These findings suggest that the MIT (and ADMIT) is a reliable and valid instrument for obtaining systematic information relevant to learning and attention in children from kindergarten through high school. Such information will be useful for clinicians and educators called on to evaluate the child who is not doing well in school.

ACKNOWLEDGMENTS

This work was supported by grants from the National Institute of Child Health and Human Development (PO1 HD 21888 and P50 HD25802). We thank Carmel Lepore for her invaluable help in the preparation of this chapter. We gratefully acknowledge the contributions of the children, families, and educators who are participating in the Connecticut Longitudinal Study.

REFERENCES

Agronin, M. E., Holahan, J. M., Shaywitz, B. A., & Shaywitz, S. E. (1992). The Multi-Grade Inventory for Teachers (MIT): Scale development, reliability, and validity of an instrument to assess children with attentional deficits and learning disabilities. In S. E. Shaywitz & B. A. Shaywitz (Eds.), *Attention deficit disorder comes of age: Toward the twenty-first century* (pp. 89–116). Austin, TX: Pro-Ed.

Atkins, M. S., & Pelham, W. E. (1991). School-based assessment of attention deficit-hyperactivity disorder. *Journal of Learning Disabilities, 24*(4), 197–204.

Barkley, R. A. (1994). The assessment of attention in children. In G. R. Lyon (Ed.), *Frames of reference for the assessment of Learning disabilities: New views on measurement issues* (pp. 69–102). Baltimore: Paul H. Brookes.

Barkley, R. A. (1996). Critical issues in research on attention. In G. R. Lyon & N. A. Krasnegor (Eds.), *Attention, memory, and executive function* (pp. 45–56). Baltimore: Paul H. Brookes.

Burgemeister, B. B., Blum, L. H., & Lorge, I. (1972). *Columbia Mental Maturity Scale.* New York: Harcourt Brace Jovanovich.

Cooley, E. L., & Morris, R. D. (1990). Attention in children: A neuropsychologically based model for assessment. *Developmental Neuropsychology, 6*(3), 239–274.

Gresham, F. M., MacMillan, D. L., & Bocian, K. M. (1997). Teachers as "tests": Differential validity of teacher judgments in identifying students at-risk for learning difficulties. *School Psychology Review, 26*(11), 47–60.

Jorm, A. F., Share, D. L., Matthews, R., & Maclean, R. (1986). Behaviour problems in specific reading retarded and general reading backward children: A longitudinal study. *Journal of Child Psychology and Psychiatry, 27*(1), 33–43.

Keogh, B. K. (1977). Early ID, selective perception or perceptive selection? *Academic Therapy, 12,* 267–274.

Keogh, B. K., & Smith, C. E. (1970). Early identification of educationally high potential and high risk children. *Journal of School Psychology 8*(4), 285–290.

Kinchla, R. A. (1992). Attention. *Annual Review of Psychology, 43,* 711–742.

Liberman, I. Y., Shankweiler, D., & Liberman, A. M. (1989). The alphabetic principle and learning to read. In D. Shankweiler & I. Y. Liberman (Eds.), *Phonology and reading disability: Solving the reading puzzle* (pp. 1–33). Ann Arbor, MI: University of Michigan Press.

McGee, R., Williams, S., Share, D. L., Anderson, J., & Silva, P. A. (1986). The relationship between specific reading retardation, general reading backwardness and behavioural problems in a large sample of Dunedin boys: A longitudinal study from five to eleven years. *Journal of Child Psychology and Psychiatry, 27*(5), 597–610.

McGee, R., Williams, S., & Silva, P. A. (1987). A comparison of girls and boys with teacher-identified problems of attention. *Journal of the American Academy of Child and Adolescent Psychiatry, 26*(5), 711–717.

Mirsky, A. F., Anthony, B. J., Duncan, C. C., Ahearn, M. B., & Kellam, S. G. (1991). Analysis of the elements of attention: A neuropsychological approach. *Neuropsychology Review, 2,* 109–145.

Morine-Dershimer, G. (1978–1979a). The anatomy of teacher prediction. *Educational Research Quarterly, 3,* 59–65.

Morine-Dershimer, G. (1978–1979b). How teachers "see" their pupils. *Educational Research Quarterly, 3,* 43–58.

Neale, M. D. (1966). *Neale Analysis of Reading Ability.* London: Macmillan.

Posner, M. (1988). Structures and functions of selective attention. In T. Boll & B. K. Bryant (Eds.), *Clinical neuropsychology and brain function: Research, measurement, and practice* (pp. 173–202). Washington, DC: American Psychological Association.

Posner, M. I., & Petersen, S. E. (1990). The attention system of the human brain. *Annual Review of Neuroscience, 13,* 25–42.

Rutter, M. (1967). A Children's Behaviour Questionnaire for completion by teachers: Preliminary findings. *Journal of Child Psychology and Psychiatry, 8,* 1–11.

Rutter, M., Tizzard, J., & Whitmore, K. (1970). *Education, health, and behavior.* London: Longman.

Scottish Council for Research in Education. (1976). *The Burt Word Reading Test—1974 Revision.* London: Hodder & Stoughton.

Shaywitz, B. A., Fletcher, J. M., Holahan, J. M., & Shaywitz, S. E. (1992). Discrepancy compared to low achievement definitions of reading disability: Results from the Connecticut Longitudinal Study. *Journal of Learning Disabilities, 25*(10), 639–648.

Shaywitz, B. A., Fletcher, J. M., Holahan, J. M., Shneider, A. E., Marchione, K. E., Stuebing, K. K., Francis, D. J., Shankweiler, D. P., Katz, L., Liberman, I. Y., & Shaywitz, S. E. (1995). Interrelationships between reading disability and attention-deficit/hyperactivity disorder. *Child Neuropsychology, 1*(3), 170–186.

Shaywitz, S. E. (1987). The Multi-Grade Inventory for Teachers.

Shaywitz, S. E. (1996). Dyslexia. *Scientific American, 275*(5), 98–104.

Shaywitz, S. E., Escobar, M. D., Shaywitz, B. A., Fletcher, J. M., & Makuch, R. (1992). Evidence that dyslexia may represent the lower tail of a normal distribution of reading ability. *New England Journal of Medicine, 326*(3), 145–150.

Shaywitz, S. E., Fletcher, J. M., & Shaywitz, B. A. (1994). Issues in the definition and classification of attention deficit disorder. *Topics in Language Disorders, 14*(4), 1–25.

Shaywitz, S. E., Shaywitz, B. A., Fletcher, J. M., & Escobar, M. D. (1990). Prevalence of reading disability in boys and girls: Results of the Connecticut longitudinal study. *Journal of the American Medical Association, 264*(8), 998–1002.

Silva, P. A., Williams, S., & McGee, R. (1987). A longitudinal study of children with developmental language delay at age three: Later intelligence, reading and behaviour problems. *Developmental Medicine and Child Neurology, 29*, 630–640.

Stanovich, K. E. (1988). The right and wrong places to look for the cognitive locus of reading disability. *Annals of Dyslexia, 38*, 154–177.

Stevenson, J., Richman, N., & Graham, P. (1985). Behaviour problems and language abilities at three years and behavioural deviance at eight years. *Journal of Child Psychology and Psychiatry, 26*(2), 215–230.

Ullmann, R. K., Sleator, E. K., & Sprague R. L. (1984). ADD children: Who is referred from the schools? *Psychopharmacology Bulletin, 20*(2), 308–312.

Wechsler, D. (1974). *Wechsler Intelligence Scale for Children–Revised*. New York: Psychological Corporation.

Werner, E. E., & Smith, R. S. (1977). *Kauai's children come of age*. Honolulu: University Press of Hawaii.

Woodcock, R. W., & Johnson, M. B. (1977). *Woodcock-Johnson Psycho-Educational Battery*. Boston: NYT Teaching Resources.

Means and Standard Deviations of MIT and ADMIT Scales

				MIT			
Grade		Academic	Language	Dexterity	Attention	Activity	Behavior
6	n	414	414	414	414	414	414
	M	1.441	.977	.665	1.341	1.015	.894
	SD	1.052	.751	.839	1.078	.938	1.267
7	n	411	411	411	411	411	410
	M	1.498	.981	.672	1.423	1.225	.883
	SD	1.066	.764	.893	1.155	.760	1.310
8	n	409	409	409	409	409	409
	M	1.378	.859	.499	1.304	1.125	.773
	SD	1.033	.746	.739	1.116	.686	1.241
9	n	408	407	407	408	408	408
	M	1.651	1.023	.817	1.413	1.186	.765
	SD	1.060	.687	.788	1.155	.705	1.267
10	n	397	397	396	397	397	396
	M	1.633	.974	.795	1.452	.863	.841
	SD	1.052	.721	.798	1.104	.826	1.248
11	n	386	386	386	388	388	386
	M	1.689	1.051	.807	1.413	.823	.846
	SD	1.041	.729	.792	1.074	.779	1.233

			ADMIT			
Grade		Academic	Activity/ Impulsivity	Attention	Behavior	ODD
9	n	408	408	408	408	406
	M	1.28	1.02	1.75	.77	.74
	SD	.78	.95	1.03	1.27	.89
10	n	395	395	395	395	395
	M	1.24	.97	1.79	.84	.71
	SD	.77	.87	1.03	1.25	.82
11	n	386	388	388	386	387
	M	1.28	.91	1.81	.85	.73
	SD	.76	.80	1.04	1.23	.84

APPENDIX B
Means and Standard Deviations of MIT and ADMIT Scales for Males and Females MIT

Grade	Gender		Academic	Language	Dexterity	Attention	Activity	Behavior	n
6	Male	M	1.640	1.072	.951	1.618	1.347	1.240	198
		SD	1.036	.752	.921	1.116	1.020	1.448	
	Female	M	1.258	.890	.402	1.088	.711	.567	216
		SD	1.035	.741	.656	.979	.736	.976	
7	Male	M	1.778	1.135	.941	1.755	1.503	1.250	196
		SD	1.094	.792	1.035	1.025	.818	1.493	
	Female	M	1.241	.839	.424	1.118	.970	.547	214
		SD	.972	.711	.648	.966	.600	1.008	
8	Male	M	1.599	.983	.726	1.608	1.348	1.056	196
		SD	1.046	.783	.905	1.186	.749	1.387	
	Female	M	1.174	.744	.290	1.025	.920	.512	213
		SD	.981	.692	.452	.968	.550	1.027	
9	Male	M	1.883	1.140	1.150	1.690	1.387	1.103	194
		SD	1.088	.715	.879	1.185	.802	1.510	
	Female	M	1.438	.915	.513	1.160	1.002	.455	213
		SD	.991	.644	.539	1.069	.542	.890	
10	Male	M	1.792	1.093	1.118	1.687	1.102	1.045	189
		SD	1.100	.796	.892	1.205	.912	1.395	
	Female	M	1.488	.865	.501	1.238	.646	.655	207
		SD	.987	.628	.559	.957	.670	1.067	
11	Male	M	1.941	1.180	1.144	1.660	.991	1.071	184
		SD	1.068	.747	.893	1.139	.853	1.361	
	Female	M	1.462	.935	.502	1.189	.670	.641	202
		SD	.964	.694	.531	.960	.671	1.066	

ADMIT

Grade	Gender		Academic	Activity/ Impulsivity	Attention	Behavior	ODD	n
9	Male	M	1.431	1.295	1.979	1.103	.895	194
		SD	.837	.962	1.076	1.395	.925	
	Female	M	1.146	.771	1.537	.455	.590	212
		SD	.716	.754	.983	.890	.770	
10	Male	M	1.368	1.232	1.975	1.037	.843	188
		SD	.837	.962	1.076	1.395	.925	
	Female	M	1.115	.740	1.622	.657	.587	207
		SD	.677	.689	.966	1.066	.694	
11	Male	M	1.469	1.088	2.066	1.071	.839	183
		SD	.808	.864	1.071	1.361	.866	
	Female	M	1.103	.744	1.577	.641	.635	203
		SD	.674	.694	.962	1.066	.808	

## CHAPTER THREE

Social Interaction Impairments

Lynn Waterhouse
The College of New Jersey

This chapter presents a model of social interaction skills. Sources of individual variation and key components of social interaction are considered. Neural and social impairments in Down syndrome, Rett syndrome, Williams syndrome and autism are described. The central claims of this chapter are (1) that brain deficits reduce variability in social interaction, and (2) that distinctive features of abnormal sociability provide clues to discovering the brain basis of social behavior.

There are three major sections in this chapter. The first outlines models of variation in behavior. The second considers the abnormal sociability in autism and Down, Rett, and Williams syndrome. The third section proposes an elaborated model of social interaction skills.

BEHAVIORAL VARIATION AND HUMAN SOCIAL INTERACTION

Sources of Variation in Behavior

A prime source of individual variation in human behavior is genetic individuality. A person's behavioral variation is determined by the expression genes in developmental interaction with the environment. Some 15,000 or more genes are thought to determine the human central nervous system (CNS). Subsets of these genes determine the brain structures, chemistry, and processes that form the control systems generating human behaviors.

Variation in individual genes (alleles) and sets of genes underwrite variation in human behavior. Genetic variation in organisms is adaptive. The greater the genetic variation within a population, the greater will be the likelihood that a subset of that population will survive and reproduce if the environment changes. Similarly, cultural variation in "memes" (units of cultural practice and innovation theorized to function as genes do) is also adaptive. The cultural memes of tools, agriculture, division of labor, writing, and laws have improved the adaptive fit of humans. Moreover, cultural memes such as clothing have extended the adaptive fit of humans to new environments (Soltis, Boyd, & Richerson, 1995).

Groups of genes underwrite control systems that fall on a continuum of malleability: (a) least malleable are autonomic system functions, such as breathing; followed by (b) reflexes, such as sneezing, blinking, and sucking; (c) fixed action programs, such as grasping; (d) fixed component triggers for specific forms of learning, such as the development of phobias or word production skills; and (e) learned programs with strong innate components such as social interaction skills; (f) learned motor skills and content knowledge; and most malleable is the (g) imagination to create new knowledge and skills.

Genetic variation in fixed programs of behavior is more limited than in learned programs: People are more like one another in breathing than they are in imagination. However, many components of each of these seven sets of control systems for behavior can vary across individuals.

Turkheimer (2000) has outlined the three "laws" of genetic influence on behavior. First, all behaviors are heritable. Second, family environment has a smaller effect on behavior than do genes. Third, a significant portion of variation in behavior is not accounted for by either genes or family environment. Turkheimer argues that environmental influences are not systematic (2000, p. 163), and therefore, research to discover causes of variation in behavior can yield only small and unpredictably changing results.

Given both the varied genetic constitution of each individual, and given the varied life experience and learning that each has encountered, the mental contents and dispositions of each person can be assumed to be quite varied. Despite this potential range of variation in behavior, there are many forces working to reduce variation in human behavior.

Forces Reducing Variation in Behavior

There are many factors that serve to limit the potentially wide range of individual variation in human behavior. Shared genes and gene groups (found in twins, siblings, families, kinships, populations, and species) maintain internal genome limits to variation. Shared features of the natural environment (the Andes, the Sahara, and the Arctic) limit gene variation through natural selection. And shared features of males and females limit gene variation in the opposite sex through sexual selection processes.

The new field of evolutionary developmental psychology has outlined still another potent force for the limitation of individual variation—innate cognitive domains of thought. For example, Geary and Bjorklund (2000) have proposed two generic domains of thought, Social and Ecological. Within the Ecological domain they have suggested two sub-domains of biology (plants and animals), and four sub-domains of physical action (movement, representation, engineering, and number processing). Within the Social domain they have proposed four sub-domains of individual sociality (nonverbal behavior, language, facial processing, and theory of mind), and four sub-domains of group sociality (kin recognition, in-group recognition, out-group recognition, and social ideologies). If universal innate "biologically primary" thinking abilities do exist as theorized, we should all share in a more limited and more similar understanding of the world.

A further source of limits to variation arises from drives that lead to reduced variation in individuals' social behaviors. First, human beings are social animals with strong needs for group social cohesion. The need for social cohesion brings people into proximity to one another, and this supports shared behaviors. Group action may be regulated by a leader or leaders, whose directions individuals share in following, thus limiting variation across those within groups. Hierarchical institutional structures in business, government, hospitals, and schools build on the forces within people for group cohesion and their acceptance of leadership regulation for limits to individual variation within group culture.

Fiske (1992) argued that there are only four forms of social cohesion in human societies.

1. Social cohesion through communal sharing. Group members give all that they have to the group without reserve. There is tight altruistic regulation of social and work behavior: Members must share food, effort, information, and behavior patterns completely or risk being ostracized from the group.

2. Social cohesion through authority ranking. A hierarchical pecking order determines the roles and rules vary by rank and power. Those with more power have greater freedom for variation in behavior.

3. Social cohesion through equality matching. Turn taking and need for matching regulates and reduces variability in the behavior of individuals.

4. Social cohesion through market valuing. Here behaviors have different value depending on their relative relevance to life needs, and this value of information must be computed by some means in order that those individuals who offer more valued information will be accorded greater value in the community. Behavioral variability is reduced through market modeling.

If there are only four forms of social exchange, then people's interaction behaviors will be limited to patterns set within these forms of exchange. Even if Fiske's model is not correct in all particulars, it is likely that only a few forms of social interaction are possible. Thus, individuals' social interaction behavior will be limited by the limits of these few frameworks for social interchange.

Another limit to variation in human behavior stems from the fact that humans are easily disturbed by behavioral novelty in others because it is inherently arousing (Insel, 1992) and potentially disruptive. Moreover, it requires greater expenditure of energy because people have to pay selective attention to the novel behavior, they have to formulate an interpretation of the behavior, and they may also have to generate a response not presently part of their habit repertoire. As a consequence, they seek interpersonal (manners) and cultural means (practices, laws) to limit novel and unpredictable variation in the behavior of others.

However, people do have one built-in mechanism to support their need for less novelty in the behavior of those around them: mimicry. People limit the variation in behavior in social interaction through mimicry. In fact, they mimic all aspects of one another's behaviors (Meltzhoff & Gopnick, 1993). Body motion mimicry leads to copied, shared, similar motor actions and hence reduces potential variability in motor patterns. Facial expression mimicry appears to lead to shared internal affect states (Ekman, 1993), thereby reducing interindividual variability in motivating dispositional states.

In addition to gene frequencies, innate Universal cognitive domains, limited social frameworks, and human needs for predictability, still another important limit to variation in social behavior is human motivation and personality. Gray (1970) early proposed that there are three innate motivation systems—the Behavioral Activation System regulating conditioned rewards, the Behavioral Inhibition System regulating conditioning of punishment, and the Fight-Flight system regulating response to unconditioned punishment and danger. Based in Gray's model Depue and Collins (1999) proposed a threshold model for dopamine as the source of individual variation in the observed trait defined as extraversion. Cloninger (Cloninger, Adolfsson, & Svrakic, 1996) proposed a model of three trait dimensions—Reward Dependence, Novelty Seeking, and Harm Avoidance. Woodward et al. (2000) have provided evidence for a high reactivity taxon in a group of 599 children. They believe that variation in the Fight/ Flight system (also identified as the Harm Avoidance trait) channels behavior in discrete types or taxons and does not exist as a spectrum of continuous variation. These models identify taxonic traits. The very limited number of such traits suggests a limit to the number of expressive personalities possible. As these models conceptualize personality as the basis for expressive behavior, such models imply reduced behavioral variability.

Overall, there is an essential conflict between the species' needs for adaptive variation in the possible range of behaviors possible and the individual's needs for variation in behavior. The species' need is for an *increase in variation* in genetic and cultural behaviors so as to enhance adaptation across all potential future environments. The individual's need is for a *decrease in variation* in the here-and-now behavior of others so that the world of human interaction will be an easier one in which to make the most adaptive survival decisions possible. The mechanisms of mimicry and social learning, the limits to the expression of personality, and people's need for social cohesion with leadership regulation may represent the outcome of a tug-of-war between opposing needs. These mechanisms suppress other aspects of individual variation in behavior, funnel preferences, delimit the execution of plans, provide greater uniformity to exploration of the environment, and channel development of ideas.

Components of Human Social Interaction

The inherent conflict between behavioral variation and behavioral uniformity is reflected most clearly in social interaction behavior. All human cultures studied have tacit rules of information exchange. A central tacit rule of information exchange is that interactants are to provide one another with relevant information (Sperber & Wilson, 1986). What is relevant is what is new. Therefore, speech acts must clearly differentiate what is new and of greatest relevance from what is "old" or already known (Clark, 1992).

In fact, people work to establish common ground in conversation (Clark, 1992). Common ground is the knowledge of the world that an individual shares with a conversation partner. Through common ground, people construct cultural systems that further limit individual variation in ideas, dispositions to act, and patterns of action. Humans in all cultures tacitly, but consistently, constrain novel beliefs, plans, and actions in others by proffering advice, episodic anecdotes, opinions, and knowledge to one another that will, when accepted, limit individual preferences, interests, ideas, and patterns of activity (Clark, 1992; Goffman, 1974; Sperber & Wilson, 1986).

Individuals are also obliged by cultural rules to share information and affect states with the least disruption to the other interactant (Leech,

1990). In *Alice in Wonderland*, the White Rabbit, the Red Queen, and the Mad Hatter provide irrelevant information in a disruptive fashion, leaving Alice to keep trying to sort out the new and relevant from the known and irrelevant. Goffman (1974) proposed that all human social behavior is an acted presentation of the self in variant roles for variant audiences in various frameworks. In Goffman's terms, the Mad Hatter throws Alice "out of the frame" of interaction by (a) never identifying the goal of their behavior or the goal of their various interactions, and (b) by never indicating what role Alice was to play in any given "scene" or "frame" of interaction.

Individuals are bound by multiple rules in conversation. These rules include not only given-new sensitivity, but sensitivity to topic, context, rank, or status of participants, as well as emotional tone and prior interactions as a specific historical basis for the current interaction. Not only is conversation rule bound, it is layered in development. Development of interaction is development of layered coregulation of interaction behaviors. And there appear to be three crucial forms of coregulation: pair bonding, imitations, and message exchange. Pair bonding is mother–child attachment based on the physiologic state regulation of mother-by-child and child-by-mother based in the physical contact of nursing. Imitation is the non-conscious motor synchrony or mimicry of facial, gestural, and postural or conscious copying of more complex motor patterns in face-to-face interaction. Message exchange is the process by which individuals develop shared mental contents through the exchange of intended verbal and nonverbal messages for complex present and future tasks (Waterhouse, 1988).

All three systems are adaptive. The coregulation involved in the mother–child nursing, bonding, and attachment process insures the physical and emotional survival of the infant. Motor synchrony and imitation provide a basis for learning, and also contribute to pair and group social cohesion by reducing the threat valence that the novel motor behaviors of others may generate. Message exchange supports the envisionment and enactment of tasks and projects that require the activity of more than one person and allows the accumulation of information across individuals and generations. As stated earlier, one key rule for message exchange is the requirement to carefully foreground new information as relevant and new (Clark, 1992; Sperber & Wilson, 1986).

Each of these three forms of social coregulation has a different neurofunctional basis. Pair bonding, in large part, depends on the physiological system involving oxytocin and vasopressin (Insel, 1992). Imitation depends on cross-modal integration in the hippocampus, along with an innate mechanism directing mimicry.

Conversation depends on a much wider variety of brain functions. These include selective attention to others and the assignment of reward value to others. They also include percept generation of faces and utterances in context in working memory, and a judgment of whether the face or utterance is novel. Most importantly, conversation requires the recognition of an individual's own message-associated emotions or feeling-states, as well as the generation of an idea of the emotions, motives, and plans of a conversation partner. Additionally, conversation requires the ability to intend to generate a response, the ability to make that response appropriate, and the ability to coordinate use of language with appropriate intonation curves and voice tones, face expression, gestures, and posture consonant with the message. Furthermore, conversation depends on a person's ability to constantly monitor the reaction of a conversation partner and shift ongoing responses in attunement to the reaction of this partner.

Conversation also requires the construction of an interpretation of the gist or message of a communication from another. For an interpretation to be constructed, people must constantly conduct some form of working memory review of words, phrases, and ideas that appeared earlier (Clark, 1992; Leech, 1990) in the interaction. This process of referent building for shared working memory information or common ground thus triggers the maintenance of the episode in working memory for the further continuance of the conversation, and the long-term storage of the salient attended to contents of that conversation. It appears that a wide range of bits of sensory information from the interaction itself will automatically index working memory records for the ongoing conversation episode. Thus information in a conversational turn will contain elements to sustain working memory control of the information from prior turns within the same conversation.

But conversational turns are not just based in working memory; they also require continuous access to long-term memory store that is being shared in the exchange of message. Thus the process of flexible redirection between working memory and long-term memory is crucial to conversation because information from long-term memory is a component in establishing the conversational common ground of shared mental contents.

Still another aspect of the complexity of human social interaction is the nature of human affect states. Buck (1999) proposed that there are two forms of primary biological affects. The first form is self-serving affects governed by the right hemisphere: arousal, approach-avoidance, and agonist. The second form is biological affects governed by the communicative left hemisphere: cooperative prosocial affect. Buck further proposed that biological affects are the primes that serve as a platform for social affects such as pride, guilt, shame, pity, or jealousy, and for cognitive affects such as curiosity and surprise. Buck proposed that prime affects arise from subcortical and limbic systems and these systems are "read out" by still other systems to generate the social affects. For Buck, the right hemisphere functions strategically for the protection of the individual, and the left hemisphere functions affiliatively for social interaction.

Luu and Tucker (1998) also presented a model of emotional behavior. However, their model is embedded in a larger model of neurolinguistic systems. Luu and Tucker claimed that the left hemisphere forms a data-driven feedback system based on anxious analytic cognition and focal attention. They argued that the right hemisphere forms a model of the world based on an expansive attentional mode with differential memory for context. For Luu and Tucker (1998), approach-avoidance behaviors are governed by the left hemisphere in its role in generating emotional action. In their model, the right hemisphere generates an emotional interpretation of ongoing behavior in interaction.

This brief sketch of a few selected theories of components of human social interaction suggests interaction is a surprisingly demanding task for the brain. In fact, social interaction appears to require the successful online functioning of many, if not all, systems of the brain. Thus, the ability to engage in a normal conversation with another person can be seen as a very powerful test of the integrity of interlinked neural functions that support the behaviors involved in human conversation. If there are many requisite brain functions, and if the brain's interacting network is complex, then it should be expected that there are many impairments disrupting the ability to engage in conversation.

SOCIAL INTERACTION IN DEVELOPMENTAL DISORDERS

By definition, children diagnosed with developmental disorders behave in ways suggesting that the function of their neural systems—especially those for learning and memory—may be impaired. As a consequence, their ability to generate variation in social behavior will be reduced, and their ability to learn limitations to their interaction behaviors is also likely to be reduced. Impaired learning will reduce the child's chance to accrue knowledge of possible variant social behaviors from the environment, and is likely to reduce their internal generation of novel behaviors via constructive imagination. Impaired learning will also constrain the child's ability to learn the limits to variation provided by mimicry, conversation, drives to social cohesion, and the implementation of interaction regulations by culture and other individuals. Most important, the specific pattern of abnormality in developmental disorders is governed by endogenous biological brain deficits not by the environmental factors that trigger variability in unaffected individuals (Steinberg & Avenovoli, 2000).

Scarr (1992) proposed that in normal development, as adolescents have increasingly more interaction outside of home, they are exposed to an increasingly wide pool of behavioral models and behavioral choices. Scarr posited that selection from this expanded pool of possible behaviors allows adolescents' behavioral expressions and patterns of choice to become increasingly true to their inherent genetic constitution.

Adolescents with developmental disorders, however, will have a reduced ability to develop that variation because they will have reduced interaction with others and reduced exploration of the environment. Therefore, they will be less able to learn what preferences and uniqueness they may inherently possess. Moreover, because they will have limited ability to express preferences, execute plans, mimic others, and to comprehend the limits imposed by others, their social peers, teachers, and family members will spend more time directly regulating interactions, and less time exchanging content or encouraging the expression of potential individual variation in behavior.

The following, social and neural variation in Down syndrome, Rett syndrome, Williams syndrome and autism are briefly reviewed, and the association between social and neural variation in developmental disabilities is explored.

Down Syndrome

Neural Dysfunctions. Down syndrome (trisomy 21) is the single most common genetic cause of retardation. It is not inherited, but occurs as a consequence of unequal chromosome segregation. The brains of Down syndrome individuals mature to about 80% of the size of normal brains (Haier et al., 1999), have fewer convolutions, and have especially small frontal lobes and hippocampal formations, with normal sized thalamic structures and basal ganglia (Hayes & Batshaw, 1993). A comparison of the brain volumes of nondemented Down syndrome adults with brain volumes of normal adults revealed that Down syndrome individuals studied had smaller hippocampal volumes but not smaller amygdala volumes than normal adults (Aylward et al., 1999).

Studies suggest that in the brains of Down syndrome individuals, neuronal development is abnormal, resulting in oddly shaped neurons with longer and thinner than normal dendrites (Wisniewski, Laure-Kamionowska, Connell, & Wen, 1986). Interestingly, one study has reported finding an overexpression of homologues to the vasopressin gene in the brains of Down syndrome individuals (Labudova et al., 1998). As vasopressin has been associated with affiliative behavior in mammals (Insel, 1992), this observation may be linked to the excessive affiliative behavior noted in many individuals with Down syndrome.

Social Impairment. As a group, Down syndrome individuals show sharply reduced variation in social interaction behavior compared to normal variation. Most all Down syndrome individuals are expressively positive, often happy, and eagerly affiliative without reserve. In a review of Down syndrome, Pulsifer (1996) reported that John Langdon Down originally described the syndrome in 1866 as characterized by cheerful personality, with the ability to mimic others, and a lively sense of humor. Their social impairment consists of being both overaffiliative and lacking in the ability to engage in self-serving strategic communicative interaction with others.

It has been argued that Down syndrome children share an abnormal social interaction persona: They are excessively and intrusively cheerful and overaffiliative. This markedly reduces variability in the form of their interactions with others.

Down syndrome individuals have slow but normal language acquisition. Although they may develop reasonable vocabularies, they have limited development of syntactic rules for sentence formation. And, as a result, their speech seems immature even in adulthood. Most Down syndrome individuals are not disaffiliative. They do not manipulate others.

Rett Syndrome

Neural Dysfunctions. There are many neural dysfunctions associated with Rett syndrome. Overall, there is a deceleration in head growth over the course of early development leading to a smaller-than-normal head size (Hagberg, Anvret, & Wahlstroem, 1993). There is evidence for abnormal cell formation in the basal ganglia, hippocampus, entorhinal cortex, frontal lobe, and temporal lobe of the brain. One study reported that cortical layers II and III are "ghost cells" that are empty and underdeveloped and layers V and VI of the cortex include cells that are hyperchromic, suggesting overdevelopment (Leontovich, Mukhina, Fedorov, & Belichenko, 1999). Comparison of Rett and Down syndrome brains showed that pyramidal neurons in prefrontal, motor, and limbic cortex in Rett syndrome brains had much less dendritic branching than did comparable pyramidal neurons in the brains of Down syndrome individuals (Armstrong, Dunn, & Antalffy, 1998).

Social Impairment. To date, only a handful of cases of Rett syndrome have been identified in boys (Hagberg et al., 1993). Thus, the syndrome is defined almost entirely through symptoms identified in females. One of the most notable social impairments in Rett syndrome is the near absence of language development. Also significant is inadequate regulation of emotional expression. Many girls diagnosed with Rett syndrome are concurrently diagnosed as autistic for a period of the course of their development. Their autistic features include both impaired language development and echolalia, as well as lack of interest in social interaction, although they may show evidence of attachment to the mother or caregiver as well as siblings.

Early development, until 6 to 9 months of age, is usually described as normal, but lack of normal language development and lack of fully normal motor development becomes apparent before the first birthday.

Williams Syndrome

Neural Dysfunctions. Gallaburda and Bellugi (2000) and Reiss et al. (2000) have reported MRI data on the brains of individuals with Williams syndrome suggesting that Williams syndrome individuals have a 13% decrease in brain volume. They also reported that Williams syndrome brains showed an unusual asymmetry in the occipital lobe tissue. While control subjects' brains had equal volumes of gray and white matter in the right and left occipital lobes, the brains of individuals with Williams syndrome had larger left than right occipital lobes (Reiss et al., 2000). This asymmetry was confined to gray matter and was not found for the white matter of the left and right occipital lobes.

Gallaburda and Bellugi (2000) reported the results of neuroanatomic study of the brains of four Williams cases. They describe the brains as being especially smaller from top to bottom, especially in the parietal and occipital lobes. They found the amygdalas of the Williams' brains to be half the size of normal amygdalas. Examination of the pattern of neurons indicated increased cell-packing density throughout (resulting from increased glial cells rather than an increase in the number of neurons), coarseness of neurons, and microvascular lesions in the dorso-parietal region and in the occipital lobes (Gallaburda & Bellugi, 2000).

Social Impairment. Individuals with Williams syndrome function in the mild to moderate range of mental retardation. Within this range Williams syndrome individuals express normal or even above average social skills, including vocabulary, verbal expression, and face recognition. Retardation is found in skills not associated with social interaction such as drawing, map reading, and spatial cognition.

Williams syndrome individuals are extremely talkative, with pressured excitable speech, and they have abnormal hypersensitivity to sounds. They interrupt people speaking to them, and thus have trouble following the tacit rules of normal social conversation. Most abnormal is their complete lack of fear of strangers.

Gallaburda and Bellugi (2000) have concluded that brain abnormalities in Williams syndrome are marked by a severe deficit in the dorsal, occipital to parietal, "where is it?" system of information processing. The ventral, occipital-temporal lobe, "what is it?" system of information processing, however, is relatively spared. They have conjectured that hypoplasia of the amygdala in Williams syndrome may account for the lack of normal fear of strangers and even lack of fear of threatening faces.

Autism

Neural Dysfunctions. Many brain deficits have been proposed as the source of autism, including brainstem, reticular activating system, cerebellum, thalamus, locus ceruleus, limbic system, hippocampus, amygdala, temporal and parietal lobe white matter, association cortex, and frontal lobes (Waterhouse, Fein, & Modahl, 1996). However, tying proposed brain deficits to specific abnormalities in autism has not been successful. The current standard diagnosis of autism (*DSM–IV*, APA, 1994) requires the presence of impaired reciprocal social interaction; absent, odd, or severely delayed language skill; and a restricted repertoire of interests and activities.

Waterhouse, Fein et al. (1996) proposed a model that outlines four systemically related neural dysfunctions that they theorized conjointly generate autistic symptoms. The first dysfunction is *canalesthesia*, wherein abnormal hippocampal system function "canalizes" sensory records, disrupting integration of information. The second dysfunction proposed is the impaired assignment of the affective significance of stimuli, wherein abnormal amygdaloid system function disrupts affect association. The third dysfunction proposed as constitutive of autism is asociality, wherein impaired oxytocin system function flattens social bonding and affiliativeness. Finally, the fourth dysfunction is extended selective attention, wherein abnormal organization of temporal and parietal polysensory regions yields aberrant overprocessing of primary representations. This model finds support in 41 studies providing separate evidence for each of these four dysfunctions in 484 cases of autism. It may be concluded that if all four were studied conjointly in a single sample, from 51% to 70% of cases of autism would be found to have all four proposed dysfunctions.

Social Impairment. The core diagnostic behaviors in autism all reflect social impairment: impaired use of nonverbal behaviors to regulate social behaviors, lack of friends, does not seek others to share an experience, lack of social or emotional reciprocity, and lack of social imitative or pretend play (*DSM–IV*, APA, 1994).

Through analysis of findings from an epidemiological study, Wing and Gould (1979) categorized social impairment in autism into three groups.

The three are aloof and indifferent to other people, passive and controllable but lacks any social initiative, and actively makes odd or bizarre social approaches to others. These groups have been validated in a variety of studies (Waterhouse, Morris et al., 1996). The subgroup of autistic children labeled Aloof has no affiliation and no strategic interaction skills. The subgroup of autistic children labeled Passive may have limited affiliation, but no strategic interaction skills. The subgroup of autistic children categorized as Active-but-Odd is affiliative in a uniquely intrusive way, and has no skills for strategic interaction.

Reduced Individual Variation in Developmental Disorders

Table 3.1 outlines the social impairments found in Down syndrome, Rett syndrome, Williams syndrome and autism. Normal individual variation in social behavior is not present for any of these groups. In fact for these developmental disorders, individual variation in social interaction behavior is largely nullified. Down syndrome, Rett syndrome, Williams syndrome, and autism must reduce normal social variation because they disable the very neural structures that determine the range of individual aspects of

TABLE 3.1
Social Impairments in Down Syndrome, Rett Syndrome,
Williams Syndrome, and Autism

	Down Syndrome	Rett Syndrome	Williams Syndrome	Autism
Dispositions re Interaction				
Pair bonding	yes	yes	yes	rare
Mimicry	yes	no	yes	no
Group social cohesion	yes	no	yes	no
Reward dependence	yes	yes	yes	abnormal
Harm avoidance	yes	no	no	variable
Novelty seeking	rare	no	yes	no
Prosocial disposition	yes	no	yes	no
Self-serving dispositions	no	no	—	abnormal
Social emotions (pride, envy)	some	none	limited	none
Cognitive emotions (surprise)	some	none	yes	variable
Information Exchange Rules				
Language rules development	slow/normal	abnormal	normal	abnormal
Relevance rules development	rare	none	abnormal	none
Turn taking rules	some	none	impaired	none
Communal sharing	some	none	some	none
Authority ranking	some	none	some	none
Equality matching	rare	none	rare	none
Market valuation	rare	none	rare	none

personality, emotional expression, and sociability. In all these disorders, a great many different things have gone wrong in developmental neurogenesis, and these dysfunctions appear to result in markedly aberrant expression of social interaction skill.

A specific range of interactive behaviors expressed by individuals within each diagnosis appears to generate a typological caricature within each disorder. The Down syndrome social persona is excessively cheerful, and is likely to be hyperattached. The Rett syndrome persona is that of a partially withdrawn and extremely emotionally labile girl. The Williams syndrome individual is overly social, chattery, and pressing in interaction, unafraid of social threats. The persona of autism may be more varied, but one core persona is that of a completely aloof and inexpressive boy seemingly unconcerned with the actions and reactions of those around him.

How Is a Diagnostic Group Persona Created?

Brain deficits in these developmental disorders must be the source of reduced variability in social behavior. The reduced variation in expression of social interaction behaviors in these syndromes suggests that these behaviors are all that are permitted by the underlying impaired brain systems of each syndrome. To create a type of group social temperament that allows little individual variation may represent a canalized simplification of the complex network of systems that form social reactivity dispositions and skills. The unanswered question is exactly how such uniform caricature personas are produced within the framework of brain disorder.

To explore specific issues based on normative models outlined in the first section, pair bonding and personality trait dimensions are considered.

Impaired Pair Bonding. Human pair bonding and human affiliativeness appear to be a discrete, innate system (Insel, 1992). It has been reported that autistic individuals have abnormal levels of oxytocin, one of the neurochemicals associated with pair bonding and affiliation (Modahl et al., 1998). There has been speculation that oxytocin abnormalities may lead to states in which autistic individuals feel no normal drive for pair bonding with those around them. It has also been reported that autistic individuals have abnormal development of limbic system tissue (Kemper & Bauman, 1998). Together these neural deficits may lead to the extreme social isolation observed for aloof autistic individuals.

Conversely, Labudova et al. (1998) reported an excess of vasopressin homologues in the brains of individuals with Down syndrome. Vasopressin and oxytocin together have been theorized to form the basis for the attachment system in humans (Insel, O'Brien, & Leckman, 1999). This, combined with the apparently normal development of the amygdala in Down syndrome, may generate excessive affiliation behavior observed consistently in Down syndrome.

In Rett syndrome, there is rudimentary attachment that rarely extends to others beyond mother or caretaker. The overall lack of brain development, including lack of development of limbic system tissue, may account for this finding. It may also be that the innate attachment system in human beings is so robust that only a severe disruption of the supporting brain tissue will disrupt attachment processes.

Impaired Reactivity. Channeled reactivity, identified as risk taking, novelty seeking, and harm avoidance is almost entirely absent from Rett syndrome, Down syndrome, and autism. Social harm avoidance is absent in Williams syndrome. This suggests that the systems theorized to provide the basis for social reactivity are impaired in all four syndromes. These neurotransmitters—dopamine, serotonin, and epinephrine—have been studied in Down syndrome, Rett syndrome, and autism. In each case there is evidence of abnormality in these transmitter systems.

The question remains as to why personality traits essentially disappear in the face of brain deficits. Harm avoidance is nearly absent in these syndromes. Novelty seeking is minimal, and risk taking is only by mistake without conscious thought of the risk taken. The meaningfulness of "harm" and "novelty" and "risk" as concepts seem to be absent from the thought of individuals with Rett syndrome, Down syndrome, and autism.

In normal individuals, are the concepts of harm, risk, and novelty learned separately from the experience of transmitter flow changes in the experience of real harm, real risk, and real novelty? Whatever the case may be for normal development, it remains true that aspects of these personality traits are absent from the expressive behavior found in Rett syndrome, Down syndrome, autism, and to a more limited extent, Williams syndrome.

The range of emotional expression is abnormal in all syndromes. Whereas Down syndrome individuals express prosocial biological prime emotions, they often fail to engage in self-serving emotional interaction behavior. Rett syndrome individuals have an extremely labile expression of emotion, as do some autistic individuals. In autism and Rett syndrome, normal emotional reactivity is extremely rare. Particularly in autism and Rett syndrome, both social (shame, pride, envy) and cognitive emotions (wonder, surprise) are absent. However, some of these social and cognitive emotions are expressed in Down syndrome. Williams syndrome and Down syndrome individuals can be hypersocial—Down syndrome clingy while Williams syndrome is "cocktail party" chatter.

As yet, the neurobiology of these emotions has not been explicitly delineated in a model, so the deficits found in these syndromes cannot be a guide for the abnormal expression of emotions.

Impaired Information Exchange.   The failure to acquire fully normal language skills, conversational skills, and exchange skills is also characteristic of these syndromes. These failures of acquisition have been attributed to failed learning processes, and have been attributed to lack of interest in learning itself. The varied impairments to cortical structure and cortical neurons in these syndromes are likely to give rise to impaired processes of learning that are observed.

However, it is important to keep in mind that the greatest information-processing load imposed on humans is social interaction (Quiatt & Reynolds, 1995). Because so many varied neural systems can contribute to the complexity of social behavior, there is greater possibility for variation in the production of social behavior. As a consequence, normal individuals have to learn how to limit variability in their behavior, both for the comfort of others, and for the successful sharing of information and work in social exchange.

The Problem of Social Skills Training

The more complex stages of interaction may involve greater individual variation precisely because of their reliance on individual learning (Anderson, 2000). There may be normal group typologies in terms of reactive personality (Kagan, 1994; Woodward et al., 2000), but fewer normal typologies in strategic interaction (Clark, 1992; Goffman, 1974; Sperber & Wilson, 1986).

It is important to consider that social learning is a key vehicle for acquisition of all sorts of behaviors (Plotkin, 1994). Thus, limitations in social interaction, such as those outlined here for autism, Rett syndrome, and Down syndrome, have wide-ranging effects on learning in all domains of behavior.

Special training programs dependent on simple and repetitive social interaction (i.e., behavior modification) have been shown to be the most effective systems of education for all three syndromes. Training has the least effect in Rett syndrome because of its degenerating course.

The difficulty with intense training in social skills is that the resulting social behavior is likely to appear as limited, repetitive, stiff, and formal— transparently the result of effortful learning. An autistic young adult with which I worked had learned to say, "Hello, how are you?" He says this at every point of greeting, with everyone he sees during the course of a day. He has not been taught the rule for offering a reduced (nod, brief smile, grunt) acknowledgment of another person after the first full-scale greeting of the day. Moreover, he is unable to learn the complex notion that repetition of the same greeting carries an additional meaning involving possible disregard for the other individual.

One mother, writing about her success in behavior modification for her autistic daughter and autistic son (Maurice, 1993), argued that behavioral techniques are just common sense made consistent: "Teaching kids by breaking down tasks into small, manageable units . . . spelling out expectations . . . praising good behavior . . . physically prompting through a behavior . . . walking a child through a task . . . having certain consequences (yes, aversives!) for disobeying the rules" (pp. 257–258).

Mrs. Maurice considered the possibility that characteristics of autistic-like behavior may remain. She reported that an evaluation of her children showed very mild residual effects. However, even with intense behavior modification programs in social and cognitive skills going on at home and at school, very few autistic individuals (and extremely few Down syndrome individuals) have a fully normal outcome.

Social skills training in autism and Down syndrome is a relatively recent application of behavior modification (L. K. Koegel & R. L. Koegel, 1995; Lord, 1995), which began as efforts to teach daily living skills and then basic cognitive functions. Until effective preventive, genetic, and pharmacological treatments are developed, such behavior modification is the most important treatment available for developmental disabilities such as mental retardation and autism.

In terms of individuation, however, it is unclear whether such social skills training programs will tend to induce another shared typological persona for each syndrome. At this point, more research in social skills training is needed to elucidate whether or not a greater range of variation would be generated within a syndrome by the application of social skills training programs. Training may reveal greater individual variation—more of the inherent individuals variation (Scarr, 1992)—through more varying, more fluid, and more complex patterns of social interaction (Maurice, 1993).

A UNIFIED MODEL OF SOCIAL
INTERACTION SKILLS IS NEEDED

As demonstrated in the first two sections of this chapter, there are many separate component skills necessary for normal social interaction. Although it is premature to propose a specific comprehensive model of social interaction skills, it is possible to attempt a meaningful list of skills. Table 3.2 is a list of skills proposed as crucial to social interaction.

The first section of Table 3.2 identifies innate traits and skills that are likely to be necessary for essential sociability. These include reward sensi-

TABLE 3.2
Component Social Interaction Skills

INNATE UNIVERSAL BASES FOR SOCIABILITY
Reward Sensitivity
Pair-Bonding
Biological Affects (experienced & expressed)
Mimicry of the Expressive Behavior of Others
Joint Attention
Altruistic Information Sharing

INNATE DOMAINS OF SOCIAL INFORMATION PROCESSING
Non-verbal behavior
Basic Language Skills
Face Processing
Theory of Mind
Kin Recognition
In-Group Recognition
Out-Group Recognition
Social Ideologies

LEARNED RULES FOR INFORMATION EXCHANGE
Turn-taking in Conversation
Construction of Common Ground in Conversation
Offering up Relevant Content in Conversation
Taking Specific Social Roles in Interaction
Equality Matching Information Exchange
Cost Benefit Valuation of Information

LEARNED DECEPTIVE STRATEGIES
Game-playing
Selective Sharing and Withholding
Creating Lies

---

tivity, pair-bonding, biological affects, mimicry, joint attention, and a drive for altruistic information sharing.

The second section of Table 3.2 lists eight hypothesized innate domains of social information processing: nonverbal behavior, basic language skills, face processing, theory of mind, kin recognition, in-group recognition, out-group recognition, social ideologies (Geary & Bjorklund, 2000).

The third section of Table 3.2 lists 6 groups of learned rules for information exchange in social interaction. These include turn-taking, construction of common ground, offering relevant content, taking social roles, equality valuation of information, and cost-benefit valuation of information in exchange. The fourth section of Table 3.2 lists three deceptive strategies in social interaction—game-playing, selective sharing, and the creation of lies.

A distinction not listed on Table 3.2 is the differentiation of goals for interaction. In general, theorists have divided goals into two categories:

affiliative goals and strategic goals. There is only a single affiliative goal: the development or maintaining of a human relationship. There are many varied strategic goals, because a strategic goal can be anything—a commodity, a change in status or rank, a service, or a promise. The social interaction is a means to obtaining the strategic goal.

Strategic goals can exist alongside the goal of maintaining affiliation. However, strategic goals can also be disaffiliative. If individuals engage in manipulative strategic interaction, then they may be seeking to gain some sort of advantage at the expense of the person who is their conversational partner. When people engage in manipulative game playing, selective sharing, or withholding of information, or engage in deceptive communication, they can behave as if they are disaffiliating themselves from the conversation partner or partners.

Innate Basis of Sociability

The bases of sociability listed in Table 3.2 require little conscious information processing. Instead, these systems rely on innate mechanisms that canalize reactivity to the environment for successful adaptation to primate social life. Reward sensitivity appears to be regulated by the hypothalamus and associated neurotransmitter systems. Rewards include human touch and social contact. Pair bonding occurs in many social mammals. Pair bonding is shown to be dependent on two neurohormones—oxytocin and vasopressin—operating within the limbic system to trigger social memory of familiar and rewarding individuals. Ferguson et al. (2000) reported that social memory is impaired in mice that are engineered to lack a normal oxytocin gene. Mimicry of others' facial expressions begins in infancy in higher primates. Nonconscious mimicry provides a mechanism for social learning through imitation. Joint attention occurs when two individuals join their attention on an external object or situation. This develops without training in "normal" children, but is missing from the repertoire of children with autism or Rett syndrome. Joint attention is another nonconscious mechanism for social learning.

Finally, altruistic information sharing is exhibited by many primates. Mother chimps share food source information with their offspring. That is, adaptive information the mother has learned is shared for the good of her family. Particular vocal displays have evolved to permit one chimp to "bark" the presence of food to others in the group. The "food bark" is a fixed action program—altruistic information sharing is not planned; it functions more like a reflex. Much pointing out of things in the environment done by healthy young children reflects an evolutionary outgrowth of altruistic information sharing.

The cognitive domains listed in Table 3.2 specify another form of canalization. If we do have social and ecological domains of information processing that are separable in brain function, the domains would provide a pre-set anchor to comprehension of things in the environment—people, food, objects, events. If true, these domains would represent a tight canalization of information about the world. Such canalization should be represented by distinct cortical regions of information processing. Research on the neural localization of these hypothesized domains is just beginning.

The sets of learned interaction rules listed in Table 3.2 presumably require evolutionarily newer, more complex forms of information processing. The types of information processing required are likely to be wide-ranging. When individuals engage in conversation, they must have access to memory representations of social structure, social roles, and memory for the assigned value of information. The specific networks of the brain's basis for maintaining common ground in a conversation must, necessarily, be complex. The frontal cortex must send projections to the hippocampal complex, exerting modulatory control of the amygdala and hippocampus, and reciprocal projections between the hippocampal complex and frontal cortex link the internal state of the individual to knowledge of external stimuli. Equally important, projections from hippocampus and amygdala are crucial to frontal processes of behavioral planning and initiation because they provide the frontal cortex with integrated sensory records and are linked to the assignment of affective significance—what can be termed an *associatively unified assessment* of the individual's current perceptions and feelings. Furthermore, normal frontal cortex projections to hippocampus modulate hippocampal function, and similar frontal projections to amygdala assist in the modulation of affective computations.

The four sections of Table 3.2 are ordered in sequence of developmental unfolding in the child and adolescent. Newborns are born with innate reward sensitivity. One-year-olds garner new information through shared attention by using domain specific cognitive processes. The social play of childhood, over the course of nearly 15 years, provides a means to learn the rules of complex social interaction, including the rules for fair and unfair deception. Humans are neotonous mammals who are dependent on pair bonding attachment for survival. In infancy, the ability to mimic others emerges. Nascent toddlers experience the emergence of the acquisition of language, of the rule of conversational exchange, and the rules of exchange because the intricate framework for social interaction is made up of many varied components.

CONCLUSIONS

This chapter has discussed a few selected models of the sources of individual variation and of limits to variation in behavior. The neural and social impairments in Down syndrome, Rett syndrome, Williams syndrome and autism were briefly outlined, and the components of social interaction have also been discussed.

The central claim of this chapter has been that developmental brain deficits can nullify normal variation in sociability, but can create distinctive patterns of aberrant social interaction. Specific overlapping brain deficits in the syndromes considered have been proposed to cause reduced variability in social behavior. In Rett syndrome, there is rudimentary attachment. Down syndrome individuals are expressively positive, often happy, and eagerly affiliative without reserve. Autistic individuals are most often aloof and indifferent to social interaction. Conversely, Williams syndrome individuals are indiscriminately social.

Autistic individuals may be aloof because they have abnormal levels of oxytocin and/or vasopressin. Autistic individuals also have been reported to have abnormal development of limbic system tissue (Kemper & Bauman, 1998). These neural deficits may be crucial sources for the isolation observed for aloof autistic individuals. For Down syndrome individuals, it may be an excess of vasopressin combined with the apparently normal development of the amygdala that contributes to the excessive affiliation behavior observed consistently in Down syndrome.

The personality trait identified as harm avoidance is almost entirely absent from Rett syndrome, Down syndrome, Williams syndrome and autism. Moreover, all syndromes have either limited expression of the normal range of emotions or abnormal skewing of the expression of emotions.

Future research in the biology of these syndromes, combined with further basic research in the nature of the neurobiology of social interaction behaviors, will help with understanding both the social impairments and their underlying source.

REFERENCES

American Psychiatric Association (1994). *Diagnostic and statistical manual of mental disorders* (4th ed.). Washington, DC: Author.

Anderson, J. R. (2000). *Learning and memory: An integrated approach* (2nd ed.). New York: Wiley.

Armstrong, D. D., Dunn, K., & Antalffy, B. (1998). Decreased dendritic branching in frontal, motor and limbic cortex in Rett syndrome compared with trisomy 21. *Journal of Neuropathology and Experimental Neurology, 57*(11), 1013–1017.

Aylward, E. H., Li, Q., Honeycutt, N. A., Warren, A. C., Pulsifer, M. B., Barta, P. E., Chan, M. D., Smith, P. D., Jerram, M., & Pearlson, G. D. (1999). MRI volumes of hippocampus and amygdala in adults with Down's syndrome with and without dementia. *American Journal of Psychiatry, 156*(4), 564–568.

Buck, R. (1999). The biological affects: A typology. *Psychological Review, 106*(2), 301–336.

Clark, H. (1992). *Arenas of language use.* Chicago: University of Chicago Press.

Cloninger, C. R., Adolfsson, R., & Svrakic, N. M. (1996). Mapping genes for human personality. *Nature Genetics, 12,* 3–4.

Depue, R. A., & Collins, P. F. (1999). Neurobiology and the structure of personality: Dopamine, facilitation of motivation, and extraversion. *Behavioral and Brain Sciences, 22*(3), 491–569.

Ekman, P. (1993). Facial expression and emotion. *American Psychologist, 48,* 384–392.

Ferguson, J. N., Young, L. J., Hearn, E. F., Matzuk, M. M., Insel, T. R., & Winslow, J. T. (2000). Social amnesia in mice lack in the oxytocin gene. *Nature Genetics, 25,* 284–288.

Fiske, A. (1992). The four elementary forms of sociality: Framework for a unified theory of social relations. *Psychological Review, 99,* 689–723.

Gallaburda, A. M., & Bellugi, U. (2000). Multi-level analysis of cortical neuroanatomy in Williams syndrome. *Journal of Cognitive Neuroscience, 12,* 74–88.

Geary, D. C., & Bjorklund, D. F. (2000). Evolutionary developmental psychology. *Child Development, 71,* 57–65.

Goffman, E. (1974). *Frame analysis.* Cambridge, MA: Harvard University Press.

Gray, J. A. (1970). A psychophysiological basis of introversion-extraversion. *Behavior Research and Therapy, 8,* 249–266.

Hagberg, B., Anvret, M., & Wahlstroem, J. (Eds.). (1993). *Rett syndrome: Clinical and biological aspects.* London: Mac Keith Press.

Haier, R. J., Chueh, D., Touchette, P., Lott, I., Buchsbaum, M. S., MacMillan, D., Sandman, C., LaCasse, L., & Sosa, E. (1995). Brain size and cerebral glucose metabolic rate in nonspecific mental retardation and Down syndrome. *Intelligence, 29,* 191–210.

Hayes, A., & Batshaw, M. L. (1993). Down syndrome. In M. Batshaw (Ed.), *Pediatric Clinics of North America: The child with developmental disabilities, 40*(3), 523–535.

Insel, T. R. (1992). Oxytocin—a neuropeptide for affiliation: Evidence from behavioral, receptor autoradiographic, and comparative studies. *Psychoneuroendocrinology, 17,* 3–5.

Insel, T. R., O'Brien, D. J., & Leckman, L. (1999). Oxytocin, vasopressin and autism: Is there a connection? *Biological Psychiatry, 45*(2), 145–157.

Kagan, J. (1994). *Galen's prophecy.* New York: Basic Books.

Kemper, T. L., & Bauman, M. (1998). Neuropathology of infantile autism. *Journal of Neuropathology and Experimental Neurology, 57*(7), 645–652.

Koegel, L. K., & Koegel R. L. (1995). Motivating communication in children with autism. In E. Schopler & G. B. Mesibov (Eds.), *Learning and cognition in autism* (pp. 73–88). New York: Plenum.

Labudova, O., Fang-Fircher, S., Cairns, N., Moenkemann, H., Yehigiazaryan, K., & Lubec, G. (1998). Brain vasopressin levels in Down syndrome and Alzheimer's disease. *Brain Research, 806*(1), 55–59.

Leech, G. (1990). *Principles of pragmatics.* New York: Longman.

Leontovich, T. A., Mukhina, J. K., Fedorov, A. A., & Belichenko, P. V. (1999). Morphological study of the entorhinal cortex, hippocampal formation, and basal ganglia in Rett syndrome patients. *Neurobiological Disorders, 6*(2), 77–91.

Lord, C. (1995). Facilitating social inclusion: Examples from peer intervention programs. In E. Schopler & G. B. Mesibov (Eds.), *Learning and cognition in autism* (pp. 221–242). New York: Plenum.

Luu, P., & Tucker, D. (1998). Vertical integration of neurolinguistic mechanisms. In H. Whitaker (Ed.), *Handbook of neurolinguistics* (pp. 159–172). New York: Academic Press.

Maurice, C. (1993). *Let me hear your voice; A family's triumph over autism.* New York: Fawcett Columbine.

Meltzoff, A. N., & Gopnik, A. (1993). The role of imitation in understanding persons and developing a theory of mind. In S. Baron-Cohen, H. Tager-Flusberg, & D. J. Cohen (Eds.), *Understanding other minds* (pp. 335–366). New York: Oxford University Press.

Modahl, C., Green, L., Fein, D., Morris, M., Waterhouse, L., Feinstein, C., & Levin, H. (1998). Plasma oxytocin levels in autistic children. *Biological Psychiatry, 43*(4), 270–277.

Plotkin, H. C. (1994). *Darwin machines and the nature of knowledge*. Cambridge, MA: Harvard University Press.

Pulsifer, M. B. (1996). The neuropsychology of mental retardation. *Journal of the International Neuropsychological Society, 2*, 146–158.

Quiatt, D., & Reynolds, V. (1995). *Primate behaviour*. Cambridge, England: Cambridge University Press.

Reiss, A. L., Eliez, S., Schmitt, J. E., Straus, E., Lai, Z., Jones, W., & Bellugi, U. (2000). Neuroanatomy of Williams Syndrome: A high resolution of MRI study. *Journal of Cognitive Neuroscience, 12*, 65–73.

Scarr, S. (1992). Developmental theories for the 1990s: Development and individual differences. *Child Development, 63*, 1–19.

Sheinberg, L., & Avenovoli, S. (2000). The role of context in the development of psychopathology: A conceptual framework and some speculative propositions. *Child Development, 71*, 66–74.

Shepherd, G. (1994). *Neurobiology* (3rd ed.). New York: Oxford University Press.

Soltis, J., Boyd, R., & Richerson, P. J. (1995). Can group-functional behaviors evolve by group selection? *Cultural Anthropology, 36*, 473–494.

Sperber, D., & Wilson, D. (1986). *Relevance: Communication and cognition*. Cambridge, MA: Harvard University Press.

Turkheimer, E. (2000). Three laws of behavior genetics and what they mean. *Current Directions in Psychological Science, 9*, 160–164.

Waterhouse, L. (1988). Aspects of the evolutionary history of human social behaviour. In L. Wing (Ed.), *Aspects of autism: Biological research* (pp. 102–114). London: Gaskell.

Waterhouse, L., & Fein, D. (1996). Perspectives on social impairment in autism. In F. Volkmar (Ed.), *Handbook of autism* (pp. 901–919) (2nd ed.). New York: Wiley.

Waterhouse, L., Fein, D., & Modahl, C. (1996). Neurofunctional mechanisms in autism. *Psychological Review, 103*(3), 457–489.

Waterhouse, L., Morris, R., Allen, D., Dunn, M., Fein, D., & Feinstein, C. (1996). Diagnosis and classification in autism. *Journal of Autism and Developmental Disorders, 26*, 59–86.

Wing, L., & Gould, J. (1979). Severe impairments of social inter-action and associated abnormalities in children: Epidemiology and classification. *Journal of Autism and Developmental Disorders, 9*, 11–30.

Wisniewski, K. E., Laure-Kamionowska, M., Connell, F., & Wen, G. Y. (1986). Neuronal density and synaptogenesis in the postnatal stage of brain maturation in Down syndrome. In C. Epstein (Ed.), *The neurobiology of Down syndrome* (pp. 29–43). New York: Raven.

Woodward, S. A., Lenzenweger, M. F., Kagan, J., Snidman, N., & Arcus, D. (2000). Taxonic structure of infant reactivity: Evidence from a taxometric perspective. *Psychological Science, 11*, 296–306.

## CHAPTER FOUR

Individual Differences in the Development of Social Communication Competency in Very Low Birthweight Children

Susan H. Landry
University of Texas Health Science Center, Houston

Cynthia L. Miller-Loncar
Brown University School of Medicine

Karen E. Smith
University of Texas Medical Branch, Galveston

Social communication development plays an important role in understanding a broad range of children's later competencies. Social interactions provide the context in which children gradually learn to share control and influence with others (Vygotsky, 1978), as well as facilitate skills that provide the basis for problem solving. Problems with the development of social communication skills across the first few years of life may cause children to be less responsive in early social exchanges, which may in turn impair their ability to learn. Social problems that persist into school-age years contribute to rejection by same-age peers and greater difficulty responding to teachers' requests (Dodge, 1985).

Social development evolves in two complementary spheres: A growing ability to respond to parental requests is coupled with an increased capacity to initiate social exchanges (Crockenberg & Litman, 1990). Although intertwined, these two aspects of social development place different demands on children. Responding socially to others involves the ability to comply with their requests as well as use eye gaze, smiles, and vocalizations to respond to caretakers' bids for attention (Schaffer, 1977). The request by others provides a certain degree of structure around which children can organize a response. In contrast, initiating social exchanges requires children to formulate a social goal and sequence their verbal and gestural activities to carry out this goal without structure from their interactive partner. Initiations, therefore, call for flexibility in a child's conceptualization of a social problem because the child must independently develop social goals that meet the changing demands of the social context.

Behaviors required for effective social initiating skills (e.g., formulating a goal, sequencing a set of behaviors) have been described by others as the types of behaviors that come under the rubric of executive function skills (Welsh & Pennington, 1988). Executive functions help operationalize the child's ability to profit from and comprehend social experiences (P. D. Rourke & Fuerst, 1991). Evidence for the link between social initiating behaviors and executive function skills can be found in studies evaluating social development and mastery motivation skills in children who have central nervous system (CNS) insults (e.g., hydrocephalus, severe intraventricular hemorrhage). When children with CNS deficits are placed in social and nonsocial situations in which they are required to independently formulate goals and sustain goal-directed activity, their performance in these areas is below that of mental age-matched comparison groups (Landry, Garner, Pirie, & Swank, 1994; Landry, Robinson, Copeland, & Garner, 1993). In contrast, when these same children are observed in situations that provide external structure (i.e., standardized tests of mental abilities or situations where they are required to respond to the specific requests of others), differences in their level of functioning are not always apparent. Therefore, in evaluating children at risk for problems in learning, it may be particularly important to consider their competence in different aspects of social communication: those that require the development of independent goals versus those that provide greater external structure.

Understanding individual differences in social communication competence for groups of children at risk for learning problems may be enhanced through evaluation of the role that parents play in early social interactions. Evaluations of parent–child interactions during the early years of the child's life may be especially important because these interactions provide the basis on which later skills are developed (Landry, Smith, Swank, & Miller-Loncar, 2000). Caretakers initially provide extensive support, but adapt their behaviors to offer more autonomy as children increase in their ability to direct their own learning (Maccoby & Martin, 1983). This form of specialized assistance is described as "scaffolding"; mothers use interactive behaviors that facilitate the young child's ability to attend and respond to components of the social interactions that are in the range of their capability (Bruner, 1982). Some aspects of mothers' specialized assistance include attention to infant cues, pacing that is appropriate to the young child's skill level, and provision of structure for aspects of the task outside the child's capability. As children become more capable of taking social initiative and directing their own behavior, mothers who are sensitive to these changes will gradually decrease their level of scaffolding (Wertsch, 1979). By gradually withdrawing their scaffolding, mothers support children's ability to function independently in social exchanges with others across a range of social situations. Understanding the parents' role in this process may provide greater insight into the reason why some children are more socially competent than others.

Studies have looked at the relation of parenting and social communication development at concurrent points in time (Barnard, Bee, & Hammond, 1984; Crawford, 1982) and/or have related early maternal behaviors with later child outcomes (Greenberg & Crnic, 1988). Longitudinal evaluations that capture the dynamic relations between children's developing social skills and mothers' adaptations to these changes are also needed.

SOCIAL COMMUNICATION COMPETENCE OF PRETERM SUBJECTS

The studies described here evaluate social communication competence across the first 3 years of life and the role parents play in determining individual differences in this area of development for very low birthweight (VLBW) preterm infants. It may be particularly important to understand social communication development for VLBW children because a number of studies report long-term delays in various aspects of their social and language development (Drillien, Thomson, & Burgoyne, 1980; Landry, Chapieski, Richardson, Palmer, & Hall, 1990; Plunkett & Meisel, 1989). Preterm infants have been reported to display more negative affect, less responsiveness in social interactions, and at later ages to be more passive and less capable socially with their peers.

Premature, VLBW infants differ dramatically in the severity of medical complications experienced at birth and during the neonatal period. Differences in their early neonatal history have not always been attended to in understanding individual differences in developmental outcomes. Inconsistencies across studies regarding whether developmental delays persist may be related to differences in the severity of early medical complications (e.g., chronic lung disease or severe intraventricular hemorrhage, IVH). Whereas some investigations have found that preterm infants with less severe medical complications (e.g., acute respiratory problems, mild IVH) show problems in social and communication behaviors only across the first year of life (Bakeman & Brown, 1980; Crawford, 1982; Greenberg & Crnic, 1988), others have found problems to persist to later ages (Drillien et al., 1980; Plunkett & Meisels, 1989). This inconsistency may be explained in part by the specific aspects of social communication development evaluated and the context in which the child's behaviors were observed. In contrast, VLBW infants with more severe medical complications (e.g., chronic lung disease, severe degrees of IVH) have been shown to have delays in motor and cognitive skills and are reported to have social problems that persist through at least age 3 (Landry et al., 1990).

When severity of complications has been considered, greater consistency across studies evaluating social outcomes has been found for VLBW infants. Results from a recent longitudinal study using growth modeling analyses provide strong support for both medical risk and environmental factors explaining individual differences in rates of growth in social communication development in VLBW infants (Landry, Denson, & Swank, 1997). In addition, this study highlights the importance of evaluating social initiations versus responsiveness as distinct aspects of social communication development. For a large group of VLBW infants ($n = 79$) subdivided into groups with more (high risk, HR) and less (low risk, LR) severe medical complications as compared to healthy full-term infants ($n = 49$), slower rates of development of social initiating skills through age 3 were found for both medically high and low risk VLBW children assessed in a mother–child toy play situation. This difference was apparent even after controlling for significant effects of socioeconomic status (SES). In contrast, SES (but not medical risk or prematurity) predicted differences in the rate of development of social responsiveness. Although the HR VLBW children also had slower rates of development in their mental and motor development through age 3, the LR children were comparable to the full-term children in rate of mental and motor development. Thus, their social initiating problems could not be explained by lower levels of cognitive functioning.

Careful analysis of this complex process may be particularly important for VLBW children, whose deficits in early attention and motor skills often lead to problems in joint learning situations (Landry, 1995). Learning through social interactions may be more difficult for these infants because they often give more ambiguous cues about their interests than healthy full-term infants (Goldberg, Lojkasek, Gartner, & Corter, 1989). Whereas full-term infants may be developmentally ready for mothers to begin to decrease some of their support during social interactions after about 6 months of age, this process may evolve more slowly for the preterm infant, who may need specialized maternal assistance considerably longer. The studies described in this chapter examine this question.

PARENTING

There are a number of maternal behaviors that have been shown to facilitate children's learning in social interactions. Three behaviors may be of special importance to the development of VLBW infants because of their specific difficulties in focusing and shifting attention as well as organizing their behavior (Landry, Garner, Swank, & Baldwin, 1996). When this type of parent scaffolding was provided across the first year of life, VLBW children showed rates of cognitive and social development that were more comparable to that of full-term children (Landry, Smith, Miller-Loncar, & Swank, 1997a). Rather than focusing on parenting behaviors that facilitate development in general, the framework is to evaluate both discrete and qualitative aspects of parenting behaviors for their ability to help buffer the special developmental problems demonstrated by VLBW infants.

One parenting behavior that may help buffer VLBW infants' early attentional difficulties is mothers' attempts to maintain their infants' interest in objects or toys rather than redirecting the infants' attention. Maintaining has been shown in previous studies of preterm infants to facilitate exploratory play (Landry et al., 1996) and language skills (Rocissano & Yatchmink, 1983). Maintaining children's interests may facilitate social communication competence by supporting their attentional focus, thus allowing young children to use their more limited cognitive resources to organize an appropriate social response (Akhtar, F. Dunham, & P. Dunham, 1991; Rocissano & Yatchmink, 1983; Tomasello & Farrar, 1986). This maternal strategy (i.e., maintaining attention) places fewer demands on VLBW infants' limited attentional capacity because it does not require the infants to inhibit a response to something they are attending to in order to redirect their attention to a different object or conversational topic (Landry & Chapieski, 1988). Social initiating also may be facilitated through maternal maintaining when mothers respond to their children's interests and bids for attention. This strategy will reinforce for the children that their interests are important, thus increasing the likelihood that the children will initiate at later times.

A parenting behavior that may buffer VLBW infants' difficulty in organizing their behavior in response to stimulation is the degree to which mothers provide information about what is expected of the child or their degree of directiveness. Positive relations between mothers' directiveness and children's interactive behaviors have been reported for infants during the first 2 years of life (Shatz, 1977) and for developmentally at risk children beyond that age (Marfo, 1990). External structure (i.e., directiveness) may provide the type of scaffolding necessary for VLBW infants to carry out a social goal at a point in their development when this is difficult to do independently. However, whereas higher degrees of external structure may support social responding for VLBW infants, it may not be providing the type of scaffolding required for the infants to learn to independently develop their own goals. In fact, high degrees of maternal direction have been negatively related to social competence for normal toddlers and preschoolers (Parpal & Maccoby, 1985). High degrees of directiveness may be important earlier in infancy for VLBW infants to learn how to respond in social interactions, but it may be important for mothers to gradually withdraw this type of support in order to facilitate these infants' ability to learn to take more active roles in directing their interactions with others. When examining the role of maintaining and directiveness on social initiative through structural modeling analyses, high levels of maintaining across the first 3 years indirectly influenced initiating at 4½ years by directly influencing the development of responsiveness. However, while high levels of directiveness up through 2 years had a positive influence, by 3 years, low levels directly supported later initiating skills (Landry et al., 2000).

Mothers' acceptance of the infants' interests, positive affective exchanges, contingent responsiveness, and a sense of pleasure in their infants may be as important in facilitating children's social development as the specific strategies mothers use, as these provide a positive emotional context for mother–child interactions (Bornstein et al., 1992). These maternal behaviors, which have been referred to as *warm responsiveness*, model specific positive social behaviors (e.g., eye gaze, smiling) that are not available through maternal behaviors such as maintaining and directiveness. Because VLBW infants have more negative affect and difficulty with eye gaze, this specific type of modeling may be important for the development of more positive social behaviors. In addition to modeling social behaviors, this construct includes greater sensitivity in reading infants' needs for more specialized stimulation. Therefore, mothers' sensitivity to children's signals and interests helps to involve them in a mutually cooperative exchange and provides an effective context for the development of social initiative (Kuczynski, Kochanska, Radke-Yarrow, & Girnius-Brown, 1987).

PRETERM CHILDREN INCLUDED
IN THE SOCIAL COMPETENCE STUDIES

The preterm VLBW children described in this chapter were subdivided according to type and severity of their early medical complications. Over 70% of preterm infants weighing < 1,600 grams have medical complications associated with prematurity (Volpe, 1981). These often lead to CNS damage, either through lack of adequate oxygenation of the brain (hypoxia) secondary to respiratory problems, such as respiratory distress syndrome (RDS) or bronchopulmonary dysplasia (BPD), or from direct brain injury, as with intraventricular hemorrhage (IVH) with associated hydrocephalus.

In the studies reported in this chapter, prematurity is defined as a gestational age at birth of ≤ 36 weeks and a birthweight of ≤ 1,600 grams. Gestational age, defined as the time from mother's last menstrual period until birth, was calculated by a neonatologist using Ballard, Novak, and Driver's (1979) scoring system. All LBW infants included in these studies had mild to severe medical complications as defined later. The presence or absence of IVH was documented by cranial ultrasonography (or occasionally CT scans) within 7–10 days of birth. Infants with IVH received successive ultrasonograms or CT scans to detect progressive ventricular dilation (e.g., dilation present on the third week ultrasound). The degree of IVH is classified by a pediatric radiologist using the system of Papile, Burstein, and Burstein (1978). For infants with respiratory illness, the presence of BPD included ≥ 28 days of oxygen and positive x-ray findings (i.e., cystic changes, hyperinflation of the lungs), while chronic lung disease was defined as oxygen required for ≥ 28 days.

A cohort of 364 urban and rural, low SES families recruited during 1990 and 1991 were evaluated in a longitudinal study of parenting and developmental outcomes in preterm VLBW children. Table 4.1 shows demographic and medical information for the three subject groups, including expected significant differences between groups for gestational age, birth-

TABLE 4.1
Demographic and Medical Characteristics by Risk Group

	Full Term (n = 128)		Low Risk (n = 123)		High Risk (n = 89)	
	Mean	(SD)	Mean	(SD)	Mean	(SD)
Medical						
Birthweight (grams)	3187[a]	(767)	1263[b]	(202)	930[c]	(233)
Gestational age (weeks)	39.1[a]	(5.9)	30.9[b]	(2.0)	28.0[c]	(2.2)
Days of hospitalization	—		44.5[a]	(47)	110[b]	(77)
Maternal						
Maternal age (years)	26[a]	(6)	29[b]	(8)	28[b]	(7)
Maternal education (years)	11.8	(1.7)	12.3	(1.9)	12.2	(2.0)
Socioeconomic status*	25.3	(10)	27.4	(12)	28.5	(12)
Marital status (%)						
Married	39.1		48.2		44.9	
Divorced	7.1		9.5		11.6	
Single	53.8		42.3		43.5	
Maternal work/school (%)						
Yes	37.0		35.0		32.0	
Ethnic (%)						
African American	62		62		57	
Caucasian	25		20		25	
Hispanic	13		15		13	
Other	—		3		5	

Note: Groups with different superscripts are significantly different from one another: "a" significantly differs from "b" and "c"; "b" significantly differs from "c" ($p < .05$).

*Hollingshead four-factor index (Hollingshead, 1965)

weight, and length of hospitalization at birth. No significant differences were found across the three groups on SES, mothers' education, ethnicity, or infant gender. The mean age of the mothers of the FT infants was approximately 2 years younger than that of the mothers of the HR and LR infants. Attrition was approximately 12% across the first 2 years of life.

Preterm infants were included if they weighed ≤ 1,600 grams and had a gestational age ≤ 36 weeks at birth. They were divided into medically high risk (HR) and low risk (LR) groups based on the presence of medical complications that have been associated with delayed or abnormal developmental outcomes in previous follow-up studies (Bendersky & Lewis, 1990; Landry, Fletcher, Denson, & Chapieski, 1993). Infants were excluded from participation in the study if they were diagnosed with significant sensory impairments, meningitis, encephalitis, symptomatic congenital syphilis, congenital abnormality of the brain, short bowel syndrome, or if they were positive for HIV antibody. They also were excluded if the primary caregiver was younger than age 16, was a drug abuser, or was non-English speaking. Eleven percent of parents approached for participation in the study declined. No differences were found on a broad range of demographic and medical characteristics between infants whose parents chose to participate and those who declined.

High Risk Preterm Children

The HR VLBW group consisted of infants diagnosed with one or more severe medical complications, including chronic pulmonary insufficiency of the premature (CPIP), bronchopulmonary dysplasia (BPD), severe intraventricular hemorrhage (IVH), and/or periventricular leukomalacia (PVL). CPIP was documented by the need for oxygen for > 28 days with no cystic lung changes observed on radiographic studies. BPD was documented by the need for oxygen for > 28 days and the presence of characteristic chest radiographic findings. Severe IVH was defined as a subependymal hemorrhage with progressive ventricular dilatation as observed on the infant's third week cranial ultrasound. PVL was also documented by cranial ultrasound with characteristic findings of ischemic lesion of the periventricular white matter. Ninety-four percent of infants in the HR group had either BPD or CPIP (45% without IVH, 40% with mild IVH, 9% with severe IVH and/or PVL). The remaining 6% had either severe IVH and/or PVL. Therefore, for this group, the main source of medical risk was chronic lung disease.

Low Risk Preterm Children

The LR VLBW group consisted of infants diagnosed with one or more less severe medical complications, including transient respiratory distress of the newborn and respiratory distress syndrome, where oxygen was required for less than 28 days. Milder grades of intraventricular hemorrhage without dilatation were also included. Previous long-term follow-up studies have documented different developmental outcomes for infants in these preterm classifications.

Full-Term Children

The FT group consisted of infants with a gestational age from 37 to 42 weeks, Apgar scores greater than 8 at 1 and 5 minutes, and a normal pregnancy history and physical examination at birth. These infants were recruited from the same hospitals as the preterm infants to ensure similar socioeconomic and ethnic backgrounds.

STUDY PROCEDURES

Maternal behaviors and infant social communication development were assessed over a 2-hour home observation that included a 60-minute naturalistic period of daily activity and a 10-minute toy play session. These two conditions were chosen because they place different demands on the infant: Daily activities typically demand less attentional capability from the infant, but require more cooperation around activities such as dressing and feeding. During toy play, cognitive and attentional demands are greater because children are required to attend to mother as well as explore toys. For the naturalistic observation period, mothers were asked to go about their daily activity for 1 hour, staying in the same room with their infants and feeding, bathing, and/or dressing their infants during that time. During the 10-minute toy play session, mothers were asked to play with their infants using age-appropriate toys that were provided by the research assistants.

During both observation sessions, one research assistant coded maternal interactive behaviors and one research assistant coded infant social communication behaviors using pencil-and-paper methods. Every 20 minutes during the naturalistic observation period and at the end of the toy play session, global ratings of warmth/acceptance, flexibility/responsiveness, and positive affect were made by the research assistant who was coding mother behaviors. After these observations, the Bayley Scales of Infant Development (Bayley, 1969) were administered to the infant at 6, 12, and 24 months of age. At 40 months, the Stanford–Binet IV Intelligence Scale was administered to children during a laboratory visit. Children's cognitive status was evaluated to determine if it related to their social development, because Kaler and Kopp (1990) described the importance of children's mental functioning when evaluating social skills.

CHILD SOCIAL COMPETENCE

Two aspects of the children's social competence were coded: *responsiveness* to mothers' attention-directing behaviors and requests and *initiations* of social interactions. Children's social competence was examined from their interactions with their mothers in the home environment rather than with an examiner because children acquire their social skills at these young ages through interactions with their primary caretaker (Marfo, 1990). This approach was, therefore, expected to provide a more valid representation of their social communication skills.

Children's social behaviors were coded as responsiveness if they followed within 3 seconds of a maternal attention-directing event and as an initiation if they occurred when the mother had not interacted with the infant for at least 3 seconds. Initiating behaviors were coded as separate events if they were separated by at least 3 seconds. Previous cross-sectional studies with children of similar ages (e.g., Landry et al., 1994) indicated that if children were going to respond to their mothers' requests, the response most often occurred within the first 2 to 3 seconds after the completion of the request. If greater amounts of time were allotted, then children's behaviors that did not seem directly responsive to the request but rather introduced a new aspect of the interaction were captured as responses rather than initiations.

Categories of Social Behaviors

At all ages, social categories for responsiveness and initiating behaviors included gestures, positive affect, eye gaze, and vocalizations/words. Two additional responsiveness categories included: the infant's orienting to the focus of mother's attention directing behavior at 6 months based on the developmental sequence of this behavior (Scaife & Bruner, 1975) and compliance and negotiating versus noncompliance to maternal requests at 24 and 40 months.

Reliability and Validity of Social Competence Constructs

Factor analysis and structural equation modeling revealed separate factors for initiating and responding across the 6- through 40-month time points, as well as a stable structure across this same developmental period. In order to establish the validity and reliability for a social competence construct, a series of confirmatory factor and structural equation modeling analyses were done. The initial measurement model specified four factors—a social competence factor at each age point from 6 to 40 months. The indicator variables included social initiating and social responsiveness scores assessed at 6, 12, 24, and 40 months of age. The initial measurement model, in which initiations and responsiveness were hypothesized to result from a single construct at each age point, indicated that the model fit the data, $\chi^2(14) = 16.5$, $p > .05$. However, the construct accounted for only .10% to .15% of the variance in each of the indicators. Further, whereas the coefficients for initiations and responsiveness showed moderate relations at 24 and 40 months, they were not related at the 6- and 12-month age points.

A new structural equation model was then examined to determine whether there were two distinct factors (i.e., responsiveness, initiations) of social competence at each age point. Confirmatory factor analyses revealed that social behaviors at 6 and 12 months for both responsiveness and initiations included four indicators (i.e., gestures, smiles, eyegaze, vocalizations/words) that were then analyzed to assess the presence of a single or multiple social construct at these early ages. Results supported the presence of two constructs at 6 and 12 months of age that accounted for significant variability in these indicators; 6 months, responsiveness ($r^2 = .46–.50$), and initiations ($r^2 = .19–.70$); 12 months, responsiveness ($r^2 = .33–.70$), and initiations ($r^2 = .26–.83$). Analyses of social behaviors at 24 and 40 months revealed the same group of indicators for responsiveness and initiations plus an additional responsiveness indicator (i.e., compliance). Results again supported the presence of two constructs (i.e., responsiveness, initiations) at these ages, which accounted for significant variability in these indicators: 24 months, responsiveness ($r^2 = .23–.80$) and initiations ($r^2 = .24–.74$); 40 months, responsiveness ($r^2 = .35–.79$) and initiations ($r^2 = .45–.77$). Finally, two models were compared using full structural equation model analyses. One had paths from responsiveness to initiating across the four age points, as well as those from responsiveness to responsiveness and initiating to initiating across time. A second model included only paths within constructs across time. A comparison of these two models indicated no significant cross construct–cross time coefficients, $\chi^2(12) = 7.81$, $p > .05$, and the model with only within construct paths over time demonstrated adequate fit, $\chi^2(343) = 686.60$, $p < .05$ (chi square to degrees of freedom ratio not greater than 2 to 1), RMSEA = .05, $p > .05$, GFI = .87, CFI = .93. Therefore, relations between parenting and social competence were modeled in two separate ways: responsiveness and initiating. The structure of initiating and responding was the same regardless of risk group.

Scoring of Social Behaviors

The points assigned to each behavior within the constructs of responsiveness and initiations were based on the developmental sequence of behaviors documented in the social literature (e.g., Butterworth, 1995; Kopp,

1982). Results from the structural analyses also were used to support points assigned to the different behaviors across ages. For example, at 24 and 40 months, the expansion of responsiveness to include three factors (i.e., use of words/gestures, compliance to parents requests, and positive affect/eye gaze) reflects the development of more complex social responsiveness skills and the need to differentially weight these behaviors.

To further validate this scoring system, expert raters viewed videotaped mother–child interactions for a subset of children at each of the four time points and ranked these children as high, medium, or low in social maturity in their social behaviors used to initiate and respond. To assure that children who had a broad range of developmental skills were included, scores from standardized testing were used to select children for inclusion in these subsets. Rankings made by experts and rankings based on the scoring system were examined for comparability.

Categories of affect, and eye gaze that emerged in early infancy were coded at all ages (one point per category). Attention-directing gestures (e.g., showing, pointing) also were coded at all ages and received two points because this is a more developmentally advanced behavior that begins to emerge at the end of the first year of life after eye gaze and positive affect (Leung & Rheingold, 1981). Children's social language skills were captured through a hierarchy of points assigned at each age based on the complexity of the verbal utterance. At 6 and 12 months of age, vocalizations were credited with one point.

Because the use of words by 24 months is a marker for more sophisticated social communicative competence, words received two points and vocalizations continued to receive one point. In order to capture the importance of language skills at 40 months for effective social interactions, points were assigned based on whether children used single words (one point), brief but incomplete utterances (three points), and complete sentences (five points). Based in part on Kuczynski and Kochanska's (1990) developmental study of noncompliance, in this study compliance at 24 and 40 months received three points, negotiating received four points, and noncompliance received negative two points. Kuczynski and Kochanska (1990) found that across the toddler period there is variability in children's ability to comply, with most children being adept at this skill by age 3 and high levels of noncompliance were a marker for immature social development. However, the ability to assert social individuality through the use of negotiations was found to be a marker for more social sophistication because it did not emerge until after age 2 and was related to competence in directing others' attention.

At each time point, an average social responsiveness score was obtained by dividing the total number of points by the total number of maternal attention-directing events, to control for the child's opportunities to show a response. A social initiating score was also obtained at each time point based on the total number of points the child received across all initiating events.

MATERNAL BEHAVIORS

A *maternal attention-directing event* was defined as any maternal verbal behavior (questions, comments, directives) or nonverbal behavior (orienting gestures, demonstrations, giving of objects) that was directed toward the child. Separate events were coded when 3 or more seconds elapsed between one maternal behavior and the next. When mothers gave rapid requests, questions, or comments that did not allow time for the child to respond, the series was considered a single event.

Two aspects of mothers' attention-directing style were coded: the proportion of events in which mothers *maintained* their infants' attention versus *redirected* their attention, and the proportion of events in which mothers used *directive* strategies. Proportions for these three behaviors were calculated based on the total number of attention-directing events and proportions were used rather than frequencies in order to control for differences in the total number of attention-directing events across mothers.

Maintaining Infants' Interests

Maintaining was defined as mothers' attention-directing behaviors that were responsive to infants' attentional signals and current interests. Decisions regarding whether mothers' attention-directing behavior maintained the children's current focus of attention were based on what each child was doing just prior to their mother's requests.

Redirecting Infant's Interest

Redirecting was defined as a mother's attention-directing behavior that required the child to change the focus of their attention from something they were already involved with to something different.

Directiveness

Directive strategies demonstrated the degree of structure or information that the mother provided to her child concerning the type of response she expected (i.e., "Put the ring here"). When the maternal attention-directing event included both directive and nondirective strategies, the event was coded as directive.

Warm Responsiveness

Five-point rating scales were used to make global ratings of mothers' positive affect, warm concern/acceptance, and responsiveness/flexibility. Positive affect was based on frequency of maternal smiles, laughs, and facial animation. Warm concern/acceptance was based on amount of physical affection, positive verbal stimulation (including tone of voice), and acceptance of children's interests, moods, and needs. Contingent responsiveness/flexibility was based on promptness and contingency of mothers' response to children's cues, degree of independence allowed, and pace of stimulation. Given high intercorrelations among the behaviors across 3 years of age ($r = .42–.80$), scores were averaged to obtain a single composite measure that was labeled *warm responsiveness*. Using Cronbach's Alpha, internal consistency measures of the composite at 6 and 12 months were .84, at 24 months, .81 and at 40 months, .80.

Interrater Reliability

Generalizability coefficients for the maternal behaviors across the four time points (6/12/24/40 months) were as follows: warm sensitivity, $r = .82/.85/.84/.84$; attention-maintaining in daily activities, $r = .92/.94/.95/.96$, and toy play, $r = .72/.73/.73/.70$; and use of directives in daily activities, $r = .95/.94/.98/.96$, and toy play, $r = .67/.60/.68/.79$. Generalizability coefficients for child social behaviors across the four time points (6/12/24/40 months) were as follows: average social responsiveness in daily activities, $r = .81/.89/.83/.94$, and toy play, $r = .67/.71/.77/.79$; and social initiations in daily activities, $r = .94/.91/.87/.92$, and toy play, $r = .83/.90/.90/.82$.

SOCIAL COMMUNICATION DEVELOPMENT
ACROSS 3 YEARS OF LIFE

The development of social skills across the first 3 years of life was evaluated for preterm VLBW children of high and low medical risk and compared with that of healthy full-term (FT) children. Because VLBW infants are reported to be more prone to passivity when having to draw on their own resources to initiate a behavior (Garner, Landry, & Richardson, 1991; Plunkett & Meisels, 1989), prematurity was expected to predict slower rates of development of initiating through the third year of life. Although VLBW children as a group are not reported to have the same degree of difficulty with responsiveness as with initiating (Landry et al., 1990), slower rates of development in responsiveness were expected to be predicted by higher levels of medical risk because of the delays HR VLBW children show in motor, attention, and early communication skills.

The First Year of Life

Across both contexts, both the HR and LR VLBW infants showed slower rates of increases from 6 to 12 months in initiations as compared to the FT infants. HR VLBW infants appeared to have both slower rates and lower levels in both contexts as compared to the FT infants. In contrast, the LR infants have both lower levels and slower rates only in the more attentionally demanding toy play context. During daily activities, LR infants also showed slower increases in initiating, but they had significantly higher 6-month initiating skills than the HR infants and skills that were somewhat higher than the FT infants, suggesting that LR infants have less difficulty initiating in this context. No significant differences across groups were found for either 6-month responsiveness scores or for the rate of increase from 6 to 12 months in responsiveness (see Table 4.2). Figure 4.1 illustrates the risk differences for initiations (for more specific information on the procedures and analyses see Landry, Smith et al., 1997b).

These results suggest that HR VLBW infants may have broader difficulties in recognizing the importance of signaling their interests. In contrast, the LR infants' may have greater difficulties with initiating when they are in situations with increased attentional demands. In support of this, LR preterm infants frequently are reported to have greater attentional problems when compared to FT infants (see Ruff, 1988). LR infants may not have the capacity to formulate a social goal when they are required to orient attention to both mother and toys. The absence of group differences in social responsiveness demonstrates that VLBW infants, even those at greater medical risk, are less likely to have difficulty in situations where mothers provide a framework by making specific requests. Because much of children's learning occurs through the active role they assume in social interactions, it will be important in future studies to evaluate the development of initiating at later ages.

The First 3 Years of Life

When evaluating the effect of prematurity and medical risk on the development of these same social skills from 6 through 40 months of age with the same groups of children, similar results were found for medical risk for growth in initiating. After accounting for the influence of mothers' behaviors, results from hierarchical linear modeling (HLM) analyses revealed that the FT children showed more of an increase in initiating than both HR and LR children. This increase was greater during toy play than daily activities (see Fig. 4.1). In contrast, the HR and LR children showed greater ac-

TABLE 4.2
Means and Standard Deviations for Social Responsiveness

	Risk Group											
	High Risk				Low Risk				Full Term			
	6	12	24	40	6	12	24	40	6	12	24	40
Daily Activities												
M	1.3	1.4	2.6	4.6	1.3	1.4	2.8	4.6	1.3	1.4	2.8	4.9
(SD)	(0.2)	(0.3)	(0.9)	(7.3)	(0.2)	(0.3)	(1.2)	(7.8)	(0.2)	(0.3)	(0.9)	(7.8)
Toy Play												
M	1.1	1.2	2.6	4.2	1.1	1.2	3.0	4.4	1.1	1.2	3.0	4.7
(SD)	(0.2)	(0.3)	(1.0)	(9.4)	(0.2)	(0.2)	(1.2)	(11.1)	(0.2)	(0.3)	(1.3)	(8.4)

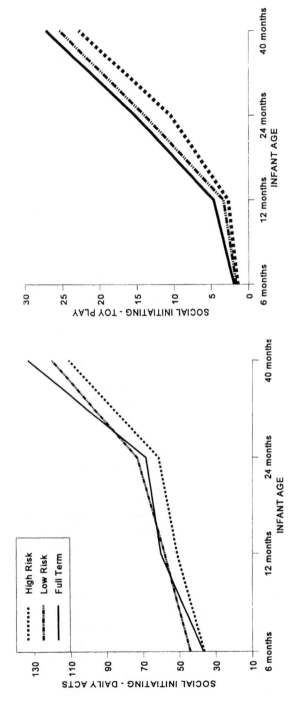

FIG. 4.1. Infant social initiating from 6 through 40 months of age by risk group for two social contexts.

celerations than the FT children, but this was most apparent during toy play, with the LR children displaying more of an acceleration in their initiating skills than the HR children. Similar to the findings across the first year of life, growth in children's responsiveness showed no significant relation with medical risk or prematurity (see Table 4.2). The VLBW children's greater accelerations in initiating suggests more unevenness in their social development. Because this unevenness was seen more in toy play than daily activities, these children's ability to learn to use gestures and verbalizations to attract their mother's attention may be more negatively affected in situations that require more joint attention. These findings demonstrate that VLBW children, as compared to FT children, show greater changes in their rate of growth of social communicative skills. Therefore, evaluating these skills at later ages may ultimately reveal appropriate levels of social functioning in these children.

RELATIONS FOR SOCIAL COMMUNICATION DEVELOPMENT AND MATERNAL BEHAVIORS ACROSS THE FIRST YEAR OF LIFE

Understanding the relation between mothers' interactive behaviors and children's social communication development across the infant's first year of life was expected to be important because of the critical nature of this period for building a base for social skill development. Increased maternal warmth and sensitivity to infants' interests provide the necessary supports for infants' active organization of social responses. These two maternal behaviors were expected to be important for infants, particularly VLBW infants, to develop early social skills. In contrast, high degrees of structure through directive strategies and attempts to redirect attention were expected to place increased demands on the infants' attentional capacities and interfere with the acquisition of social skills, particularly social initiating. These behaviors were expected to have a more significant impact on the VLBW infants because of their attentional difficulties (see Landry, Smith, Miller-Loncar, & Swank, 1998). Table 4.3 contains means and standard deviations for all three maternal behaviors.

Because the frequency of mothers' interactions and infants' cognitive levels may be important in understanding individual differences in social development, these variables were included when examining relations between maternal interactive behaviors and infant social development. Results are shown in Tables 4.4 and 4.5. For all infants, higher Bayley mental scores were associated with increased competency in initiating and this was more apparent for the LR VLBW infants than the HR infants. In addition, maternal maintaining was an important predictor of both 6-month social responsiveness (see Table 4.4) and growth in this skill across the

TABLE 4.3
Comparison of Maternal Interactive Behaviors by Risk Group

	Risk Group											
	High Risk				Low Risk				Full Term			
Maternal Behavior	6	12	24	40	6	12	24	40	6	12	24	40
Warm Sensitivity[1]												
M	3.68	3.62	3.26	4.81	3.60	3.53	3.25	4.72	3.66	3.50	3.26	4.73
(SD)	(.71)	(.76)	(.74)	(1.0)	(.72)	(.80)	(.65)	(.91)	(.73)	(.78)	(.68)	(1.0)
Maintaining[2]												
Daily Activities												
M	28.3	29.5	45.2	69.1	28.6	29.2	45.5	71.7	25.7	33.3	44.7	65.0
(SD)	(14.0)	(13.5)	(16.2)	(17.9)	(15.0)	(13.2)	(16.5)	(18.1)	(14.4)	(14.5)	(17.7)	(19.1)
Toy Play												
M	26.4	49.9	59.3	81.4	23.6	53.2	59.8	80.7	27.1	56.2	56.4	79.3
(SD)	(18.3)	(18.1)	(16.4)	(14.6)	(15.6)	(16.3)	(15.4)	(13.4)	(15.2)	(17.0)	(18.4)	(13.1)
Directiveness												
Daily Activities												
M	48.0	51.7	52.9	44.9	47.1	51.6	47.8	40.1	47.1	50.9	47.0	40.8
(SD)	(14.5)	(12.7)	(12.7)	(14.4)	(14.0)	(14.0)	(14.0)	(14.6)	(15.8)	(14.3)	(12.8)	(14.8)
Toy Play												
M	50.0	55.9	49.6	44.3	49.2	53.4	45.1	40.7	46.0	54.2	45.8	41.9
(SD)	(15.4)	(14.8)	(14.7)	(18.1)	(15.0)	(16.0)	(18.0)	(17.9)	(14.2)	(14.2)	(18.8)	(16.4)

[1]Ratings range from 1 to 5, with higher ratings indicate higher levels of behavior.
[2]Data are proportions (expressed as percentages) based on total number of maternal attention-directing events.

TABLE 4.4
Multivariate and Univariate Relations
for Infant Social Competence at 6 Months

BETWEEN CONTEXT EFFECTS

Multivariate Model	Wilks's Lambda	F	df	p value
Warm sensitivity	.94	3.15	6,606	.01
Maintain—DA	.95	2.38	6,606	.03
Control variables (Bayley & maternal stimulation)	.87	2.41	18,606	.01

Model for Initiations	R²	F	df	p value
	.20	2.45	32,304	.0001

Univariate		t	df	p value
Warm sensitivity		-2.10	304	.05
Maternal stimulation—DA		-2.24	304	.03
Bayley mental—6 months		2.65	304	.01

Model for Responsiveness	R²	F	df	p value
	.22	2.62	32,304	.0001

Univariate		t	df	p value
Warm sensitivity		2.75	304	.01
Maintaining—DA		3.27	304	.01
Maintaining—DA × HR/LR vs. FT²		-1.79	304	.04*
Maternal stimulation—DA		-3.39	304	.01

Note: DA = daily activities; HR/LR vs. FT = High Risk/Low Risk vs. Full-term
*Indicates one-tailed test of significance

first year of life during both contexts (see Table 4.5). A stronger relation of maintaining with social responsiveness for the VLBW versus the FT infants at 6 months of age indicated that maintaining may be a particularly important strategy for mothers to use early in VLBW infants' development.

In contrast, when at 6 months mothers are not sensitive to their infants' cues and attempt to redirect their attention, all infants show slower development across 6 to 12 months in their social initiating skills (see Table 4.5). Maternal redirecting at 6 months of age may be particularly detrimental for the development of social communication skills because this is a period in which infants are beginning to learn how to organize their social behaviors and to attract another's attention. When infants are just developing their ability to coordinate their attention with another person, mothers' insensitivity to their infants' interests may impede the communicative process.

TABLE 4.5
Multivariate and Univariate Relations for Infant
Social Competence Across 6 to 12 Months

BETWEEN CONTEXT EFFECTS

Multivariate Model	Wilks's Lambda	F	df	p value
Redirect—DA	.93	1.75	12,562	.05
Maintain—DA	.92	1.94	12,562	.03
Warm sensitivity	.93	1.82	12,562	.04
Directiveness—DA	.91	2.26	12,562	.01
Control variables (Bayley & maternal stimulation)	.88	2.07	18,562	.01

Model for Initiations	R^2	F	df	p value
	.28	2.04	53,282	.01

Univariate		t	df	p value
Redirecting (6 months)—DA		−2.40	282	.03
Warm sensitivity (6–12 months) × HR vs. LR		−2.78	282	.01
Directiveness (6 months)—DA		−2.82	282	.01
Directiveness (6–12 months)—DA		−4.19	282	.01
Maternal interactions—DA		2.06	282	.04
Bayley Mental (6 months) × HR vs. LR		2.49	282	.03

Model for Responsiveness	R^2	F	df	p value
	.30	2.26	53,282	.01

Univariate		t	df	p value
Maintaining (6–12 months)—DA		2.25	282	.04
Maternal Interactions—DA		2.46	282	.02
Maternal Interactions—TP		2.49	282	.02

WITHIN CONTEXT EFFECTS

Multivariate Model	Wilks's Lambda	F	df	p value
Directiveness—DA	.92	1.90	12,562	.05

Model for Initiations	R^2	F	df	p value
	.28	2.08	53,282	.01

Univariate		t	df	p value
Directiveness (6 months)—DA		−3.28	282	.01
Directiveness (6–12 months)—DA		−4.58	282	.01

Note: DA = Daily Activities; HR vs. LR = High Risk vs. Low Risk; TP = Toy Play

Maternal use of directiveness during early infancy (i.e., 6 months of age), as well as increases in this maternal behavior across the first year of life, were related to slower increases in development of infants' social initiating skills over the first year of life for all infants, particularly during daily activities (see Table 4.5). This maternal strategy may not provide the infant with adequate opportunities to take initiative in social interactions. A high degree of maternal control also may fail to promote social initiative because it does not provide a context in which the child can develop an adequate sense of autonomy.

Although mothers' specific interactive strategies (i.e., maintaining, redirecting, directiveness) were expected to be important in understanding infants' social development, qualitative aspects (i.e., positive affect, contingent responsiveness to infants' cues) also were expected to be facilitative of early infant development. These findings support those of other studies, because mothers who displayed high degrees of warm responsiveness had infants who displayed greater social competence. Mothers' warmth at 6 months related to higher levels of infants' social responsiveness at the same point of time (see Table 4.4), and greater increases in this maternal behavior from 6 to 12 months were associated with greater increases in infants' social initiating over the first year of life (see Table 4.5). Of particular interest is that mothers' warm responsiveness seemed to be especially important for the development of initiating skills for the HR infants as compared with the LR and FT infants. These results are correlational in nature and, therefore, do not indicate direction of influence. However, a plausible explanation is that because HR infants have greater difficulty organizing their social world, mothers' warm sensitivity facilitates social development by modeling specific features of positive social exchanges at a pace that fits the infants' attentional and regulating skills. Infants who are showing more normal patterns of development may not require this form of early specialized support to the same extent as infants who are having greater difficulty in social development.

RELATIONS FOR SOCIAL COMMUNICATION DEVELOPMENT AND MATERNAL BEHAVIORS ACROSS 3 YEARS OF LIFE

In examining relations of maternal behaviors to social communicative development through age 3, particular interest was in maternal behaviors and changes in these behaviors that facilitated accelerated growth in responsiveness and initiating skills. HLM was used to examine these relations, examining maternal behavior as a time-varying covariate (Bryk & Raudenbush, 1992). Higher levels and further increases in the rates with which mothers attempted to maintain infants' attention were expected to relate positively to accelerations in infants' social responsiveness and initiative. Because of the VLBW infants' greater difficulty in shifting attention and need for more assistance in this area (Landry, 1995), these relations were expected to be stronger for both VLBW groups compared to the FT infants, and stronger for the HR than the LR VLBW infants. Although directiveness was not expected to facilitate social skills in early infancy, higher levels in this behavior over time were expected to be supportive of VLBW infants' development of social responsiveness. The VLBW infants were expected to require more information across longer periods of time about what response was expected of them. High degrees of directiveness were not expected to provide adequate opportunities for children to take social initiative, but higher levels and further increases in directiveness were expected to show negative relations with growth in social initiating for all infants, but more so for the VLBW infants. Although a decrease was predicted in maternal warm responsiveness across the three groups through age 3, it was expected that higher levels in this behavior across this period would relate to greater accelerations in infants' responsiveness and initiations. This relation was expected to be stronger for the VLBW infants because of their need for more sensitive interactive styles across a longer period.

These findings showed that higher levels of mothers' *maintaining* and further increases in this behavior over 6 through 40 months related to growth in *initiating* skills for FT children but supported the VLBW children in making greater gains in initiations ($p < .01$), because there was an interaction between maintaining and prematurity (see Fig. 4.2). Also, as mothers showed even higher levels of maintaining, the HR children showed greater acceleration in their initiating as compared to the LR and FT ($p < .001$). Maintaining also supported a child's *responsiveness* to maternal requests; however, this was true for all children ($p < .001$). Contrary to expectations, these relations were greater during daily activities than during toy play. A number of studies describe mothers' sensitivity to their children's focus of interest as important for understanding a range of developmental outcomes (Akhtar et al., 1991; Schaffer & Crook, 1980; Tomasello & Farrar, 1986). From the perspective of the child's cognitive development, mothers' attempts to maintain attentional focus provides support for young children's immature attentional skills by not requiring them to shift their attentional focus. When mothers make requests that are complementary to children's interests, children can then use their attentional and cognitive capacity to respond appropriately and initiate social exchanges. Although maintaining has been related to social skills at early ages, the present results demonstrate that increases in the rate at which children develop these skills also depends on mothers increasing their use of this supportive strategy across the early childhood period.

Across both contexts and for all groups, higher levels of maternal directiveness across 6 to 40 months predicted slower rates of initiating (p

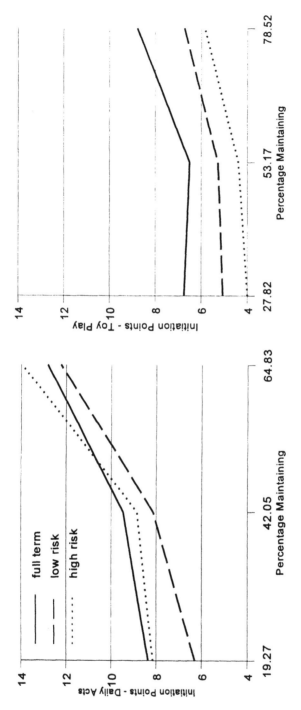

FIG. 4.2. Relation of mothers' maintaining with children's development of initiating. This illustrates how different levels of mothers' maintaining relate to the children's average rate of growth in initiating for each of the three risk groups in each context. The midpoint on the x-axis is the grand mean of mothers' maintaining, which is based on maintaining across all times and on all mother–child dyads. Points on either side represent ± 1 SD from this grand mean.

< .05) (see Fig. 4.3). Across this developmental period, when mothers show high amounts of direction about what their children should do, they may not promote the development of more active roles in social interactions (Kuczynski et al., 1987). It was expected that the information provided by directiveness about what was expected of a child would facilitate the children's ability to respond. However, high levels of directiveness across this time period also predicted slower increases in the children's responsiveness ($p < .05$). This finding suggests that high amounts of control and structure interfere with children developing a willingness to work with mother in a cooperative manner. This negative influence of directiveness was found to be more apparent during daily activities than toy play, possibly because the contextual demands of the toy play situation result in children needing increased structure in order to respond.

As predicted, there was a positive effect on children's growth in initiating when mothers showed high levels of warm responsiveness ($p < .001$) and this effect was stronger for mothers who had even higher levels ($p < .01$). These relations were seen during daily activities but not during toy play (see Fig. 4.4). We expected that relations with warm responsiveness would influence both VLBW children differently than the FT children. However, whereas all groups appeared to respond more positively (i.e., as evidenced by their increased initiating behaviors) to higher levels of this maternal style during daily activities than during toy play, the LR children showed the greatest difference across these contexts ($p < .01$). It is unclear why this relation was different across contexts for the LR children.

When evaluating growth in the children's social responsiveness, mothers' warmth supported all children's growth, but again, this was most apparent during daily activities ($p < .001$). Positive relations during daily activities may be due to the fact that parenting, which is warm and responsive, fosters reciprocal interactions in a manner that allows the child to have a degree of control. During daily activities, children have many opportunities to elicit their mother's attention to various play and self-help activities. A parenting style that is responsive to children's signals and need for autonomy encourages children to learn that they can have a more active role in social interactions (Bornstein & Tamis-LeMonda, 1989; Lewis & Goldberg, 1969). Also, this parenting behavior is thought to have a motivational effect because it promotes cooperation as the child learns that mother is attentive to their cues and needs (MacDonald, 1992).

CONCLUSIONS

These results demonstrate the importance of evaluating different aspects of social communication development for VLBW children of varying degrees of medical risk. Although VLBW children showed competency in

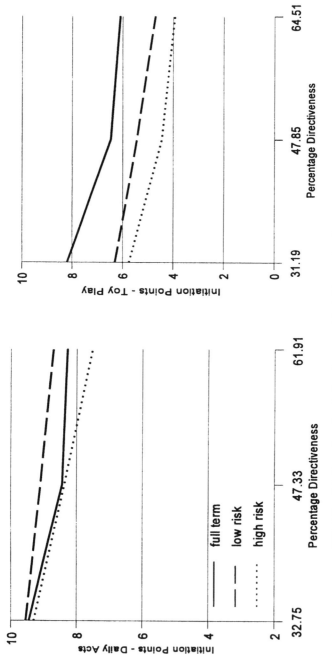

FIG. 4.3. Relation of mothers' directiveness with children's development of initiating. This illustrates how different levels of mothers' directiveness relate to the children's average rate of growth in initiating for each of the three risk groups in each context. The midpoint on the x-axis is the grand mean of mothers' directiveness, which is based on maintaining across all times and on all mother–child dyads. Points on either side represent ± 1 SD from this grand mean.

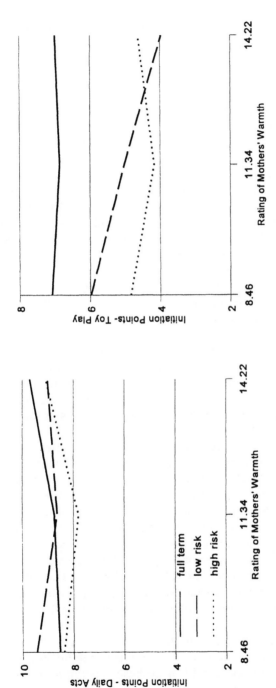

FIG. 4.4. Relation of mothers' warm sensitivity with children's development of initiating. This illustrates how different levels of mothers' warm sensitivity relate to the children's average rate of growth in initiating for each of the three risk groups during daily activities. The midpoint on the x-axis is the grand mean of mothers' warm sensitivity, which is based on maintaining across all times and on all mother–child dyads. Points on either side represent ± 1 SD from this grand mean.

responsiveness skills, they did not show normal rates of development in initiating across the first 3 years of life. The ability to initiate social interactions independently appears to be a more difficult skill for young children who have experienced medical complications at birth. Behaviors required to initiate include setting social goals and sequencing behaviors to achieve the goal, as well as flexibility in adapting to the changing demands of social situations. These behaviors have been described under the rubric of self-regulation (Kopp, 1982), as well as executive function skills (Welsch & Pennington, 1988). One aspect of executive functions for young children is the ability to understand their role in relation to what is occurring in the social interactions around them, including the ability to determine and carry out a behavior to satisfy a specific social need. Children with CNS-related deficits have been shown in other studies to have particular problems with these types of skills (Landry et al., 1993) and the results of current studies provide further support for deficits in this area for medically compromised children. Because this aspect of children's social communication development plays an important role in understanding children's cognitive development, their competency with peers, and ability to direct their own learning, it is essential to identify factors that facilitate this development.

Findings from recent studies demonstrate that parenting behaviors may be an important factor that influences children's social development. Both qualitative aspects (i.e., warm responsiveness) and specific interactive styles (i.e., maintaining attentional focus), which demonstrate sensitivity to children's signals and needs, are related to greater gains in social competency, particularly for VLBW children.

Mothers' provision of increased structure (e.g., directiveness) was also an important maternal behavior in understanding individual differences in the VLBW infants, and especially the HR infants' social development. Increased structure may facilitate social responding in the first year, possibly because it gives the HR infant specific information about the type of response that is expected. However, higher levels of structure were not facilitative of social development beyond the second year of life. Specifically, social initiating skills are not supported by maternal styles of interacting that are high in structure for VLBW or FT infants. The child's ability to independently initiate social contacts develops when mothers establish a cooperative exchange by offering choices rather than directing children's behavior.

It was expected that changes in mothers' behaviors across the first 3 years of life would be important in understanding variability in children's rates of development. Support for this hypothesis was found through the use of methodologies allowing for evaluation of change in a mother with change in the child. Increases in maternal behaviors that more closely matched children's changing developmental needs related to greater accelerations in children's social development across 6 to 40 months of age. An interesting question not addressed by these studies is whether there are critical points in the child's development in which one member of the mother–child dyad is more influential in triggering changes in the other's behavior. This will be an important question to address in future research.

In addition to the parents' interactive behaviors and the child's medical risk status, the child's cognitive abilities, the type of social behavior, and the demands of the social context were also important in understanding individual differences in the children's development of social communication abilities. The relative importance of these factors for understanding individual differences in children's social development varies as a result of the child's biological risk status. The aspects of social development that appear most vulnerable to higher degrees of biological risk are those requiring the child to perceive, integrate, and respond in a flexible way to changing social demands. These skills represent a critical area of social communication development that warrants further investigation.

ACKNOWLEDGMENTS

This study was supported by NIH Grant HD24128. We are grateful to the research staff for their assistance in data collection.

REFERENCES

Akhtar, N., Dunham, F., & Dunham, P. (1991). Directive interactions and early vocabulary development: The role of joint attentional focus. *Journal of Child Language, 18*, 41–49.

Bakeman, R., & Brown, J. V. (1980). Early interaction: Consequences for social and mental development at three years. *Child Development, 51*, 437–447.

Ballard, J. L., Novak, K. K., & Driver, M. (1979). A simplified score for assessment of fetal maturation of newly born infants. *Journal of Pediatrics, 95*, 769–774.

Barnard, K. E., Bee, H. L., & Hammond, M. A. (1984). Developmental changes in maternal interactions with term and preterm infants. *Infant Behavior and Development, 7*, 101–114.

Bayley, N. (1969). *Bayley Scales of Infant Development*. New York: Psychological Corporation.

Bendersky, M., & Lewis, M. (1990). Early language ability as a function of ventricular dilatation associated with intraventricular hemorrhage. *Developmental and Behavioral Pediatrics, 11*, 17–21.

Bornstein, M. A., Tamis-LeMonda, C. S., Tal, J., Ludemann, P., Sueko, T., Rahn, C. W., Pecheux, M. G., Azuma, H., & Vardi, D. (1992). Maternal responsiveness to infants in three societies: The United States, France, and Japan. *Child Development, 63*, 808–821.

Bornstein, M., & Tamis-LeMonda, C. S. (1989). Maternal responsiveness and cognitive development in children. In M. H. Bornstein (Ed.), *Maternal responsiveness: Characteristics and consequences* (pp. 49–61). San Francisco: Jossey-Bass.

Bruner, J. S. (1982). The organization of action and the nature of the adult–infant interaction. In E. Tronick (Ed.), *Social interchange in infancy: Affect, cognition, and communication* (pp. 23–35). Baltimore: University Park Press.

Bryk, A. S., & Raudenbush, S. W. (1992). *Hierarchical linear models: Applications and data analysis methods.* London: Sage.

Butterworth, G. (1995). Origins of mind in perception and action. In C. Moore & P. J. Dunham (Eds.), *Joint attention: Its origins and role in development* (pp. 29–40). Hillsdale, NJ: Lawrence Erlbaum Associates.

Crawford, J. W. (1982). Mother–infant interaction in premature and full-term infants. *Child Development, 53,* 957–962.

Crockenberg, S., & Litman, C. (1990). Autonomy as competence in 2-year-olds: Maternal correlates of child defiance, compliance, and self-assertion. *Developmental Psychology, 26*(6), 961–971.

Dodge, K. (1985). Facets of social interaction and the assessment of social competence in children. In B. Schneider, K. Rubin, & S. Ledingham (Eds.), *Children's peer relations: Issues in assessment and intervention* (pp. 3–22). New York: Springer-Verlag.

Drillien, C. M., Thomson, A., & Burgoyne, K. (1980). Low-birthweight children at school age: A longitudinal study. *Developmental Medicine and Child Neurology, 22,* 26–47.

Garner, P. W., Landry, S. H., & Richardson, M. A. (1991). The development of joint attention skills in very low birth weight infants across the first two years. *Infant Behavior and Development, 14,* 489–495.

Goldberg, S., Lojkasek, M., Gartner, G., & Corter, C. (1989). Maternal responsiveness and social development in preterm infants. In M. H. Bornstein (Ed.), *Maternal responsiveness: Characteristics and consequences* (pp. 89–103). San Francisco: Jossey-Bass.

Greenberg, M. T., & Crnic, K. A. (1988). Longitudinal predictors of developmental status and social interaction in premature and full-term infants at age two. *Child Development, 59,* 554–570.

Hollingshead, A. B. (1965). *Four factor index of social status.* Unpublished manuscript, Yale University Department of Sociology, New Haven, CT.

Kaler, S. R., & Kopp, C. B. (1990). Compliance and comprehension in very young toddlers. *Child Development, 61,* 1997–2003.

Kopp, C. B. (1982). The growth of self-regulation: A developmental perspective. *Developmental Psychology, 18,* 199–214.

Kuczynski, L., & Kochanska, G. (1990). Development of children's noncompliance strategies: From toddlerhood to age 5. *Developmental Psychology, 26,* 398–408.

Kuczynski, L., Kochanska, G., Radke-Yarrow, M., & Girnius-Brown, O. (1987). A developmental interpretation of young children's noncompliance. *Developmental Psycholgy, 23,* 799–806.

Landry, S. H. (1995). The development of joint attention in premature low birth weight infants: Effects of early medical complications and maternal attention-directing behaviors. In C. Moore & P. Dunham (Eds.), *Joint attention: Its origins and role in development* (pp. 223–250). Hillsdale, NJ: Lawrence Erlbaum Associates.

Landry, S. H., & Chapieski, M. L. (1988). Visual attention skills and preterm infant risk. *Infant Behavior and Development, 11,* 177–185.

Landry, S. H., Chapieski, M. L., Richardson, M., Palmer, J., & Hall, S. (1990). The social competence of children born prematurely: Effects of medical complications and parent behaviors. *Child Development, 61,* 1605–1616.

Landry, S. H., Denson, S. E., & Swank, P. R. (1997). Effects of early medical risk and socioeconomic status on the cognitive development and social communication skills of low birth weight infants. *Journal of Clinical and Experimental Neuropsychology, 19*(3), 261–274.

Landry, S. H., Fletcher, J. M., Denson, S., & Chapieski, L. (1993). Longitudinal outcome for low birth weight infants: Effects of intraventricular hemorrhage and bronchopulmonary dysplasia. *Journal of Clinical and Experimental Neuropsychology, 15*(2), 205–218.

Landry, S. H., Garner, P., Swank, P., & Baldwin, C. (1996). Effects of maternal scaffolding during joint toy play with preterm and full-term infants. *Merrill-Palmer Quarterly, 42,* 1–23.

Landry, S. H., Garner, P. W., Pirie, D., & Swank, P. R. (1994). Effects of social context and mothers' requesting strategies on Down's syndrome children's social responsiveness. *Developmental Psychology, 30,* 293–302.

Landry, S. H., Robinson, S. S., Copeland, D., & Garner, P. W. (1993). Goal-directed behavior and perception of self-competence in children with Spina Bifida. *Journal of Pediatric Psychology, 18,* 389–396.

Landry, S. H., Smith, K. E., Miller-Loncar, C. L., & Swank, P. R. (1997a). Predicting cognitive-language and social growth curves from early maternal behaviors in children at varying degrees of biologic risk. *Developmental Psychology, 33,* 1–14.

Landry, S. H., Smith, K. E., Miller-Loncar, C. L., & Swank, P. R. (1997b). Responsiveness and initiative: Two aspects of social compentence. *Infant Behavior and Development, 20,* 259–262.

Landry, S. H., Smith, K. E., Miller-Loncar, C. L., & Swank, P. R. (1998). The relation of change in maternal interactive styles to the developing social competence of full-term and preterm children. *Child Development, 69,* 105–123.

Landry, S. H., Smith, K. E., Swank, P. R., & Miller-Loncar, C. L. (2000). Early maternal and child influences on children's later independent cognitive and social functioning. *Child Development, 71,* 358–375.

Leung, E. H. L., & Rheingold, H. (1981). Development of pointing as a social gesture. *Developmental Psychology, 172,* 215–220.

Lewis, M., & Goldberg, S. (1969). Perceptual-cognitive development in infancy: A generalized expectancy model as a function of mother–infant interaction. *Merrill-Palmer Quarterly, 15,* 81–100.

Maccoby, E., & Martin, J. A. (1983). Socialization in the context of the family. In E. M. Hetherington (Ed.), P. H. Mussen (Series Ed.), *Handbook of child psychology: Vol. 4. Socialization, personality, and social development* (pp. 1–102). New York: Wiley.

MacDonald, K. (1992). Warmth as a developmental construct: An evolutionary analysis. *Child Development, 63,* 753–773.

Marfo, K. (1990). Maternal directiveness in interactions with mentally handicapped children: An analytical commentary. *Journal of Child Psychology and Psychiatry, 31,* 531–549.

Papile, L., Burstein, V., & Burstein, R. (1978). Incidence and evolution of subependymal and intraventricular hemorrhage: A study of infants with birth weight less than 1500 grams. *Journal of Pediatrics, 92,* 529–534.

Parpal, M., & Maccoby, E. E. (1985). Maternal responsiveness and subsequent child compliance. *Child Development, 56,* 1326–1334.

Plunkett, J. W., & Meisels, S. J. (1989). Socioemotional adaptation of preterm infants at three years. *Infant Mental Health Journal, 10,* 117–131.

Rocissano, L., & Yatchmink, Y. (1983). Language skill and interactive patterns in prematurely born toddlers. *Child Development, 54,* 1229–1241.

Rourke, P. D., & Fuerst, D. R. (1991). *Learning disabilitiesand psychosocial functioning: A neuropsychological perspective.* New York: Guilford.

Ruff, H. A. (1988). The measurement of attention in high-risk infants. In P. Vietze & H. G. Vaughan (Eds.), *Early identification of infants at risk for mental retardation* (pp. 282–296). New York: Grune & Stratton.

Scaife, M., & Bruner, J. S. (1975). The capacity for joint visual attention in the infant. *Nature, 253,* 265–266.

Schaffer, H. R. (1977). *Studies in mother–infant interactions.* New York: Academic Press.

Schaffer, H. R., & Crook, C. K. (1980). Child compliance and maternal control techniques. *Developmental Psychology, 16,* 54–61.

Shatz, M. (1977). On the development of communicative understandings: An early strategy for interpreting and responding to messages. In J. Glick & A. Clarke-Stewart (Eds.), *Studies in social and communicative development* (pp. 24–65). New York: Gardner.

Tomasello, M., & Farrar, J. (1986). Joint attention and early language. *Child Development, 57*, 1454–1463.

Volpe, J. J. (1981). Neonatal intraventricular hemorrhage. *New England Journal of Medicine, 304*, 886–891.

Vygotsky, L. S. (1978). *Mind in society: The development of higher psychological processes.* Cambridge, MA: Harvard University Press.

Welsch, M. C., & Pennington, B. F. (1988). Assessing frontal lobe functioning in children: Views from developmental psychology. *Developmental Neuropsychology, 4*(3), 199–230.

Wertsch, J. V. (1979). From social interaction to higher psychological processes. *Human Development, 22*, 1–22.

## CHAPTER FIVE

Individual Differences in the Development of Executive Function in Children: Lessons From the Delayed Response and A-not-B Tasks

Kimberly Andrews Espy
Southern Illinois University School of Medicine

Paul M. Kaufmann
Clyde L. Choate Mental Health and Developmental Center

An explosion of research activity in the area of attention, memory, and executive function has been noted since the mid-1980s (Lyon & Krasnegor, 1996). The bulk of this activity, however, has focused on the examination of group differences in executive skills, with less attention devoted to the manner by which individual children differ in executive skills from their peers. This chapter explores individual differences from a developmental perspective, that is, by returning to the emergence of basic executive functions and tracing the subsequent manifestations by examining the individual patterns of change. Therefore, it first reviews the history of executive function through critical case study descriptions and then discusses the current conceptualizations of executive functions. Traditional frameworks for understanding individual differences are described with emphasis on quasi-experimental designs commonly used in developmental neuropsychology. Finally, investigations concerning the performance of infants and young children on a particular executive function paradigm are reviewed because, according to the position herein, executive behavior is readily observable early in development.

WHERE DID THE CONCEPT OF EXECUTIVE FUNCTIONS DEVELOP? A CASE STUDY REVIEW

Historically, case study has been a useful approach to investigate individual differences in adult and child populations. The strength of this approach lies in its sensitivity to individual variation and its breadth of quali-

113

tative descriptions. Many authors identify the unique clinical presentation of Phineas Gage, an otherwise unremarkable railroad worker, as the dawning of modern interest in the brain–behavior relations associated with executive functions (Harlow, 1848, 1868). Gage made history when an accidental explosion sent a large tamping iron traversing through his left frontal lobe, causing focal, yet extensive damage. Harlow's behavioral observations are the only record of the psychological changes characterized by reduced inhibition and altered personality:

> The equilibrium or balance, so to speak, between his intellectual faculties and his animal propensities, seems to have been destroyed. He is fitful, irreverent, indulging at times in the grossest profanity (which was not previously his custom), manifesting but little deference for his fellows, impatient of restraint or advice when it conflicts with his desires, at times pertinaciously obstinate, yet capricious and vacillating, devising many plans for future operations, which are no sooner arranged than they are abandoned in turn for others appearing more feasible. (Harlow, 1868, p. 344).

Soon after the injury, Harlow (1848) concluded that Gage's memory was unimpaired. However, extended observations noted that Gage would entertain his nieces and nephews with fabulous stories of "his wonderful feats and hairbreadth escapes, without any foundation except in his fancy" (Harlow, 1868, p. 334).

Using a formal, psychometric approach, Eslinger and Damasio (1985) investigated patient EVR, whose orbital frontal surface and the frontal pole were excised bilaterally, due to a large orbitofrontal meningioma. Traditional neuropsychological batteries, which included measures of executive functions, such as the Wisconsin Card Sorting Test (WCST; Heaton, 1981), demonstrated little, if any, evidence of disturbed higher cortical functions following recovery from surgery. Protocols from repeated follow-up examinations are noteworthy in that EVR's performance was strategic, sophisticated, and almost flawless. However, information provided by family members, along with observations of EVR's decision making in everyday life, clearly demonstrated a significant disability associated with his frontal lobe tumor and excision, which A. R. Damasio, Tranel, and H. Damasio (1990) labeled acquired sociopathy.

In children, the investigation of executive skills has a much shorter history. Until the 1980s, many neuropsychologists believed that executive skills did not "turn on" or become functional until puberty (Golden, 1981). However, recent studies with various methods and measurement tools have demonstrated repeatedly that children possess executive functions (Chelune & Baer, 1986; Levin et al., 1991; Welsh, Pennington, & Groisser, 1991). In addition, lesions to the prefrontal cortex early in life may be less likely to mimic impairments observed acutely following prefrontal lesions in adulthood (Eslinger, Biddle, & Grattan, 1997). This observation is not surprising, considering that the children's behavior and intact central nervous systems differ from those of adults. It is well established that brain–behavior relations from adult neuropsychology do not generalize well to children (Fletcher & Taylor, 1984).

Eslinger and colleagues (1997) reviewed several cases of early prefrontal cortex lesions in children, including JC. JC, a 7-year-old right-handed boy, had an unremarkable medical, developmental, and early academic history when he suddenly developed severe headache, vomiting, seizures, and subsequent loss of consciousness. He underwent emergency surgery, resulting in right middle frontal gyrus topectomy and excision of an arteriovenous malformation located just superior and lateral to the head of the caudate (see Eslinger et al., 1997, for specific MRI localization). Neuropsychological evaluation 6 months after surgery revealed specific dissociations in cognitive, memory, and executive functions similar to that observed in Gage and EVR. Unlike these cases, JC's damage was localized to right frontal cortex, therefore, specific difficulties in spatial planning, sequencing, constructional praxis, and monitoring during multistep tasks were prominent, in addition to a classic "adult-like" left hemi-spatial neglect. Measured intelligence was in the High Average Range and consistent with premorbid expectations (Wechsler Intelligence Scale for Children–Revised, WISC–R Full Scale IQ = 111; VIQ = 113, PIQ = 106). Patterns of distracted, impulsive, and disinhibited behavior, with tangential speech, were noted. One of the more idiosyncratic behaviors displayed by JC was an obsessive propensity to sniff everything.

Follow-up neuropsychological evaluation of JC, 4 years after surgery, revealed greatly diminished—yet residual evidence of—spatial planning and spatial attention deficits. Interestingly, these mild persisting deficits were not apparent when external organizational strategies were provided. Performance on an executive function battery indicated executive function impairments on many measures, but noteworthy exceptions included age-appropriate performance on the WCST and the Tower of Hanoi (TOH; Simon, 1975). Socially, JC denied any behavioral problems and commented "I'm nice. I'm a good friend, I'm nice to other people." However, reports from his parents and teachers revealed persisting difficulties with concentration, restlessness, and carelessness in his work. Social problems and aggressive behavior were noted, with JC showing poor appreciation or compliance with age-appropriate nuance and finesse in social situations. His parents reported that, "JC doesn't seem to understand a lot of the dynamics of his peer groups. He takes things very literally and personally," but described him as a happy, loving boy, who was sociable, outgoing, and responsive to his family life (Eslinger et al., 1997).

These cases share several commonalties. First, general intellectual and other neuropsychological functions, such as language, sensory abilities, and visuospatial skills were not impaired. In contrast, deficits in inhibition, maintaining information over time, judgment, planning, and social skills were prominent. Furthermore, performance on tasks considered to "measure" executive and frontal lobe function was in the normal range. Comparing the findings from these cases suggests that the nature of executive processes may be elusive (i.e., not easily captured or quantified), at least on traditional psychometric measures.

WHAT ARE EXECUTIVE FUNCTIONS?
A CONSTRUCT REVIEW

The study of executive function in children is comprised of a patchwork of tasks and in various populations, with some investigations focusing on neuropathological correlates and others on cognitive or behavioral interrelations (Pennington, 1997). Many of the tasks purported to measure executive function have been linked speculatively to frontal lobe function without direct measurement of the brain. Pennington labeled this inferred brain–behavior relation as the "frontal metaphor." He noted the indiscriminant use of this metaphor to explain a wide range of normal developmental phenomena and clinical presentations. The power of the frontal metaphor is in the application of neuroscience to integrate an understanding of normal developmental progression, developmental disabilities, and outcome following acquired frontal lobe lesions. The unique patterns of behavioral disturbance associated with frontal lobe lesions in both adults and children markedly reduce daily living skills and are frequently the source of distress to patient's family members seeking clinical services. However, discussions of global psychological constructs, like executive functions, rapidly deteriorate into vague analogies without the elucidation of component processes and corresponding operational definitions.

There is no universally accepted operational definition of executive functions. Luria (1973) originally proposed a "functional brain unit for programming, regulation, and verification of activity," in which "man not only reacts passively to incoming information but creates intentions, forms plans and programs of his actions, inspects their performance, regulates his behavior so that it conforms to these plans and programs, finally he verifies his conscious activity comparing the effects of his actions with the original intentions and correcting any mistakes that he has made" (pp. 79–80). More recently, theorists from different traditions have emphasized diverse aspects of cognition in order to define executive functions (Eslinger, 1996). For example, in Lyon and Krasnegor (1996), Borkowski and Burke (1996) took an information-processing approach, emphasizing that executive functions are comprised of three main components: task analysis, strategy control, and strategy monitoring. Pennington, Bennetto, McAleer, and Roberts (1996) focused on planning, maintaining such plans online, and inhibiting other actions in order to problem solve to achieve a future goal. Executive functions have been defined behaviorally by Hayes, Gifford, and Ruckstahl (1996) to include the complex control of stimuli, responses, and derived properties in a given context. In contrast, Graham and Harris (1996) focused on the self-regulatory strategies, including metacognition, goal-setting, monitoring, strategy deployment, and action plans. Barkley (1996) proposed that executive functions overlap heavily with attention mechanisms. He identified four criteria that must be present for a given behavior to be "executive": behavior–behavior response chains, relation to the probability of a subsequent response, a delay between events and actions, and finally, inhibition of other responses.

All of these cognitive theories included at least semi-independent component processes of executive skills. The validity of these processes has been investigated either by manipulating task demands or by examining patterns of associations among various tasks (Embretson, 1983). Problems arise because neuropsychologists, both in clinical practice and research investigations, interpret patterns of task performance on the basis of face validity, where isolated deficits represent distinct component process impairments (Taylor, 1996). In fact, the underlying measurement characteristics of many executive function tasks have not been well studied and may not reflect distinct cognitive phenomena. Pennington (1997) identified at least three dimensions of executive functions with demonstrated validity in normal and clinical populations: verbal working memory, cognitive flexibility or set-shifting, and motor inhibition. Somewhat different components (i.e., fluid/speeded response, hypothesis testing/impulse control, and planning) have been reported in normal school-age children (Welsh et al., 1991). Moreover, Levin and associates (1991) found that three underlying factors best described executive task performance: semantic association/concept formation, freedom from perseveration, and planning/ strategy.

Executive function tasks, therefore, may not map onto component constructs in a one-to-one, linear manner. Executive functions, by the very nature of any definition, involve higher order, integrative control-type skills, where the translation of the definition into measurement tools is somewhat more difficult than with a more discrete skill (e.g., language). These definitional issues render the study of individual differences in executive skill in children difficult. However, there are other measurement issues from the broader individual differences literature that also affect the study of such differences in executive functions in children.

WHAT ARE INDIVIDUAL DIFFERENCES?
MEASUREMENT AND RELEVANCE

Differences among individual children have become increasingly important in neuropsychological research. Clinicians predict neuropsychological outcome, educational progress, and/or therapeutic needs of an individual, not of a diaphanous average of a group. Research studies focusing on the average of a group process provide a rich base and may illuminate fruitful subsequent directions for investigation. These relatively crude prognostications, however, may be of little comfort to parents who are seeking a better understanding of their child's problems and/or assistance in remediating these problems.

Individual differences traditionally have been conceptualized as factors that cause an individual to deviate from the "average" or mean group performance (Keppel, 1982). In randomized experimental designs, the degree to which an individual varies from the expected group mean is considered error variance. The goal in this type of investigation is to minimize error variance, that is, to reduce differences among individuals in order to maximize the hypothesized group effect. In practice, at least in quasi-experimental, clinical neuropsychological research, whether the hypothesized effect concerns a "group" or an "individual" is somewhat arbitrary. For example, the presence of a medical condition, such as traumatic brain injury, influences the manner by which an individual child deviates from expectations of normally developing peers. Children who have sustained traumatic brain injury also can be grouped according to injury severity in order to determine the risk for cognitive sequelae (Fletcher & Levin, 1988). Moreover, within severely brain injured children, those with pupillary abnormalities exhibit greater developmental differences in visuomotor skill relative to those without such eye findings (Francis, Fletcher, Steubing, Davidson, & Thompson, 1991). Which level or dimension represents the "individual difference": presence of brain injury, brain injury severity, or pupillary abnormality? This example illustrates that individual differences in almost any outcome can be demonstrated depending on the manner and/or level at which the independent variable is conceptualized.

The conceptualization of many neuropsychological phenomena has been driven by the reliance on medical, disease-based models of clinical phenomena in children. For example, dyslexia is the term often used in medical settings to describe children who are poor readers (Menkes, 1985). Dyslexia historically has been defined as "specific"—that is, as a discrete, biologically uniform category of children who presumably differ from children who read poorly for nonspecific, but "explainable" reasons, such as low intelligence (Rutter & Yule, 1975). This conceptualization is disease based, as it is thought to be present or absent in a manner such as infection (e.g., World Federation of Neurology definition; Critchley, 1970). More modern conceptualizations view poor readers as comprising the natural tail end of the normal distribution of reading skills (S. E. Shaywitz, Escobar, B. A. Shaywitz, Fletcher, & Makuch, 1992). In fact, other medical "disease" states also may represent a continuum of neuropathology and associated cognitive sequelae, for example, the degree of white matter damage is related linearly with cognitive outcome children with hydrocephalus (Fletcher et al., 1992).

Readily accessible, relatively simple, traditional statistics, such as *t* test and analysis of variance (ANOVA), also have promulgated discrete, group-based designs that focus on average performance differences between groups. The researcher may be compelled to form "artificial" groups in order to conduct these analyses. The problem is not in the statistics, in that the artificial grouping may not reflect the phenomena under study. In fact, many independent variables in neuropsychological research are continuously distributed and therefore are amenable to designs that relate individual differences in the independent variable to differences in outcome. Multiple regression is one such design that utilizes the inherent variability in both the independent and dependent measures. There are many naturally occurring grouping variables in quasi-experimental research, which when considered in more detail can be analyzed as a continuum.

When a child's neuropsychological development is considered in a longitudinal context, individual variability occurs at many levels. Individuals may differ in the age of onset of the emergence of skill development, the rate of development, the level of proficiency at any given age, and the shape of the trajectory of skill acquisition. When taken together, these individual differences yield various developmental patterns (Satz, Fletcher, Clark, & Morris, 1981). It is only recently with the advent of flexible and relatively accessible hierarchical or multilevel modeling techniques (Bryk & Raudenbush, 1992; Goldstein, 1995) that these individual differences in the patterns of skill development can be studied (e.g., Espy, Riese, & Francis, 1997; Francis, S. E. Shaywitz, Stuebing, B. A. Shaywitz, & Fletcher, 1996). Furthermore, these techniques can be used to investigate individual differences, which are nondevelopmental, but that also are nested at several levels (e.g., individual children in various classrooms within different schools).

Presumably, it is these individual differences in development that comprise important variability in outcome. Fletcher (1997) proposed that the fundamental structure–function relations and the mechanisms for individual variability differ. Individual variability, then, may result from phenomena not related to a given structure–function relation, but nevertheless are important in predicting outcome. For example, the relation of injury severity in traumatically brain injured children and outcome is well known

(Fletcher & Levin, 1988). The diffuse axonal injury due to shear strains and tearing of subcortical white matter tracts from impact (Strich, 1970) is associated with reduced information processing and impaired motor speed (Kaufmann, Fletcher, Levin, Miner, & Ewing-Cobbs, 1993; Levin et al., 1994; Yeates, Blumenstein, Patterson, & Delis, 1995). However, variability in outcome, such as school performance, is not a direct function of injury severity (Taylor & Schatschneider, 1992). Despite comparable injury severity, children with larger frontal lesions/contusions demonstrate greater problems on tasks involving judgment and planning (Levin et al., 1994). These differences in executive function performance may be important markers of poorer functional outcome at school and/or work in these children, but are not a direct consequence of the diffuse axonal injury to white matter.

Alternatively, there may be observed performance differences among individuals that actually do not result from differences in underlying psychological skill. For example, when performance variability on a given instrument changes with age, it may be inferred that as children mature, individual differences in performance become more prominent. Children may differ in the rate of skill development, which over time increases variability in the level of performance when measured at the chosen endpoint age. However, differential variability at different ages also may signify that the instrument does not adequately measure the underlying construct at all ages (Hertzog, 1985). Therefore, it is critical to thoroughly understand the underlying neuropsychological phenomena and the pertinent developmental manifestations prior to examining how and why individual children vary.

HOW MAY EXECUTIVE FUNCTIONS BE CHARACTERIZED IN INDIVIDUALS? DELAYED RESPONSE AND A-NOT-B TASKS

Given the unresolved issues of measurement and construct definition already discussed, one approach to disentangle some of the complexity in the study of executive functions in children is to trace the ontogeny "backward," that is, to return to the early emergence of these skills in infancy. At this point in development, executive skills presumably are less differentiated, less sophisticated, and more able to be mapped onto meaningful cognitive components. Once the origin of executive skills is better understood, the manner in which these executive functions subsequently differentiate in development can be investigated more fruitfully. It is our hope, then, that a review of studies of executive functions in infancy may shed light on the manifestation of the more complex executive skills later in childhood. This review is limited to studies of individual differences on one particular executive function paradigm, the delayed response (DR) and the variant, A-not-B (AB) tasks. This paradigm was chosen because of its parallel roots in both the developmental neuroscience and cognitive literature bases. DR and AB have been used to investigate the relation between brain–behavior relations in animals (Goldman-Rakic, 1987) and, more recently, in infants and young children (Diamond, 1985; Espy, Kaufmann, & Glisky, 1999; Kaufmann, Leckman, & Ort, 1989; Wellman, Cross, & Bartsch, 1986). Table 5.1 contains a summary of the studies reviewed below.

In the classic DR task, a well is baited with a reward while the subject watches. A delay is imposed and then the subject searches for the reward. The side of hiding is switched randomly across trials. In order to maximize reward, the subject must remember where the reward was hidden on this trial and not search at the location that was rewarded on the previous trial. For AB, the infant observes a reward hidden at a location (A). The infant then retrieves the reward at location A for several trials. The reward is switched then to the alternative location (B). Between 8 and 12 months of age, the infant continues to search for the reward at location A, despite direct observation of the hiding of the reward at location B (the AB error). However, by 12 months of age, the infant searches at correct location B, regardless of where the reward was hidden on the previous trial (Piaget, 1954).

Diamond and Goldman-Rakic (1989) argued that AB and DR depend on "working memory" and on the inhibition of a prepotent response. Working memory has been defined as "the process by which symbolic representations are accessed and held on-line to guide a response" (Goldman-Rakic, 1987, p. 604). The AB error results when the location of the reward at the observed location B is not maintained across the temporal gap (Fuster, 1985). The imposition of a delay appears to be critical in order to activate working memory (Goldman-Rakic, 1987; Gratch, Appel, Evans, LeCompte, & Wright, 1974; Harris, 1973). If there is not a temporal interval between hiding and retrieval during which the representation must be held "online," neither infants nor monkeys with prefrontal lesions err (Diamond, 1985; Goldman & Rosvold, 1970). The infant, then, must rely on associative memory to find the reward, and therefore, searches at location A.

Differences in AB performance among individuals can be categorized in several ways. Because this chapter focuses on infants and children, one major source of individual differences in performance is that related to development, often operationalized as age effects. Howe (1994) proposed that individual differences could be construed also as those occurring between individuals (interindividual) and within individuals (intraindi-

TABLE 5.1

Studies Using AB or DR to Investigate Executive Functions in Infants

Study	Subjects	Design	Task	Delay	Results
Baillargeon & Graber (1988)	24 infants 7 & 8 months	Looking Time	Possible/ Impossible Paired 2 Location Discrimination	15 sec	8 months infants looked longer at impossible location 7 months infants looked at each location equally 8 months only looked at impossible location after hand appeared to retrieve object
Baillargeon, DeVos, & Graber (1989)	24 infants 7 & 8 months	Looking Time	Paired 2 Location Discrimination	30 sec 70 sec	Infants looked longer at impossible location Infants looked longer at first location
Baillargeon, Graber, DeVos, & Black (1990)	32 infants 5 months	Looking Time	Paired Means-End Discrimination (from vs. under vs. behind)	13 sec 17 sec	Infants looked longer at impossible location Infants looked less reliably at later conditions
Bell & Fox (1992)	13 infants (7–12 months) 36 infants 7, 8, 9, 10, 11, & 12 months	Longitudinal & Cross- sectional	AB Object Retrieval Response Inhibition Resting EEG	Incremental	AB delay increased with age Wide variability in delay—Long group M = 13 sec Short group M = 3 sec (at 12 months) Long group had decreased right frontal power at 7–8 months, increased left frontal coherence between 10 & 12 months Only short group showed decrease in right frontal power between 10 & 11 months Infants who passed AB early had greater power at 8 months at right frontal lead

Study	Sample	Design	Task	Delay	Results
Diamond (1985)	25 infants (approximately 6½–12 months)	Longitudinal	AB	Incremental	AB delay increased by 2 sec for each month of age Best performance on repeat following correct trials No differences on reversal following correct or reversal following error trials Girls outperformed boys in AB emergence 10-sec delay at 12 months; 2-sec delay at 7½ months No evidence of side preference
Diamond & Doar (1989)	12 infants (6–12 months) 36 infants 8, 10, & 12 months	Longitudinal & Cross-sectional	DR	Incremental	DR performance = AB (Diamond, 1985) Girls outperformed boys in DR emergence Best performance on repeat following correct trials No differences on reversal following error and reversal following correct trials Cross-sectional data pattern was similar, but wider individual variability (e.g., only 50% of 12 months passed 8-sec delay) No evidence of side preference
Espy, Kaufmann, & Glisky (1999)	17 cocaine-exposed 17 normal control toddlers (17–21 months)	Cross-sectional	AB Self-control	10 sec	Cocaine-exposed toddlers made more perseverative errors, perseverated on more trials, and achieved fewer sets than nonexposed toddlers Only set difference was related to cognitive skills
Espy, Kaufmann, McDiarmid, & Glisky (1999)	117 preschool children (23–66 months)	Cross-sectional	AB Self-control Delayed Alternation Spatial & Color Reversal	10 sec	AB performance improved with age Individual variability observed Older children had less performance variability

(Continued)

TABLE 5.1
(Continued)

Study	Subjects	Design	Task	Delay	Results
Hostadter & Reznick (1996)	24 7 months 48 9 months 48 11 months 12 5 months	Cross-sectional Reach vs. Gaze	DR	3 sec	Gaze more likely to be correct than reach 7 months—significant percentage of AB errors Perseverative reach were more common than gaze Perseverations decreased with age Infants perseverated more following a correct rather than an incorrect response Perseverations were more likely on incorrect reach Reaching was more laterally perseverative to left 5 months—identified location with gaze Significant tendency to err on repeat correct trials
Matthews, Ellis, & Nelson (1996)	10 preterm 10 full term 28–60 weeks (corrected age)	Longitudinal Reach vs. Gaze	AB Object Retrieval Means–End	Incremental	Longer delays in reach for preterms No effect of term on gaze 2-sec difference between reach and gaze conditions OR performance improved with age, no term effect Low error rates on Means–End, no term effect
McEvoy, Rogers, & Pennington (1993)	17 autistic children 13 developmentally delayed children 16 normal control (10–80 months)	Matched Cross-sectional	AB DR	None 6 sec	No group differences on AB or DR Ceiling effects on AB
Ross, Tesman, Auld, & Nass (1992)	30 preterm infants with hemorrhage 30 preterm infants without hemorrhage 30 full-term infants (10 months)	Cross-sectional	AB	Incremental	AB errors differed by term birth status No differences among preterm infants 60% of premature infants were unable to find the reward on two out of three reversal trials; only 13% of full-term infants demonstrated this pattern

Note: Please see Wellman, Cross, and Bartsch (1986) for a complete listing of studies using the traditional Piagetian AB format (with few B trials).

vidual). It is this framework that will be used in order to review the pertinent findings regarding individual differences in AB performance.

Developmental Differences

Diamond (1985) found large individual differences in the delay at which AB error was demonstrated. Infants demonstrated the AB error at delays that increased by two additional seconds per month of age, on average. However, at 8 months of age, infants exhibited the AB error at delays ranging from 0 to 8 seconds, where at 12 months of age the range of delays were from 5 to 12 seconds. When this variability is expressed in terms of individual children, "Todd" was not able to perform the task until 8 months of age, and then only with no delay between hiding and retrieval. Until 10½ months, Todd demonstrated the AB error at a 5-second delay. At the last evaluation (11½), Todd demonstrated the AB error at a delay of 8 seconds. "Nina," on the other hand, was able to complete the task at 6½ months. At ages 8½ through 10½ months, she exhibited AB error at 10 seconds. By 11 months, Nina required 12 seconds of delay in order to demonstrate the AB error. The performance of these children illustrates the remarkable variability that is not captured by presentation of the group mean. A similar pattern of performance also has been observed on DR (Diamond & Doar, 1989).

Bell and Fox (1992) confirmed the marked individual variability in AB performance with a different analytic method. Bell and Fox utilized cluster analysis in order to group subjects according to their pattern of performance on AB across the testing period. Two groups emerged. The short delay infants tolerated a delay of almost 3 seconds at 12 months of age before making the AB error, and almost half of which were unable to perform the task at 7 months of age. In the long delay infant group, the delays tolerated prior to making the AB error were on the order of 13 seconds at 12 months of age, with the majority of the children able to complete the task and sustain a short delay at 7 months of age.

Findings from the studies by Diamond (1985; Diamond & Doar, 1989) and Bell and Fox (1992) indicate that AB skills emerge around 7 to 8 months in most infants, consistent with the original observation by Piaget (1954). However, Baillargeon and associates (Baillargeon, DeVos, & Graber, 1989; Baillargeon & Graber, 1988; Baillargeon, Graber, DeVos, & Black, 1990) demonstrated that young infants have the ability to "find" the location of an object if visual gaze, rather than manual reaching, is used as the dependent measure. In these studies, a preferential looking paradigm was used in order to evaluate whether infants identify the correct location of the reward. Younger (5½-month-old) and older (8-month-old) infants identified the location of the reward, that is, looked longer at location B at a comparatively long delay intervals (15 and 70 seconds) (Baillargeon et al., 1989; Baillargeon et ai., 1990). Hofstadter and Reznick (1996) also found that in DR, 5-month-old infants identified reliably object location, if gaze direction is used as the dependent measure.

In terms of skill maturation, Piaget (1954) observed that infants, at about 12 months of age, no longer make the AB error. He proposed that at this age, infants are able to represent the object as independent of their own search strategy (i.e., object permanence), and therefore are able to find the reward at any given location. However, Diamond (1990a) proposed that the AB error could be demonstrated in older children, given a sufficiently long delay between hiding and retrieval. Espy, Kaufmann, McDiarmid, and Glisky (1999) found that 2- to 5-year-old children made the AB error with a 10-second delay. Out of 10 trials, the 2-year-old children made from 0 to 7 errors. The 5-year-old children, on the other hand, made 0 to 2 errors. There was some indication that performance was constrained at the older ages as a ceiling was reached, however, the age at which perfect performance was achieved varied markedly among preschool children. These findings lend support to Diamond's hypothesis.

Taken together, these studies suggest that individual variability in AB performance can be parsed to differences in skill onset, level of proficiency at the given age endpoint, rate of skill change, and shape of the developmental trajectory. Researchers, to this point at least, have not examined formally the rates and patterns of change in individual performance differences on AB. Given that the unit of measure is on a ratio scale (the number of trials, or seconds of delay), such data are well suited in recently developed techniques such as hierarchical modeling. These longitudinal modeling techniques allow the examination of developmental patterns of change and permit a more sensitive measure of individual differences, which may illuminate the underlying developmental process of executive function development in infants and young children.

Interindividual Differences

Individual differences occur as a result of phenomena other than those solely related to development. Sex differences are probably the most widely studied individual difference (Stumpf, 1995). AB performance has been demonstrated to differ in infants by sex. Girls outperformed boys in the age at which the AB error was demonstrated. Diamond (1985) found that 86% of the girls made the AB error at 7½ months, whereas 45% of the males could not search for the hidden reward. A longer delay was necessary in order to elicit the AB error in female infants, by an average margin of 2 seconds (Diamond, 1985). The same, sex-dependent pattern has been observed on DR (Diamond & Doar, 1989).

Other interindividual influences also affect AB performance. Matthews, Ellis, and Nelson (1996) found that healthy, low risk preterm infants tolerated longer delays before exhibiting the AB error than full-term infants. Matthews et al. concluded that better AB performance by preterm infants was related to the greater extra-utero experience (testing was conducted at the corrected age). Furthermore, Ross, Tesman, Auld, and Nass (1992) found that approximately two thirds of their sample of 10-month-old preterm infants with and without subependymal or intraventricular hemorrhages were unable to find the reward on two out of three reversal trials. Only 13% of full-term infants exhibited this response pattern. Of the children who succeeded on this task, however, there were no differences in the delays required to consistently exhibit the AB error.

Espy, Kaufmann, and Glisky (1999) examined AB performance in prenatally cocaine-exposed toddlers. Cocaine-exposed toddlers made more perseverative errors and erred perseveratively for more consecutive trials on AB relative to nonexposed controls. Toddlers who were exposed in utero to cocaine also obtained fewer correct sets, but this effect was nonsignificant when verbal intellectual abilities were controlled statistically. In a sample of infants with early and continuously treated phenylketonuria, mild hyperphenylalaniemia, siblings, and matched and general population controls, Diamond, Prevor, Callendar, and Druin (1997) found that infants with either phenylketonuria or mild hyperphenylalaniemia required longer delays to successfully retrieve the reward and performed more poorly compared to all control comparison groups. As toddlers, performance differences only were apparent in children with phenylketonuria with high phenylalanine levels after 21 months of age, compared to toddlers with lower phenylalanine levels and control groups. McEvoy, Rogers, and Pennington (1992), however, found no differences in DR or AB performance among autistic, chronologically age-matched developmentally delayed, and verbal ability-matched preschool control children. In this study, no delay was used between hiding and retrieval, which may have contributed to the null findings. To our knowledge, the impact of other individual difference variables, such as race or socioeconomic status, has not been examined, which is critical in order to understand the effects of the environment on AB and DR performance variability.

Intraindividual Differences

When individuals perform similarly on two tasks, the tasks often are inferred to be related, sharing some common measurement characteristic. Many studies have examined patterns of performance on AB and on pertinent comparison tasks in order to understand what cognitive ability underlies AB performance. For example, Diamond (1990b) compared performance on AB to that on the Object Retrieval (OR) task in order to assess the contribution of inhibition in AB performance. In this task, the infant retrieved an object from beneath a clear, plexiglass box with an opening on one lateral side. Similar to AB, a manual reaching response is required. However, performance on OR is not considered to depend on working memory processes because there is no delay and the object is in full view while the infant responds. The infant must inhibit the tendency to reach straight at the sight of the object (where there is a clear, but solid top), and reach obliquely through the side opening (out of direct sight of the object). Infants, age 6 to 12 months, showed the same pattern of improvement with age on AB and OR (Diamond, 1990b; Matthews et al., 1996). In addition, adult monkeys with lesions to the dorsolateral prefrontal cortex evidenced deficits on this task; they scratched repeatedly at the solid top and retrieved the object only when looking through the open side (Diamond, 1990b).

Although performance on two tasks may be related on average, not all individuals will exhibit the same performance. In this vein, although using a somewhat different procedure, Bell and Fox (1992) found no relation between the age at which maximal OR performance was achieved in the long and short delay groups, although the length of delay tolerated on AB was positively correlated with OR performance. Bell and Fox also examined performance on a Response Inhibition to Novelty task, where the infant had to inhibit reaching for a moving, novel toy. Infants differed on this task, however; the infants who performed well on this task and on AB were not the same infants. More studies should utilize this type of approach in order to study performance on other executive function tasks, particularly in clinical populations, where performance variability may be high.

Another important comparison within individuals is comparative task performance with differing dependent measures. For example, Hofstadter and Reznick (1996) utilized both gaze direction and reaching response as the dependent measures in DR. Perseverative errors were more common in the reach condition than in the gaze condition. Perseverative reaching responses also were significantly more likely on trials following incorrect responses, however, the number of perseverative gaze and reaching responses did not differ following correct responses. Hofstadter and Reznick concluded that reinforcement affected the likelihood of perseverative gaze and reach responses equally. However, the increase in perseverative manual responding was considered a priming effect, perhaps related to the proximity of the efferent connections from dorsolateral prefrontal cortex to the caudate nucleus. Hofstadter and Reznick did not report whether all individual infants manifested better performance in the gaze condition. It may be that those children who performed equivalently across conditions differed in important ways from those with discrepant performance.

Relation to Brain Structure and Function

Both AB and DR share a well-defined relation to dorsolateral prefrontal cortical function (Diamond & Goldman-Rakic, 1989; Goldman-Rakic, 1987). For example, perseverative searching behavior on AB and/or DR has been observed in frontally ablated adult monkeys (Diamond & Goldman-Rakic, 1989), intact and frontally ablated infant monkeys (Diamond & Goldman-Rakic, 1986), and intact human infants, from age 7½ to 12 months (Diamond, 1985; Diamond & Doar, 1989). On the basis of these findings, Diamond (1990a) concluded that AB and DR performances in 8- to 12-month-old infants are related to frontal lobe immaturity.

Individual differences in AB performance also have been related to variability in frontal lobe function, as measured by resting frontal EEG activity and increased anterior to posterior EEG coherence (Bell & Fox, 1992). Bell and Fox (1992) found that the infants who required the long delay in order to display the AB error evidenced: decreased right frontal power in the resting EEG signal between 7 and 8 months of age, greater increases in bilateral frontal EEG power each month between 9 and 10 months of age, and greater power in the EEG signal from the left occipital lead across the 6 months of the study, relative to the infants who displayed the AB error after a short delay. There were no differences in signal power from the parietal recording sites. When averaged across the frontal/parietal and frontal/occipital leads, signal coherence initially decreased between 8 and 9 months of age and then increased in the left hemisphere between 10 and 12 months of age. Coherence did not change between 9 and 10 months. The length of F3/P3 coherence was U-shaped in left hemisphere, whereas the length of the F3/O1 coherence was stable. In the right hemisphere, F4/02 sites were more coherent than F4/P4. The short-delay group, who tolerated, on average, a 3-second delay before exhibiting the AB error at 12 months of age, showed decreased power at the right frontal lead site only between 10 and 11 months of age. These findings suggest that the individual differences in executive behavior also are manifested in brain function, however, the ongoing relation between development of the prefrontal cortex and changes in AB or DR performance remains to be investigated.

There are many changes in the structure and function of the dorsolateral prefrontal cortex that occur during late infancy, concurrent with the emergence of AB performance. Maximal synaptic density is achieved (Huttenlocher & Dabholkar, 1997), glucose metabolism is increased (Chugani & Phelps, 1990), and myelination of the prefrontal, subcortical brain regions is completed, at least at the level visualized by magnetic resonance imaging (Barkovich, 1995). Goldman-Rakic (1987; Diamond & Goldman-Rakic, 1989) suggested that it is the emergence of function in the prefrontal cortex that drives the emergence of AB and DR performance in young infants. Bell and Fox (1992) found infants who solved the AB problem without a delay before 8 months of age, differed in the amount of signal power at the right frontal lead at 8 months of age from those infants who solved the AB problem at older ages. However, Bell and Fox did not find that EEG power or coherence differed between the last age at which AB was unable to be solved and the age at which AB was solved initially on any lead site.

Bell and Fox (1992) found no relation between the age at which maximal OR performance was achieved and the delay tolerated on AB. Furthermore, frontal EEG power and coherence among frontal and other electrode sites were unrelated to performance on OR and response inhibition to novelty tasks. Bell and Fox concluded that the dorsolateral prefrontal cortex was unrelated to performance on OR. In light of Fletcher's (1997) formulation of individual differences, it may be that differences in OR performance may, in fact, be related to the inhibition component of AB and DR performance. Inhibition, however, may not be subserved by the dorsolateral prefrontal cortex, but may remain an important contributor to executive function performance differences among individual children.

The well-developed relation of AB/DR and the dorsolateral prefrontal cortex is unusual in most neuropsychological work. The application of such neuroscience paradigms offers a rich methodology by which to study executive function development in individual children (Kaufmann et al., 1989). However, tasks must be developmentally sensitive, in a like manner as AB and DR. For example, Espy, Kaufmann, McDiarmid, and Glisky (1999) found that performance on a Delayed Alternation task was sensitive to development in preschool children and was not related to verbal intellectual skill. Performance on this task, however, was not successful in discriminating among school-age traumatically brain-injured children with frontal lobe lesions (Levin et al., 1994). In that study, Levin cautioned that the task may not have been valid in this age range, as children tried to "out think" the simple alternation problem. The demand characteristics of any given task may influence heavily the sensitivity to individual performance differences.

HOW DO AB/DR INVESTIGATIONS INFORM THE STUDY OF INDIVIDUAL DIFFERENCES IN PERFORMANCE ON EXECUTIVE FUNCTION TASKS? FUTURE DIRECTIONS

The investigations reviewed suggest several directions of inquiry that should be pursued in order to better understand the nature of individual differences in executive function in children. First, the findings from AB and DR indicate that individual differences are manifest at several levels.

Individuals may differ in the age of skill acquisition, the level of proficiency at a given age, the rate of development, or more complex developmental parameters. The differences were apparent on AB/DR because behavior was examined longitudinally (Bell & Fox, 1992; Diamond, 1985; Hofstadter & Reznik, 1996; Matthews et al., 1996). The next step is to examine how other components of executive function, measured by other tasks, may change with development. In order to accomplish this goal, multiple tasks must be administered at each age and sophisticated analytic techniques, such as structural equation or multilevel modeling, should be used (Goldstein, 1995; McArdle, 1996).

There are, however, inherent difficulties in using other executive function measures in longitudinal studies. For example, one hallmark of several of the executive function definitions is the synthesis of novel information. The repeated administration of any executive function instrument may render the task less novel, especially in older children. After the task has become familiar, the task may no longer measure executive skills. Perhaps a mixed cross-sectional, longitudinal design would be more useful in disentangling the developmental and practice effects. Alternatively, the delayed response paradigm may be suited uniquely for longitudinal use. In the latter case, the delay between hiding and retrieval may be adjusted incrementally in order to maintain sensitivity across a wide age range, presumably without grossly distorting the measurement characteristics (Diamond, 1990a; Espy, Kaufmann, McDiarmid, & Glisky, 1999). In addition, the complexity of the retrieval principle also may be increased with age (Kaufmann et al., 1989). For example, in AB/DR, the infant simply retrieves the reward at the observed location across trials. In the more complex variant, Delayed Matching to Sample, familiar and novel are placed on top of the well covers as cues to signal reward location. Invariably, the increased task complexity will produce different patterns of developmental proficiencies (Janowsky, 1993), which may be related somewhat differently to brain function than the more simple tasks. However, this paradigm is a powerful tool by which to investigate executive skill development across age.

Second, given the diverse definitions of executive function (Lyon & Krasnegor, 1996), one way to better understand how individual children differ in executive functions is to trace skill development back to that which is observable early in development. Investigations of performance on AB/DR represent such efforts. Unlike some of the other executive function tasks, AB/DR has not been used extensively to document interindividual differences in performance, perhaps related to its history in the developmental and neuroscientific literatures. Other more complex tasks, such as TOH (Simon, 1975) and WCST (Heaton, 1981), have been used routinely in studies of interindividual differences, particularly in various clinical populations (Pennington, 1997). Similar developmental task analyses are being employed with these tasks in order to elucidate the nature of individual performance differences (Welsh et al., 1991; Zelazo, Reznick, & Pinion, 1995). Other interindividual differences in executive function remain to be investigated on all tasks, such as the impact of environmental risk (e.g., socioeconomic status or parenting effects). Such interindividual differences in executive skill would be particularly relevant to the clinician when trying to distinguish one child from another, particularly for the purposes of diagnosis or prognosis.

Individual differences within the individual—the intraindividual—generally have not been investigated. Bell and Fox (1992) used cluster analysis in order to group infants according to AB performance and then examined differences in performance on comparison tasks and in resting brain electrophysiology. Cluster analysis is the method of choice by which to quantify and group how individuals differ across tasks (Aldenderfer & Blashfield, 1984). Such methods have been used successfully in the learning disabled population, where problematic definitional issues have clouded the identification of particular children (Morris, Blashfield, & Satz, 1986). The study of executive functions in older children also could benefit from utilization of cluster analytic approaches. Discriminating among individuals may be important, particularly for intervention research. It is likely that the pattern of skill discrepancies among various components of executive function may limit or enhance intervention efficacy in both normal and clinically identified children.

Finally, individual differences are apparent at all levels of analysis. The brain also undergoes remarkable development, concurrent with behavioral maturation. Thatcher (1997) characterized three major growth cycles in brain electrical activity across childhood. Individual differences in brain electricity were related to AB/DR performance differences (Bell & Fox, 1992). However, Goldman (1974) observed that the expression of behavioral deficits after early lesions to the prefrontal cortex varies with time since injury. The manner by which changes in the brain dynamically underlie behavioral changes in discrete groups of children is just beginning to be known. Unfortunately, the present knowledge of how these brain–behavior relations vary among individual children is primitive at best. Individual differences in performance may be subserved by brain structures other than those related to the prominent deficit of the group (Fletcher, 1997). In fact, the dissociation of the structure–function relations of individual differences from that of the group process may be more common for higher order skills that integrate diverse information, such as executive functions. It is this level of analysis that will ultimately inform the clinician who faces the anxious parent of a brain injured child.

Ultimately, individual variability in childhood executive functions may be a consequence of the cumulative effects of both the particular genetic predispositions of the infant interacting with the unique environmental condition. This interaction predates birth and continues through senescence. Consequently, Pennington's (1997) observation of increasing interest in the "frontal metaphor" for understanding normal development, developmental disabilities, behavioral disturbance following acquired lesions of the central nervous system, although overapplied, may be of heuristic value. If neuropsychology is to meet the challenge of

> determining whether or not organic factors were playing a role in an older person's behavioral difficulties; the need to devise ways to help a patient who had sustained a stroke to recovery his/her lost functions; the need to fathom why a school child of adequate general intelligence was failing academically or engaging in self-defeating behavior; the need to understand seemingly inexplicable disturbances in mood in persons of all ages (Benton, 1987, p. 7).

then the case for investing resources in studying the early emergence of executive functions cannot be overstated.

ACKNOWLEDGMENTS

This research was supported in part by grants from the University of Arizona Foundation and the Office of Research Development and Administration, Southern Illinois University at Carbondale to K. A. Espy.

REFERENCES

Aldenderfer, M. S., & Blashfield, R. K. (1984). *Cluster analysis* (Vol. 44). Newbury Park, CA: Sage.

Baillargeon, R., DeVos, J., & Graber, M. (1989). Location memory in 8-month-old infants in a nonsearch AB task: Further evidence. *Cognitive Development, 4,* 345–367.

Baillargeon, R., & Graber, M. (1988). Evidence of location memory in 8-month-old infants in a nonsearch AB task. *Developmental Psychology, 24*(4), 502–511.

Baillargeon, R., Graber, M., DeVos, J., & Black, J. (1990). Why do young infants fail to search for hidden objects? *Cognition, 36,* 255–284.

Barkley, R. A. (1996). Linkages between attention and executive functions. In G. R. Lyon & N. A. Krasnegor (Eds.), *Attention, memory, and executive function* (pp. 307–326). Baltimore: Paul H. Brookes.

Barkovich, A. J. (1995). *Pediatric neuroimaging* (2nd ed.). New York: Raven.

Bell, M. A., & Fox, N. A. (1992). The relations between frontal brain electrical activity and cognitive development during infancy. *Child Development, 63,* 1142–1163.

Benton, A. (1987). Evolution of a clinical specialty. *Clinical Neuropsychologist, 1,* 5–8.

Borkowski, J. G., & Burke, J. E. (1996). Theories, models, and measurements of executive functioning: An information processing perspective. In G. R. Lyon & N. A. Krasnegor (Eds.), *Attention, memory, and executive function* (pp. 235–262). Baltimore: Paul H. Brookes.

Bryk, A. S., & Raudenbush, S. W. (1992). *Hierarchical linear models.* Newbury Park, CA: Sage.

Chelune, G. J., & Baer, R. A. (1986). Developmental norms for the Wisconsin Card Sorting Test. *Journal of Clinical and Experimental Neuropsychology, 8,* 219–228.

Chugani, H. T., & Phelps, M. E. (1990). Imaging human brain development with positron emission tomography. *Journal of Nuclear Medicine, 32,* 23–25.

Critchley, M. (1970). *The dyslexic child.* Springfield, IL: Thomas.

Damasio, A. R., Tranel, D., & Damasio, H. (1990). Individuals with sociopathic behavior caused by frontal damage fail to respond autonomically to social stimuli. *Behaviour Brain Research, 41*(2), 81–94.

Diamond, A. (1985). Development of the ability to use recall to guide action, as indicated by infants' performance on AB. *Child Development, 56,* 868–883.

Diamond, A. (1990a). The development and neural bases of memory functions as indexed by AB and delayed response tasks in human infants and infant monkeys. *Annals of the New York Academy of Sciences, 608,* 267–317.

Diamond, A. (1990b). Developmental time course in human infants and infant monkeys, and the neural bases of inhibitory control in reaching. *Annals of the New York Academy of Sciences, 608,* 637–676.

Diamond, A., & Doar, B. (1989). The performance of human infants on a measure of frontal cortex function, the delayed response task. *Developmental Psychobiology, 22,* 271–294.

Diamond, A., & Goldman-Rakic, P. S. (1986). Comparative development of human infants and infant rhesus monkeys of cognitive functions that depend on the prefrontal cortex. *Neuropsychological Abstracts, 12,* 274.

Diamond, A., & Goldman-Rakic, P. S. (1989). Comparison of human infants and rhesus monkeys on Piaget's AB task: Evidence for dependence on dorsolateral prefrontal cortex. *Experimental Brain Research, 74,* 24–40.

Diamond, A., Prevor, M. B., Callendar, G., & Druin, D. P. (1997). Prefrontal cortex cognitive deficits in children treated early and continuously for PKU. *Monographs for the Society for Research in Child Development, 62*(Serial 252).

Embretson, S. (1983). Construct validity: Construct representation versus nomothetic span. *Psychological Bulletin, 93,* 179–197.

Eslinger, P. J. (1996). Conceptualizing, describing, and measuring components of executive function: A summary. In G. R. Lyon & N. A. Krasnegor (Eds.), *Attention, memory, and executive function* (pp. 367–396). Baltimore: Paul H. Brookes.

Eslinger, P. J., Biddle, K. R., & Grattan, L. M. (1997). Cognitive and social development in children with prefrontal cortex lesions. In N. A. Krasnegor, G. R. Lyon, & P. S. Goldman-Rakic (Eds.), *Development of the prefrontal cortex: Evolution, neurobiology, and behavior* (pp. 295–336). Baltimore: Paul H. Brookes.

Eslinger, P. J., & Damasio, A. R. (1985). Severe disturbance of higher cognition after bilateral frontal lobe ablation: Patient EVR. *Neurology, 35,* 1731–1741.

Espy, K. A., Kaufmann, P. M., & Glisky, M. L. (1999). Neuropsychological function in toddlers exposed to cocaine in utero: A preliminary study. *Developmental Neuropsychology, 15,* 447–460.

Espy, K. A., Kaufmann, P. M., McDiarmid, M. D., & Glisky, M. L. (1999). Executive functioning in preschool children: A-not-B and other delayed response format task performance. *Brain and Cognition, 41,* 178–199.

Espy, K. A., Riese, M. L., & Francis, D. J. (1997). Neuropsychological development in preterm neonates prenatally exposed to cocaine. *Infant Behavior and Development, 20,* 297–309.

Fletcher, J. M. (1997, August). *Brain–behavior relationships in children with developmental disabilities: concepts and methods.* Paper presented at the American Psychological Association, Chicago, IL.

Fletcher, J. M., Bohan, T. P., Brandt, M. E., Brookshire, B. L., Beaver, S. R., Francis, D. J., Davidson, K. C., Thompson, N. M., & Miner, M. E. (1992). Cerebral white matter and cognition in hydrocephalic children. *Archives of Neurology, 49*, 818–834.

Fletcher, J. M., & Levin, H. S. (1988). Neurobehavioral effects of brain injury in children. In D. K. Routh (Ed.), *Handbook of pediatric psychology* (pp. 258–298). New York: Guilford.

Fletcher, J. M., & Taylor, H. G. (1984). Neuropsychological approaches to children: Towards a developmental neuropsychology. *Journal of Clinical Neuropsychology, 6*, 39–56.

Francis, D. J., Fletcher, J. M., Steubing, K. K., Davidson, K. C., & Thompson, N. M. (1991). Analysis of change: Modeling individual growth. *Journal of Consulting and Clinical Psychology, 59*, 27–37.

Francis, D. J., Shaywitz, S. E., Stuebing, K. K., Shaywitz, B. A., & Fletcher, J. M. (1996). Developmental lag vs. deficit models of reading disabilities: A longitudinal, individual, and growth curves analysis. *Journal of Educational Psychology, 88*, 3–17.

Fuster, J. M. (1985). The prefrontal cortex and temporal integration. In A. Jones (Ed.), *Cerebral cortex* (Vol. 4, pp. 151–177). New York: Plenum.

Golden, C. J. (1981). The Luria–Nebraska Children's Battery; theory and formulation. In G. W. Hynd & J. E. Obrzut (Eds.), *Neuropsychological assessment and the school-age child* (pp. 277–302). New York: Grune & Stratton.

Goldman, P. S. (1974). An alternative to developmental plasticity: Heterology of CNS structures in infants and adults. In D. Stein, J. Rosen, & N. Butters (Eds.), *Plasticity and recovery of function in the central nervous system* (pp. 149–174). New York: Academic Press.

Goldman, P. S., & Rosvold, H. E. (1970). Localization of function within the dorsolateral prefrontal cortex of the rhesus monkey. *Experimental Neurology, 27*, 291–304.

Goldman-Rakic, P. S. (1987). Development of cortical circuitry and cognitive function. *Child Development, 58*, 601–622.

Goldstein, H. (1995). *Multilevel statistical models* (2nd ed.). New York: Wiley.

Graham, S., & Harris, K. R. (1996). Addressing problems in attention, memory, and executive functioning: An example from self-regulated strategy development. In G. R. Lyons & N. A. Krasnegor (Eds.), *Attention, memory, and executive function* (pp. 349–366). Baltimore: Paul H. Brookes.

Gratch, G., Appel, K. J., Evans, W. F., LeCompte, G. K., & Wright, N. A. (1974). Piaget's stage IV object concept error: Evidence of forgetting or object conception. *Child Development, 45*, 71–77.

Harlow, J. M. (1848). Passage of an iron bar through the head. *Boston Medical and Surgical Journal, 39*, 389–393.

Harlow, J. M. (1868). Recovery from the passage of an iron bar through the head. *Publication of the Massachusetts Medical Society, 2*, 327–347.

Harris, P. L. (1973). Perseverative errors in search by young infants. *Child Development, 44*, 28–33.

Hayes, S. C., Gifford, E. V., & Ruckstuhl, L. E. (1996). Relational frame theory and executive function: A behavioral approach. In G. R. Lyons & N. A. Krasnegor (Eds.), *Attention, memory, and executive function* (pp. 279–306). Baltimore: Paul H. Brookes.

Heaton, R. K. (1981). *Wisconsin Card Sorting Test manual.* Odessa, FL: Psychological Assessment Resources.

Hertzog, C. (1985). An individual difference perspective: Implications for cognitive research in gerontology. *Research on Aging, 7*, 7–45.

Hofstadter, M., & Reznick, J. S. (1996). Response modality affects human infant delayed-response performance. *Child Development, 67*, 646–658.

Howe, M. L. (1994). Dynamics of cognitive development: A unifying approach to universal trends and individual differences. Special Issue: Developmental perspectives on individual differences in learning and memory. *Learning and Individual Differences, 6*(3), 365–367.

Huttenlocher, P. R., & Dabholkar, A. S. (1997). Developmental anatomy of prefrontal cortex. In N. A. Krasnegor, G. R. Lyon, & P. S. Goldman-Rakic (Eds.), *Development of the prefrontal cortex: Evolution, neurobiology, and behavior* (pp. 69–83). Baltimore: Paul H. Brookes.

Janowsky, J. S. (1993). The development of neural basis of memory systems. In M. H. Johnson (Ed.), *Brain development and cognition* (pp. 665–678). Cambridge, England: Basil Blackwell.

Kaufmann, P., Leckman, J. M., & Ort, S. I. (1989). Delayed response performance in males with Fragile-X. *Journal of Clinical and Experimental Neuropsychology, 12*, 69.

Kaufmann, P. M., Fletcher, J. M., Levin, H. S., Miner, M. E., & Ewing-Cobbs, L. (1993). Attentional disturbance following pediatric closed head injury. *Journal of Child Neurology, 8*, 348–353.

Keppel, G. (1982). *Design & analysis: Researcher's handbook* (2nd ed.). Englewood Cliffs, NJ: Prentice-Hall.

Levin, H. S., Culhane, K. A., Fletcher, J. M., Mendelsohn, D. B., Lilly, M. A., Harward, H., Chapman, S. B., Bruce, D. A., Bertolino-Kusnerik, L., & Eisenberg, H. M. (1994). Dissociation between delayed alternation and memory after pediatric head injury: Relationship to MRI findings. *Journal of Child Neurology, 9*, 81–89.

Levin, H. S., Culhane, K. A., Hartmann, J., Evankovich, K., Mattson, A. J., Harward, H., Ringholtz, G., Ewing-Cobbs, L., & Fletcher, J. M. (1991). Developmental changes in performance on tests of purported frontal lobe functioning. *Developmental Neuropsychology, 7*, 377–395.

Luria, A. R. (1973). *The working brain*. New York: Basic Books.

Lyon, G. R., & Krasnegor, N. A. (Eds.). (1996). *Attention, memory, and executive function*. Baltimore: Paul H. Brookes.

Matthews, A., Ellis, A. E., & Nelson, C. A. (1996). Development of preterm and full-term infant ability on AB, recall memory, transparent barrier detour, and means-end tasks. *Child Development, 67*, 2658–2676.

McArdle, J. J. (1996). Current directions in structural factor analysis. *Current Directions in Psychological Science, 5*(1), 11–18.

McEvoy, R. E., Rogers, S. J., & Pennington, B. F. (1993). Executive function and social communication deficits in young autistic children. *Journal of Child Psychology and Psychiatry, 34*(4), 563–578.

Menkes, J. H. (1985). *Textbook of child neurology* (3rd ed.). Philadelphia: Lea & Febiger.

Morris, R., Blashfield, R., & Satz, P. (1986). Developmental classification of reading-disabled children. *Journal of Clinical and Experimental Neuropsychology, 8*(4), 371–392.

Pennington, B. F. (1997). Dimensions of executive functions in normal and abnormal development. In N. A. Krasnegor, G. R. Lyon, & P. S. Goldman-Rakic (Eds.), *Development of the prefrontal cortex: Evolution, neurobiology, and behavior* (pp. 265–282). Baltimore: Paul H. Brookes.

Pennington, B. F., Bennetto, L., McAleer, O., & Roberts, R. J. (1996). Executive functions and working memory: Theoretical and measurement issues. In G. R. Lyons & N. A. Krasnegor (Eds.), *Attention, memory, and executive function* (pp. 327–348). Baltimore: Paul H. Brookes.

Piaget, J. (1954). *The construction of reality in the child*. New York: Basic Books.

Ross, G., Tesman, J., Auld, P., & Nass, R. (1992). Effects of subependymal and mild intraventricular lesions on visual attention and memory in premature infants. *Developmental Psychology, 28*, 1067–1074.

Rutter, M., & Yule, W. (1975). The concept of specific reading retardation. *Journal of Child Psychology and Psychiatry, 16*, 181–197.

Satz, P., Fletcher, J. M., Clark, W., & Morris, R. (1981). Lag, deficit, rate and delay constructs in specific learning disabilities: A re-examination. In A. Ansara (Ed.), *Sex differences in dyslexia* (pp. 129–150). New York: Orton Dyslexia Society.

Shaywitz, S. E., Escobar, M. D., Shaywitz, B. A., Fletcher, J. M., & Makuch, R. (1992). Evidence that dyslexia may represent the lower tail of a normal distribution of reading ability. *New England Journal of Medicine, 326*(3), 145–150.

Simon, H. A. (1975). The functional equivalence of problem solving skills. *Cognitive Psychology, 7,* 268–288.

Strich, S. J. (1970). Lesions in the cerebral hemisphere after blunt head injury. In S. Sevitt & H. B. Stoner (Eds.), *The pathology of trauma* (pp. 166–171). London: BMA House.

Stumpf, H. (1995). Gender differences in performance on tests of cognitive abilities: Experimental design issues and empirical results. Special issue: Psychological and psychobiological perspectives on sex differences in cognition: I. Theory and research. *Learning and Individual Differences, 7*(4), 275–287.

Taylor, H. G. (1996). Critical issues and future directions in the development of theories, models, and measurements of attention, memory, and executive function. In G. R. Lyons & N. A. Krasnegor (Eds.), *Attention, memory, and executive function* (pp. 399–412). Baltimore: Paul H. Brookes.

Taylor, H. G., & Schatschneider, C. (1992). Clinical neuropsychological assessment: A test of basic assumptions. *The Clinical Neuropsychologist, 6,* 259–275.

Thatcher, R. W. (1997). Human frontal lobe development: A theory of cyclical cortical reorganization. In N. A. Krasnegor, G. R. Lyon, & P. S. Goldman-Rakic (Eds.), *Development of the prefrontal cortex: Evolution, neurobiology, and behavior* (pp. 85–113). Baltimore: Paul H. Brookes.

Wellman, H. M., Cross, D., & Bartsch, K. (1986). Infant search and object permanence: A meta-analysis of the A-not-B error. *Monographs of the Society for Research in Child Development, 51*(Serial No. 214).

Welsh, M. C., Pennington, B. F., & Groisser, D. B. (1991). A normative-developmental study of executive function: A window on prefrontal function in children. *Developmental Neuropsychology, 7*(2), 131–149.

Yeates, K. O., Blumenstein, E., Patterson, C. M., & Delis, D. C. (1995). Verbal learning and memory following pediatric closed-head injury. *Journal of the International Neuropsychological Society, 1,* 78–87.

Zelazo, P. D., Reznick, J. S., & Pinion, D. E. (1995). Response control and the execution of verbal roles. *Developmental Psychology, 31,* 508–517.

## CHAPTER SIX

Developmental and Clinical Variations in Executive Functions

Marilyn C. Welsh
University of Northern Colorado

You drive along the same route every evening as you return home from work. As you drive, you can engage in conversation with a passenger, sing along to the radio or argue with the talk-radio host, plan dinner, daydream, and so on. This kind of routinized activity does not demand a great deal of conscious attention, strategic thinking, or flexible action, although this is not an endorsement for engaging in such concurrent activities. In contrast, if this routine drive is perturbed by a traffic accident, a snowstorm, last minute errands that must be completed on the way home, then the task has now become an activity that engages executive functions (e.g., planning, generating and monitoring strategies, inhibiting maladaptive actions, and flexible shifting to more appropriate ones). For those people who normally adopt a "defensive driving" strategy, in which other drivers' actions are anticipated and their own potential responses are planned, the executive function system is continuously active.

Although still somewhat controversial, it is proposed in this chapter as it has been elsewhere (e.g., Welsh & Pennington, 1988) that infants and young children utilize executive functions, albeit primitive versions of the adult activities that subserve goal-directed, future-oriented behavior. When a 9-month-old reaches for a stuffed toy, the behavior is driven by the basic goal of play. However, executive functions are tapped to a greater extent when the infant must generate and flexibly execute the plan in order to retrieve the toy (e.g., push away a pillow, pull on the blanket on which the toy lies). Similarly, once the rules of a simple board game are learned by a pair of 8-year-olds, playing the game may not require executive functions. However, when critical pieces of the game are invariably lost, executive function skills are recruited to find substitute pieces, generate new rules, and monitor the success of the new game.

The cognitive construct of executive function has been the subject of intense research interest over the last several years (Krasnegor, Lyon, & Goldman-Rakic, 1997; Levin, Eisenberg, & Benton, 1991, Perecman, 1987). However, its status as a "construct" is certainly open to debate (Gnys & Willis, 1991) and on which side of this controversy researchers fall depends to a large extent on which of a myriad of tasks they select to measure executive function. There is no current consensus on a single yardstick (or set of tests) that best assesses executive functions. Table 6.1 displays a sampling of some of the most widely used executive function tasks and the particular cognitive component of executive function (e.g., planning, inhibition) it is purported to measure. It is important to note that the construct validity of most of the tasks has not been well established empirically. For example, although most researchers describe the Tower of Hanoi (TOH) as a measure of planning, working memory, and/or inhibition (Goel & Grafman, 1995; Goldman-Rakic, 1987; Welsh, 1991), empirical evidence of links between this task and measures of these cognitive processes is weak at best (Welsh, Satterlee-Cartmell, & Stine, 1999).

TABLE 6.1
Widely Used Executive Function Tasks

Task	EF Component	Representative Studies
TOH	P; I; WM?	Welsh et al. (1990)
		Goel & Grafman (1995)
TOL	P; I; WM	Levin et al. (1994)
		Welsh et al. (1999)
		Luciana & Nelson (1999)
Porteus Maze	P	Grodzinsky & Diamond (1992)
WCST	I; F; WM	Milner (1964)
		Kimberg & Farah (1993)
Stroop	I; WM	Cohen & Servan-Schreiber (1992)
CPT	I; WM	Cohen & Servan-Schreiber (1992)
Fluency	OR; I; F	Welsh et al. (1990)
ROCF	OR; P; WM?	Reader et al. (1994)
Antisaccade	I	Roberts et al. (1994)

Note: EF component abbreviations: P = planning; I = inhibition; F = flexible set shifting; WM = working memory; OR = organization. Task abbreviations: TOH = Tower of Hanoi; TOL = Tower of London; WCST = Wisconsin Card Sorting Test; CPT = Continuous Performance Test; ROCF = Rey–Osterrieth Complex Figure.

Despite the conceptual and measurement problems inherent in the study of executive functions, the topic has compelled such wide interest for several reasons. First, it has been assumed for decades that measuring executive functions—such as planning, inhibition, and flexibility—provides a window on neurologic function, specifically the integrity of the frontal cortex. The literature is replete with case studies of frontal damaged individuals who cannot generate and sustain strategic, goal-directed behavior, especially in the face of simpler, competing, routinized responses (Luria, 1973; Tueber, 1964). More recently, research has documented impaired performance in patient populations with known or suspected frontal damage on executive function tasks, such as the Tower of London (Owen, Downes, Sahakian, Polkey, & Robbins, 1990), Tower of Hanoi (Goel & Grafman, 1995), Wisconsin Card Sorting Test (Milner, 1964), and Stroop (Perret, 1974; cited in Kolb & Whishaw, 1985). Second, developmentalists have long recognized that cognitive mechanisms—such as working memory capacity, inhibition, and strategic problem solving—may underlie age-related improvements in a broad range of intellectual and social behaviors (Case, 1985; Flavell, 1971; Siegler, 1983). Third, although the precise characteristics defining the domain of executive function are in dispute (Pennington, Bennetto, McAleer, & Roberts, 1996), there is likely universal agreement regarding the importance of executive function skills to everyday function. Researchers may not know exactly what executive function is, but they are painfully aware when there is a breakdown or lapse in its operation.

WHAT IS EXECUTIVE FUNCTION?

A Cluster of Skills

The term *executive function* derives from a long and storied history of experimental and clinical neuropsychological investigations of frontal lobe function, described in vivid detail by Benton (1991). For example, Bianchi (1895, 1920/1922; as cited in Benton, 1991) performed unilateral surgical ablations of the prefrontal cortex in monkeys and dogs, observing in their consequent behavior a very important dissociation. Although basic motor and sensory functions remained intact, the animals exhibited severe disruptions in what he referred to as global personality function, including difficulties with impulse control and the serial and parallel processing of mental representations.

Benton (1991) described the early clinical work of Feuchtwanger (1923; as cited in Benton, 1991) in which he compared two groups of brain damaged patients: those with frontal lesions and those with non-frontal lesions. Feuchtwanger characterized the frontal group as showing mood disturbances, impulsivity, attentional problems, and a general inability to control and integrate behavior. Like Bianchi, he attributed these deficits to an organic personality disorder and highlighted the fact that sensorimotor, perceptual, linguistic, and mnemonic skills were unimpaired. Following this work, Goldstein (1936, 1944; as cited in Benton, 1991) shifted the focus from personality to cognitive function by suggesting that the prefrontal cortex mediated a set of functions, including initiative, anticipation and planning, resistance to suggestion, flexibility, self-monitoring, and an analytical approach to problem solving. Although this set of skills was referred to as "abstract attitude," it comes very close to current definitions of executive function.

Perhaps the greatest influence on the working definition of executive function, both its cognitive components and its neurologic underpinnings, comes from Luria's theory of the brain's functional systems (Luria, 1966, 1973). In Luria's model, each functional system involved three basic brain-based units that mirror the sequence of information processing: the arousal unit, the sensory input unit, and the output/planning unit. The latter two units were further subdivided into primary, secondary, and tertiary areas that represented increasing levels of information complexity and integration (Spreen, Risser, & Edgell, 1995). Luria noted that a behavioral manifestation of the output/planning unit seen as early as age 6 was the use of internalized language to plan, monitor, and control behavior (e.g., inhibit maladaptive responses). However, the tertiary area of this unit that presumably plans and executes more abstract and complex problem-solving behavior was thought to develop between age 12 and 24 (Luria, 1973; cited in Spreen et al., 1995).

Welsh and Pennington (1988) defined executive function as the ability to adopt and maintain an appropriate problem-solving set to obtain a future goal. This set could include one or more of the following characteristics: an intention to inhibit a maladaptive response or to defer it to a more appropriate time, a strategic plan of action sequences, and a mental representation of the task that could involve rules, constraints, subgoals, and final goals. This definition dovetailed nicely with a model of prefrontal function proposed by Fuster (1985) in which he suggested that three functions were mediated by different loci within the prefrontal cortex: a temporally retrospective function of working memory (related to the idea of online mental representation), a temporally prospective function of anticipatory set (related to the planning process), and an interference-control mechanism that suppresses behavior incompatible with the current goal (similar to the inhibition function).

Some other current theories of executive function include those by Stuss and Benson and Norman and Shallice. Stuss and Benson (1984,

1986, 1987) suggested that much of overt behavior is directed by "organized integrated fixed functional systems" (p. 142) that are localized in posterior or subcortical brain regions and operate independently of frontal lobe influence. That is, in routine situations and on familiar tasks, such functional systems will recruit the necessary arousal mechanisms, and perceptual, language, and memory processes without the intervention of the frontal cortex. However, when the situation is novel and nonroutine, these functional systems must be directed by the frontal cortex in order to achieve well-coordinated and efficient information processing and response execution. Stuss and Benson (1987) referred to such direction as executive function and included anticipation, goal selection, planning, and monitoring. A similar distinction between routine and nonroutine environmental contingencies has been the focus of the theory by Norman and Shallice (1986; Shallice & Burgess, 1991). Their model involves a two-level system, including a lower level contention scheduling function and a higher level supervisory attentional function. The contention scheduling function works well in familiar, routine, overlearned situations in which particular stimulus inputs trigger specific and appropriate behavioral outputs in a more or less automatic way. The general operation of the contention scheduling function is overseen by the supervisory attentional function that modulates activation levels such that certain input–output units will be favored for selection over others. Norman and Shallice (1986) proposed that the situations in which the supervisory attentional function is particularly needed include those that require: planning or decision making; error detection or correction; the generation of novel action sequences; or the inhibition of strong, overlearned responses.

To summarize, the various working definitions of executive function used today share a common theme. Executive function is viewed as a cluster of skills that are necessary for efficient and effective future-oriented behavior, whether that behavior involves an infant retrieving a toy or a 30-year-old attorney planning the perfect closing argument. The executive functions of planning, inhibition, monitoring, and flexibility recruit a range of basic cognitive processes such as attention, perception, language, and memory. The essence of executive function is that these basic processes are coordinated for a very specific purpose: to subserve goal-directed behavior.

Inhibition and Working Memory

Pennington (1994, 1998; Pennington et al., 1996) discussed the problem of the "unconstrained frontal metaphor" (p. 6). That is, there is a veritable laundry list of symptoms that can follow frontal injury or dysfunction and these have been subsumed under the umbrella of executive function. Cognitive processes such as planning, inhibition, working memory, and flexibility are presumably interrelated in the sense that they each contribute to goal-directed behavior. However, empirical evidence of the convergent and discriminant validity of the executive function construct must still be demonstrated. To what degree do measures of various executive function skills converge to form a single factor, or even multiple factors, that are distinct from the other cognitive domains (e.g., verbal comprehension, long-term memory, spatial processing, etc.)? Recent factor analytic studies of executive function have identified factors tentatively named "cognitive flexibility," "speeded processing," and "basic/divided attention and short-term memory" (Boone, Ponton, Gorsuch, Gonzalez, & Miller, 1998) or "executive concept formation/flexibility" and "executive planning/inhibition" (Culbertson & Zillmer, 1998). It is important to note that in exploratory factor analyses such as these, the factors identified are highly influenced by the experimental measures chosen, as well as the makeup of the samples tested (children with attention deficit hyperactivity disorder, ADHD, in Culberton and Zillmer; neurologically impaired adults in Boone et al.).

Recent theoretical and computational accounts of executive functions have proposed that two cognitive processes, working memory and inhibition, may be sufficient to characterize the entire domain (e.g., Cohen & Servan-Schreiber, 1992; Dehaene & Changeux, 1991; Diamond, 1991; Kimberg & Farah, 1993; Pennington, 1994; Pennington et al., 1996; Roberts & Pennington, 1996; Roberts, Hager, & Heron, 1994). As defined by Roberts et al. (1994), working memory is the maintenance of transient information over brief temporal intervals to direct future-oriented activity, and inhibition is the ability to engage in the appropriate response instead of the more likely, albeit maladaptive, response. Roberts and colleagues (Roberts et al., 1994; Roberts & Pennington, 1996) argued convincingly that many, if not all, of the commonly used executive function tasks appear to require both cognitive processes. The authors suggested that the tasks may demand two *independent* processes, working memory and inhibition, with one or the other predominating depending on the task. The alternative position suggests that the two processes *interact*; for example, it is necessary to activate and maintain task-relevant information in working memory in order to inhibit prepotent, inappropriate responses.

Theories consistent with this notion of the interaction between working memory and inhibition generally follow a "limited capacity, central pool of mental resources" model. In this model, there is a basic assumption of a limited-capacity pool of resources from which both working memory and inhibition mechanisms must draw. Thus, imposing a large working memory load on a person will interfere with inhibition; conversely, confronting the person with a task that elicits strong competing responses (requiring the inhibition of all but one) will disrupt working memory performance. This interaction is illustrated in recent research by Conway and Engle (1994). These researchers defined working memory span as the ability to activate information from long-term memory. They found that high and low span subjects differed in their ability to activate information in a conflict situation, but there were no differences in a nonconflict situation. They explained these results by suggesting that individuals differ in their available attentional resources; this singular pool of resources is used for the working memory function (activation of LTM information) and for the inhibition function (dealing with the conflict situation). When no conflict was presented, both groups of subjects had sufficient available resources to execute the working memory operations. However, when a conflict situation required that the resources be used for inhibition and working memory, the more limited pool of resources characteristic of the low span subjects was exposed in the form of compromised working memory performance.

Bjorklund and Harnishfeger (1990) discussed a similar resource model of working memory and inhibition within a developmental framework. They followed Case's description of total mental capacity as a "processing space" consisting of an operating space and a storage space (Case, 1985). As the child's operational efficiency improves with development and knowledge, more of the total processing space will be available for storage. According to Bjorklund and Harnishfeger, one of these operations would presumably be a particular type of inhibition: keeping irrelevant information out of the processing space. As inhibition improves with development, practice, instruction, and so on, more of the available resources can be dedicated to the storage function, otherwise known as working memory. The Conway and Engle (1994) results can be interpreted within this framework: The conflict situation required that operating space be used for inhibition, leaving relatively less total space available for storage or working memory.

Several recent connectionist models have yielded data supporting the notion that working memory and inhibition interact to contribute to goal-directed behavior. Although different executive function tasks are modeled in different ways by these research teams, the consistent finding is that there is a direct association between the activation of working memory information and the tendency to inhibit prepotent responses (Cohen & Servan-Schreiber, 1992; Dehaene & Changeux, 1991; Kimberg & Farah, 1993; Levine & Prueitt, 1989). Essentially, the stronger the prepotency, or pull, to engage in the well-established, but incorrect, response, the greater the need for activation of task-relevant information in working memory. If inhibition and working memory are part of an interactive system, then the converse should also be true: When heavy demands are placed on working memory resources, there are fewer resources available to dedicate to inhibition.

Such a result was found by Roberts et al. (1994) on the antisaccade task, a behavioral measure of inhibition. The authors observed that increasing the working memory load via a concurrent task interfered with the inhibition required by the antisaccade task. Importantly, the working memory load did not interfere with performance on the prosaccade task (in which inhibition is not involved), and a concurrent task that did not require working memory resources failed to interfere with antisaccade performance. Thus, a very specific interaction between working memory and inhibitory control was found. However, individual differences in working memory (as measured by separate span tasks) did not correlate with inhibition as reflected by antisaccade performance. The authors suggested that there may be different aspects of working memory, capacity, and temporary vigilance that are demanded by the span and antisaccade tasks, respectively, and therefore, normal individual differences in each may not be expected to correlate. This begs the question: If different measures of working memory do not intercorrelate because they measure independent expressions of this cognitive process, then how likely is it that researchers will ever discover a unified construct of executive function that includes working memory, as well as other cognitive functions?

Therefore, there is a current trend to characterize executive function in a more parsimonious manner, that is, in terms of two potentially interactive subfunctions of inhibition and working memory. Whether the construct of executive function as it has been defined can be reduced to these two core processes makes for a lively theoretical debate, but ultimately must be demonstrated empirically. One way to examine the usefulness of the two-process approach to executive function would be to compare what is known about the development of inhibition and working memory to the small literature on the development of executive function. If the two processes can serve as a proxy of sorts for executive function, then the developmental patterns and clinical manifestations in children should be similar.

Plan of the Chapter

The purpose of this chapter is to explore the typical and atypical development of executive functions. Given the current controversy regarding how executive function should be conceptualized, three separate literatures are reviewed: research specifically designed to explore executive functions, as broadly defined here; research investigating both visual and verbal working memory; and research examining inhibition. First, these three domains are discussed with regard to typical development from early childhood through the school-age years. Second, the clinical variations in executive function, working memory, and inhibition are explored. The objective of reviewing these three literatures "side-by-side" is to evaluate the degree to which there is convergence, in terms of normal development and clinical variations. If, as has been suggested (Pennington et al., 1996; Roberts et al., 1994; Roberts & Pennington, 1996), a working memory/inhibition metaphor should replace the current broad executive function concept, a relatively a high level of convergence would be expected. In the final section, the similarities in both typical and atypical development across executive function, working memory, and inhibition are discussed, as well as the implications of these for the measurement of executive function in children.

DEVELOPMENTAL VARIATIONS
IN EXECUTIVE FUNCTIONS

Studying Frontal Lobe Function in Children

As Benton's (1991) early history of frontal lobe research nicely illustrates, there has been continuous active research examining the neuropsychologic function of this large cortical region since the closing decades of the 19th century. However, his review of the most seminal studies through the middle of the 20th century mentioned no studies of frontal lobe function in children. The current excitement surrounding the development of frontal lobe function is a phenomenon that is, at most, two decades old. Today there is a flurry of empirical activity focused on developing age-appropriate neuropsychological measures of frontal lobe function so as to understand both its normal development and relevant clinical variations.

Whereas the history of experimental animal model research and clinical neuropsychological examinations of frontal damaged adults has been enormously important to painting a general picture of the behaviors mediated by the prefrontal cortex, this database is no substitute for research with developing humans (e.g., Bolter & Long, 1985; Diamond, 1991; Tramontana & Hooper, 1988). Research exploring the function of the frontal cortex in children has been a relatively late-developing phenomenon for reasons that generally can be categorized as methodological and theoretical.

With regard to methodology, studies of adults with focal frontal lesions have provided the foundation of the current knowledge regarding frontal lobe function. These focal lesions were typically caused by gunshot wounds sustained during wartime. Children are much less likely to suffer discrete missile wounds of this type. Instead, they more frequently experience closed-head injury that results in diffusely represented brain damage, rather than focal damage to the frontal cortex alone. It is certainly the case that, with the introduction of modern neuroimaging technologies, clinical neuropsychological investigation is no longer limited to naturally occurring lesion case studies. However, many of the neuroimaging techniques that have proven so powerful with respect to revealing brain–behavior relations (e.g., PET, rCBF) are considered too invasive to be used routinely with normal children (e.g., Chugani, 1994).

Another explanation for the lack of research on the development of frontal lobe function is theoretical. There has been an assumption, and there still is to a certain extent (e.g., Bolter & Long, 1985), that the frontal lobes are essentially nonfunctional until sometime between age 10 and 12. In fact, damage to the frontal cortex before this time was thought to be "silent," with symptoms manifesting only at such time that the frontal cortex came "on line" with the rest of the functional brain. This assumption that frontal cortical function does not emerge until preadolescence comes from three lines of reasoning. First, based on data regarding myelination of cortical regions (Yakolev & Lecours, 1967), it has been assumed that the frontal cortex is not structurally mature until late in childhood. It is now widely believed that synaptogenesis and the "pruning" of these synaptic connections are the structural parameters that underlie many important functional developments (e.g., Chugani, 1994; Huttenlocher, 1994). Dendritic and synaptic density in the frontal lobes appear to reach a peak in the first few years of life, with selective pruning of excess connections occurring throughout childhood and adolescence (Huttenlocher, 1990).

Second, since the seminal work of Milner in the 1960s, performance on the Wisconsin Card Sorting Test (WCST) has been considered the sin quo non of frontal lobe function. Several studies (e.g., Chelune & Baer, 1986; Welsh, Pennington, & Groisser, 1991) have found that 6- and 7-year-old children perform like frontal damaged adults on this task. Normal adult-level performance is achieved at about age 10. Hence, the conclusion has been drawn that frontal lobe function (as reflected by mature WCST performance) emerges in preadolescence. A cursory examination of the WCST would reveal that there is another compelling reason that young children perform poorly on the task. Executive function skills of inhibition, flexible set shifting, and working memory are demanded within a context that also requires relatively sophisticated rule induction strategies. Therefore, a more age-appropriate task that still required the previous executive function skills might yield substantial evidence of "frontal lobe function" in children under age 7 (see the next section).

Third, prior to the 1990s, there was very little integration of theory and data across the two disciplines of neuropsychology and developmental psychology (e.g., Case, 1992; Dawson & Fischer, 1994; Welsh & Pennington, 1988). For decades, the typical clinical neuropsychologist's understanding of child development was limited to Jean Piaget, the dominant theory of cognitive development of the 20th century. Piaget's description of the fourth stage of cognitive development, formal operations, sounded strikingly similar to frontal lobe function to the neuropsychologist, with its emphasis on abstract and hypothetical thought, organized and planful strategies, and the newly emerging abilities to introspect and self-monitor. In Piaget's theory, formal operational thought emerged at about age 11. The presumption that formal operational thought was an observable manifestation of frontal lobe function fueled the notion that the frontal cortex began to subserve behavior between age 10 and 12.

Although there has been a long tradition in the field of neuropsychology to consider the study of the development of frontal lobe function in children both theoretically unsound and methodologically difficult, the trend has been reversing of late. With advances in knowledge of child development, as well as in methodological creativity and technological sophistication, there has been a burgeoning interest in describing the nature of frontal lobe function in developing children, using the construct of executive function as the organizing principle.

Development of Executive Functions

As previously discussed, studies specifically designed to track the normal development of cognitive processes attributed to prefrontal cortex function have been a relatively recent phenomenon. The studies generally adopt a common approach: Children are tested on tasks selected from either neuropsychology or cognitive psychology because they are presumed to measure one or more of the executive functions described earlier. The authors of these studies begin with a conception of frontal lobe function that derives from the adult clinical neuropsychological literature and then select or create age-appropriate tasks that might reveal the "child versions" of the same executive function skills.

Five studies are discussed that illustrate the aforementioned strategy. Each was designed specifically to address the question: What is the normal developmental pattern exhibited by behaviors attributed to the prefrontal cortex? Passler, Isaac, and Hynd (1985) selected a battery of tasks that assessed inhibition and flexible set shifting of motoric responses and mnemonic representations utilizing both verbal and nonverbal stimuli. The six tasks were administered to 64 children representing four age groups: 6-year-olds, 8-year-olds, 10-year-olds, and 12-year-olds. Passler et al. found a multistage pattern of development in which the most active period of development occurred between age 6 and 8, inhibitory control improved on other tasks by age 10, and mastery on most of the tasks was evident by age 12.

In a follow-up study, Becker, Isaac, and Hynd (1987) assessed the development of frontal lobe functions of 80 children representing the same age groups as the Passler et al. study. They selected a battery of nonverbal tasks designed to tap three skills areas: the inhibition of motor actions in the face of distractor stimuli; the inhibition of routinized, prepotent responses; and the ability to make recency judgments from temporally ordered working memory representations. Their results were very consistent with those of Passler et al. (1985). Again, the most striking developmental advances in these skills occurred between age 6 and 8. As in the Passler et al. study, inhibitory control with respect to mnemonic representations achieved maturity relatively late in development, at about age 12. Although both studies focused on inhibition, the performance on the recency memory task could be interpreted as reflecting the interaction of working memory and inhibition. That is, the children had to actively maintain temporal-order information in working memory, as well as inhibit inappropriate responses during the recency judgment trials.

Fiducia and O'Leary (1990) selected two tasks with which to measure the development of frontal lobe function in normal children. The verbal retroactive inhibition (VRI) task was selected based on clinical neuropsychological evidence of its sensitivity to frontal lobe damage. The central-incidental (C-I) learning paradigm was drawn from the developmental psychology literature because of its apparent demands for executive function skills. Such skills could be described as the ability to generate a working memory representation consisting of task-relevant information, while inhibiting the tendency to include irrelevant, distractor stimuli. Administering both tasks to 90 children at three age groups (7-, 10-, and 13-year-olds), Fiducia and O'Leary found that performance on the VRI improved significantly at two points in development, age 7 to 10 and age 10 to 13, replicating and extending the findings of Passler et al. (1985). Performance on the C-I task improved between age 10 and 13, and a significant correlation that emerged between the VRI and the C-I at age 13 suggested that a common ability to inhibit the processing of irrelevant stimuli may mature at this age. Again, these tasks fit the Bjorklund and Harnishfeger (1990) model in which inhibitory and working memory processes interact to affect problem-solving performance.

In a fourth study designed to explore the normal development of frontal lobe behaviors, Welsh, Pennington, and Groisser (1991) utilized a more wide-ranging battery of executive function tasks. Tests were selected from both the neuropsychology and developmental literatures in order to measure executive functions such as planning, organized search, and inhibition. Performance of 100 children ranging from age 3 to 12 and a sample of 10 adults indicated a multistage pattern of development as observed by Passler et al. (1985). The age at which adult-level performance was achieved depended on the nature of the task, in terms of the cognitive processes required and the difficulty level. Tasks that tapped simple planning and organized search of an external stimulus display exhibited adult-level performance as early as age 6. The two tasks that primarily demanded inhibition skills matured by age 10. However, tasks that required more complex planning and the organized search of long-term memory information did not reach adult-level performance by age 12.

Finally, a recent study by Luciana and Nelson (1999) explored the development of "prefrontally-guided working memory systems" in young, normal children ranging from age 4 to 8. Although the authors referred to the cognitive domain examined as "working memory," the broad range of tasks used in this study presumably required a variety of executive function skills, such as planning, inhibition, and flexibility, in addition to working memory. A sample of 181 children between age 4 and 8 and a smaller sample of teenagers and young adults were tested on a set of measures from the Cambridge Neuropsychological Test Automated Battery (CANTAB). The experimental tasks included spatial memory span, spatial working memory, Tower of London, and a intradimensional/extradimensional set shifting. Consistent with the earlier studies of the development of executive function, the improvements observed in performance were dependent on the nature and demands of the particular task. Four-year-olds performed more poorly than 5- to 7-year-olds on all of the measures, and the latter group was as proficient as older children and adults on the least demanding executive function measures (spatial span, simple problems from the TOL). However, a significant improvement was seen at age 8 on more complex tasks that seemed to introduce additional demands for planning, inhibition, and flexibility (e.g., more difficult problems from the TOL, spatial working memory). Moreover, 8-year-olds did not exhibit an adult level of performance on these more difficult executive function tasks, suggesting a later developmental shift or shifts in performance.

Other studies have explored the development of executive function skills by examining developmental trends on established neuropsychological measures of frontal lobe function. The task most closely associated with frontal lobe function is the WCST, and three studies have yielded very consistent results with regard to development of performance. Chelune and colleagues (Chelune & Baer, 1986; Chelune & Thompson, 1987) and Welsh et al. (1991) found that adult-level performance on the most meaningful index of performance, perseverative errors, was achieved by age 10. Levin et al. (1991) found a significant decrease in perseverative errors between their 7- to 8-year-old group and their 9- to 12-year-old group.

Disk-transfer tasks, such as the Tower of London (TOL) and the Tower of Hanoi (TOH), are relatively recent additions to the frontal assessment literature. These tasks require that a start state is transformed to a goal state via a correct sequence of moves. Although the TOH and TOL have face validity as planning tasks, there is a need for empirical validation of the underlying cognitive processes contributing to performance (Welsh et al., 1997). P. Anderson, V. Anderson, and Lajoie (1996) found that number correct and solution times improved on the TOL between age 7 and 9 and again between age 11 and 12. Somewhat surprisingly, the number of failed attempts, which might be avoided with better inhibitory control, did not change with age. Levin et al. (1991) investigated performance on the TOL in three age groups: 7- to 8-year-olds, 9- to 12-year-olds, and 13- to 15-year-olds. There was significantly better performance in the oldest age group, as compared with the youngest age group, in terms of percentage of problems solved on the first trial and average number of trials to solution. In a recent study, Kepler (1998) found a significant improvement in TOL performance between 7- and 9-year-olds and no difference between 9- and 11-year-olds. These children were administered a new, expanded version of the TOL that appears to have good reliability. Therefore, recent evidence converges on an early developmental shift toward improved performance between age 7 and 9 (P. Anderson et al., 1996; Kepler, 1998; Luciano & Nelson, 1999), as well as a later improvement in skill between age 12 and 13 (P. Anderson et al., 1996; Levin et al., 1991).

With regard to the TOH, Welsh and colleagues (Welsh, 1991; Welsh et al., 1991) found 6-year-olds to exhibit mature performance on the relatively simple 3-disk task, whereas 12-year-olds had not achieved adult-level performance on the more complex 4-disk version. It is important to note that procedural changes in the administration of the TOH can substantially affect these developmental patterns. When the 3-disk TOH was administered in different formats by Borys, Spitz, and Dorans (1982) and by Klahr (1978), 6-year-olds did not perform up to the standard found by Welsh.

What common developmental patterns emerge from this review of the literature on executive functions in children? Taken together, the studies indicate a multistage pattern of development with some executive function skills displayed by relatively young children and other skills not maturing until 6 or more years later. For example, some simple planning, organized search, spatial working memory, and inhibitory control are seen in children as young as age 6 (Luciana & Nelson, 1999; Passler et al., 1985; Welsh et al., 1990). There is substantial development of inhibition and flexible set shifting abilities between age 6 and 8 (Becker et al., 1987; Luciana & Nelson, 1999; Passler et al., 1985). This is followed by a consolidation of sorts in which inhibitory control on a range of tasks (WCST, Matching Familiar Figures Test, conflict, perseveration, etc.) attain maturity by age 10 (P. Anderson et al., 1996; Passler et al., 1985; Welsh et al., 1991). Finally, tasks that require more complex planning strategies and the manipulation of mnemonic information appear to show an early developmental shift between approximately age 7 to 10, as well as a more protracted course of development extending into adolescence (P. Anderson et al., 1996; Fiducia & O'Leary, 1990; Kepler, 1998; Levin et al., 1991; Welsh et al., 1991).

Development of Working Memory

The issues surrounding the difficulty defining and measuring executive function are similar when the concept of working memory is considered. As Hulme and Mackenzie (1992) pointed out, working memory is a functional term, often defined by what it does and in what contexts it is used. In the broadest sense, working memory can be defined as the system or complex of systems that is engaged for the transient maintenance of information during the performance of cognitive tasks (Hulme & Mackenzie, 1992). This definition is obviously problematic with regard to the measurement of the efficacy of working memory. Presumably, working memory would be involved in every cognitive performance, and some portion of the variance in that performance would be the result of the operation of working memory. Contributing to the variance in performance would be a multitude of other cognitive processes (e.g., Long Term Memory, language, spatial skills, etc.) and how much and which of the variance is due to working memory, per se, would be unknown.

In the now classic structural model proposed by Baddeley and Hitch (1974; Baddeley, 1992), working memory is characterized as a system of memory stores including a limited-capacity central executive and two slave subsystems, the articulatory loop and the visuospatial scratchpad, that processes verbal and nonverbal material, respectively. Information can be passively stored in the slave subsystems without utilizing limited processing resources. In contrast, the central executive uses its limited energy to direct the input and output of information to these subsystems, online manipulation of information, integration with other permanently stored information, and selection of relevant information, while ignoring distractors. The Baddeley and Hitch description is reminiscent of Norman and Shallice's proposed supervisory system and also highlights the intimate connection between working memory and inhibition. Pennington (1994) suggested that the "computational throughput" (Carpenter & Just, 1989) that results from working memory processes involves information integration, action selection, and the inhibition of related, but maladaptive, actions. In a similar vein, Case (1992) proposed that tests of working memory should include three specific requirements: execution of a repetitive pattern of operations, storage of the products of these operations in the face of interfering stimuli, and the output of these products in a precise sequence. Therefore, the essence of the role of working memory in Case's view is the maintenance of a temporally ordered sequence of information while inhibiting the intrusion of potentially competing sequences of information.

The development of working memory abilities in children have been explored in both the verbal and visuospatial domains. According to the Baddeley and Hitch (1974) model, verbal working memory tasks reflect the operation of the articulatory loop in conjunction with the central executive, whereas the nonverbal tasks are mediated by the visuospatial scratchpad and the central executive. Hitch and colleagues (Hitch, Halliday, Schaafstal, & Schraagen, 1988; Hitch, Woodin, & Barker, 1989) suggested that visual working memory develops at an earlier age than verbal working memory. They proposed that by age 5, visual stimuli are automatically processed by the visual working memory system. However, it takes another 5 or 6 years for control processes to develop that mediate a transfer of visual information from the visual to the phonological working memory system (Hitch et al., 1989). The authors maintain that by age 10 to 11, children are more likely to translate visual information into an auditory-verbal code for processing in verbal working memory (Hitch et al., 1988). Unlike the gradual development of verbal working memory over the school years, Hitch and colleagues suggested in 1989 that there was surprisingly little, if any, maturational change in visual working memory after age 5.

There is relatively little recent literature exploring visuospatial working memory in young children; however, the findings of one study are consistent with the notion of very early functional development of this system. Using the radial maze task as a measure of spatial working memory, Foreman, Warry, and Murray (1990) found some evidence of working memory ability in children as young as 18 months; however, there was a linear increase in performance from 18 months to about 5 years of age. It is interesting to note that the radial maze task not only requires the child to maintain and manipulate the search plan in spatial working memory, but it also demands inhibition of the prepotent response to return to previously rewarded locations. Mutter (1998) explored spatial working memory in young children with the Mr. Cucui task (Diaz, 1974; cited in Case, 1985). This is a spatial span task in which the children were shown the Mr. Cucui clown with certain body parts marked and, following a delay, had to point to the previously marked locations on a blank model. Mutter (1998) found a linear developmental pattern of performance on this task between age 3 and 5. Therefore, the results of two studies that explored visuospatial working memory in the first 5 years of life converged on the notion that there is a gradual improvement in skill.

In contrast with the Hitch et al. (1989) proposal that there is little developmental improvement in visual working memory after age 5, Case (1992) discussed studies by Crammond (1992) and Menna (1989) that demonstrate an increase in spatial working memory span from age 4 to 15. In the spatial span task, subjects are shown a random spatial arrangement of marked cells in a matrix and, after a brief delay, must recall all the locations of the marked cells. Luciana and Nelson (1999) observed development of spatial span performance from age 4 to 7, and when demands for inhibition were increased in their spatial working memory test, a further improvement between 7 and 8 years was found. Morra, Moizo, and Scopesi (1988) found similar improvements in spatial working memory capacity from age 7 to 11 using related tasks. In a study by Walker, Hitch, Doyle, and Porter (1994), development of spatial working memory was observed after age 5 (specifically between ages 5 and 7) utilizing another task that required recall of the spatiotemporal information. There is a clear inhibition component in these various spatial working memory tasks. That is, the relevant spatial information is constantly changing across trials, introducing interference and competing responses that must be inhibited to perform well.

In fact, Case (1992) proposed that a demand for inhibition of responses to irrelevant stimuli is a requirement for a test to be considered a measure of working memory. Whereas the tasks used in the studies cited earlier included this requirement, the visual working memory task used in the earlier work by Hitch and colleagues did not. Hitch et al. (1988) did acknowledge that their picture memory task probably assessed the "passive storage component" (p. 131) of visual working memory; this is what Baddeley and Hitch referred to as the visual scratchpad. This visual memory store has similar properties in younger and older children (and perhaps adults, as well) and thus exhibits little developmental change (Hitch et al., 1988). However, when the visuospatial working memory task demands updating, manipulation, and inhibition of competing responses, developmental change can be expected across the school years.

Verbal working memory has been investigated in children primarily through the use of span tasks that vary in the apparent demands for the processing requirements Case (1992) suggested are necessary to effectively tap working memory. Phonological working memory is typically assessed via tasks such as digit span, letter span, and word/nonword repetition. Such tasks include relatively little demand for inhibition and may primarily tap "passive" articulatory loop, the verbal analogue of the visual scratchpad discussed earlier. Nevertheless, research by Adams and Gathercole (1995, 1996; Gathercole & Adams, 1993) highlighted the critical importance of phonological working memory to a range of skills in very young children. First, they demonstrated that phonological working memory can be assessed in children as young as age 2 with both word and nonword repetition tasks. Their studies of children from age 3 to 5 have demonstrated that phonological working memory skills predict expressive language ability with regard to complexity of both vocabulary and grammar. Stage and Wagner (1992) found that limited phonological working memory capacity, as measured by letter span, adversely affects spelling performance in young children (kindergarten and first grade), but not in older children (second and third grade). This appears to be consistent with the Hitch et al. (1989) proposal that the transfer of information between verbal working memory (e.g., letter sounds) and visual working memory (e.g., written letter symbols) is primitive, at best, in young children.

Word span, as measured by word repetition tasks, appears to show substantial improvement over the school years. Case (1982) reported an increase in word span between age 4 and 5. Engle, Carullo, and Collins (1991) revealed a spurt in development between age 9 and 12. Hulme (1984) found what appeared to be a linear increase in word span from age 4 to 10 (although paired comparisons of means were not conducted). In a 5-year longitudinal study, Hulme and Mackenzie (1992) demonstrated a significant increase in auditory sequential memory (i.e., digit span) from age 4 to 9. Gualin and Cambell (1994) studied the development of verbal working memory with a task that incorporated demands for inhibition and interference control. In the Competing Language Processing Task, the subject was required to hold words in verbal working memory while analyzing and responding to True and False statements. These authors found evidence for word span increases over the range of age 6 to 10; in contrast with the Engle et al. (1991) results, there was no improvement from age 10 to 12.

To summarize, this selective review of research on the development of working memory skills provides evidence for a very early emergence of visual working memory skills. Children under age 2 exhibit some ability to execute an efficient spatial search that requires updating working memory, as well as resisting the impulse to return to earlier locations (Foreman et al., 1990). Various types of visuospatial search continues to develop during the preschool years, and performance on tasks that primarily tap the passive visuospatial scratchpad appears to mature by age 5 (Hitch et al., 1988). However, visual working memory tasks that recruit the central executive to a greater degree will exhibit developmental improvements in performance across childhood and into adolescence (Case, 1992).

With regard to verbal working memory, a similar distinction can be made between tasks that seem to involve the central executive in conjunction with the passive "slave system" to a greater or lesser degree. Although traditional span tasks would seem to involve the central executive to a smaller degree than other working memory tasks, Adams and Gathercole (1996) demonstrated that young children's "capacity" as measured by span tasks is highly predictive of a range of language-related abilities. Emerging phonological working memory skill is measurable as early as age 2 and continues its development in proficiency until at least age 10. As Hulme and Mackenzie (1992) proposed, these developmental improvements in verbal working memory do not appear to be the result of an increase in the sheer capacity of the store. Instead, it is likely due to increases in articulation speed that allows for the processing of more information into the limited capacity system. Regarding verbal working memory tests that involve interference control and inhibition mediated by the central executive, there is some evidence of developmental improvements through age 10 to 12. However, most of the research with more complex sentence span tasks has explored individual, not developmental, differences (e.g., Daneman & Carpenter, 1980, 1983).

Development of Inhibition

As has been the case for constructs such as executive function and working memory, there is little consensus regarding the definition of inhibition. At first blush it would seem that inhibition could be defined simply as "appropriately withholding a response" in a given situation. However, inhibition is not always seen as an "appropriate" behavior. In research on personality traits, inhibition is viewed as one of several broad behavioral dimensions that is related to a neurotic and anxious response to novel or threatening environments (Costa & McCrae, 1988). Certainly, there must be a distinction between this type of pervasive behavioral style and the type of task-specific, adaptive, response inhibition subsumed under the rubric of executive function. Interestingly, there may be frontal cortex mediation of both types of inhibition; Sutton and Davidson (1997) found that the tendency toward the former type of behavioral inhibition is correlated with increased electrical activation in the right prefrontal cortex.

The working definition of inhibition relevant to this chapter is frequently discussed in the clinical and developmental literatures in terms of impulsivity. That is, a child who is impulsive lacks the ability to appropriately inhibit a response when the situation demands it. In their review of research and measures of impulsivity, Milich and Kramer (1984) pointed out that "impulsivity is not clearly or comprehensively defined" (p. 58) and highlighted a range of descriptions and operational definitions. Some of these ("inability to inhibit motor actions," "inability to delay gratification," "poor self control") are consistent with the working definition of inhibition used in this section. However, other conceptualizations of impulsivity ("poor judgement," "poor planning ability," "lack of foresight") are reminiscent of the more general construct of executive function. Typically, impulsivity and inhibition have been viewed as two sides of the same coin. This basic ability to stay on task and resist interference has long been identified with frontal cortex mediation of executive function.

This is reflected by the incorporation of traditional measures of impulsivity, such as the Matching Familiar Figures Test (Kagan, Rosman, Day, Albert, & Phillips, 1964) and self-control tasks, into executive function assessment batteries for children (Diamond et al., 1993; Diamond, Prevor, Callender, & Druin, 1977; Welsh et al., 1991).

Another complication when describing inhibition is its close association with the idea of flexibility and set shifting. For example, the classic neuropsychological description of frontal damage sequelae includes "impaired response inhibition and inflexible behavior (Kolb & Whishaw, 1985). That is, on neuropsychological tests (e.g., WCST, Stroop), as well as in more naturalistic contexts, individuals with frontal damage not only have difficulty inhibiting a prepotent, well-established, or previously reinforced response, but they also cannot flexibly switch to a more appropriate response. In essence, the concept of inhibition and the tasks designed to measure it usually include both stopping a behavior and shifting to another behavior. Pennington (1998) elegantly demonstrated this distinction between inhibition (stopping and doing "nothing" in its place) and flexibility (stopping and doing something else) through a factor analysis of a range of executive function tasks used in his laboratory with both normal and abnormal populations. This analysis revealed two independent factors: the "Inhibition" factor was comprised of tasks demanding that a response be withheld, whereas the "Cognitive Flexibility" factor included tasks requiring that a shift to a new response be made (e.g., in the Stroop, the individual must resist reading the word and shift to naming the color). Interestingly, this factor analysis also revealed a third independent factor, "Working Memory," on which three span tasks (digit, counting, and sentence) loaded. It is unclear how the separability of inhibition and working memory can be reconciled with the limited resources hypothesis of an interactive working memory-inhibition system described earlier.

Dempster (1993) pointed out that the activation of knowledge and rule-based strategies has captured the attention of researchers in the field of cognitive development; however, the role of inhibitory processes has been relatively ignored. An example that illustrates this position is the long-standing view that the correlations between infant performance on habituation and recognition memory tasks and later intellectual ability is mediated by rate of information processing (an "activation" component). McCall (1994) argued that it may be the infant's ability to inhibit attention to familiar and/or less salient stimuli in these tasks that, in addition to rate of information processing, contributes to the prediction of IQ variance during childhood.

The following selective review of literature will operationally define inhibition both in terms of withholding or stopping a response, as well as with regard to flexibly switching to another, more appropriate response.

Development of inhibitory processes in young children primarily has been studied with self-control and resistance to temptation paradigms and these generally tap the "withholding" dimension of inhibition. Research exploring inhibition that requires a withholding response and cognitive flexibility generally has focused on school-age children, although some recent studies have examined this component of inhibition in young children as well (Cuneo & Welsh, 1992; Gerstadt, Hong, & Diamond, 1994).

Inhibition in early childhood traditionally has been assessed by means of self-control paradigms, also referred to as delay of gratification or resistance to temptation (Mischel & Patterson, 1979). In the typical task, children are presented with an attractive stimulus or activity and is told that they must wait for a period of time before approaching the object or engaging in the activity, frequently with an added incentive to do so. Self-control is operationalized as the amount of time the child can delay various approach behaviors (touching, eating, etc.). According to Olson and colleagues (Olson, 1989; Olson, Bates, & Bayles, 1990), self-control behavior in children may reflect two relatively independent sources of normal variation: an inhibitory control ability that is closely tied to cognitive development and a predisposition toward complying with internalized social expectations.

Kopp (1982) proposed a developmental model of self-regulation behavior, suggesting that it emerges at about age 2 in conjunction with representational thought and the ability to recall information (e.g., social rules, prohibitions, expectations) from long-term memory. This early manifestation of self-control was confirmed by the research of Vaughn and colleagues (Vaughn, Kopp, & Krakow, 1984; Vaughn, Krakow, Kopp, Johnson, & Schwartz, 1986) in which a very rudimentary and unstable form of delay behavior was observed as early as 18 months and a significant improvement in self-control was demonstrated between age 2 and 3. According to Kopp's model, a more flexible form of self-regulation that includes self-monitoring and appropriate adjustments to changing contingencies would not be apparent until age 3 to 4. Interestingly, Cournoyer and Trudel (1991) found that, among children as young as age 2½, those who performed the best on self-control tasks did so by using a flexible strategy of shifting their attention during the delay period. Therefore, tasks that primarily require the withholding of a response elicit evidence of inhibition in children from as early as 18 months and this skill appears to develop until about age 4. Flexible shifting can help a very young child inhibit an approach response, but this strategy is usually not seen until the preschool years. The classic self-control paradigm is an effective means of demonstrating inhibition in young children, but there appears to be little development in the behaviors elicited by this type of task after age 4 (Logue & Chararro, 1992).

Inhibition also has been studied in young children by means of a variety of tasks that assess the withholding of a response, as well as a greater demand for shifting to an alternative behavior. Zelazo, Kearsley, and Stack (1995) examined the memory skills of young children (22–32 months) that involved recognizing a series of visual stimuli and assimilating transformations of these stimuli. Although speed of processing increased across this age range, the authors concluded that it was speed of processing and the increasing ability to inhibit expectations set up from past information (proactive inhibition) that contributed to improved performance. It is interesting to note the similarity between their conclusions and McCall's interpretation of the infant habituation data discussed earlier in this section. That is, both speed of processing and inhibition contribute to the quality of cognitive performance. The poor performance of children under age 5 on discrimination learning tasks (Bell & Livesey, 1985; Gholson, Levine, & Phillips, 1972) has been attributed, not to a lack of conceptual understanding, but to problems inhibiting inappropriate responses (Livesey & Morgan, 1991). Similarly, the spatial layout and cues of a task have been found to "drive" the search strategy of a 3-year-old, whereas a 4-year-old can inhibit this external control and follow an internalized search plan (Cuneo & Welsh, 1992; Miller & Harris, 1988; Mutter, 1998). Finally, in a child version of the classic Stroop task, Gerstadt et al. (1994) found that 3½- to 4-year-old children performed more poorly than children between age 5 and 7. Although the younger age group could maintain a working memory representation of the rules, it was the demand to inhibit a response (or perhaps the combination of working memory and inhibition demands) that was beyond the capacity of the 3- to 4-year-olds. Taken together, these results suggest that inhibition of responses to salient external stimuli may improve between age 3 and 4, but when the task involves the addition of working memory demands (remembering rules, as in discrimination learning and the Stroop), further development is seen between age 4 and 6 (Baron-Cohen, Cross, Crowson, & Robertson, 1994).

The development of inhibitory processes in school-age children was recently reviewed by Harnishfeger and Bjorklund (1993) with regard to motor inhibition, inhibition of external distractors (e.g., visual search), and inhibition of internal distractors (e.g., memory tasks). It is clear from this review that the age at which effective inhibition is observed depends to a large degree on the processing requirements and response demands of the particular task. Drawing some general conclusions from the extensive array of studies discussed, it appears that the inhibition of simple motor actions may be mature by age 7, whereas inhibition of external distractors in visual search and Stroop-like tasks does not attain adult-level performance at this young age. With regard to the inhibition of internal distractors, evidence from a range of memory studies indicate efficient inhibition by about age 8 to 9. A look at three studies that were not reviewed by Harnishfeger and Bjorklund illustrate that importance of considering the domain and type of task when evaluating the development of inhibitory processes. Halberstadt, Grotjohn, Johnson, and Furth (1992) found that children as young as age 7 could easily inhibit the facial expressions corresponding to a felt emotion both on command and spontaneously. In contrast, the use of sentence context to inhibit the activation of inappropriate object names was not exhibited consistently until age 9 (Johnson, 1994). Similarly, Kepler (1998) found a linear pattern of development of inhibitory processes on the Stroop task from age 7 to 11. One could speculate that the inhibition of motor movements (including facial expressions) may operate on a more primitive, even survival-based, level and would be expected to reach maturity at an earlier point in development. Inhibition in the context of linguistic, conceptual, and mnemonic information would be expected to show a more protracted course of development across the school years.

Therefore, when considering the development of inhibitory processes, it is useful to recognize the distinction between pure withholding of response and cognitive flexibility delineated by Pennington (1998). It appears that children as young as 18 months show a primitive form of inhibition; however, flexible strategies to aid the inhibition of responses are more likely to emerge in the 3- to 4-year-old range. The development of inhibition skills on tasks that require the additional demand of cognitive flexibility may be domain and task specific, with motor inhibition developing prior to age 7 and inhibition of irrelevant linguistic and mnemonic information maturing a few years later. As is discussed in the last section, performance on tasks that include the demand for cognitive flexibility may develop more slowly because of the need to represent the rules in working memory.

CLINICAL VARIATIONS IN EXECUTIVE FUNCTIONS

Another approach to examining the convergence of the literatures on executive function, working memory, and inhibition is to evaluate the degree to which there are similarities in the clinical manifestations of the three constructs. That is, do the same childhood disorders exhibit deficits of executive function, working memory, and inhibition, or do impairments in these three domains appear to "load" on different clinical conditions? This section begins with those studies that were designed specifically to address the possibility of executive function deficits in disorders in which a prefrontal cortical dysfunction is suspected. This is followed by two subsections on research that has explored working memory and inhibition impairments in child clinical groups, with an emphasis on how these literatures converge with, and diverge from, the literature on executive function deficits.

Studies Specifically Exploring Executive Function

Research exploring specific executive function impairments in disorders of childhood primarily has focused on three clinical groups that vary in the specificity with which the neurologic dysfunction has been identified. Of the three conditions, the genetic disorder phenylketonuria (PKU) reflects the most well-specified model of a prefrontal dysfunction (e.g., Chamove & Molinaro, 1978; Diamond et al., 1993; Diamond et al., 1997; Welsh, 1996). The subtle prefrontal dysfunction is assumed to be the result of the neurochemical consequences of a very specific genetic mutation that appears to reduce levels of functional dopamine (Krause et al., 1985). It has been proposed by several research groups that the second clinical condition, Attention Deficit Hyperactivity Disorder, may represent a frontal lobe dysfunction disorder (Gualtieri & Hicks, 1978; Mattes, 1980; Rosenthal & Allen, 1978; Stamm & Kreder, 1979; Welsh, 1994). This hypothesis has been based on behavioral symptomatology (Douglas, 1983, 1988), dopamine deficiencies (S. E. Shaywitz, B. A. Shaywitz, Cohen, & Young, 1983), and neuroimaging evidence of hypofrontality (Lou, Henriksen, & Bruhn, 1984); however, it is not without its critics (e.g., Oades, 1987; Zametkin & Rapoport, 1987). The third child clinical condition, autism, has been controversial with regard to the core neuropsychological impairment (e.g., language, social cognition, or executive function), which has led to different hypotheses regarding neurobiological mechanisms (Pennington & Welsh, 1995). However, recent research has converged on a possible prefrontal cortex dysfunction as manifested by executive function deficits (e.g., Ozonoff, Pennington, & Rogers, 1991).

Research specifically designed to examine the prefrontal dysfunction model of early treated PKU generally has revealed significant executive function impairments that are unrelated to general intelligence. Welsh, Pennington, Ozonoff, Rouse, and McCabe (1990) found executive function deficits in a group of early treated 4- and 5-year-old PKU children as compared to IQ-matched controls. Poor performance was observed on such tasks as TOH, visual search, and verbal fluency, and many performance scores were negatively correlated with plasma phenylalanine (Phe) level at the time of testing. In a longitudinal study, Diamond and colleagues (1993, 1997) revealed executive function impairments during the infancy, toddler, and preschool periods of development, and again, these related to concurrent Phe level in the early treated PKU group. The executive function measures used in this study could be characterized as demanding a combination of inhibitory control and working memory (e.g., object retrieval for infants, Stroop for young children). Recent dissertation research by Stemerdink (Stemerdink et al., 1999) found that a group of early treated PKU subjects (ranging from age 8 to 19) had a significantly lower scores on three of four executive function measures than an age- and IQ-matched control group. Unlike the Welsh et al. (1990) study, Stemerdink did not find impairments on a modified version of the TOH; however, she did find significant group differences on two other executive function tasks, the WCST and the Corsi-Miller test of temporal memory. Whereas most of the findings have consistently shown executive function deficits in early treated PKU, one study did not (Mazzocco, Nord, Van Doorninck, Greene, Kovar, & Pennington, 1994).

Recent reviews of executive function performance in children diagnosed with ADHD indicate a fairly clear pattern of specific deficits in this cognitive domain (Barkley, Grodzinsky, & DuPaul, 1992; Pennington, 1998; Pennington & Ozonoff, 1996; Welsh, 1994). In their meta-analysis of 18 studies examining executive function and ADHD, Pennington and Ozonoff (1996) found evidence for consistent impairments on tasks such as letter fluency, TOH, Matching Familiar Test, Trailmaking Test, and Stroop, as well as less consistent deficits on the WCST. It is important to note that these tasks represent a range of executive functions, including organization, planning, flexibility, and inhibition. Based on an analysis of data from his own laboratory, Pennington (1998) concluded that the executive function profile that best fits children with ADHD is characterized by deficits in inhibition and planning, but not in cognitive flexibility. A pattern of executive function impairments has been an important factor for discriminating the ADHD group from other clinical conditions, such as reading disability (Pennington, Groisser, & Welsh, 1993), autism (Ozonoff & Jensen, 1999), and Tourette syndrome (Harris et al., 1995; Ozonoff & Jensen, 1999).

The Pennington and Ozonoff (1996) meta-analysis of executive function impairments and child psychopathology also examined the evidence for autism. They reviewed early research documenting in autistic children the type of inflexible, perseverative behavior characteristic of individuals with frontal lobe damage (Boucher, 1977; Frith, 1972; Hermelin & O'Connor, 1970; cited in Pennington & Ozonoff, 1996). Of the 14 empirical investigations of executive function performance in autistic children that were meta-analyzed, Pennington and Ozonoff found significant group differences on 78% of the 32 different measures utilized. Somewhat different from the findings in the ADHD population, autistic children appear to be particularly impaired on the WCST, so much so that this deficit in flexibility can discriminate the autistic group from dyslexia (Rumsey & Hamburger, 1990), Tourette syndrome (Ozonoff & Jensen, 1999; Ozonoff, Strayer, McMahon, & Filloux, 1994), and ADHD (Ozonoff & Jensen, 1999; Szatmari, Tuff, Finlayson, & Bartolucci, 1990). Similar to the research with ADHD children, the TOH measure of executive function appears to be sensitive to the cognitive deficits of autistic subjects (Ozonoff et al., 1991; Ozonoff & McEvoy, 1994). These observed impairments in executive function processes are consistent with evidence of regional cerebral blood flow (rCBF) patterns seen in the brains of autistic children that is suggestive of a maturational delay of the frontal cortex (Zibovicius et al., 1995).

To summarize, recent research has documented a pattern of executive function deficits in three clinical conditions of childhood, early treated PKU, ADHD, and autism. Given the broad range of cognitive skills subsumed within the rubric of executive function, deficits in this domain may show a variety of profiles and this appears to be the case for these three clinical groups. The few studies examining early treated PKU have indicated a relatively wide range of executive functions, including planning, organized search, flexibility, inhibition, and working memory. A greater number of studies has assessed executive function skills in ADHD; there appears to be more convergence on a few executive function deficits in the areas of planning and inhibition. Finally, recent explorations of executive functions in autism suggest that planning and flexibility of strategies are particular weaknesses.

Studies Exploring Working Memory Deficits

The preceding section discussed research designed to test the hypothesis of specific executive function/prefrontal cortical deficits underlying clinical conditions of childhood. This section concentrates on studies that focused primarily on the effectiveness of verbal and nonverbal working memory skills. Two questions are addressed: To what degree do the three groups characterized with executive function deficits (PKU, ADHD, and autism) also exhibit working memory impairments? And, have other clinical conditions, not typically identified with frontal lobe dysfunction, also been found to demonstrate impairments in working memory?

There have been relatively few studies exploring working memory performance in early treated PKU individuals; for the most part, these have been conducted on adolescents and adults and the interpretation of results is complicated by variations in dietary treatment regimens across studies. Another problem is that the memory tasks used are often not identified as working memory tasks, yet they are consistent with the criteria typically associated with such tasks (Case, 1992). For example, Faust, Libon, and Pueschel (1986–1987) indicated "reduced channel capacity" (p. 174) in their PKU subjects, and Stemerdink (1996) revealed poor memory for recency information in her PKU subjects in the same age range. Although the Corsi-Miller test of recency memory has not been called a working memory task explicitly, the demand to encode and continuously update the temporal order of visual stimuli seems, on the face of it, to require working memory processes.

Evidence for working memory deficits in ADHD is quite a bit weaker than the data suggesting general executive function or inhibition (next section) impairments. In the meta-analysis conducted by Pennington and Ozonoff (1996), only 2 of 16 relevant studies used what the authors considered to be working memory measures; significant group differences were found on the Sequential Memory task (Gorenstein, Mammato, & Sandy, 1989) and on the Self-ordered Pointing task (Shue & Douglas, 1992). Whether these two tasks tap verbal or visual working memory is unclear. Both use pictorial stimuli of representational material and the information potentially could be coded in the articulatory loop or the visuospatial scratchpad. Siegel and Ryan (1989) found evidence of a verbal working memory deficit only in their 7- to 8-year-old ADHD group and not in the 9- to 10-year-old group. Pennington (1998) concluded from research in his own laboratory that the evidence for a verbal working memory deficit in ADHD is not very strong. However, it is important to note that there appears to be a dearth of studies specifically exploring the possibility of a nonverbal working memory deficit. Given the range of primarily visuospatial tasks on which ADHD children perform poorly (e.g., TOH, MFFT, Trails), the hypothesis that a nonverbal working memory deficit exists should be examined more extensively.

Pennington and colleagues (Pennington & Ozonoff, 1996; Pennington, 1998) suggested that verbal working memory is an area of impairment for children diagnosed with autism. However, there have been relatively few studies to date that have tested a hypothesized working memory deficit in this population. Of the 14 relevant executive function studies reviewed by Pennington and Ozonoff, only one utilized measures that were considered by the authors to qualify as working memory tasks (i.e., digit span was excluded). Bennetto, Pennington, and Rogers (1996) examined working memory performance in high-functioning autistic adolescents and adults as compared to age- and IQ-matched controls. They found striking evidence of a working memory deficit on several tasks, in the context of intact skills in rote short-term memory (e.g., digit span), verbal long-term memory, and recognition memory. Although these results are impressive, more work needs to be done to replicate this finding, particularly in groups of autistic individuals representing different ages and levels of intellectual functioning.

Working memory skills have also been studied extensively in clinical populations that are not typically thought of as reflecting a prefrontal cortical dysfunction. There is a great deal of evidence that verbal working memory, as measured by digit and letter span tasks, is impaired in severe, low IQ learning disabilities such as Down syndrome (see review by Hulme & MacKenzie, 1992). These types of span tasks may tap the function of the articulatory loop (rather than the central executive), and might not fit the processing requirements for a prefrontally mediated working memory task (Case, 1992; Pennington et al., 1995). However, other studies have used more complex sentence, counting and spatial span tasks of working memory; these have revealed significantly poorer performance of reading disabled, learning disabled, and math disabled children (Hitch & McAuley, 1991; Swanson, Ashbaker, & Lee, 1996; Swanson, Cochran, & Ewers, 1990; Swanson & Trahan, 1990).

Therefore, there is some evidence of working memory impairments in the three clinical groups that have been identified in terms of executive dysfunction. Currently, this evidence is based on relatively few studies and, although the data are intriguing (e.g., Bennetto et al., 1996), further study of this specific phenomenon is needed. On the other hand, working memory deficits have been identified in a rather broad range of clinical syndromes of childhood that implicate the involvement of several brain systems other than the frontal cortex. Denckla (1996) suggested that working memory deficiencies are characteristic of both the ADHD and LD populations, but that intention and inhibition are additional problem areas for the former group.

Studies Exploring Inhibition Deficits

An examination of the literature regarding inhibition impairments in children overlaps to a large degree with the literature on clinical manifestations of executive function (described earlier). Inhibition and flexibility, more so than working memory, traditionally have been subsumed under the umbrella term of executive function. Thus, the question of whether inhibitory deficits have been found in the three key clinical groups will often refer to these executive function studies, with a sharper focus on those tasks assessing inhibition and flexibility. In addition, the literature exploring the range of clinical conditions in which a problem with inhibition and flexible set-shifting is found is examined.

Inhibition deficits in early treated PKU have been investigated with tasks that demand both inhibition and flexibility of action. For example, in the longitudinal study by Diamond and colleagues (1993, 1997), infants and toddlers were tested on object search and retrieval tasks and young children were tested on a child version of the Stroop test. These measures require the inhibition of a strong, prepotent response and a switch to a more adaptive, albeit less likely, response. Early treated PKU children were selectively impaired on these tasks at all three age periods and this was especially true for the subjects whose plasma Phe level was at the high end of the "safe" range. Poor inhibition and lack of flexibility also has been operationalized as perseveration on the Wisconsin Card Sort and other experimental tasks. Children and young adults with early treated PKU have been found to be more perseverative on the Wisconsin (Pennington, van Doorninck, & McCabe, 1985; Ris, Williams, Hunt, Berry, & Leslie, 1994), as well as on visual search and verbal fluency tasks (Welsh et al., 1990). In terms of cognitive style, these children have been described as more impulsive (Davis, McIntyre, Murray, & Mims, 1986).

There is a long tradition of research identifying inhibition impairments in children with ADHD (e.g., Barkley, 1981; Douglas, 1985); in fact, pervasive impulsive behavior is considered one of the diagnostic features of the disorder. In empirical studies contrasting children with ADHD and those diagnosed with a range of learning disabilities, problems with self-regulation and inhibition appear to typify the former group (Denkla, 1996; Robbins, 1992). The question of whether ADHD children have more difficulty with "pure" inhibition tasks or those that include the additional demand of cognitive flexibility is far from resolved. Pennington and colleagues (Pennington, 1998; Pennington & Ozonoff, 1996) suggest that cognitive flexibility is less of a problem for these children than is the basic inhibition of motor responses (i.e., stopping, but not shifting to a new response). Aman, Roberts, and Pennington (1998), Logan and colleagues (Schachar & Logan, 1990; Schachar, Tannock, & Logan, 1993; Schachar, Tannock, Marriott, & Logan, 1995; Tannock, Schachar, Carr, Chajczyk, & Logan, 1989), and Ozonoff and Jensen (1999) found such pure motor inhibition deficits. These are frequently reversible with methylphenidate treatment. However, there is also substantial evidence of cognitive inflexibility in this population (Pearson, Yaffee, Loveland, & Norton, 1995; Tannock, Schachar, & Logan, 1995), as seen on such tasks as the WCST (Boucugnani & Jones, 1989; Chelune, Ferguson, Koon, & Dickey, 1986; Gorenstein et al., 1989; Reader, Harris, Schuerholz, & Denckla, 1994) and the Stroop (Boucugnani & Jones, 1989; Everett, Thomas, Cote, Levesque, & Michaud, 1991; Grodzinsky & Diamond, 1992).

With regard to inhibition impairments in autism, Pennington (1998; Pennington, & Ozonoff, 1996) concluded that the evidence is strong for a particular flexibility deficit in this clinical group. There have been consistent findings of perseveration on the WSCT (Bennetto et al., 1996; Ozonoff & McEvoy, 1994; Ozonoff et al., 1991; Prior & Hoffman, 1990; Rumsey, 1985; Rumsey & Hamburger, 1988, 1990), and inflexibility on other experimental measures (Hughes, Russell, & Robbins, 1994; Ozonoff & Jensen, 1999; Ozonoff, Strayer, McMahon, & Filloux, 1994). This lack of flexibility is consistent with some of the classic symptoms of autistic disorder such as behavioral stereotypies and poor adaptability to changes in daily routines (Spreen et al., 1995). In contrast, impairments in pure inhibition in autism have not been the focus of research until very recently. Ozonoff and Strayer (1997) found no evidence of deficits on two measures of inhibition that did not demand flexibility: the Stopping Task (Schachar & Logan, 1990) and the Negative Priming Task (Tipper, 1985).

Finally, impairments in inhibition have been explored in a range of clinical conditions of childhood; deficits on tasks of inhibition with the added demand for flexibility have been observed. For example, perseverative responding on a discrimination shift learning task has been observed in mentally retarded children (Bhattacharyya & Chattopadhyay, 1983; Umetani, Kitao, & Katada, 1985). School-age boys diagnosed with soft neurological signs and disruptive behavior disorders also exhibited cognitive impulsivity on the Matching Familiar Figures Test (Vitiello, Stoff, Atkins, & Mahoney, 1990). Poor performance on the color–word interference component of the Stroop Test has been documented in children diagnosed with learning disabilities (Barkley et al., 1992), and reading disabilities (Das, Mensink, & Mishra, 1990; Kelly, Best, & Kirk, 1989). Longer latency and increased number of errors on the interference portion of the Stroop is assumed to reflect a problem inhibiting word reading and shifting to color naming. However, because the prepotent response that must be inhibited is verbal (i.e., reading), some have suggested that deficient speech-related processes (e.g., subvocal articulation) may contribute to poor performance. This line of reasoning would help to explain why reading disabled children exhibit impaired performance on the Stroop.

In summary, the three clinical groups that have been identified with executive function impairments have also been found to exhibit inhibition deficits. Children with early treated PKU and those diagnosed as autistic do poorly on tasks that demand inhibition and cognitive flexibility. However, whether or not they would show "pure" inhibition impairments is an empirical question that has been explored only recently in autism (Ozonoff & Jensen, 1999; Ozonoff & Strayer, 1997) and has not been pursued in PKU. The meta-analysis by Pennington and Ozonoff (1996) suggests that children diagnosed with ADHD have the most consistent problems with such pure inhibition tasks; various studies also indicate deficits on cognitive flexibility measures as well.

CONCLUSIONS AND FUTURE DIRECTIONS

In this final section, the convergence among the executive function, working memory, and inhibition domains are examined by addressing the following two questions: To what degree do similar normative age trends emerge across these three domains? What is the evidence that the three clinical groups identified with executive dysfunction (PKU, ADHD, and autism) also exhibit specific deficits in working memory and inhibition? An exploration of the points of intersection among these domains has direct implications for the measurement of executive function across childhood. For example, what do the literatures pertaining to the early development of working memory and inhibition have to offer to the development of measures of executive function for very young children? To what extent do experimental and clinical tasks tend to demand both working memory and inhibition (either as independent or interactive processes) and what are the implications for a working definition of executive function and its measurement? Finally, how does the TOH, an executive function measure that has proven to have good sensitivity in clinical research, fit into the discussion of working memory and inhibition?

Developmental Patterns

What can be concluded regarding the developmental trends observed in executive functions, working memory, and inhibition? Synthesizing such a wide array of literatures can be problematic, and this is the first attempt to do so in order to examine the construct of executive function. The major difficulties one confronts when comparing a variety of studies in a given domain (e.g., inhibition) concern the diversity of conceptualizations that inevitably leads to a broad range of experimental tasks. As should be clear from the earlier review, there is not an agreed on task or set of tasks to assess each of these cognitive domains, and the particular tasks chosen by different researchers will tap different variations of a given domain.

Table 6.2 summarizes the developmental research reviewed in this chapter with an appreciation that somewhat different aspects of the cognitive construct have been explored. The objective is to combine the results across a wide variety of recent developmental studies of executive function, working memory, and inhibition to examine, in a preliminary fashion, whether consistent developmental patterns emerge. To the extent that studies have explored skills in very young children, these results have been noted in terms of the emergence (E) of the process. However, this term should be interpreted cautiously, because generally these studies did not investigate the performance of younger children on the particular tasks. That is, future research may reveal even earlier emergence of skill on these tasks. The maturation (M) of a process means either that the performance at this age is equivalent to adult-level performance (e.g., visual search) or that no further development of the skill is apparent in older children (e.g., motor inhibition). Finally, the developmental transitions (T) in performance typically represent a synthesis of age effects across several studies of that particular aspect of the cognitive domain.

With these caveats in mind, what consistent developmental trends emerge across these three literatures? First, the period between about 18

TABLE 6.2

A Summary of Age Transitions for Executive Function, Working Memory, and Inhibition

Domains	<2	2	3	4	5	6	7	8	9	10	11	12	13	>13
Executive Function														
visual search			E	T		M								
semantic search			E											T+
planning			E	T		T			T			T+		
inhibition/flexibility								T		M		M		
WM & inhibition										T		T		
Working Memory														
visual WM	E				T		T+							
vis. WM (no interf)					M									
verbal WM		E			T			M		M				
Inhibition														
self-control		E	T	M										
motor inhibition							M							
flexibility		E			T		T		M					

Note: E = some evidence of emergence of the skill; T = a significant age transition; T+ = age changes beyond this point are assumed; M = some evidence of maturity of the skill; WM = working memory; WM & inhibition = tasks that appear to require both skills; no interf = task does not include an interference component requiring inhibition.

months and 4 years seems to be a time when the emergence of certain executive functions, working memory, inhibitory processes can be observed. Again, it is important to note that the focus of this chapter is on research conducted with children from toddlerhood through the school years and on the types of tasks appropriate for this age range. On these tasks (e.g., visual search, radial maze test of WM, self-control paradigms, etc.), reliable and relatively effective performance can be measured during these early years. However, there is substantial evidence that more primitive forms of these skills are exhibited on age-appropriate tasks even earlier in development (Diamond, Werker, LaLonde, 1994; Willatts, 1980). Within each domain, certain aspects have a relatively short period of development. For example, organized visual search (Welsh et al., 1991) emerged at age 3, improved at age 4, and showed maturity by age 6. The maturation of performance on this task was facilitated by a developing ability to inhibit the tendency to point to previous targets and to completely switch the focus to the new target at about age 4 (Cuneo & Welsh, 1992; Mutter, 1998). Interestingly, the developmental pattern seen on this single task of executive function dovetails with the development of self-control and motor inhibition skills (both required by the visual search task), which exhibit maturity between age 4 and 7.

Across all three domains, there is evidence of significant developmental improvements between ages 5 and 9 to 12. There are consistent findings that the executive functions of inhibition and flexibility mature between age 10 and 12; performance on verbal working memory tests mature in this same age range. Skill exhibited on verbal and memory tasks requiring cognitive flexibility seems to plateau at about age 9. Interestingly, those skills that appear to show a protracted period of development beyond age 12, visual working memory and the coordination of working memory and inhibition, may be just the processes underlying performance on the planning tasks. Performance on tasks presumed to require planning skills, TOH and TOL, also show a similarly protracted period of development.

How do these age trends relate to some of the new evidence on the functional development of the brain during the school years? Chugani (1994) conducted research that has tracked the development of local cerebral metabolic rates for glucose (lCMRGlc). He suggested that the increase in glucose metabolic rates reflects the overproduction of synaptic connections and neuronal processes that occurs during postnatal development. The decline in lCMRGlc to more adult levels correlates with the selective elimination of excess connectivity; this "sculpting" of the neuronal substrate eventually results in more efficient information processing. Chugani reported that the low rates of cortical lCMRGlc observed in newborns continues to rise until it exceeds adult levels at age 3, plateaus at this high level between ages 4 and 9, and declines thereafter, reaching adult values in the second decade of life. This pattern of energy demand by the brain corresponds fairly well to the developmental patterns seen in executive function, working memory- and inhibition: Skills emerge during the first 4 years of life, with many reaching maturity between age 9 and 12.

Clinical Manifestations

The second major question addressed in this chapter concerns the degree to which research has documented working memory and inhibition deficits in the three clinical conditions typically regarded as manifesting an executive dysfunction. Table 6.3 indicates the particular executive function deficits that research has revealed so far in the three clinical groups: PKU, ADHD, and autism. Specific executive function studies of these three groups were reviewed to establish that these diagnostic conditions have been, to the greatest extent, identified with executive function deficits. It was not relevant here to explore the existence of specific executive function deficits in other clinical conditions.

Table 6.3 also summarizes the clinical literature reviewed with regard to the domains of working memory and inhibition to evaluate the degree of convergence with the executive function literature. Regarding the first clinical condition, PKU, there is some evidence of deficits on tasks of visual working memory and inhibition plus cognitive flexibility. More re-

TABLE 6.3
Executive Function, Working Memory, and Inhibition
Impairments in Clinical Conditions of Childhood

	Clinical Groups							
Deficits	PKU	ADHD	Autism	LD	RD	MathLD	EP	DS
E F								
planning	X	X	X					
search	X							
inhibition	X	X						
flexibility	X	?	X					
WM	X							
W M								
visual WM	X	X	X					
verbal WM	?	?	X	X	X	X		X
INHIBITION								
"pure" inhib		X						
flexibility	X	?	X	X	X		X	X

Note: EF = executive function; WM = working memory; "pure" inhib = inhibition that does not include the demand for flexibility; PKU = phenylketonuria; ADHD = attention deficit hyperactivity disorder; LD = learning disability; RD = reading disability; MathLD = math disability; EP = epilepsy; DS = Downs Syndrome; X = evidence of impairment; ? = some inconsistency in research findings of impairment.

search is needed to explore the quality of performance on tasks assessing verbal working memory and pure motor inhibition. In the case of ADHD, there are fairly clear findings indicating visual working memory and pure inhibition impairments; there is less consistent evidence of problems with verbal working memory and cognitive flexibility. Finally, autism is the one group in which verbal working memory impairments typically are observed along with difficulties in flexible set shifting.

Taken together, there is accumulating evidence that there are working memory and inhibition impairments in the same clinical conditions that have been identified with executive dysfunction. To some degree, the existence of certain inhibition deficits (e.g., inflexibility on the WCST) has served as evidence of both executive function and inhibition impairments. The domain of inhibition needs to be explored in these three groups in its own right, with a more specific focus on relevant variations such as pure motor inhibition, inhibition plus cognitive flexibility, and so on. Evaluation of working memory deficits in these groups has been somewhat more separate from the investigation of executive function; however, a more comprehensive and fine-grained analysis of both the visual and verbal working memory performances of these children would help to resolve current inconsistencies in the literature.

As previously discussed, converging neuroimaging, neurochemical, and behavioral data have characterized PKU, ADHD, and autism as possible prefrontal dysfunction conditions. The cognitive manifestation of prefrontal dysfunction has been referred to as difficulties with executive function, and the evidence reviewed here suggests that difficulties with working memory and inhibition also typify these conditions. However, it is important to note that other clinical conditions, presumably not the outcome of a specific frontal lobe dysfunction, also exhibit impairments in working memory and inhibition. In particular, verbal working memory and cognitive flexibility deficits have been observed in groups in which the neurological insult may be global (e.g., LD, epilepsy, Down syndrome) or primarily localized to the posterior cortex (e.g., RD). This contradiction between the presumed frontal mediation of working memory and inhibition and the deficiencies observed in such clinical groups has not been resolved adequately in the theoretical literature. It is possible that this apparent contradiction reflects the perennial problems with the precise behavioral measurement of these cognitive domains, complicating the direct comparison across studies.

Measurement Issues

This side-by-side comparison of executive function, working memory, and inhibition highlights some important issues with regard to the measurement of the skills attributed to the frontal cortex. First, the relatively small set of studies that has been designed specifically to track the normal development of executive functions has utilized a wide array of tasks, including measures of planning, organized search, motor inhibition, flexible set-shifting, and working memory. The apparent convergences across the three cognitive domains in terms of development and clinical manifestations suggests that it might be helpful to "mine" the working memory and inhibition literatures for more precise and specific measures of executive function. Furthermore, although the executive function research generally has not tested children under age 6 (see Diamond et al., 1997; Luciano & Nelson, 1999; Welsh et al., 1991, for exceptions), the apparent early emergence of some aspects of working memory and inhibition indicate ways in which the early functional development of executive functions might be assessed.

Second, the potential interaction between working memory and inhibition processes is one that deserves further consideration in the context of the development of new measures of executive function. Examining tasks that have been specifically referred to as tapping either working memory or inhibition, it becomes clear that it is often the case that both skills are required to a greater or lesser degree. For example, in many measures of working memory, optimal performance demands that the child inhibit the tendency to incorporate irrelevant information into the current working memory representation. Similarly, in nearly all measures of inhibition, children must maintain in working memory the rules governing their responses. That is, even in the simplest "pure" motor inhibition task, the rule that states "Do not respond to X" must be kept active in working memory. In the more complex inhibition task that also requires flexibility, there are more rules to be activated in working memory (i.e., "Do not respond to X with response A, but with response B."). Therefore, it is possible that the increasing demands for inhibition in such tasks is confounded with an increasing working memory load.

In the wide variety of tasks that appear to require both inhibition and working memory, the developmental transitions and clinical manifestations are more difficult to interpret. Are the age changes occurring in inhibition or working memory? Do children diagnosed with a particular clinical condition have a core deficit in inhibition or working memory? Of course, these questions are germane only if these two processes are actually independent contributors to performance on the task. Theoretical accounts reviewed earlier in the chapter have suggested that working memory and inhibition interact because they both draw on the same limited pool of resources, and experiments specifically designed to examine this interaction (e.g., Roberts et al., 1994) have supported this view. Whether there is an interaction of working memory and inhibition in the developmental tasks reviewed in this chapter is an empirical question; it might be speculated that measures of flexibility are contexts in which this interaction occurs.

Finally, the degree to which other measures of executive function, such as visual search, verbal fluency, and planning tasks demand working memory and/or inhibition processes must be addressed. For example, the TOH has been referred to as a planning task, but the cognitive components comprising "planning" have never been entirely clear (e.g., Scholnick, Friedman, & Wallner-Allen, 1997). It would appear that planning a sequence of moves prior to action, as is required by the TOH, would necessitate working memory resources for generating, monitoring, and revising the plan (Goldman-Rakic, 1987). However, empirical evidence of an association between working memory and TOH performance has been mixed; one study found a significant correlation between TOH and one verbal working memory (Humes, Welsh, Retzlaff, & Cookson, 1997) and another study found no relation with spatial working memory tests (Welsh et al., 1999). Furthermore, there is evidence that subjects who perform well on the TOH are able to inhibit direct moves to the goal, and defer them to a later time (Goel & Grafman, 1995; Welsh, 1991; Welsh, Cicerello, Cuneo, & Brennan, 1995). There is some evidence that inhibition and flexible shifting is related to TOH performance (Welsh et al., 1999). Given the protracted course of development and the clear pattern of deficits in the three "frontal dysfunction" groups, it would be of great value to understand the cognitive processes underlying performance on this task.

Summary

The objective of this chapter was to explore the developmental and clinical variations in executive function, a nascent construct for which several operational definitions exist. The controversy surrounding the conceptualization of executive function was reviewed, with a specific focus on the proposal that working memory and inhibition might serve as a more parsimonious description of the cognitive functions mediated by the frontal cortex. To examine this proposal, the intersections among the three domains in terms of developmental patterns and clinical manifestations were explored, and it appears that there are interesting convergences. An understanding of the typical and atypical development of frontal lobe function will be facilitated by a more precise definition of the executive function construct, which should include closer attention to the working memory and inhibition components. Current and future executive function tasks must be examined more carefully with respect to their demands for these component processes. Moreover, there must be an appreciation for the complex nature of the developmental emergence of executive function processes in order to design tasks that will reliably and validly assess this domain of cognitive function across the life span.

REFERENCES

Adams, A. M., & Gathercole, S. E. (1995). Phonological working memory and speech production in preschool children. *Journal of Speech & Hearing Research, 38*, 403–414.

Adams, A. M., & Gathercole, S. E. (1996). Phonological working memory and spoken language development in young children. *Quarterly Journal of Experimental Psychology, 49A*, 216–233.

Aman, C. J., Roberts, R. J., Jr., & Pennington, B. F. (1998). A neuropsychological examination of the underlying deficit in ADHD: The frontal lobe vs right parietal lobe theories. *Developmental Psychology, 34*, 956–969.

Anderson, P., Anderson, V., & Lajoie, G. (1996). The Tower of London test: Validation and standardization for pediatric populations. *Clinical Neuropsychology, 10*, 54–56.

Baddeley, A. D. (1992). Working memory. *Science, 255*, 556–559.

Baddeley, A. D., & Hitch, G. J. (1974). Working memory. In G. H. Bower (Ed.), *The psychology of learning and motivation* (Vol. 8, pp. 47–89). New York: Academic Press.

Barkley, R. A. (1981). *Hyperactive children: A handbook for diagnosis and treatment.* New York: Guilford.

Barkley, R. A., Grodzinsky, G., DuPaul, G. J. (1992). Frontal lobe functions in attention deficit disorder with and without hyperactivity: A review and research report. *Journal of Abnormal Child Psychology, 20*, 163–188.

Baron-Cohen, S., Cross, P., Crowson, M., & Robertson, M. (1994). Can children with Gilles de la Tourette syndrome edit their intentions? *Psychological Medicine, 24*, 29–40.

Becker, M. G., Isaac, W., & Hynd, G. W. (1987). Neuropsychological development of nonverbal behaviors attributed to "frontal lobe" functioning. *Developmental Neuropsychology, 3*, 275–298.

Bell, J. A., & Livesey, P. J. (1985). Cue significance and response regulation in 3- to 6-year-old children's learning of multiple choice discrimination tasks. *Developmental Psychobiology, 18*, 229–245.

Bennetto, L., Pennington, B. F., & Rogers, S. J. (1996). Intact and impaired memory functions in autism. *Child Development, 67*, 1816–1835.

Benton, A. L. (1991). The prefrontal region: Its early history. In H. S. Levin, H. M. Eisenberg, & A. L. Benton (Eds.), *Frontal lobe function and dysfunction* (pp. 3–32). New York: Oxford University Press.

Bhanttacharyya, A. K., & Chattopadhyay, P. K. (1983). Response-inhibition deficit in mentally retarded children. *Indian Psychologist, 2*, 50–56.

Bjorklund, D. F., & Harnishfeger, K. K. (1990). The resources construct in cognitive development: Diverse sources of evidence and a theory of inefficient inhibition. *Developmental Review, 10*, 48–71.

Bolter, J. F., & Long, C. J. (1985). Methodological issues in research in developmental neuropsychology. In L. C. Hartlage & C. F. Telzrow (Eds.), *The neuropsychology of individual differences: A developmental perspective* (pp. 41–59). New York: Plenum.

Boone, K. B., Ponton, M. O., Gorsuch, R. L., Gonzalez, J. J., & Miller, B. L. (1998). Factor analysis of four measures of prefrontal lobe functioning. *Archives of Clinical Neuropsychology, 13*, 585–595.

Borys, S. V., Spitz, H. H., & Dorans, B. A. (1982). Tower of Hanoi performance of retarded young adults and nonretarded as a function of solution length and goal state. *Journal of Experimental Child Psychology*, *33*, 87–110.

Boucher, J. (1977). Alternation and sequencing behavior and response to novelty in autistic children. *Journal of Child Psychology & Psychiatry*, *18*, 67–72.

Boucugnani, L. L., & Jones, R. W. (1989). Behaviors analogous to frontal lobe dysfunction in children with attention deficit hyperactivity disorder. *Archives of Clinical Neuropsychology*, *4*, 161, 173.

Carpenter, P. A., & Just, M. A. (1989). The role of working memory in language comprehension. In D. Klahr & K. Kotovsky (Eds.), *Complex information processing: The impact of Herbert A. Simpson* (pp. 31–68). Hillsdale, NJ: Lawrence Erlbaum Associates.

Case, R. (1985). *Intellectual development*. New York: Academic Press.

Case, R. (1992). The role of the frontal lobes in the regulation of cognitive development. *Brain & Cognition*, *20*, 51–73.

Chamove, A. S., & Molinario, T. J. (1978). Monkey retarded learning analysis. *Journal of Mental Deficiency Research*, *22*, 223.

Chelune, G. J., & Baer, R. L. (1986). Developmental norms for the Wisconsin Card Sorting Test. *Journal of Clinical & Experimental Neuropsychology*, *8*, 219–228.

Chelune, G. J., Ferguson, W., Koon, R., & Dickey, T. O. (1986). Frontal lobe disinhibition in attention deficit disorder. *Child Psychiatry and Human Development*, *16*, 221–234.

Chelune, G. J., & Thompson, L. L. (1987). Evaluation of the general sensitivity of the Wisconsin Card Sorting Test among young and older children. *Developmental Neuropsychology*, *3*, 81–90.

Chugani, H. T. (1994). Development of regional brain glucose metabolism in relation to behavior and plasticity. In G. Dawson & K. W. Fischer (Eds.), *Human behavior and the developing brain* (pp. 153–175). New York: Guilford.

Cohen, J. D., & Servan-Schreiber, D. (1992). Context, cortex, and dopamine: A connectionist approach to behavior and biology in schizophrenia. *Psychological Review*, *99*, 45–77.

Conway, A. R., & Engle, R. W. (1994). Working memory and retrieval: A resource dependent inhibition model. *Journal of Experimental Psychology: General*, *123*, 254–373.

Costa, P. T., Jr., & McCrae, R. R. (1988). Personality in adulthood: A six-year longitudinal study of self-reports and spouse ratings on the NEO personality inventory. *Journal of Personality and Social Psychology*, *38*, 793–800.

Cournoyer, M., & Trudel, M. (1991). Behavioral correlates of self-control at 33 months. *Infant Behavior & Development*, *14*, 497–503.

Crammond, J. (1992). Analyzing the basic cognitive developmental processes of children with specific types of learning disability. In R. Case (Ed.), *The mind's staircase: Exploring the conceptual underpinnings of human thought and knowledge* (pp. 285–303). Hillsdale, NJ: Lawrence Erlbaum Associates.

Culbertson, W. C., & Zillmer, E. A. (1998). The Tower of London-sub(DX): A standardized approach to assessing executive functioning in children. *Archives of Clinical Neuropsychology*, *13*, 285–301.

Cuneo, K. M., & Welsh, M. C. (1992). Perseveration in young children: Developmental and neuropsychological perspectives. *Child Study Journal*, *22*, 73–91.

Daneman, M., & Carpenter, P. A, (1980). Individual differences in working memory and reading. *Journal of Verbal Learning & Verbal Behavior*, *19*, 450–466.

Daneman, M., & Carpenter, P. A. (1983). Individual differences in integrating information between and within sentences. *Journal of Experimental Psychology: Learning, Memory & Cognition*, *9*, 561–584.

Das, J. P., Mensink, D., & Mishra, R. K. (1990). Cognitive processes separating good and poor readers when IQ is covaried. *Learning & Individual Differences*, *2*, 423–436.

Davis, D. D., McIntyre, C. W., Murray, M. E., & Mims, S. K. S. (1986). Cognitive styles in children with dietary treated phenylketonuria. *Educational and Psychological Research, 6,* 9–15.

Dawson, G., & Fischer, K. W. (Eds.). (1994). *Human behavior and the developing brain.* New York: Guilford.

Dehaene, S., & Changeux, J. P. (1991). The Wisconsin Card Sorting Test: Theoretical analysis and modeling in a neuronal network. *Cerebral Cortex, 1,* 62–79.

Dempster, F. (1993). Resistance to interference: Developmental changes in a basic processing mechanism. In M. L. Howe & R. Pasnack (Eds.), *Emerging themes in cognitive development: Vol. I. Foundations* (pp. 3–27). New York: Springer-Verlag.

Denckla, M. B. (1996). Biological correlates of learning and attention: What is relevant to learning disability and attention deficit hyperactivity disorder?. *Journal of Developmental & Behavioral Pediatrics, 17,* 114–119.

Diamond, A. (1991). Guidelines for the study of brain–behavior relationships during development. In H. S. Levin, H. M. Eisenberg, & A. L. Benton (Eds.), *Frontal lobe function and dysfunction* (pp. 339–378). New York: Oxford University Press.

Diamond, A., Hurwitz, W., Lee, E. Y., Bockes, T., Grover, W., & Minarcik, C. (1993, April). *Cognitive deficits on frontal cortex tasks in children with early-treated PKU: Results of two years of longitudinal study.* Paper presented at SRCD, Los Angeles, CA.

Diamond, A., Prevor, M. B., Callender, G., & Druin, D. P. (1997). Prefrontal cortex cognitive deficits in children treated early and continuously for PKU. *Monographs of the Society for Research in Child Development, 62*(4, Serial No. 252).

Diamond, A., Werker, J. F., & Lalonde, C. (1994). Toward understanding commonalities in the development of object search, detour navigation, categorization, and speech perception. In G. Dawson & K. W. Fischer (Eds.), *Human behavior and the developing brain* (pp. 380–426). New York: Guilford.

Diaz, S. (1974). *Cucui scale: Technical Manual Multilingual Assessment Program.* Stockton Unified School District, Stockton, CA.

Douglas, V. I. (1983). Attentional and cognitive problems. In M. Rutter (Ed.), *Developmental neuropsychiatry* (pp. 280–329). New York: Guilford.

Douglas, V. I. (1985, April). *Attention deficit disorder.* Invited address at the annual meeting of the Society for Research in Child Development, Toronto, Ontario, Canada.

Douglas, V. I. (1988). Cognitive deficits in children with attention deficit disorder with hyperactivity. In L. M. Bloomingdale & J. Sergeant (Eds.), *Attention deficit disorder: Criteria, cognition, intervention. A book supplement of the Journal of Child Psychology and Psychiatry (No. 5).* New York: Pergamon.

Engle, R. W., Carullo, J. J., & Collins, K. W. (1991). Individual differences in working memory for comprehension and following directions. *Journal of Educational Research, 84,* 253–262.

Everett, J., Thomas, J., Cote, F., Levesque, J., & Michaud, D. (1991). Cognitive effects of psychostimulant medication in hyperactive children. *Child Psychiatry & Human Development, 22,* 79–87.

Faust, D., Libon, D., & Pueschel, S. (1986–1987). Neuropsychological functioning in treated phenylketonuria. *International Journal of Psychiatry in Medicine, 16,* 169–177.

Fiducia, D., & O'Leary, D. S. (1990). Development of a behavior attributed to the frontal lobes and the relationship to other cognitive functions. *Developmental Neuropsychology, 6,* 85–94.

Flavell, J. H. (1971). First discussant's comments. What is memory development the development of? *Human Development, 14,* 272–278.

Foreman, N., Warry, R., & Murray, P. (1990). Development of reference and working spatial memory in preschool children. *Journal of General Psychology, 117,* 267–276.

Frith, U. (1972). Cognitive mechanisms in autism: Experiments with color and tone sequence production. *Journal of Autism & Child Schizophrenia, 2,* 160–173.

Fuster, J. M. (1985). The prefrontal cortex, mediator of cross-temporal contingencies. *Human Neurobiology, 4,* 169–179.

Gathercole, S. E., & Adams, A. M. (1993). Phonological working memory in very young children. *Developmental Psychology, 29,* 770–778.

Gerstadt, C. L., Hong, Y. J., & Diamond, A. (1994). The relationship between cognition and action: Performance of children 3½–7 years old on a Stroop-like day-night test. *Cognition, 53,* 129–153.

Gholson, B., Levine, M., & Phillips, S. (1972). Hypothesis, strategies and stereotypes in discrimination learning. *Journal of Experimental Child Psychology, 13,* 423–446.

Gnys, J. A., & Willis, G. (1991). Validation of executive function tasks with young children. *Developmental Neuropsychology, 7,* 487–501.

Goel, V., & Grafman, J. (1995). Are the frontal lobes implicated in "planning" functions? Interpreting data from the Tower of Hanoi. *Neuropsychologia, 33,* 623–642.

Goldman-Rakic, P. S. (1987). Development of cortical circuitry and cognitive function. *Child Development, 58,* 601–622.

Gorenstein, E. E., Mammato, C. A., & Sandy, J. M. (1989). Performance of inattentive-overactive children on selected measures of prefrontal-type function. *Journal of Clinical Psychology, 45,* 619–632.

Grodzinsky, G. M., & Diamond, R. (1992). Frontal lobe functioning in boys with attention-deficit hyperactivity disorder. *Developmental Neuropsychology, 8,* 427–445.

Gualin, C. A., & Campbell, T. F. (1994). Procedure for assessing verbal working memory in normal school-age children: Some preliminary data. *Perceptual & Motor Skills, 79,* 55–64.

Gualtieri, C. T., & Hicks, R. E. (1978). Neuropharmacology of methylphenidate and a neural substrate for childhood hyperactivity. *Psychiatric Clinics of North America, 6,* 875–892.

Halberstadt, A. G., Grotjohn, D. K., Johnson, C. A., & Fruth, M. S. (1992). Children's abilities and strategies in managing the facial display of affect. *Journal of Nonverbal Behavior, 16,* 215–230.

Harnishfeger, K. K., & Bjorklund, D. F. (1993). The ontogeny of inhibition mechanisms: A renewed approach to cognitive development. In M. L. Howe & R. Pasnack (Eds.), *Emerging themes in cognitive development: Vol. I. Foundations* (pp. 28–49). New York: Springer-Verlag.

Harris, E. L., Schuerholz, L. J., Singer, H. S., Reader, M. J., Brown, J. E., Cox, C., Mohr, J., Chase, G. A., & Denckla, M. B. (1995). Executive function in children with Tourette syndrome and/or attention deficit hyperactivity disorder. *Journal of the International Neuropsychological Society, 1,* 511–516.

Hermelin, B., & O'Connor, N. (1970). *Psychological experiments with autistic children.* New York: Pergamon.

Hitch, G. J., Halliday, S., Scaafstal, A. M., & Schraagen, J. M. (1988). Visual working memory in young children. *Memory & Cognition, 16,* 120–132.

Hitch, G. J., & McAuley, E. (1991). Working memory in children with specific arithmetical learning difficulties. *British Journal of Psychology, 82,* 375–386.

Hitch, G. J., Woodin, M. E., & Baker, S. (1989). Visual and phonological components of working memory in children. *Memory & Cognition, 17,* 175–185.

Hughes, C., Russell, J., & Robbins, T. W. (1994). Evidence for executive dysfunction in autism. *Neuropsychologia, 32,* 477, 492.

Hulme, C. (1984). Developmental differences in the effects of acoustic similarity on memory span. *Developmental Psychology, 20,* 650–652.

Hulme, C., & Mackenzie, S. (1992). *Working memory and severe learning difficulties.* Hillsdale, NJ: Lawrence Erlbaum Associates.

Humes, G. E., Welsh, M. C., Retzlaff, P. D., & Cookson, N. (1997). Towers of Hanoi and London: Reliability and validity of two executive function tasks. *Assessment, 4,* 249–257.

Huttenlocher, P. R. (1990). Morphometric study of human cerebral cortex development. *Neuropsychologia, 28,* 517–527.

Huttenlocher, P. R. (1994). Synaptogenesis in human cerebral cortex. In G. Dawson & K. W. Fischer (Eds.), *Human behavior and the developing brain* (pp. 137–152). New York: Guilford.

Johnson, C. J. (1994). Inhibitory mechanisms in selection among multiple object names. *Cognitive Development, 9,* 293–309.

Kagan, J., Rosman, B. L., Day, L., Albert, J., & Phillips, W. (1964). Information processing in the child: Significance of analytic and reflective attitudes. *Psychological Monographs, 78*(1, Whole No. 578).

Kelly, M. S., Best, C. T., & Kirk, U. (1989). Cognitive processing deficits in reading disabilities: A prefrontal cortical hypotheses. *Brain & Cognition, 11,* 275–293.

Kepler, M. D. (1998). *Assessing executive functions using the Stroop, Tower of London, Children's Behavior Questionnaire, and Behavior Rating Inventory of Executive Functions.* Unpublished master's thesis, University of Northern Colorado, Greeley, CO.

Kimberg, D. Y., & Farah, M. J. (1993). A unified account of cognitive impairments following frontal lobe damage: The role of working memory in complex, organized behavior. *Journal of Experimental Psychology: General, 122,* 411–428.

Klahr, D. (1978). Goal formation, planning, and learning by preschool problem solvers or: "My socks are in the dryer". In R. S. Siegler (Ed.), *Children's thinking: What develops?* (pp. 181–212). Hillsdale, NJ: Lawrence Erlbaum Associates.

Kolb, B., & Whishaw, I. (1985). *Fundamentals of human neuropsychology.* New York: Freeman.

Kopp, C. B. (1982). Antecedents of self-regulation: A developmental perspective. *Developmental Psychology, 18,* 199–214.

Krause, W. L., Halminski, M., McDonald, L., Dembure, P., Salvo, R., Freides, D., & Elsas, L. J. (1985). Biochemical and neuropsychological effects of elevated plasma phenylalanine in patients with treated phenylketonuria: A model for the study of phenylalanine and brain function in man. *Journal of Clinical Investigation, 75,* 40–48.

Krasnegor, N., Lyon, R., & Goldman-Rakic, P. S. (Eds.). (1998). *Development of the prefrontal cortex: Evolution, neurobiology, and behavior.* Baltimore: Brookes.

Levin, H. S., Eisenberg, H. M., & Benton, A. L. (Eds.). (1991). *Frontal lobe function and dysfunction.* New York: Oxford University Press.

Levin, H. S., Mendelsohn, D., Lilly, M. J., Fletcher, J. M., Culhane, K. A., Chapman, S. B., Harward, H., Kusnerick, L., Bruce, D., & Eisenberg, H. M. (1994). Tower of London performance in relation to magnetic resonance imaging following closed head injury to children. *Neuropsychologia, 28,* 126–140.

Levine, D. J., & Prueitt, P. S. (1989). Modeling some effects of frontal lobe damage: Novelty and perseveration. *Neural Networks, 2,* 103–116.

Livesey, D. J., & Morgan, G. A. (1991). The development of response inhibition in 4- and 5-year-old children. *Australian Journal of Psychology, 43,* 133–137.

Logue, A. W., & Charraro, A. (1992). Self-control and impulsiveness in preschool children. *The Psychological Record, 42,* 189–204.

Lou, H. C., Henriksen, L., & Bruhn, P. (1984). Focal cerebral hypoperfusion in children with dysphasia and/or attention deficit disorder. *Archives of Neurology, 41,* 825–829.

Luciana, M., & Nelson, C. A. (1999). The functional emergence of prefrontally-guided working memory systems in four-to-eight-year-old children. *Neuropsychologia, 36,* 273–293.

Luria, A. R. (1966). *Higher cortical functions in man.* New York: Basic Books.

Luria, A. R. (1973). *The working brain.* New York: Basic Books.

Mattes, J. A. (1980). The role of frontal lobe dysfunction in childhood hyperkinesis. *Comprehensive Psychiatry, 21,* 358–369.

Mazzocco, M. M., Nord, A. M., van Doorninck, W. J., Greene, C. L., Kovar, C. G., & Pennington, B. F. (1994). Cognitive development among children with early treated phenylketonuria. *Developmental Neuropsychology, 10,* 133–151.

McCall, R. B. (1994). What process mediates prediction of childhood IQ from infant habituation and recognition memory? Speculations on the roles of inhibition and rate of information processing. *Intelligence, 18,* 107–125.

Menna, R. (1989). *Working memory development: An EEG investigation.* Unpublished master's thesis, University of Toronto, Toronto, Canada.

Milich, R., & Kramer, J. (1984). Reflections on impulsivity: An empirical investigation of impulsivity as a construct. *Advances in Learning & Behavioral Disabilities, 3,* 57–94.

Miller, P. H., & Harris, Y. R. (1988). Preschoolers' strategies of attention on a same-different task. *Developmental Psychology, 24,* 628–633.

Milner, B. (1964). Some effects of frontal lobectomy in man. In J. Warren & K. Akert (Eds.), *The frontal granular cortex and behavior* (pp. 313–334). New York: McGraw-Hill.

Mischel, W., & Patterson, C. J. (1979). Effective plans for self-control in children. In W. A. Collins (Ed.), *Minnesota symposia on child psychology* (Vol. 11, pp. 199–230). Hillsdale, NJ: Lawrence Erlbaum Associates.

Morra, S., Moizo, C., & Scopesi, A. (1988). Working memory (or the M operator) and the planning of children's drawings. *Journal of Experimental Child Psychology, 46,* 41–73.

Mutter, B. S. (1998). *Why do three-year-olds fail false-belief tasks: Inhibition or working memory?* Unpublished master's thesis, University of Northern Colorado, Greeley, CO.

Norman, D., & Shallice, T. (1986). Attention to action: Willed and automatic control of behaviour. Center for human information processing (Technical Report No. 99). Reprinted in revised form in R. J. Davidson, G. E. Schwartz, & D. Shapiro (Eds.), *Consciousness and self-regulation* (Vol. 4). New York: Plenum.

Oades, R. D. (1987). Attention deficit disorder with hyperactivity: The contribution of chatecholaminergic activity. *Progress in Neurobiology, 29,* 365–391.

Olson, S. L. (1989). Assessment of impulsivity in preschoolers: Cross measure convergences, longitudinal stability, and relevance to social competence. *Journal of Clinical Child Psychology, 18,* 176–183.

Olson, S. L., Baytes, J. E., & Bayles, K. (1990). Early antecedent of childhood impulsivity: The role of parent–child interaction, cognitive competence and temperament. *Journal of Abnormal Child Psychology, 18,* 317–334.

Owen, A. M., Downes, J. J., Sahakian, B. J., Polkey, C. E., & Robbins, T. W. (1990). Planning and spatial working memory following frontal lobe lesions in man. *Neuropsychologia, 28,* 1021–1034.

Ozonoff, S., & Jensen, J. (1999). Specific executive function profiles in three neurodevelopmental disorders. *Journal of Autism and Developmental Disorders, 29,* 171–177.

Ozonoff, S., & McEvoy, R. E. (1994). A longitudinal study of executive function and theory of mind development in autism. *Development & Psychopathology, 6,* 415–431.

Ozonoff, S., Pennington, B. F., & Rogers, S. J. (1991). Executive function deficits in high-functioning autistic individuals: Relationships to theory of mind. *Journal of Child Psychology & Psychiatry & Allied Disciplines, 32,* 1081–1105.

Ozonoff, S., & Strayer, D. L. (1997). Inhibitory function in nonretarded children with autism. *Journal of Autism and Developmental Disorders, 27,* 59–77.

Ozonoff, S., Strayer, D. L., McMahon, W. M., & Filloux, F. (1994). Executive function abilities in autism and Tourette syndrome: An information-processing approach. *Journal of Child Psychology & Psychiatry & Allied Disciplines, 35,* 1015–1032.

Passler, M. A., Isaac, W., & Hynd, G. W. (1985). Neuropsychological development of behavior attributed to frontal lobe functioning in children. *Developmental Neuropsychology, 1,* 349–370.

Pearson, D. A., Yafee, L. S., Loveland, K. A., & Norton, A. (1995). Covert visual attention in children with attention deficit hyperactivity disorder: Evidence for developmental immaturity?. *Development & Psychopathology, 7,* 351–367.

Pennington, B. F. (1994). The working memory function of the prefrontal cortices: Implications for developmental and individual differences. In M. M. Haith, J. B. Benson, R. Roberts, & B. F. Pennington (Eds.), *The development of future-oriented processes* (pp. 243–289). Chicago: U. of Chicago Press.

Pennington, B. F. (1998). Dimensions of executive functions in normal and abnormal development. In N. A. Krasnegor, G. R. Lyon, & P. S. Goldman-Rakic (Eds.), *Development of the prefrontal cortex: Evolution, neurobiology, and behavior* (pp. 265–281). Baltimore: Brookes.

Pennington, B. F., Benneto, L., McAleer, O. K., & Roberts, R. J. (1996). Executive functions and working memory: Theoretical and measurement issues. In G. R. Lyon & N. A. Krasnegor (Eds.), *Attention, memory, and executive function* (pp. 327–348). Baltimore: Brookes.

Pennington, B. F., Groisser, D., & Welsh, M. C. (1993). Contrasting cognitive deficits in attention deficit hyperactivity disorder versus reading disability. *Developmental Psychology, 29,* 511–523.

Pennington, B. F., & Ozonoff, S. (1996). Executive functions and developmental psychopathology. *Journal of Child Psychology & Psychiatry & Allied Disciplines, 37,* 51–87.

Pennington, B. F., van Doornick, W. J., & McCabe, E. R. B. (1985). Neuropsychological deficits in early treated phenylketonuric children. *American Journal of Mental Deficiency, 89,* 467–474.

Pennington, B. F., & Welsh, M. C. (1985). Neuropsychology and developmental psychopathology. In D. Cicchetti & D. J. Cohen (Eds.), *Manual of developmental psychopathology* (Vol. 1, pp. 254–290). New York: Wiley.

Perecman, E. (Ed.). (1987). *The frontal lobes revisited.* New York: IRBN Press.

Perret, E. (1974). The left frontal lobe of man and the suppression of habitual responses in verbal categorical behavior. *Neuropsychologia, 16,* 527–537.

Prior, M. R., & Hoffman, W. (1990). Neuropsychological testing of autistic children through an exploration with frontal lobe tests. *Journal of Autism and Developmental Disorders, 20,* 581–590.

Reader, M. J., Harris, E. L., Schuerholz, L. J., & Denckla, M. B. (1994). Attention deficit hyperactivity disorder and executive dysfunction. *Developmental Neuropsychology, 10,* 493–512.

Ris, M. D., Williams, S. E., Hunt, M. M., Berry, H. K., & Leslie, N. (1994). Early-treated phenylketonuria: Adult neuropsychologic outcome. *Journal of Pediatrics, 124,* 388–392.

Robbins, P. M. (1992). A comparison of behavioral and attentional functioning in children diagnosed as hyperactive or learning-disabled. *Journal of Abnormal Child Psychology, 20,* 65–82.

Roberts, R. J., Hager, L. D., & Heron, C. (1994). Prefrontal cognitive processes: Working memory and inhibition in the antisaccade task. *Journal of Experimental Psychology: General, 123,* 374–393.

Roberts, R. J., & Pennington, B. F. (1996). An interactive framework for examining prefrontal cognitive processes. *Developmental Neuropsychology, 12,* 105–126.

Rosenthal, R. H., & Allen, T. W. (1978). An examination of attention, arousal, and learning dysfunctions of hyperkinetic children. *Psychological Bulletin, 85,* 689–715.

Rumsey, J. M. (1985). Conceptual problem-solving in highly verbal, nonretarded autistic men. *Journal of Autism and Developmental Disorders, 15,* 23–36.

Rumsey, J. M., & Hamburger, S. D. (1988). Neuropsychological findings in high-functioning autistic men with infantile autism, residual state. *Journal of Clinical and Experimental Neuropsychology, 10,* 201–221.

Rumsey, J. M., & Hamburger, S. D. (1990). Neuropsychological divergence of high-level autism and severe dyslexia. *Journal of Autism and Developmental Disorders, 20,* 155–168.

Schachar, R., & Logan, G. D. (1990). Impulsivity and inhibitory control in normal development and childhood psychopathology. *Developmental Psychology, 26,* 710–720.

Schachar, R. J., Tannock, R., & Logan, C. (1993). Inhibitory control, impulsiveness, and attention deficit hyperactivity disorder. *Clinical Psychology Review, 13,* 721–739.

Schachar, R., Tannock, R., Marriot, M., & Logan, G. D. (1995). Deficient inhibitory control in attention deficit hyperactivity disorder. *Journal of Abnormal Child Psychology, 23,* 411–437.

Scholnick, E. K., Friedman, S. L., & Wallner-Allen, K. E. (1997). What do they really measure? A comparative analysis of planning tasks. In S. L. Friedman & E. K. Scholnick (Eds.), *The developmental psychology of planning: When, how and why do we plan?* (pp. 127–156). Hillsdale: NJ: Lawrence Erlbaum Associates.

Shallice, T., & Burgess, P. (1991). Higher-order cognitive impairments and frontal lobe lesions in man. In H. S. Levin, H. M. Eisenberg, & A. L. Benton (Eds.), *Frontal lobe function and dysfunction* (pp. 125–138). New York: Oxford University Press.

Shaywitz, S. E., Shaywitz, B. A., Cohen, D. J., & Young, J. G. (1983). Monoaminergic mechanisms in hyperactivity. In M. Rutter (Ed.), *Developmental neuropsychiatry* (pp. 330–347). New York: Guilford.

Shue, K. L., & Douglas, V. I. (1992). Attention deficit hyperactivity disorder and the frontal lobe syndrome. *Brain & Cognition, 20,* 104–124.

Siegler, R. S. (1983). Information processing approaches to development. In W. Kessen (Ed.), *Paul H. Mussen handbook of child psychology: Vol 1. History, theory, and methods* (pp. 129–211). New York: Wiley.

Siegel, L. S., & Ryan, E. B. (1989). The development of working memory in normally achieving and subtypes of learning disabled children. *Child Development, 60,* 973–980.

Spreen, O., Risser, A. H., & Edgell, D. (1995). *Developmental neuropsychology.* New York: Oxford University Press.

Stage, S. A., & Wagner, R. K. (1992). Development of young children's phonological and orthographic knowledge as revealed by their spellings. *Developmental Psychology, 28,* 287–296.

Stamm, J. S., & Kreder, S. V. (1979). Minimal brain dysfunction: Psychological and neuropsychological disorders in hyperkinetic children. In M. S. Gazzaniga (Ed.), *Handbook of behavioral neurology: Vol. 2. Neuropsychology* (pp. 119–150). New York: Plenum.

Stemerdink, N. B. A., van der Molen, M. W., Kalverboer, A. F., van der Meere, J. J., Huisman, J., de Jong, L. W., Slijper, F. M. E., Verkerk, P. H., & van Spronsen, F. J. (1999). Prefrontal dysfunction in early and continuously treated Phenylketonuria. *Developmental Neuropsychology, 16,* 29–57.

Stuss, D. T., & Benson, D. F. (1984). Neuropsychological studies of frontal lobes. *Psychological Bulletin, 95,* 3–28.

Stuss, D. T., & Benson, D. F. (1986). *The frontal lobes.* New York: Raven.

Stuss, D. T., & Benson, D. F. (1987). The frontal lobes and the control of cognition and memory. In E. Perceman (Ed.), *The frontal lobes revisited* (pp. 141–158). New York: IRBN Press.

Sutton, S. K., & Davidson, R. J. (1997). Prefrontal brain asymmetry: A biological substrate of the behavioral approach and inhibition systems. *Psychological Science, 8,* 204–210.

Swanson, H. L., Ashbaker, M. H., & Lee, C. (1996). Learning-disabled readers' working memory as a function of processing demands. *Journal of Experimental Child Psychology, 61,* 242, 275.

Swanson, H. L., Cochran, K. F., & Ewers, C. A. (1990). Can learning disabilities be determined from working memory performance? *Journal of Learning Disabilities, 23,* 59–67.

Swanson, H. L., & Trahan, M. (1990). Naturalistic memory in learning disabled children. *Learning Disability Quarterly, 13*, 82–95.

Szatmari, P., Tuff, L., Finlayson, M. A. J., & Bartolucci, G. (1990). Asperger's syndrome and autism: Neurocognitive aspects. *Journal of the American Academy of Child and Adolescent Psychiatry, 29*, 130–136.

Tannock, R., Schachar, R., Carr, R. P., Chajczyk, D., & Logan, G. D. (1989). Effects of methylphenidate on inhibitory control in hyperactive children. *Journal of Abnormal Child Psychology, 17*, 473–491.

Tannock, R., Schachar, R., & Logan, G. D. (1995). Methylphenidate and cognitive flexibility: Dissociated dose effects in hyperactive children. *Journal of Abnormal Child Psychology, 23*, 235–266.

Tipper, S. (1985). The negative priming effect: Inhibitory priming by ignored objects. *Quarterly Journal of Experimental Psychology, 37A*, 571–590.

Tramontana, M. G., & Hooper, S. R. (1988). Child neuropsychological assessment: Overview of current status. In M. Tramontana & S. Hooper (Eds.), *Assessment issues in child neuropsychology* (pp. 3–38). New York: Plenum.

Tueber, H. L. (1964). The riddle of frontal lobe function in man. In J. Warren & K. Akert (Eds.), *The frontal granular cortex and behavior* (pp. 410–440). New York: McGraw-Hill.

Umetani, T., Kitao, S., & Katada, A. (1985). Discrimination shift learning and response inhibition of moderately and severely mentally retarded and non-retarded children. *Journal of Mental Deficiency Research, 29*, 219–224.

Vaughn, B. E., Kopp, C. B., & Krakow, J. B. (1984). The emergence and consolidation of self-control from 18 to 30 months of age: Normative trends and individual differences. *Child Development, 55*, 990–1004.

Vaughn, B. E., Krakow, J. B., Kopp, C. B., Johnson, K., & Schwartz, S. S. (1986). Process analysis of the behavior of very young children in delay tasks. *Developmental Psychology, 22*, 752–759.

Vitiello, B., Stoff, D., Atkins, M., & Mahoney, A. (1990). Soft neurological signs and impulsivity in children. *Journal of Developmental & Behavioral Pediatrics, 11*, 112–115.

Walker, P., Hitch, G., Doyle, A., & Porter, T. (1994). The development of short-term visual memory in young children. Special issue: The development of working memory. *International Journal of Behavioral Development, 17*, 73–89.

Welsh, M. C. (1991). Rule-guided behavior and self-monitoring on the Tower of Hanoi disk-transfer task. *Cognitive Development, 6*, 59–76.

Welsh, M. C. (1994). Executive function and the assessment of attention deficits. In N. Jordan & J. Goldsmith-Phillips (Eds.), *New directions in the assessment and treatment of learning disabilities* (pp. 21–42). New York: Allyn & Bacon.

Welsh, M. C. (1996). A prefrontal dysfunction model or early-treated phenylketonuria. *European Journal of Pediatrics (Special Section), 155*, 87–89.

Welsh, M. C., Cicerello, A., Cuneo, K., & Brennan, M. (1995). Error and temporal patterns on the Tower of Hanoi disk-transfer task: Cognitive mechanisms and individual differences. *Journal of General Psychology, 122*, 69–81.

Welsh, M. C., & Pennington, B. F. (1988). Assessing frontal lobe functioning in children: Views from developmental psychology. *Developmental Neuropsychology, 4*, 199–230.

Welsh, M. C., Pennington, B. F., & Groisser, D. B. (1991). A normative-developmental study of executive function: A window on prefrontal function in children. *Developmental Neuropsychology, 7*, 131–149.

Welsh, M. C. Pennington, B. F., Ozonoff, S., Rouse, B., & McCabe, E. R. B. (1990). Neuropsychology of early-treated phenylketonuria: Specific executive function deficits. *Child Development, 61*, 1697–1713.

Welsh, M. C., Satterlee-Cartmell, T. S., & Stine, M. K. (1999). Towers of Hanoi and London: Contribution of working memory and inhibition to performance. *Brain and Cognition*, *41*, 231–242.

Willats, P. (1980). Development of problem-solving strategies in infancy. In D. F. Bjorklund (Ed.), *Children's strategies: Contemporary views of cognitive development* (pp. 23–66). Hillsdale, NJ: Lawrence Erlbaum Associates.

Yakolev, P., & Lecours, A. (1967). The myelogenetic cycles of regional maturation of the brain. In A. Minkowski (Ed.), *Regional development of the brain in early life* (pp. 3–64). Oxford, England: Blackwell.

Zametkin, A., & Rapoport, J. (1987). Neurobiology of attention deficit disorder with hyperactivity: Where have we come in 50 years? *Journal of the American Academy of Child and Adolescent Psychiatry*, *26*, 676–678.

Zelazo, P. R., Kearsley, R. B., & Stack, D. M. (1995). Mental representations for visual sequences: Increased speed of central processing from 22 to 32 months. *Intelligence*, *20*, 41–63.

Zibovicius, M., Garreau, B., Samson, Y., Remy, P., Barthelemy, C., Syrota, A., & Lelord, G. (1995). Delayed maturation of the frontal cortex in childhood autism. *American Journal of Psychiatry*, *152*, 248–252.

## CHAPTER SEVEN

The Relation Between Language Development and Brain Activity

Dennis L. Molfese
University of Louisville
Dana B. Narter
Arlene Modglin
Southern Illinois University at Carbondale

For decades, investigators believed that if they could accurately identify a child's potential for language and cognitive disorders early in development, then the opportunity for intervention to correct such problems, as well as the likelihood of success resulting from that intervention, would be greater. Such a belief has spawned many attempts to predict language and cognitive skills in the preschool and early elementary school periods based on a variety of behavioral, medical, and physiological measures obtained in the neonatal period (D. L. Molfese, 1989; Pederson, Evans, Bento, Chance, & Fox, 1987; Sostek, Smith, Katz, & Grant, 1987). However, few procedures have accomplished the traditional screening goals of high true positive and low false negative rates in their identifications. That is, no projects have successfully identified only those children who would later experience poor developmental outcomes while not identifying other children for later intervention who did not require it. Most procedures, although sometimes yielding statistically significant results, have produced low correlations between measures obtained in early infancy and later scores on childhood language and cognitive tests (Siegel, 1982). When regression models are constructed using these language and cognitive scores as the criterion measures and the various behavioral, medical, and physiological measures as the predictors, it becomes clear that the predictors typically identify differences in the performances of relatively small proportions of the children tested. This accuracy in prediction does not improve significantly even when tests are used to distinguish between categories of children: for example, those classified as at risk (e.g., respiratory distress, premature, intraventricular hemorrhage) and those not identified with these problems (Cohen & Beckwith, 1979; Cohen & Parmelee, 1983; Cohen, Parmelee, Sigman, & Beckwith, 1982; Silva, McGee, & Williams, 1984). However, recent findings from neuropsychological studies provide new hope that scientists and clinicians will one day be able to screen children early in life for later cognitive and linguistic developmental problems.

The following review is a critical evaluation of a series of neuroelectrophysiological studies published over the past 30 years that attempt to predict language and cognitive abilities of children using measures obtained at birth or in early infancy. These studies make it clear that some measures obtained in the neonatal period are predictive of later cognitive and language performance and may provide useful techniques for the early identification of certain types of cognitive disabilities.

THE SEARCH FOR THE RELATION BETWEEN IQ AND BRAIN WAVE ACTIVITY

There have been many changes over the past half century regarding the relation between measures of intelligence and measures of brain wave activity. Based on an early, critical review of the literature focusing on the relation between electroencephalogram (EEG) activity and test intelligence, Vogel and Broverman (1964) concluded that a strong relation exists between these two variables among children, the mentally retarded, institutionalized geriatric patients, and brain damaged patients. However, they noted that such a relation appeared to be attenuated in normal adults. Additionally, they concluded that electrophysiological indices are more strongly correlated with mental age than with IQ.

Vogel and Broverman noted that a variety of factors contributed to the absence of significant findings in some research attempts to find a link between intelligence and neuroelectrophysiological measures. First, they objected to the manner in which intelligence was measured. They argued that investigators focused more efforts on measuring EEG instead of intelligence. Investigators often failed to justify the selection of one test over another and, in fact, failed to report the actual intelligence tests used. Other investigators, in contrast, often failed to use standardized test batteries, but selected tests they reasoned measured different types of intelligence. This approach, of course, greatly reduced opportunities for comparisons across studies and methods, as well as the possibility of comparing the population tested and the study results to other published research not involving electrophysiological measures. Second, Vogel and

Broverman commented on the restricted placement of electrodes on the scalp in such studies. Most used only occipital leads; however, it had long been argued throughout the clinical neuropsychology literature (as summarized in Lenneberg, 1967) that intellectual functions are distributed throughout the brain in the frontal, temporal, and parietal lobes. To focus on a restricted set of electrode placements, particularly those that often failed to demonstrate differences even in standard experimental studies, seemed misguided at best. Third, Vogel and Broverman discussed the restricted conditions under which EEG recordings were collected. Generally, subjects were physically and mentally inactive during recording procedures and were not required to solve cognitive tasks during EEG recordings. Thus, there was no way to control for the mental concentration level of study participants, identify the evoking stimuli, or even to identify their cognitive or emotional state. Fourth, previous studies failed to control for sex, although sex differences in EEG patterns had been reported previously in the literature. Thus, in addition to the types of error variance described earlier, sex differences were added to the list. Finally, the authors commented on the EEG indices utilized. Traditionally, EEG measures have included frequency and amplitude measures of alpha, delta, or theta waves. Instead, Vogel and Broverman suggested that more complex, composite indices should be used when investigating the relation between brain neural activity and test intelligence. Although they appeared optimistic regarding the potential for identifying a relation between brain and intelligence measures, Vogel and Broverman concluded that the field had failed to adequately investigate the potential relations between these two measures.

In contrast to Vogel and Broverman, Ellingson (1966) argued that the evidence concerning relations between normal brain wave activity and intelligence in both child and mentally retarded populations was contradictory and often inconclusive. Ellingson cited several studies of the mentally retarded in which either no relations or only weak relations were found between brain and intelligence variables. He also reviewed studies in which only a small proportion of the correlations between EEG and intelligence were statistically significant, reinforcing the impression that no relation existed. Ellingson noted that the evidence available at that time suggested there was no relation between brain waves and IQ in normal adults. Rather, he argued that EEG abnormality and decreased intellectual capacity both are the effects of organic brain disorders. Thus, marked differences would be expected in neuroelectrical activity between these two populations. However, the techniques themselves may not be sensitive enough to detect reliable differences within those domains. Ellingson (1966) and Vogel and Broverman (1964) reached their conclusions regarding this relation by working through the scientific literature from different perspectives, but there is a sense of frustration from both regarding the state of the science and its failure to adequately address this question.

This chapter focuses attention on studies investigating the relation between intelligence and the event-related potential (ERP). Some discussion includes the results of adult studies, but the specific focus is on the development of the individual from early in infancy and whether the ERP can be used to predict future intellectual performance.

ERP Measures

The auditory ERP has been used extensively to study language and cognitive processes (D. L. Molfese, 1983). The ERP is a synchronized portion of the ongoing EEG pattern that is detectable at the scalp and occurs immediately in response to some auditory stimulus (Callaway, Tueting, & Koslow, 1978; Rockstroh, Elbert, Birbaumer, & Lutzenberger, 1982). Because of its time-locked relation to the evoking stimulus, the ERP has been demonstrated to reflect both general and specific aspects of the evoking stimulus and the perceptions and decisions regarding it (D. L. Molfese, 1983; D. Molfese & Betz, 1988; D. L. Molfese & V. J. Molfese, 1979a, 1979b, 1980, 1985, 1986; Nelson & Salapatek, 1986; Ruchkin, Sutton, Munson, & Macar, 1981).

Relations Between IQ and ERPs in Children

Work conducted in the late 1960s generally indicated the presence of some relations between IQ, intelligence, and language during the early and middle childhood years. These studies are summarized in Table 7.1. Ertl and Schafer (1969) tested 317 males and 256 females from grades 2 through 8, and did find a relation between visual event-related potential (VERP) characteristics and IQ. Children were administered the Weschler Intelligence Scales for Children (WISC), the Primary Mental Abilities Test (PMA), and the Otis Quick Scoring Mental Ability Test. VERPs then were recorded from bipolar electrodes 6 cm apart and parallel to midline and astride the C4 site referred to the right ear lobe, A2 (see Jasper, 1958), to 400 flashes recorded over a 625 ms period. Analyses involved both ERP amplitude summation and zero crossing analysis, a second method to establish ERP component identification reliability. Four peaks between 60 ms and 275 ms were identified in this manner and were found to correlate inversely with Intelligence test scores. In general, negative correlations between these ERP amplitude and measures of intelligence were better for the last three ERP peak components at 100 ms, 190 ms, and 275 ms. ERPs recorded from the high performing subjects were generally more com-

TABLE 7.1
The Relationship Between IQ and ERPs in Children

Study	Subjects	Electrode	Task	Results
Kraus et al. (1996)	90 normal children age 6–15 91 learning disabled children $n = 181$	Fz referred to A2	Computer synthesized speech syllable pairs (ba, wa and da, ga) presented to right ear Oddball paradigm: infrequent syllable intermixed with presentations of a frequent syllable	Good Perceivers had robust grand average MMN responses whereas Poor Perceivers did not MMN area and duration were smaller for Poor than for Good group da–ga discrimination scores were correlated with MMN duration and area
Engel & Henderson (1973)	7- to 8-year-old children $n = 119$	14 electrodes positioned symmetrically over both hemispheres; 15th electrode over inion	Visual ERPs to light flashes WISC (Information, Comprehension, Vocabulary, Digit Span, Picture Arrangement, Block Design, Coding) Bender Visual Motor Gestalt Test	The latency of the VERP peaks did not contribute to prediction of IQ None of the VERPs correlated significantly with behavioral measures alone at 7–8 years
Ertl & Schafer (1969)	Students from grades 2, 3, 4, 5, 7 and 8 $n = 573$	Bipolar electrodes 6 cm apart parallel to midline and astride C4; referred to A2	Visual ERPs to light flashes at birth ERPs to 400 flashes recorded for 625 ms WISC, primary mental abilities test (PMA), Otis quick scoring mental ability test	IQ inversely correlated to ERP latencies ERPs of high performing individuals more complex and had high frequency components in the first 100 ms than ERPs of low performers
Rhodes, Dustman, & Beck (1969)	Children age 10–11 20 "bright" (WISC IQ = 120–140) 20 "dull" children (WISC IQ = 70–90) $n = 40$	C3, C4, O1, O2 referred to earlobes	Visual ERPs to 100 light flashes Button press after 4th and 6th flashes in sequence of 10 flashes Subject tested again 2 months later	VERPs of bright children correlate with VERPs of older children VERPs of dull children fail to correlate with VERPs of younger children or same age children

plex, were smaller in amplitude, and had higher frequency components in the first 100 ms, unlike the low performing subjects.

Rhodes, Dustman, and Beck (1969) attempted to address the question of a relation between VERP and IQ by testing 20 bright (WISC IQ: 120–140, $M = 130$) and 20 dull (WISC IQ: 70–90, $M = 79$) children who were between age 10 and 11. Electrodes were placed at the central scalp locations, C3, C4, O1, O2, which were all referred to "ear lobes." VERPs were recorded to 100 reflected flashes presented at less than 2 Hz. Each child was tested in two sessions, 2 months apart. Electrodes placed on the child's thumb served as a gross control to monitor for variations in attention to monitor mental task used. Each child was instructed to press a button after the 4th and 6th flashes in a sequence of 10 flashes. After 2 months, the tests were repeated for reliability. The VERP measures included recording the latencies from flash onset to each of eight peaks (labeled A through H by Rhodes, Dustman, and Beck), which varied in their polarity. Amplitude of the ERPs was measured from the preceding peak-to-following peak as well as three excursions (i.e., the total length of the waveform as determined by placing a string over the line graph and the placing of this string along a ruler to measure its total length). The measures included string length from stimulus onset to 250 ms, stimulus onset to the D-peak at about 100 ms, and the latency from the D wave at about 100 ms to 250 ms. Analyses noted that three middle peaks between 100 and 250 ms (D, E, F peaks) were larger for bright than they were for dull children at all sites. Hemisphere asymmetries were also found for these same three ERP components. The bright children had a larger ERP response over the left hemisphere (LH) than the right hemisphere (RH), whereas no such difference was noted for the dull children, regardless of changes in luminance levels. At the occipital sites, the G wave occurred earlier for bright children than it did for dull children. Waveform correlations (as a measure of similarity) were significantly better for the bright children, suggesting that bright children were a more homogeneous group.

When Rhodes, Dustman, and Beck compared these data with those obtained by Dustman and Beck (1969a, 1969b), they found that the ERPs obtained from the bright children correlated with those obtained from older children. However, the VERPs from dull children did not correlate with and were smaller than those recorded from younger or even same age children. Rhodes, Dustman, and Beck interpreted this finding to suggest that the bright versus dull differences reflected more than just maturational differences.

In contrast to the positive results between ERPs and IQ noted earlier, Engel and Henderson (1973) failed to find such a relation between VERPs and concurrent IQ measures. They recorded visual evoked responses and IQ scores from 66 boys and 53 girls between age 7 and 8 and attempted to relate them to each other. The VERPs were recorded to 50 repeated photic flashes from 14 scalp electrodes and referred to the inion. In addition, a variety of psychological tests was administered, which were adaptations of the WISC (4 verbal subtests: Information, Comprehension, Vocabulary, and Digit Span; 3 performance subtests: Picture Arrangement, Block Design, and Coding) and the Bender Visual-Motor Gestalt Test. Multiple regression procedures were used to assess the contribution of race, sex, and each VERP peak to simple and multiple correlations with the Bender and with WISC Verbal, Performance, and Full Scale IQ scores. However, no significant relations were found between VERP measures and intellectual function. Although no mention is made of what VERP measures were used in their analysis, given the other published studies by Engel and his colleagues, it is likely that they focused exclusively on the early N1 component latency.

The bulk of the studies reviewed suggest a relation between ERP activity and IQ-related measures in children, although such findings are not ubiquitous. However, one striking observation is in order. The studies analyzing multiple regions of the ERP waveform reported finding relations between VERP measures and IQ or language measures (Ertl & Shafer, 1969; Rhodes, Dustman, & Beck, 1969). However, studies focusing only on a single peak failed to find such relations (Engel & Henderson, 1973).

Relations Between IQ and ERPs in Adults

Some researchers, although noting reliable relations early in life between IQ and brain wave activity, failed to find continued relations between these two factors in adulthood (Shucard & Callaway, 1973). Others, in contrast, have continued to find such relations (Chalke & Ertl, 1965; Galbraith, Gliddon, & Busk, 1970; Shucard & Horn, 1972). These results are summarized in Table 7.2.

Chalke and Ertl (1965) noted a relation between IQ and ERP latency. Specifically, they found that high psychomotor intelligence was associated with short delays in the late occurring ERP components. Chalke and Ertl tested three groups of adults, age 17 to 41, which included 33 postgraduate students "with I.Q.'s in the superior range," 11 Army cadets "with I.Q.'s in the low average range," and 4 mentally retarded subjects "with I.Q.'s ranging from 50 to 65." Unfortunately, no information was included regarding the IQ test used or the specific subtests employed. Bipolar recording electrodes were placed "over the left motor area of each subject," and visual ERPs were recorded to light flashes for 500 ms periods.

Five ERP components were identified within this period, E1 (peak latency at 47–52 ms), E2 (peak latency at 90–102 ms), E3 (peak latency 142–205 ms), E4 (peak latency at 223–278 ms), and E5 (peak latency at

TABLE 7.2
The Relationship between IQ and ERPs in Adults

Study	Subjects	Electrodes	Task	Results
Chalke & Ertl (1965)	Adults age 17–41, n = 48 3 groups: (1) graduate students with "IQs in the superior range" (n = 33) (2) Army cadets with "IQs in the low average range" (n = 11) (3) mentally retarded with "IQs ranging from 50 to 65" (n = 4)	Bipolar electrodes placed over left motor area	Visual ERPs recorded to light flashes for 500 ms periods No IQ test information	Five ERP components identified: E1 (47–52 ms) E2 (90–102 ms) E3 (42–205 ms) E4 (223–278 ms) E5 (302–374 ms) Found relation between high psychomotor intelligence and latency changes in late ERP components
Weinberg (1969)	Adults age 18–39 with IQs ranging from 77 to 146 n = 42	Bipolar electrodes at medial and lateral sites on the left and right sides of the head, with each pair separated by 2.5 cm; about 2.5 cm above the inion Medial electrodes placed 2.5 cm lateral to the midline	Visual ERPs recorded for 500 ms while participants attended to light flashes 70 trials from one hemisphere, then 70 trials from the other hemisphere	The density of frequencies between 2 and 50 Hz correlated with IQ Individual spectra components at 12 and 14 Hz correlated with IQ in only low IQ group

| Shucard & Horn (1972) | Adults age 16–68 $n = 108$ | Bipolar recording sites: F4-C4, C4-P4, P4-O2, F4-P4, F3-P3, F3-C3, C3-P3, P3-O1 | Battery included 16 measures of intellectual abilities to calculate 3 types of intelligence:
—Fluid Intelligence
—Crystallized Intelligence
—General Ability
VERs to light flashes over 500 ms period averaged from 100 responses
24 adapting trials, then 3 conditions:
—high extrinsic activation (HEA)
—medium extrinsic activation (MEA)
—intrinsic activation (IA) | ERP latency correlated with IQ
Effects best seen under low arousal
No relation between IQ and ERP amplitude |
| Shucard & Callaway (1973) | Adults age 16–68 $n = 107$ | Bipolar recording sites: F4-P4 F3-P3 | Battery same as used by Shucard and Horn (1972) Ability
VERs averaged to light flashes over 500 ms period | No correlation between IQ and ERP frequency measures for either hemisphere |

302–374 ms). Although no differences were found between groups for the first two peaks, E1 and E2, the High group had shortened latencies for later occurring ERP components, beginning at E3 (post 142 ms). The High and Low groups differed at peaks E3, E4, and E5. The High group also differed from the Average group at E4 and the Average group differed from the Low group at E3. A retest of a small subset of only participants from the High group found comparable results. Based on these results, Chalke and Ertl concluded that there was a relation between high psychomotor intelligence and latency changes in late ERP components.

Shucard and Horn (1972) also noted a relation between ERP frequency, latency, and IQ. They recorded VERPs to light flashes from a series of bipolar sites, including F4-C4, C4-P4, P4-O2, F4-P4, F3-P3, F3-C3, C3-P3, P3-O1 from 60 males and 48 females between age 16 and 68. The large age range and varied IQ status of their population were deliberately recruited in order to test subjects of different sexes over a wide age and SES range "to provide a broad range of abilities and ERP measurements."

Following 24 adaptation trials, subjects were presented with three conditions: HEA (high extrinsic activation), during which subjects pressed a button to indicate a light flash for 100 trials; MEA (medium extrinsic activation), during which subjects counted light flashes after the HEA condition; and IA (intrinsic activation), during which subjects lied quietly and attended to lights after the MEA condition. For analyses, EEGs were rated for arousal by a technician on a 1 (low alert) to 6 (hi alert) scale. Questionnaires were also administered after each condition to assess alertness. The latency and amplitude of the first five peaks and troughs were then measured. VERPs to the light flashes over a 500 ms period were averaged from 100 responses. They then calculated peak frequency, power at peak frequency, and power at 14.04 Hz for both the left and right electrode sites.

These VERP measures were then compared with a battery that included 16 measures of intellectual abilities, some used by others and others were newly constructed by the investigators. Thus, the final IQ scores derived were based largely on their own and not standardized tests. Three types of measures were then calculated: Gf (fluid intelligence), which was the sum of unweighted standard scores for number span backward, induction, conceptual figure relations, and conceptual semantic relations; Gc (crystallized intelligence), which was the unweighted sum of standardized scores including verbal comprehension, formal reasoning, esoteric conceptual relations, numbers, general reasoning, and association fluency; and G (general ability), which was the unweighted sum of standardized scores including Gf and Gc plus perceptual speediness and visualization.

Shucard and Horn (1972), like Chalke and Ertl (1965), noted that long ERP latencies were associated with low IQ scores and short latencies were correlated with high ability. Interestingly, the numbers of significant correlations varied across the three tasks, suggesting that the ERP measures were differentially sensitive to the different tasks. The HEA task was characterized by 9 significant correlations for positive peaks 3, 4, and 5, the MEA task had 11 significant correlations, and the IA task had 32. Correlations of ERP latency with IQ were better for low arousal and amplitude was not found to be related to IQ. Gf and Gc yielded correlations to each other with comparable ERP latency measures. Shucard and Horn concluded that ERP latency correlated with intellectual functions and these effects were best seen under low arousal situations. Thus, the correlation between IQ and VERPs reflected in part variations in alertness. With low alertness levels, ERP latencies showed better correlations with IQ-related factors.

In a subsequent but closely related paper, Shucard and Callaway (1973) also assessed the relation between ERP frequency and IQ, but found no IQ-related effects. The subjects included 60 males and 47 females between age 16 and 68. As in Shucard and Horn, subjects varied widely in age, sex, and SES. The researchers collected VERP data from two electrode sets, F4-P4 and F3-P3, to light flashes over a 500 ms period. VERPs were then averaged from 100 such responses. The IQ measures were identical to those reported by Shucard and Horn (1972). For the ERP analyses, they calculated peak frequency, power at peak frequency, and power at 14.04 Hz for both left and right hemisphere sites. No correlations were found between IQ and ERP frequency measures for either hemisphere. Additionally, although frequency measures did correlate between hemispheres, they did not correlate with IQ. Shucard and Horn suggested, in part, that electrode placement differences from Bennett (1968) and Weinberg (1969) might have contributed to their own failure to replicate their earlier results. Additionally, they suggested that it may be better, as Ertl suggests, to look at specific peak measures for relations to IQ.

Galbraith et al. (1970) noted that IQ scores correlated with a posterior, lateral right hemisphere site in retardates only. They tested 24 retarded (mean IQ = 46.7, range = 26–66, mean CA = 16.3, range = 9–27), and 16 nonretarded adults (mean IQ = unavailable, mean CA = 20.0, range = 7–32 years). The target population included 6 Downs, 1 PKU, 1 asphyxia, 1 galactosemia, 1 hydrocephalic, 5 uncertain-functional, and 5 uncertain-structural based individuals, although no specific information is included concerning the nature of these problems. Thus, the mentally disabled population is heterogeneous at best.

All subjects were dark adapted for 10 minutes and then focused on a center fixation light. Within a 3.3 degree circular lighted area, black line triangles (2.2 degrees) were then each randomly presented 80 times for 100 ms (240 total stimuli were presented) to left (L) or right (R) or on both sides (B) of fixation. Visual ERPs were recorded from 6 positions over the back of the head and referenced to a midline posterior scalp lead. These electrode positions, which were positioned largely over the occipital area, were identified as PM (posterior midline), AL (anterior left), AR (anterior right), AM (anterior midline), LL (lower left), and LR (lower right). All electrodes were referred to an electrode 5 cm above PM on the midline. The VERPs were sampled at 5 ms intervals for 500 ms.

Lateral differences in mean latency were found between the normal (55.2 ms) and retarded subjects (75.3 ms), although five of the retardates had P1 latencies equivalent to the normals. In addition, at an electrode just superior to the inion in the midline (PM), the P3 latency was shorter for normals (279 ms) than retardates (322 ms), suggesting that processing speed was longer in the latter group. Galbraith et al. next calculated an amplitude ratio for the Late Positive Component (LPC) where peak-to-peak amplitude was represented as a percentage of PM amplitude noted. Nonretardates produced greater amplitude ratios in sites identified as LL, LR, AL, and were smaller in AM and AR than PM. Overall, the VERPs of the retardates were smaller at all sites than they were at PM. Larger ratios were found for normals and thus were correlated with higher IQs.

In general, the studies reviewed here found relations between intelligence and ERP activity. The one measure that did not correlate with intelligence was frequency. However, even here there is some ambiguity. Shucard and Callaway (1973) suggested their study could have been limited by their selection of very few electrode sites and their decision not to include other measures of the ERP besides frequency. Additionally, given the heterogeneity of their population, it might be suspected that this was also a factor in their failure to find a relation between ERP frequency and IQ.

PREDICTING LATER DEVELOPMENTAL OUTCOMES

Two sets of studies, building on the argument of a relation between IQ and ERP activity, have investigated whether ERPs could predict later skills. However, the outcomes of these two attempts have been quite different. In the earlier series of studies, although such relations appear to occur between birth and later infancy (Butler & Engel, 1969), the correlations between ERP activity and IQ at later ages were not consistently found (Engel & Fay, 1972; Henderson & Engel, 1974). The second set of studies, which undertook a different approach (D. Molfese & V. Molfese, 1985, 1997; Molfese & Searock, 1986), although noting relations between birth measures and later performance at age 1, continued to show relations between

TABLE 7.3

ERP Studies Predicting Later Developmental Outcomes

Study	Subjects	Electrodes	Task	Results
Butler & Engel (1969)	ERPs recorded within first 5 days after birth Retested 8 months of age on Bayley Scales $n = 433$	6 electrodes per hemisphere (no specific sites identified)	Visual ERPs to light flashes 3 variables: photic latency, gestational age, birthweight Modified version of the Bayley Scales at 8 months of age (Mental, Gross Motor, Fine Motor)	Correlations involving photic response latency and gestational age were higher than the correlations involving birthweight Mental test score had higher correlations with neonatal measures than fine motor or gross motor scores
Engel & Fay (1972)	Tested at birth, 3 years, 4 years $n = 828$	Placed over the inion of both occipital areas	Visual ERPs to light flashes at birth Separated into 3 Reactor groups: Fast, Average, Slow 3 measures of speech and language (pronunciation of initial consonants, pronunciation of final consonants, verbal comprehension) at age 3 y Stanford–Binet at age 4 y	Articulation of initial and final consonants at age 3 y was significantly greater in the fast reactors No significant correlation was found between neonatal VER and verbal comprehension at age 3 y or with IQ at age 4 y
Henderson & Engel (1974)	Tested within first week after birth Tested again at age 7 y $n = 809$	Oz referred to C3, Oz referred to C4, or O1 referred to C3 O2 referred to C4	Visual ERPs to light flashes at birth WISC (Information, Comprehension, Vocabulary, Digit Span, Picture Arrangement, Block Design Coding)	No relation found between Neonatal VERPs and IQ, perceptual measures, or achievement measures

(Continued)

TABLE 7.3
(Continued)

Study	Subjects	Electrode	Task	Results
			Bender Gestalt Test using the Koppitz system Tactile Finger Recognition Test (from Reitan Neuropsychological Battery for Children) WRAT (Spelling, Arithmetic, Reading)	
D. Molfese & V. Molfese (1985)	Infants studied longitudinally from birth through age 3 y *n* = 16	T3, T4 referenced to linked ears	ERPs recorded to speech and nonspeech consonant–vowel sounds at birth McCarthy Scales of Children's Abilities administered at age 3 y	Newborn ERPs identified children performing better or worse on language tasks 3 years later ERPs 88–240 ms discriminated High vs. Low Groups on McCarthy Verbal Index at age 3 y ERP component, with peak latency of 664 ms also discriminated High vs. Low Groups at age 3 y
D. Molfese & Searock (1986)	1-year-old infants retested at age 3 y *n* = 16	T3, T4 referenced to linked ears	At age 1 y, ERPs recorded to speech and non speech vowel sounds McCarthy test administered at age 3 y	Children with above-average language skills at age 3 y exhibited ERPs at age 1 y that discriminated different vowel sounds
D. Molfese (1989)	Newborns retested at age 3 y (15 with McCarthy scores below 50 and 15 with scores above 50) *n* = 30	T3, T4 referenced to linked ears	At birth, ERPs to speech and nonspeech consonant–vowel sounds were recorded McCarthy test administered at age 3 y	Discriminant function correctly classified 68.6% of the ERPs recorded from children with McCarthy scores higher than 50 and 69.7% of the ERPs recorded from those with McCarthy scores less than 50

D. Molfese & V. Molfese (1994)	Newborns retested at age 3 y (27 with McCarthy scores below 50 and 27 with McCarthy scores above 54) n = 54	FL, FR, T3, T4, PL, PR referenced to linked ears	At birth, ERPs recorded to speech and nonspeech consonant–vowel sounds McCarthy test administered at age 3 y	Positive peak of neonatal LH responses 70–210 ms discriminated consonant sounds for above-average language users at age 3 y Positive peak of neonatal parietal response between 470 and 670 ms discriminated consonants for above-average language users at age 3 y
D. L. Molfese, Gill, Simos, & Tan (1995)	Newborns tested again at age 5 y n = 79	T3, T4, FL, FR, PL, PR referenced to linked ears	At birth, ERPs were collected to 9 consonant–vowel syllables Stanford–Binet was administered at 5 years of age	PCA-discriminant function analysis performed 3 groups based on Stanford–Binet Verbal reasoning subtest scores at age 5 y 2 discriminant functions classified children 81% accuracy
D. L. Molfese (1995)	Newborns tested again at age 3 y n = 79	T3, T4, FL, FR, PL, PR referenced to linked ears	At birth, ERPs collected to 9 consonant–vowel syllables Stanford–Binet administered at age 3 y	PCA-discriminant function analysis 3 groups based on Stanford–Binet Verbal reasoning subtest scores at age 3 y 2 discriminant functions classified at 100% accuracy
D. L. Molfese & V. J. Molfese (1997)	Newborns tested again at age 5 y n = 71	T3, T4, FL, FR, PL, PR referenced to linked ears	At birth, ERPs collected to 9 consonant–vowel syllables Stanford–Binet administered at age 5 y	2 groups based on Stanford–Binet Verbal reasoning subtest scores at age 5 y: 62 > 100 VIQ, 9 < 100 VIQ 3 discriminant functions classified children at 78.9%, 91.6%, & 95.8% accuracy using 3, 6, 7 variables

(Continued)

TABLE 7.3
(Continued)

Study	Subjects	Electrode	Task	Results
Molfese (2000)	Newborns tested again at 8 years of age when 17 are dyslexic, 7 have lower FSIQ with reading problems, 24 matched Controls n = 48	T3, T4, Fl, FR, PL, PR referenced to linked ears	At birth, ERPs collected to 9 consonant–vowel syllables WRAT3 administered at age 8 y	3 groups based on WRAT 3 Reading scores at age 8 y 2 discriminant functions classified children at 82.1%
Molfese (In press)	Newborns tested again at age 8 y n = 102	T3, T4, Fl, FR, PL, PR referenced to linked ears	At birth, ERPs collected to 9 consonant–vowel syllables WRAT3 administered at age 8 y	3 groups based on WRAT 3 Reading scores at 8 years: Low Group with 11 children, Average Group with 75 children, High Group with 16 children 2 discriminant functions classified children at 66.67% accuracy, Low Group 90% accurate, High group 75& accurate, Average Group 67% accurate

early brain electrical measures and later language performance even up to age 5. These studies are outlined in Table 7.3.

The earliest set of studies to investigate birth measures as predictors of later development began when Butler and Engel (1969) recorded visual ERPs from six electrodes applied over each hemisphere of 216 males and 217 females within the first 5 days of life. The VERPs were recorded to repeated light flashes while the infants were awake, drowsy, and at different depths of sleep. Newborn data included 3 variables: photic latency (PL), gestational age (GA), and birthweight (BW). Additional data were collected from these infants again at 8 months of age using a modified version of the Bayley scales (Bayley, 1969). Three ratings were obtained: mental, gross motor, and fine motor. Photic latency was defined as the length of the interval in ms between flash onset and the takeoff point (N1) that led to the following large P2 peak. Correlations between neonatal photic latency and Bayley scores at 8 months were found to be significant ($p < .001$) for all 3 subtests ($r = .33$ for mental; $r = .24$ for fine motor; $r = .23$ for gross motor) ($n = 433$); when low birthweight infants were removed from the sample (reducing it to an n of 400), the correlations between photic latency and Bayley scores were still significant at the .001 level ($r = .31$ for mental; $r = .19$ for fine motor; $r = .20$ gross motor). Correlations involving PL and GA were higher than correlations involving BW. Interestingly, when the effect of both GA and BW were parcelled out, the correlation between PL and the 8-month mental score remained significant with $r = -.24$, suggesting that PL is significantly related to mental scores independent of the other two variables. As in the case of Shucard and Horn, as well as Chalke and Ertl, shorter peak latencies were noted for infants with higher mental scores. These shorter latencies, because they are normally associated with faster processing times or more mature nervous systems, support the view that the better performing infants had more mature motor systems at birth that might be expected to at least maintain this developmental advantage later in infancy—if not develop at a more accelerated rate—than infants with more immature systems.

In a follow-up to this work, Engel and Fay (1972) further examined the relation between these visual evoked responses at birth and the preschool child's verbal scores at ages 3 and 4. VERPs were recorded to flashes of light using electrodes placed over inion of the occipital areas of a group of newborns. N1 latency was again used as the VERP variable. Engel and Fay administered standard speech, language, and hearing examination to 828 of these same children when they reached 3 years and from 1,046 children at age 4 using the Stanford–Binet short-form (Form LM; Terman & Merrill, 1960). Newborns were separated into three groups based on their VERPs: fast reactors (those with N1 latencies of 145 ms or less); average reactors (N1 latencies between 146 ms and 175 ms); and slow reactors (N1 latencies greater than or equal to 175 ms). The language measures at age 3 included the 14 items of a standard comprehension subtest, plus 5 vocal identifications of familiar objects in real or toy form; speech criteria were scores of correct articulation of one-syllable words as spoken by the examining speech pathologist and repeated in imitation by the child. Analyses relating newborn VERP measures to performance measures at age 3 found that infants with shorter peak latencies at birth performed better ($p < .05$) at age 3 than the neonatal slow reactors. In further analyses, race, sex, and VERP contributed significantly ($p < .0001$) to the clear production of final consonants. However, neonatal VERP latency and sex did not contribute significantly to the verbal comprehension results in 3-year-olds. Furthermore, neonatal VERPs did not predict Stanford–Binet test scores at 4 years. These findings at ages 3 and 4 suggest that whereas neonatal VERP might be a good predictor of subsequent motor speech development even up to age 3, they do not predict later symbolic or intellectual development.

This failure to make long-term predictions of language or cognitive abilities is reinforced in a related study by Henderson and Engel (1974), who followed these children to age 7. Neonatal VERPs to light flashes from 809 children at birth were used in an attempt to discriminate these same children at age 7 on a variety of psychological measures, including the WISC (including 7 subtests on information, comprehension, vocabulary, digit span, picture arrangement, block design, and coding), Full Scale (FS) IQ, Verbal IQ, Performance IQ, Bender Gestalt Test (Koppitz system), Tactile Finger Recognition Test (from the Reitan Neuropsychology Battery for Children), and the Wide Range Achievement Test (WRAT; spelling, arithmetic, reading). Partial data also were obtained at age 7 for an additional 40 children. Final analyses included 809 children who had all tests and were within the 2.5 SD of the mean for their sex and race.

Neonatal measures, including the VERP measures of N1 latency, came from two thirds of subjects on the second or third day of life, and one third came from the first day or after the third day but within the first week. The VERPs were recorded from Oz referred to C3, Oz referred to C4 or O1 referred to C3 and O2 referred to C4. The dependent variable of the VERP was again the latency between flash onset and the takeoff point (N1) that led to the P2 peak. The scores of 809 children were stepwise regressed on their VERPs and multiple regressions were calculated separately for race and sex. Twelve test scores were thus obtained for the four groups, resulting in 48 "independent" regression coefficients. Of the 60 correlations conducted between VERPs and other outcome variables, only one was significant: The VERP measure correlated significantly with arithmetic achievement for Black females. No other effects related to intelligence measures and VERPs were found. Thus, Henderson and Engel, like

Engel and Fay (1972), concluded that neonatal VERPs do not correlate with various IQ tests, perceptual, or achievement measures later in development.

Recent Efforts to Find a Relation Between Cognitive Performance and Neuroelectrophysiological Measures

It appears from this review that several studies report some early relation between one component of the visual evoked response, the latency or length of the interval between stimulus onset and the N1 peak, and subsequent motor, cognitive-motor, or language-related abilities during the first year of life. However, further research comparing neonatal evoked responses with later intelligence scores measured after the first year of life failed to demonstrate such a relation. Although the drawing of any conclusions concerning the usefulness of evoked potential measures as predictors of later functioning may appear discouraging, more recent studies suggest that such relations in fact exist (D. L. Molfese, 1989; D. Molfese & V. Molfese, 1985, 1997; Molfese & Searock, 1986). Such disparity in findings first appears puzzling, but closer inspection suggests that the differences in success between such studies most likely reflect a number of major differences in both methodology and experimental design. First, like Chalke and Ertl (1965) and Ertl and Shafer (1969), Molfese and his associates analyzed the entire evoked potential waveform, whereas the other researchers cited (Butler & Engel, 1969; Engel & Fay, 1972; Engel & Henderson, 1973; Henderson & Engel, 1974) typically confined their analysis to the latency measure of a single, early occurring peak in the waveform. This contrast between the analysis of a single peak versus multiple peaks and between a single measure of these peaks (latency) versus multiple measures (latency and amplitude) is striking. Molfese and colleagues argued that the analysis of all data collected instead of only a small subset will increase the likelihood of isolating a relation between early brain responses and later development—if such relations in fact exist. Second, the frequency range of the evoked potential studied by Molfese includes a lower range of frequencies (below 3 Hz) than those employed by earlier investigators (Shucard & Callaway, 1973; Shucard & Horn, 1972). Given that the brain wave frequencies characterizing the evoked potentials of young infants are concentrated in the frequency range below 3 Hz, such a strategy should measure more of the neonate's brain wave activity. Third, these later studies employ language-related speech sounds as the evoking stimuli rather than the photic flashes used by the researchers who have employed the visual-evoked response procedure. The relatedness of photic flashes to the types of cognitive processing thought to be reflected in intelligence tests is not known. However, there are data available that suggest that speech perception abilities are related to language development. Engel and Fay (1972), as already noted, did find a relation between phonetic production and VERPs. Because predictors of successful performance are generally better if they measure predicted skills, the inclusion of more language relevant materials as the evoking stimuli should increase the likelihood for predicting later language-related skills. That the inclusion of speech materials per se might enhance predictability is supported by a recent study (Kraus et al., 1996) noting that differences may exist in the phonetic processing abilities of learning-disabled versus normal readers.

Such differences in ERP measures, electrode placements, IQ-related measures, and the selection of relevant stimuli could all contribute to the greater success found in some of the studies reviewed, as well as the more recent studies using auditory ERPs recorded at birth to predict later cognitive and language functioning.

Multivariate Approaches to Language Prediction
Using ERPs to Predict Later Development

Stimulus selection, as noted earlier, may be one important dimension in the effort to identify long-term predictors of developmental outcomes. Although light flashes have been used in the past, the use of language-related stimuli (e.g., speech sounds) appears a better choice as a predictive stimulus for several reasons. First, it accesses and stimulates the auditory channel, which is a primary channel for language input during the early years of life. Second, the phonological skills, which the child will ultimately develop, are based on their ability to hear differences between different speech sounds and eventually relate these different sounds to different orthographic characters.

A great deal of research has been conducted over the past three decades investigating the development of speech perception abilities in young infants (Eimas, Siqueland, Juscyk, & Vigorito, 1971). Such studies indicate that infants at the earliest ages tested show some ability to discriminate speech sounds. A parallel set of studies investigating the neuroelectrical correlates of speech perception development noted a similar pattern, although the procedure has enabled investigators to observe speech sound discrimination abilities even in newborn infants. D. L. Molfese and V. J. Molfese (1979a, 1979b, 1980, 1985, 1988) isolated and identified electrophysiological correlates of various speech perception cues across and within a number of developmental periods. A number of studies conducted over the past three decades have indicated that ERPs are sensitive to phonetic variations (Kraus et al., 1996; D. Molfese, 1978a, 1978b; D. L. Molfese & V. J. Molfese, 1979a, 1979b, 1980, 1985, 1988). This research has investigated, for the most part, two major speech cues—voice onset time (VOT) and place of articulation (POA).

Voice Onset Time. In a prelude to studying speech perception in young infants, Molfese first studied whether ERP correlates of phonetic effects occurred in adults. To this end, D. Molfese (1978a) recorded ERPs from the left and right temporal regions of 16 adults during a standard phoneme identification task. Randomly ordered sequences of synthesized bilabial stop consonants with VOT values of +0 ms, +20 ms, +40 ms, and +60 ms elicited scalp recorded ERPs while adults pressed keys to identify each sound. Two regions of the ERP (at 135 ms and between 300 and 500 ms following stimulus onset) changed systematically as a function of the sound's phonetic category. ERPs to stop consonant sounds with VOT values of +0 and +20 ms (sounds identified as *ba*) differed from those with VOT values of +40 and +60 ms (sounds identified as *pa*). However, ERPs did not discriminate between sounds from the same phonetic category, suggesting that the ERPs were sensitive to discriminations between, but not within, different phonetic categories. These findings parallel those previously reporting categorical speech perception with behavioral techniques (Liberman, Cooper, Shankweiler, & Studdert-Kennedy, 1967). Electrophysiological studies employing similar stimuli have replicated this finding with 2- to 5-month-old infants (D. L. Molfese & V. J. Molfese, 1979b), two different groups of preschool children (D. L. Molfese & Hess, 1978; D. Molfese & V. Molfese, 1988), and adults (Molfese, 1978a), and were later replicated by Segalowitz and Cohen (1989). Findings with newborn infants, however, have been more mixed. An early study with newborns failed to find a categorical like effect for VOT until 2 to 5 months of age (D. L. Molfese & V. J. Molfese, 1979b). Such findings suggest that a speech sound discriminator for VOT develops after birth but early in infancy.

Place of Articulation. Other studies focused on the development of a different phonetic cue, place of articulation (POA). In an initial study with adults, D. Molfese (1978a) recorded ERPs while adults listened to series of consonant–vowel syllables that differed in the second formant transition (F2, which signaled POA information), and formant bandwidth. Two regions of the auditory ERP that peaked at 70 ms (and occurred over both hemispheres) and 300 ms (only over the left hemisphere temporal electrode site) following stimulus onset discriminated POA. In a replication/extension of this POA discrimination work with newborn and young infants, D. L. Molfese and V. J. Molfese (1979a) noted a similar pattern of lateralized and bilateral responses. Analyses identified two regions of the auditory ERP that discriminated the POA. One region, with a peak latency of 168 ms, detected only over the left hemisphere site discriminated between the two different consonant sounds; a second region with a peak latency of 664 ms discriminated this POA difference and was detected by electrodes placed over both hemispheres. A replication and extension of this work, which involved recorded ERPs from 6 scalp locations of 38 newborn infants to a somewhat different stimulus set, reported comparable effects at similar latencies (Molfese, Burger-Judisch, & Hans, 1991). Unlike the VOT studies, these show a relatively stable pattern of development from infancy into adulthood (Gelfer, 1987; D. L. Molfese, 1978a, 1980b, 1983; D. L. Molfese, Buhrke, & Wang; 1985; D. L. Molfese, Linnville, Wetzel, & Leicht, 1985; D. Molfese & V. Molfese, 1979a, 1985; D. L. Molfese & Schmidt, 1983). These effects have also been replicated independently by other laboratories (Gelfer, 1987; Segalowitz & Cohen, 1989).

Building Predictive Models Based on ERPs. Several consistent trends in this data can be noted. First, it is clear that discrimination of different speech cues emerge at different times in early development. This is true from both the standpoint of behavioral research (Eimas et al., 1971), as well as ERP research (D. Molfese & V. Molfese, 1979a, 1979b, 1985, 1997). For example, relatively stable and reliable ERP correlates of consonant place of articulation (POA) discrimination occur in newborn infants. At the same time, however, discrimination of a different speech cue, voice onset time (VOT), does not appear to develop until sometime after birth, at least in the majority of the population (D. Molfese & V. Molfese, 1979b; Simos & D. L. Molfese, 1997). Second, the scalp distributions for ERP effects in relation to speech sound discrimination change with development. Thus, for example, D. Molfese and V. Molfese (1979a) noted temporal lateral effects in newborn infants, and more pronounced frontal effects are noted in 12- to 16-month-old infants (D. L. Molfese, 1989, 1990), and temporal-parietal effects in children (D. Molfese & V. Molfese, 1988) and adults (D. Molfese, 1978a). The third point is that different temporal regions of the ERP waveform appear sensitive to phonetic contrasts at different developmental stages. Thus, shortly after birth, speech sound discriminations are noted to occur at relatively long latencies (520–920 ms, see D. L. Molfese & V. J. Molfese, 1979a; Simos & D. L. Molfese, 1997), and these effects shift forward in the ERP wave to 180–400 ms for preschoolers (D. L. Molfese & Hess, 1978; D. Molfese & V. Molfese, 1988), and from 50–350 ms for elementary school children and adults. Developmental variations in these three areas, the age of appearance of these ERP phonetic-related effects, their scalp distributions, and their latencies within the ERP waveforms can be expected to influence the stability of the models used to predict different levels of language and cognitive skills across different developmental periods. Furthermore, given the types of tasks and measures used to measure language and cognition also change developmentally (as well as the very characteristics of those areas), the task of developing a predictive model across different developmental periods presents the appearance of being nearly Herculean. One factor seems evident—that is, attempts to develop static predictive models that are accurate from infancy to adulthood would be limited in their success. Instead, it appears likely that any successful model must employ at least some different predictor variables at different ages in order to be successful.

Such lateralized patterns may have important implications for later language development. Of particular concern are questions, such as: Are these patterns of lateralized responses related to later language development or do they reflect only some basic pattern of auditory processing in the brain that has little relation to language development? Given Lenneberg's (1967) notion that lateralization is a biological sign of language, could such early patterns of lateralized discrimination for speech sounds predict later language outcomes? Theoreticians have speculated that the absence of hemispheric differences in a child indicates that the child is at risk for cognitive or language disabilities (Travis, 1931). Although the data generally have not supported such a position with regard to the absence of hemispheric differences and disabilities, predictions concerning later performance could be enhanced when hemispheric differences are considered in light of specific language or speech processing capacities.

In this regard, D. Molfese and V. Molfese (1985, 1986) attempted to establish the predictive validity of a variety of factors in predicting long-term outcomes in language development from measures taken shortly after birth and during the first years of life. In the first study, 16 infants were studied longitudinally from birth through age 3. Information was collected on gender, birthweight, length at birth, gestational age, scores on the Obstetric Complications Scale (Littman & Parmelee, 1978), the Brazelton Neonatal Assessment Scale (Als, Tronick, Lester, & Brazelton, 1977; Brazelton, 1973), the Bayley Scales of Infant Development (Bayley, 1969), the Peabody Picture Vocabulary Test (Dunn, 1965), and the McCarthy Scales of Children's Abilities (McCarthy, 1972). Information on parental ages, incomes, educational levels, and occupations was also obtained. In addition, ERPs were recorded from the left and right temporal areas (T3 and T4, referenced to linked ears) at birth and again at 6-month intervals until the child's third birthday. These ERPs were elicited in response to speech stimuli chosen because they produced reliable general hemispheric difference effects as well as bilateral and lateralized discrimination effects. Eight other stimuli were added to facilitate tests of generalizability across different consonant and vowel contrasts. Such stimuli appeared ideally suited for determining whether general hemispheric differences, per se, or specific lateralized discrimination abilities were the best predictors of later language skills.

Analyses of the ERP data indicated that electrophysiological measures recorded at birth could identify children who performed better or worse on language tasks 3 years later. Two particularly important components in the brain waves were identified. One component of the auditory ERP that occurred between 88 and 240 ms reliably discriminated between children whose McCarthy Verbal Index scores were above 50 (the High group) and those with lower scores (i.e., the Low group). Only ERPs recorded over the left hemisphere of the High group systematically discriminated between the different consonant speech sounds. The right hemisphere responses of this group, on the other hand, discriminated between the different nonspeech stimuli. The Low group displayed no such lateralized discrimination for either the speech or the nonspeech sounds. A second component of the ERP with a late peak latency of 664 ms also discriminated between the High and Low groups. Unlike the earlier component, however, the second component occurred over both hemispheres and, consequently, reflected bilateral activity. This second component differed in other ways from the first component. Whereas the second component discriminated between speech and nonspeech sounds, this discrimination depended on which vowel followed the consonant. A third component of the ERP (peak latency = 450 ms) that only varied across hemispheres failed to discriminate between the two different language performance groups. Thus, hemispheric differences at birth by themselves did not discriminate between infants who would develop better or poorer language skills 3 years later. Furthermore, given that the ERP components discriminating between the two groups were sensitive to certain speech and nonspeech contrasts but not to others, it appears that the ERPs reflected the infant's sensitivity to specific language-related cues rather than the overall readiness of the brain to respond to any general stimulus in its environment.

In subsequent analyses of these data, a stepwise multiple regression model was developed in which the Peabody scores and McCarthy Verbal Index scores were used as the dependent variables and the ERP components obtained at birth that best discriminated the different consonant sounds were used as the independent variables. This model accounted for 78% of the total variance in predicting McCarthy scores from the brain responses, whereas 69% of the variance was accounted for in predicting Peabody scores (Molfese, 1989). Clearly, there appears to be a strong relation between early ERP discrimination of speech-related stimuli and later language skills. Efforts to improve the amount of variance accounted for were undertaken in which perinatal measures and Brazelton scores were also entered into the equations. These regression models were significant, but the improvement in the amount of variance accounted for less than 3%.

D. Molfese and Searock (1986) noted that the relation between neonatal ERP activity and later language also exists using ERPs recorded at age 1. In this study, ERPs were recorded from 16 infants at birth and again within

2 weeks of their first birthday. A series of three vowel sounds with normal speech formant structure bandwidths and 3 nonspeech tokens containing 1-Hz wide formants that matched the mean frequencies of the speech sounds were presented to these infants, and their ERPs were recorded in response to each sound. Two regions of the ERPs, one centered between 300 and 400 ms, and another centered around 200 ms following stimulus onset, discriminated between the 1-year-old infants, who 2 years later would perform better or worse on the McCarthy language tasks. Infants who were able to discriminate between more vowel sounds at age 1 performed better on the language tasks at age 3. Thus, it appears that ERPs at birth and at 1 year can both be successfully used as the basis for making predictions concerning language performance at age 3.

Subsequently, D. L. Molfese (1989) utilized a different type of statistical procedures with a different longitudinal sample of infants. ERPs were recorded at birth from frontal, temporal, and parietal scalp areas over the left and right hemispheres in response to speech and nonspeech sounds (consisting of speech syllables [bi, gi] and nonspeech analogues for the consonant–vowel sounds). The sample consisted of 30 infants with McCarthy verbal scores at age 3 ranging from 32 to 69 (mean = 53, SD = 9.41). The mean for the infants who scored 50 or below on the McCarthy test was 45 (SD = 4.97, range = 32-50). The mean for the infants who scored above 50 was 61 (SD = 4.95, range = 54–69). Overall, both groups of children possessed largely average language scores. A Discriminant Function Procedure used the time points of the averaged ERPs to discriminate the language scores. The stepwise analysis, with an F-to-enter of 3.0, selected 17 points in order of their effectiveness in classifying each of the 720 original averaged ERPs into one of the two groups (Low or High language performance). These points clustered in four regions of the ERP— the first between 20 and 140 ms, the second between 230 and 270 ms, the third between 410 and 490 ms, and the fourth between 600 and 700 ms. The likelihood of correctly classifying a brain response as belonging to a Low or High language performance child was 50%, but the actual classification accuracy was significantly higher than chance. For the High group, the classification was accurate 68.6% of the time, whereas it was accurate 69.7% of the time for the Low group. A z test of proportions indicated that the actual classification was significantly better than chance for each group (z = 10.57, p < .001, and z < 9.98, p < .001, respectively). Applying a rule that at least 51% of an individual's ERPs must be classified into the Low group before that infant would be classified as a lower than average language performing child, Molfese noted that only one infant from each group would be misclassified.

More recently, D. L. Molfese (1992) collected data from a second and larger longitudinal sample of infants. Analyses involving one subset of data included a sample of 1,296 ERPs recorded from 54 neonates. The language performance of these children was measured with the McCarthy Verbal Index at age 3. The children were divided into two groups, such that half of the children scored above 54 (High group: M = 61, SD = 4.95, range = 54–72) on the McCarthy test and half scored 50 or below (Low group M = 45, SD = 4.97, range = 32–50). The early region of the ERP was again found to vary as a function of 3-year language performance scores (Low vs. High). As in the case of D. Molfese and V. Molfese (1985), the region between 70 and 210 ms with a peak latency of 140 ms discriminated between groups. The left hemisphere auditory-evoked responses from the High language group discriminated between the two consonant sounds, /b/ and /g/, $F(1, 52) = 8.37, p < .0057$. This was not the case for the Low language group. These findings are especially exciting because they are similar in both latency and lateralized effect to the results reported from the earlier D. Molfese and V. Molfese (1985) study, even though D. L. Molfese (1992) used a different population of infants and the stimuli comprised a smaller subset of that employed earlier by D. Molfese and V. Molfese (1985).

Another striking aspect of this replication concerns the range of language abilities assessed at age 3 years between the D. Molfese and V. Molfese (1985) study and D. L. Molfese (1992). Although the language skills of the earlier study covered a considerable range from relatively poor receptive and productive skills to well above average skills, the language skills in the D. L. Molfese (1992) study are from a sample of children whose language skills cover a much narrower range. In spite of the dissimilarity of the two samples, the brain responses continue to be fairly robust in their ability to distinguish groups of children who perform differently on language tasks.

One overall interpretation of these results is that neonatal discrimination abilities, as measured by ERPs, relate directly to later language development. The children who performed better on language tasks at age 3, as newborn infants could discriminate between consonant sounds alone and consonant sounds in combination with different vowel sounds. Such a pattern of responding suggests that more linguistically advanced children are already at an advantage at birth because their nervous systems can make finer discriminations along a variety of different dimensions. As D. Molfese (1989) suggested, "Perhaps the earlier an infant can discriminate between speech sounds in its environment, the more likely that infant will be able to use such information to discriminate word sound differences" (p. 55). Such early discrimination abilities may later play a major role in the infant and young child's vocabulary and syntax development.

D. L. Molfese and V. J. Molfese (1997) noted that this relation between early neonatal ERPs and later language performance measures continues into the kindergarten years. In fact, Molfese and Molfese presented data indicating that this relation remains a strong one over this longer time period. D. L. Molfese and V. J. Molfese tested a sample of 71 term Caucasian infants (39 females, 32 males) within 36 hours of birth using auditory ERPs. The ERPs were recorded to 9 consonant–vowel (CV) syllables, which combined the initial consonants (b, d, or g) with a following vowel (a, i, or u). Twenty repetitions of each CV were presented in blocked random order with the other sounds. Electrodes were placed at FL, FR, T3, T4, PL, and PR, with linked ears serving as the reference. In this manner, 3,834 ERPs were obtained from the 71 infants and then submitted to a PCA, which generated 7 factors that accounted for 89.02% of the total variance. These children were subsequently tested again at age 5 using the Stanford–Binet verbal score. These 71 children were then divided into two groups based on their verbal scores: 62 children with verbal IQ above 100 (High group) and 9 with verbal IQ less than 100. Comparisons of these groups indicated no differences in birthweight, Apgar scores, or gestational ages.

The investigators selected two factors in their analysis with the same temporal characteristics of that previously identified by D. Molfese and V. Molfese (1985) as discriminating children at age 3 in terms of their verbal skills. Using discriminant function analyses to discriminate between these two groups based on their newborn ERPs, D. Molfese and V. Molfese correctly classified 78.87% of the children (56 of 71 children) in terms of their verbal skills at age 5 based on three variables (LTBG2, RTBG2, RPBD2), which reflected variations in the ERP waveform between 170 and 320 ms as elicited by different CV sounds. LTBG2 was derived by subtracting the left temporal hemisphere factor score for /g/ initial syllables from those obtained for the left temporal hemisphere response to /b/ initial syllables); and RTBG2 reflected the same difference score obtained for the right temporal hemisphere. RPBD2 was derived by subtracting right hemisphere parietal factor scores obtained for /d/ initial syllables from those obtained at this electrode site from /b/ initial syllables.

The inclusion of three additional variables (RTDG6, RTA6, HAU6) for the region between 70 and 210 ms allowed D. Molfese and V. Molfese to correctly classify 91.55% of the children (65 of 71 children). In this case, 7 of 9 children were correctly identified as scoring below 100 and 58 of 62 children were correctly classified as scoring above 100. RTDG2 reflected the difference score obtained by subtracting the right temporal hemisphere factor score for /g/ initial syllables from those obtained for the right temporal hemisphere response to /d/ initial syllables; RTA6 reflected the right hemisphere temporal response to the vowel /a/, and HAU6 summarized the difference in the way the two hemispheres responded to the /a/ versus /u/ vowels.

A final discriminant analysis was conducted using one additional variable, LTA6, which summarized the left hemisphere temporal response to all CV syllables ending in /a/. In this analysis, 68 of 71 children were correctly classified at age 5 based on their newborn brain responses. Virtually all of the children belonging to the Low group (8 of 9 for 88.9%) were correctly classified along with 60 of 62 children (96.8%) belonging to the High group.

These results indicate that auditory ERPs recorded at birth can successfully discriminate the verbal performance of children even up to 5 years later with high accuracy. These results extend the predictive accuracy of neonatal ERPs 2 years beyond that first demonstrated by D. Molfese and V. Molfese (1985). Confirmation in this study of the findings from D. Molfese and V. Molfese (1985) regarding the use of neonatal ERPs to predict later language performance outcomes are especially intriguing when it is remembered that different verbal performance measures were used across these two studies. The McCarthy verbal scores were used by D. Molfese and V. Molfese (1985) and the verbal scores derived from the Stanford–Binet were used in the present study. Thus, given this ability to classify children across different performance measures, it is clear that ERP factor scores obtained from similar brain regions can provide an effective and powerful means to discriminate performance on different standardized tests and at different ages. In addition, D. L. Molfese and V. J. Molfese (1997) were able to accurately classify children's language performance on verbal tests based on their birth measures, despite a narrower range of verbal skills. Indeed, the children in the D. L. Molfese and V. J. Molfese (1997) study showed a narrower range of scores than that shown by the children originally tested by D. Molfese and V. Molfese (1985). Children in the previous study were characterized by McCarthy verbal scores that ranged from 12 to 99, a range of approximately nine standard deviations. For the present sample, the ranges of Stanford–Binet verbal IQ scores extending from 80 to 129, a difference of approximately four standard deviations. Nevertheless, despite this relatively narrow range of scores, their measures continued to show high classification accuracy.

The D. L. Molfese and V. J. Molfese (1997) study varied in other ways from their earlier study with 3-year-old children. In contrast to D. Molfese and V. Molfese (1985), who used ERPs recorded from only the left and right temporal regions, T3 and T4, the 1997 study employed a total of six scalp recording sites, two of which were identical to those used in the original study. As in their previous study, factor scores derived from the temporal sites were important in discriminating between children with different levels of verbal skills. In fact, for the most part, the discriminative models in D. L. Molfese and V. J. Molfese (1997) included ERPs recorded primarily from the temporal sites and comprised two of three components in the three variable model, four of six in the second model, and five of seven in the third model. However, it is clear that the additional factor scores derived from frontal and parietal leads improved the classification accuracy beyond that produced by the temporal sites alone. The ability of the right parietal region to discriminate between consonant sounds also contributed to the discrimination between variations in language skills. Another variable that collapsed electrode sites within each hemisphere and then subtracted the contribution of the right hemisphere from that of the left also contributed to this discrimination. A final variable that characterized a more general level of hemisphere difference related to vowel discrimination further served to improve the discrimination. Thus, although ERPs recorded from over the temporal regions of the two hemispheres continued to play a prominent role in predicting later developmental outcomes, additional contributions were noted at other electrode sites.

More recent work indicates that such long-term prediction continues through age 8. Molfese (in press) assessed the relationship between neonatal brain responses and reading performance at 8 years of age in 102 children. He recorded 5508 auditory event related potentials (ERPs) that were from the left and right hemisphere frontal, temporal, and parietal scalp regions (linked ear references) of 102 newborn term infants to a series of 9 consonant–vowel syllables composed of the consonants /b, d, g/ and the vowels /i, a, u/. These children were subsequently tested within two weeks of their eighth birthday using these ERP procedures as well as a variety of language and cognitive measures. Data presented in this report focus on results obtained at age 8 using the WRAT-3 to assess general reading performance.

Following artifact rejection, the ERPs were averaged by condition and electrode site and then submitted to a principal components analysis procedure employing a correlation matrix with varimax rotation. Seven factors describing variability in different ERP wave regions characterized 85% of the total variance in the ERP data set. These were input to a discriminant function procedure to classify 3 groups of children defined by their WRAT 3 reading subtest scores at 8 years-of-age: (1) a Low group comprised responses from 11 children who performed one standard deviation below the mean (range = 50–82), (2) a Mean group included 75 children who scored within one standard deviation of the population mean (range = 83–113), and (3) a High group included 16 children who scored one standard deviation above the mean (range = 114–126). Six factor scores representing ERP discriminations of the consonants /b/, /d/, and /g/ at left hemisphere parietal and temporal were entered into the discriminant function procedure from two factors that matched the peak latencies previously identified by Molfese and Molfese (1985) with a different longitudinal sample of children. Two discriminant functions classified these children at eight years of age with 66.67% accuracy. Ten of 11 children (90.9%) were correctly classified as members of the Low group, 46 of 75 children (61.3%) were correctly classified as Average, and 12 of 16 children were correctly classified as High performers (75%). Thus, neonatal brain responses discriminated individual children's level of performance at 8 years of age on the WRAT-3 test of reading abilities. Given overall WRAT-3 reading scores at 8 years were generally within the normal range, these newborn brain response data made relatively fine distinctions in predicting later reading skills. These data extend findings which previously reported strong relationships between neonatal speech discrimination and verbal performance measures at 3 and 5 years. This work extends those findings and indicates that a strong relationship exists between the ability of newborn infants to discriminate speech sounds and their reading level at 8 years of age. Such findings raise the hope that early identification could lead to early successful intervention for reading problems. If infants can be identified shortly after birth as "at risk" for later poor reading skills, interventions could be started much earlier in development than is now considered feasible. The additional time to address potential shortfalls in development, when coupled with the early plasticity that cognitive and linguistic systems appear to possess, could potentially lead to the elimination of some types of reading disabilities. A subsequent study by Molfese (2000) that applied this approach to a group of children including those with reading problems suggests that these procedures may in fact be useful in identifying early in life children with potential reading problems.

Molfese (2000) used traditional latency and amplitude measures of the newborn infant's brain responses to speech syllable to predict outcomes in reading skills at eight years of age. This work extended the findings of Molfese and Molfese (1997) to the prediction of reading performance by assessing the relationship between neonatal brain responses and reading performance at 8 years of age in 48 children. This sample consisted of 17 Dyslexics, 7 Poor Readers, and 24 Controls. The dyslexic children at eight years of age had normal full scale IQ (FSIQ) scores (mean FSIQ = 110.0) as measured by the Wechsler Intelligence Scales for Children–3 (Wechsler, 1991, WISC-3), although their reading scores from the Wide Range Achievement Test 3 (Wilkinson, 1993, WRAT) were markedly below average (mean = 80.6). The Poor Readers had both low reading scores (mean WRAT = 85.4) and low WISC Full Scale IQ scores (mean FSIQ = 96.9). Although the FSIQ scores of the Poor Readers and Dyslexics differed from each other, their reading scores did not. The Control children were matched to the Full Scale IQ scores of the Dyslexic children (mean WISC FSIQ = 111.7), although their WRAT reading scores were higher than those obtained by both the Poor Readers and Dyslexics (mean WRAT = 103.75).

Auditory event related potentials (ERPs) were recorded from the left and right hemisphere frontal, temporal, and parietal scalp regions (linked ear references) of these 48 infants within 36 hours of birth to a series of two consonant–vowel syllables, /bi/ and /gi/, and non-speech homologues of these sounds. These children were subsequently tested within two weeks of their eighth birthday using these ERP procedures as well as a variety of language and cognitive measures including the reading subtest of the WRAT3 (mean = 97.66, SD = 12.6, range = 50–126) that was used to assess general reading performance.

Following artifact rejection for eye and muscle artifacts (rejection levels across infants < 15%), the ERPs were averaged by condition and electrode site. Next, baseline-to-peak amplitude (calculated from the average prestimulus period to a peak within the brainwave) as well as peak latency measures (calculated from stimulus onset to the maximum point of a peak within the brainwave) were calculated for three component peaks of each neonatal ERP. These peak measures of the neonatal brain responses then served as dependent measures in a discriminant function analysis to classify children's reading performance at 8 years of age. These peaks included (a) the initial negative–positive shift in the ERP in the region from the first large negative peak (N1, mean peak latency = 174.3 ms, SD = 31.2, mean baseline-to-peak amplitude = –2.4 V, SD = 1.2 V) to the following positive peak (P2, mean peak latency = 308.7 ms, SD = 38.2, mean peak amplitude = 3.3 V, SD = 1.2 V), and (b) a second large negative peak (N2, mean peak latency = 458.0 ms, SD = 32.8, mean peak amplitude = –3.5 V, SD = 1.2 V).

The discriminant function used six neonatal ERP responses to discriminate between the Control, Dyslexic, and Poor Reader groups at eight years of age. These variables included three amplitude measures that included (1) the second large negative peak (N2) that differed between groups in response to the /gi/ speech syllable at the right hemisphere frontal electrode site; (2) the N1 amplitude change recorded at the right temporal hemisphere electrode site elicited in response to the /bi/ non-speech syllable; and (3) the second large positive peak amplitude (P2) elicited in response to the /bi/ speech syllable. The three peak latency measures included the first large negative peak latency (N1) to the speech syllable, /gi/, recorded at both the left hemisphere frontal and parietal electrode sites, and at the right temporal hemisphere.

These six measures resulted in the identification of two significant canonical discriminant functions which correctly classified 81.25% of the entire sample (39 of 48 children) at eight years of age. Using the neonatal ERP measures, seven of seven Poor Readers were correctly classified (100%), 13 of 17 Dyslexic children were correctly classified (76.5%), and 19 of 24 of Control children (79.2%). These classifications are approximately two times greater than chance levels. If reading interventions were attempted shortly after birth on the basis of these data, 22 of 24 children in need of intervention at 8 years of age could have been targeted to receive intervention beginning at birth while only 5 of 24 children who did not require intervention would have received it. Thus, ERP measures shortly after birth demonstrate high accuracy (identifying nearly 92% of children in need of intervention by eight years) and generate relatively few false positives in predicting reading problems eight years later.

Brain responses collected at birth discriminated individual children's level of performance at 8 years of age on the WRAT-3 test of reading abilities. Given overall WRAT-3 reading scores at 8 years were generally within the normal range, these newborn brain response data made relatively fine distinctions in predicting later reading skills. These data extend findings which previously reported strong relationships between neonatal speech discrimination and verbal performance measures at 3, 5, and 8 years of age. This work extends those findings and indicates that a strong relationship exists between the ability of newborn infants to discriminate speech sounds and their reading level at 8 years of age.

Such findings raise the hope that early identification could lead to early successful intervention for reading problems. If infants can be identified shortly after birth as "at risk" for later reading skills, intervention could be started much earlier in development than is currently considered feasible. The additional time to address potential shortfalls in development, coupled with the early plasticity that cognitive and linguistic systems appear to possess, could potentially lead to the elimination of some types of reading disabilities. These data are discussed further in terms of early assessment approaches and potential interventions for reading disabilities.

From the review already provided, it is clear that studies conducted over the past four decades have varied in their ability to predict later development based on neonatal-evoked potential measures certainly (Table 7.3). However, it is equally clear that some relations have been noted. In general, those studies restricting their analyses of the evoked potential response to a single early peak in the brain wave or to a specific peak latency (i.e., usually the N1 component) achieved some modest success in short-term prediction, but failed to find a long-term relation between various measures of intelligence and the ERP waveform. The more successful long-term prediction studies, in contrast, analyzed more of the ERP waveform, that is, analyzed three to four peaks, and recorded ERPs from scalp locations anterior to the occipital areas.

The obvious question that arises from such highly predictive results as these is why any type of measure, behavioral or brain, should discriminate developmental outcomes over a large age range with such high accuracy. Are human accomplishments predetermined from birth? Are genetic factors so potent that they all but force certain developmental outcomes despite the influence of any environmental factors? Rather, D. L. Molfese and V. J. Molfese (1997) hypothesized that these data reflect the state of an underlying perceptual mechanism on which some aspects of later developing and emerging verbal and cognitive processes are based. As a result of genetic and intrauterine factors, the developing organism develops a set of perceptual abilities responsive to variations in its environment. For most individuals, these perceptual abilities are similar and readily enable them to discriminate elements within their environment in quite similar ways. For others, however, aspects of these perceptual skills may not respond to environmental elements in the same way. It is these fundamental differences in perceptual skills that set the stage for early detection of responses that influence later language development.

Such findings as those outlined earlier raise exciting possibilities regarding the early identification of children with potential language problems and enhance the possibility that successful intervention for such language problems could be carried out before they become fully manifested in the child's behavior. At present, the identification of children with language and other cognitive problems occurs relatively late, often occurring in the elementary school years after it is established that the child is performing below grade level. One consequence of this delayed identification strategy is that it occurs so late in the child's overall cognitive and linguistic development. Thus, it may already be pushing the edge of the child's cognitive flexibility and its ability to master new skills. Witelson and Swallow (1987) noted that age 10 could mark an important transition, or major "breaking point," in development because there are marked changes in abilities such as spatial pattern recognition, Braille, and map reading after this time. Others (e.g., Curtis, 1977) have shown that the onset of puberty appears to set limits on the acquisition of certain language and cognitive skills. Thus, interventions begun at approximately age 10 could face ceiling limits placed on their success by the child's developmental level and age. If, however, potential problems in language or cognitive development could be identified much earlier in time, the planned interventions could be introduced earlier to the child and, consequently, be more successful in remediating the child's emerging language or cognitive problems.

CONCLUSIONS

These data obtained using ERP measures from neonates are supportive of the position that these early physiological indices are highly predictive of later emerging language skills over a 3-year time period. The utilization of several brain wave components rather than one component or one latency measure seems to impact importantly on the effectiveness of brain waves as predictors of later functioning. The identification of these brain wave components as related to specific stimulus conditions permits them to be used in analyses in a theory driven manner to predict specific types of later language functioning. These analysis procedures, which have been described by D. Molfese (1978a), have also been effective in attempts to use brain wave components to assess other aspects of cognitive functioning and performance abilities (D. Molfese, 1978a, 1978b, 1980a, 1980b, 1983, 1984).

It remains to be determined how neonatal ERP measures can be effectively combined with other measures, such as medical and behavioral measures obtained in the neonatal period, to identify even more accurately infants who are at risk for cognitive and language disabilities. Although previous attempts to combine ERP measures with perinatal and neonatal behavioral measures were not impressive, it seems reasonable that perinatal and behavioral measures should complement the ERP measures, possibly adding additional information on which predictions of functioning in later infancy can be based. Efforts are currently underway to combine different types of perinatal risk measures with ERP measures to predict outcomes in the longitudinal sample currently under investigation.

Further work is underway to identify when in development the best predictions of later functioning can be made. The use of a longitudinal sample makes this work feasible because measures appropriate for use across the birth to age 13 range are being used. Unlike some measures, ERP methods can be used with infants and children to provide measures of brain processing. Further, the ERP methods have shown promise as providing a basis by which accurate predictions of language and cognitive status can be made even when the scales used for assessments of cognitive and language functioning must change as the children mature. We are very hopeful that ERP measures, in combination with other measures, will provide a highly accurate assessment methodology for use with neonates.

ACKNOWLEDGMENTS

The work presented in this chapter was supported by grants from the March of Dimes Birth Defects Foundation (12-142) and National Institutes of Health (R01 HD17860).

REFERENCES

Als, H., Tronick, E., Lester, B., & Brazelton, T. (1977). The Brazelton Neonatal Behavioral Assessment Scale. *Journal of Abnormal Child Psychology, 5,* 215–231.
Bayley, N. (1969). *Bayley scales of infant development: Birth to two years.* New York: Psychological Corporation.

Bennett, W. F. (1968). Human perception: A network theory approach. *Nature, 220*, 1147–1148.

Brazelton, T. (1973). Neonatal behavior assessment scale. *Clinics in Developmental Medicine*, No. 50. Philadelphia: Lippincott.

Butler, B., & Engel, R. (1969). Mental and motor scores at 8 months in relation to neonatal photic responses. *Developmental Medicine and Child Neurology, 11*, 77–82.

Callaway, C., Tueting, P., & Koslow, S. (1978). *Event-related brain potentials and behavior.* New York: Academic Press.

Chalke, F. C. R., & Ertl, J. (1965). Evoked potentials and intelligence. *Life Sciences, 4*, 1319–1322.

Cohen, S., & Beckwith, L. (1979). Preterm infant interactions with the caregiver in the first year of life and competence at age two. *Child Development, 50*, 767–777.

Cohen, S., & Parmelee, A. (1983). Prediction of five-year Stanford–Binet scores in preterm infants. *Child Development, 54*, 1242–1253.

Cohen, S., Parmelee, A., Sigman, M., & Beckwith, L. (1982). Neonatal risk factors in preterm infants. *Applied Research in Mental Retardation, 3*, 265–278.

Curtis, S. (1977). *Genie: A psycholinguistic study of a modern day "wild child."* New York: Academic Press.

Dunn, D. (1965). *Peabody Picture Vocabulary Test.* Circle Pines: American Guidance Series.

Dustman, R. E., & Beck, E. C. (1969a). The effects of maturation and aging on the wave form of visually evoked potentials. *Journal of Electroencephalography and Clinical Neurophysiology, 26*, 2–11.

Dustman, R. E., & Beck, E. C. (1969b). Visually evoked potentials: Amplitude changes with age. *Science, 151*, 1013–1015.

Eimas, P. D., Siqueland, E., Jusczyk, P., & Vigorito, J. (1971). Speech perception in infants. *Science, 171*, 303–306.

Ellingson, R. J. (1966). Relationship between EEG and test intelligence: A commentary. *Psychological Bulletin, 65*, 91–98.

Engel, R., & Fay, W. (1972). Visual evoked responses at birth, verbal scores at three years and IQ at four years. *Developmental Medicine and Child Neurology, 14*, 283–289.

Engel, R., & Henderson, N. (1973). Visual evoked responses and IQ scores at school age. *Developmental Medicine and Child Neurology, 15*, 136–145.

Ertl, J. P., & Schafer, E. W. P. (1969). Brain response correlates of psychometric intelligence. *Nature, 223*, 421–422.

Galbraith, G. C., Gliddon, J. B., & Busk, J. (1970). Visual evoked responses in mentally retarded and nonretarded subjects. *American Journal of Mental Deficiency, 75*(3), 341–348.

Gelfer, M. (1987). An AER study of stop-consonant discrimination. *Perception & Psychophysics, 42*, 318–327.

Henderson, N., & Engel, R. (1974). Neonatal visual evoked potentials as predictors of psychoeducational testing at age seven. *Developmental Psychology, 10*, 269–276.

Jasper, H. (1958). The ten-twenty electrode system of the International Federation of Societies for Electroencephalography: Appendix to report of the committee on methods and clinical examination of electroencephalography. *Journal of Electroencephalography and Clinical Neurophysiology, 10*, 371–375.

Kraus, N., McGee, T. J., Carrell, T. D., Zecker, S. G., Nicol, T. G., & Koch, D. B. (1996). Auditory neurophysiologic responses and discrimination deficits in children with learning problems. *Science, 273*, 971–973.

Lenneberg, E. (1967). *Biological foundations of language.* New York: Wiley.

Liberman, A. M., Cooper, F. S., Shankweiler, D., & Studdert-Kennedy, M. (1967). Perception of the speech code. *Psychological Review, 74*, 431–461.

Littman, B., & Parmelee, A. (1978). Medical correlation of infant development. *Pediatrics, 61,* 470–474.

McCarthy, D. (1972). *Manual for the McCarthy scales of children's abilities.* New York: Psychological Corporation.

Molfese, D. (1978a). Left and right hemisphere involvement in speech perception: Electrophysiological correlates. *Perception and Psychophysics, 23,* 237–243.

Molfese, D. L. (1978b). Neuroelectrical correlates of categorical speech perception in adults. *Brain and Language, 5,* 25–35.

Molfese, D. L. (1980a). Hemispheric specialization for temporal information: Implications for the perception of voicing cues during speech perception. *Brain and Language, 11,* 285–299.

Molfese, D. L. (1980b). The phoneme and the engram: Electrophysiological evidence for the acoustic invariant in stop consonants. *Brain and Language, 9,* 372–376.

Molfese, D. L. (1983). Event related potentials and language processes. In A. W. K. Gaillard & W. Ritter (Eds.), *Tutorials in ERP Research: Endogenous Components* (pp. 345–368). The Netherlands: North Holland.

Molfese, D. L. (1989). The use of auditory evoked responses recorded from newborns to predict later language skills. In N. Paul (Ed.), *Research in infant assessment* (Vol. 25, No. 6). White Plains, NY: March of Dimes.

Molfese, D. L. (1992). The use of auditory evoked responses recorded from newborn infants to predict language skills. In M. G. Tramontana & S. R. Hooper (Eds.), *Advances in child neuropsychology* (Vol. 1, pp. 1–23). New York: Springer-Verlag.

Molfese, D. L. (1995). Electrophysiological responses obtained during infancy and their relation to later language development: Further findings. In M. G. Tramontana & S. R. Hooper (Eds.), *Advances in child neuropsychology* (Vol. 3, pp. 1–11). New York: Springer-Verlag

Molfese, D. L. (1990). Auditory evoked responses recorded from 16-month-old human infants to words they did and did not know. *Brain and Language, 38,* 345–363.

Molfese, D. L. (1984). Left hemisphere sensitivity to consonant sounds not displayed by the right hemisphere: Electrophysiological correlates. *Brain and Language, 22,* 109–127.

Molfese, D. L. (in press). Newborn brain responses predict language development skills which emerge eight years later. *Brain and Language.*

Molfese, D. L. (2000). Predicting Dyslexia at 8 Years of Age Using Neonatal Brain Responses. *Brain and Language, 72,* 238–245.

Molfese, D., & Betz, J. (1988). Electrophysiological indices of the early development of lateralization of language and cognition, and their implication for predicting later development. In D. L. Molfese & S. J. Segalowitz (Eds.), *Brain lateralization in children: Developmental implications* (pp. 171–190). New York: Guilford.

Molfese, D. L., Buhrke, R. A., & Wang, S. L. (1985). The right hemisphere and temporal processing of consonant transition durations: Electrophysiological correlates. *Brain and Language. 26,* 289–299.

Molfese, D., Burger-Judisch, L., & Hans, L. (1991). Consonant discrimination by newborn infants: Electrophysiological differences. *Developmental Neuropsychology, 7,* 177–195.

Molfese, D., Freeman, R., & Palermo, D. (1975). The ontogeny of lateralization for speech and nonspeech stimuli. *Brain and Language, 2,* 356–368.

Molfese, D. L., Gill, L. A., Simos, P. G., & Tan, A. (1995). Implications resulting from the use of biological techniques to assess development. In L. F. DiLalla & S. M. Clancy-Dollinger (Eds.), *Assessment and intervention across the lifespan* (pp. 173–190). Hillsdale, NJ: Lawrence Erlbaum Associates.

Molfese, D. L., & Hess, T. (1978). Speech perception in nursery school age children: Sex and hemisphere differences. *Journal of Experimental Child Psychology, 26,* 71–84.

Molfese, D. L., Linnville, S. E., Wetzel, W. F., & Leicht, D. (1985). Electrophysiological correlates of handedness and speech perception contrasts. *Neuropsychologia, 23*, 77–86.

Molfese, D. L., & Molfese, V. J. (1979a). Hemisphere and stimulus differences as reflected in the cortical responses of newborn infants to speech stimuli. *Developmental Psychology, 15*, 505–511.

Molfese, D., & Molfese, V. (1979b). Infant speech perception: Learned or innate? In H. Whitaker & H. Whitaker (Eds.), *Advances in neurolinguistics* (Vol. 4, pp. 225–240). New York: Academic Press.

Molfese, D., & Molfese, V. (1980). Cortical responses of preterm infants to phonetic and nonphonetic speech stimuli. *Developmental Psychology, 16*, 574–581.

Moflese, D., & Molfese, V. (1985). Electrophysiological indices of auditory discrimination in newborn infants: The bases for predicting later language development. *Infant Behavior and Development, 8*, 197–211.

Molfese, D., & Molfese, V. (1986). Psychophysical indices of early cognitive processes and their relationship to language. In J. E. Obrzut & G. W. Hynd (Eds.), *Child neuropsychology: Theory and research* (Vol. 1, pp. 95–115). New York: Academic Press.

Molfese, D., & Molfese, V. (1988). Right hemisphere responses from preschool children to temporal cues contained in speech and nonspeech materials. Electrophysiological correlates. *Brain and Language, 33*, 245–259.

Molfese, D. L., & Molfese, V. J. (1994). Short-term and long-term developmental outcomes. In G. Dawson & K. Fischer (Eds.), *Human behavior and the developing brain* (pp. 493–517). New York: Guilford Press.

Molfese, D. L., & Molfese, V. J. (1997). Discrimination of language skills at five years of age using event-related potentials recorded at birth. *Developmental Neuropsychology, 13*(2), 135–156.

Molfese, D. L., & Schmidt, A. L. (1983). An auditory evoked potential study of consonant perception. *Brain and Language, 18*, 57–70.

Molfese, D., & Searock, K. (1986). The use of auditory evoked responses at one year of age to predict language skills at 3 years. *Australian Journal of Communication Disorders, 14*, 35–46.

Nelson, C., & Salapatek, P. (1986). Electrophysiological correlates of infant recognition memory. *Child Development, 57*, 1483–1497.

Pederson, D., Evans, B., Bento, S., Chance, G., & Fox, A. (1987, April). *Invulnerable high risk preterm infants.* Poster presented at the Society for Research in Child Development, Baltimore.

Rhodes, L. E., Dustman, R. E., & Beck, E. C. (1969). The visual evoked response: A comparison of bright and dull children. *Journal of Electroencephalography and Clinical Neurophysiology, 27*, 364–372.

Rockstroh, B., Elbert, T., Birbaumer, N., & Lutzenberger, W. (1982). *Slow brain potentials and behavior.* Baltimore: Urban-Schwarzenberg.

Ruchkin, D., Sutton, S., Munson, R., & Macar, F. (1981). P300 and feedback provided by the absence of the stimuli. *Psychophysiology, 18*, 271–282.

Segalowitz, S., & Cohen, H. (1989). Right hemisphere EEG sensitivity to speech. *Brain and Language, 37*, 220–231.

Shucard, D. W., & Callaway, E., III. (1973). Relationship between human intelligence and frequency analysis of cortical evoked responses. *Perceptual and Motor Skills, 36*, 147–151.

Shucard, D. W., & Horn, J. L. (1972). Evoked cortical potentials and measurement of human abilities. *Journal of Comparative and Physiological Psychology, 78*(1), 59–68.

Siegel, L. (1982). Reproductive, perinatal and environmental variables as predictors of development of preterm (< 1500 grams) and full term infants at 5 years. *Seminars and Perinatology, 6*, 274–279.

Silva, P., McGee, R., & Williams, S. (1984). A seven year follow-up study of the cognitive development of children who experienced common perinatal problems. *Australian Pediatric Journal, 20*, 23–28.

Simos, P. G., & Molfese, D. L. (1997). Electrophysiological responses from a temporal order continuum in the newborn infant. *Neuropsychologia, 35*, 89–98.

Sostek, A., Smith, Y., Katz, K., & Grant, E. (1987). Developmental outcome of preterm infants with intraventricular hemorrhage at one and two years of age. *Child Development, 58*, 779–786.

Terman, L. M., & Merrill, M. A. (1960). *Stanford–Binet Scale, Form L. M.* Cambridge, MA: Houghton Mifflin.

Travis, L. (1931). *Speech pathology.* New York: Appleton-Century.

Vogel, W., & Broverman, D. M. (1964). Relationship between EEG and test intelligence: A critical review. *Psychological Bulletin, 62*(2), 132–144.

Weinberg, H. (1969). Correlation of frequency spectra of averaged visual evoked potentials with verbal intelligence. *Science, 224*, 813–815.

Witelson, S., & Swallow, J. A. (1987). Neuropsychological study of the development of spatial cognition. In J. Stiles-Davis, M. Kritchevsky, & U. Bellugi (Eds.), *Spatial cognition: Brain bases and development* (pp. 373–409). Hillsdale, NJ: Lawrence Erlbaum Associates.

## CHAPTER EIGHT

Naming Abilities in Children With Brain Tumors

Robin D. Morris
Lorna Lazarus-Benbenisty
Georgia State University

Nicolas Krawiecki
Emory University School of Medicine

Maryanne Wolf
Tufts University

Naming refers to the ability to access and retrieve words in lexical storage (German, 1992, 1993). The act of finding a name or word is the "deceptively simple" end of a complex set of perceptual, linguistic, cognitive, and motoric operations (Caramazza & Berndt, 1978; Gardner, 1974; Liederman, Kohn, Wolf, & Goodglass, 1983; Wolf, 1982, 1995; Wolf & Obregon, 1992). Qualitatively different types of naming disorders have been reported in adults with anterior and posterior brain injuries. Patients with focal damage to the anterior portion of the dominant hemisphere have many concrete and picturable nouns available for retrieval; they often perform accurately, but with an increased latency, on naming tasks. This type of naming disruption appears to be part of a more generalized speech/language disturbance, because other symptoms often include laborious articulation and a severe disruption of productive syntax. Patients with posterior lesions in the dominant hemisphere often display a deficit in the naming of concrete, picturable nouns, although the errors are frequently semantically or phonologically related to target (Goodglass, 1980). This impairment carries over into spontaneous speech, which is characterized by fluent articulation and intact syntax but reduction of content words. Although these patterns in adult naming performance are found in anterior versus posterior lesion comparisons, comparisons at a more differentiated level of lesion site have not yielded clear differences in naming performance (Goodglass, personal communication, 1995).

225

In the past, children with focal cerebral lesions were not considered to present with patterns in speech and language disorders similar to adults (Lenneberg, 1967). Later studies, however, demonstrated that young children with left brain lesions are impaired in various aspects of lexical, syntactic, and narrative discourse development (Aram, Ekelman, & Whitaker, 1986; Biddle, McCabe, & Bliss, 1996; Chapman et al., 1992; Dennis, 1980; Dennis & Lovett, 1990; Kiessling, Denckla, & Carlton, 1983; Vargha-Khadem, O'Gorman, & Watters, 1985), whereas children with right brain lesions have relatively less impaired syntax, but are impaired (like adult patients) in "paralinguistic communicative abilities" (e.g., speech prosody, facial and body gestures in communication) (Gross-Tsur, Shalev, Manor, & Amir, 1995). Case studies of lexical ability in hemidecorticate children (Dennis & Kohn, 1975; Dennis & Whitaker, 1976) have also shown a reduction in syntactic abilities in children with left hemidecortication, but no significant differences have been observed between children with left and right hemidecortication on phonemic or semantic tasks.

Children with traumatic brain injury (TBI) offer another important source of information. With these children traditional language measures appear insufficient to detect their linguistic deficits: For example, they appear within normal limits on most language batteries using any decontextualized tests of language (Biddle et al., 1996; Chapman et al., 1992; Jordan, Cannon, & Murdoch, 1992). However, when the discourse and personal narrative skills of TBI children have been examined, significant differences in cohension ability, dysfluency, and rate have been uncovered (Biddle et al., 1996; Chapman et al., 1992). Biddle and her colleagues contended that these narrative impairments appear more the "result of problems with planning, producing, and monitoring discourse," than to language impairments per se (Biddle et al., 1996, p. 459). The notion that these disturbances are related more to higher order, executive processes than language function is supported by other researchers' work (e.g., Ylvisaker, 1993; Ylvisaker & Szekeres, 1989), by the fact that TBI often involves frontal lobe and subcortical damage, and by the frequent finding that TBI children evidence qualitatively different language profiles than other childhood populations with known language disorders (Glosser & Deser, 1990; McDonald, 1993).

The information regarding the specific lexical retrieval abilities of non-hemidecorticate children with brain lesions is mixed. Vargha-Khadem et al. (1985) administered the Oldfield and Wingfield Naming Test to 53 children, 28 of whom had left hemisphere lesions and 25 of whom had right hemisphere lesions. Results showed impaired naming in all children with left lesions (prenatal, early postnatal, and late postnatal) and in the children with early postnatal, right lesions when compared to control subjects. Aram, Ekelman, Rose, and Whitaker (1985) also demonstrated that children with left and right lesions were impaired on global lexical measures when compared to control groups.

Aram et al. (1986) suggested that children with left and right lesions may be impaired on lexical tasks for different reasons, such as the semantic category or stimulus cues provided. In addition, the Oldfield and Wingfield test was normed in England with words and items more typical of British adult populations. Aram et al. (1986), therefore, examined lexical retrieval in 19 children with left brain lesions and 13 with right brain lesions, using the Word-Finding Test developed by Wiegel-Crump and Dennis (1984). The latter task elicits naming across three conditions (semantic, rhyming, and visual). They found that the left lesioned group was slower in word retrieval on the semantic and visual conditions, and produced significantly more errors in naming on the rhyming condition than their matched controls. Qualitatively, their error responses were similar to the left control children and to normals, with the exceptions of a slight tendency of the left lesioned group to produce more repetitive responses, to show a low occurrence of unrelated and category only responses, and to show a provocatively high percentage of association errors. On the Rapid Automatic Naming Test (Denckla & Rudel, 1974, 1976; Wolf, Bally, & Morris, 1986), which elicits naming for the most basic letters, digits, colors, and objects in a visual, serial format, children with left but not right lesions were significantly slower than controls in responding to all categories tested. The order of difficulty was comparable to the normal control group (in order of decreasing latency: objects, colors, numbers, and letters were produced most rapidly), and replicated developmental studies (Wolf et al., 1986). The actual incidence of naming errors was low, and data analysis failed to indicate a pronounced or category-specific naming deficit. Overall, Aram et al. (1986) noted that lesion laterality is related to lexical-retrieval speed rather than error rate, with children with left lesions responding slower, and children with right lesions faster, than their respective controls. Age or lesion site failed to differentiate error rate or latency. Aram et al. concluded that children's lexical retrieval is differentially affected by lesions to the left, but not to the right, hemisphere.

The majority of reported studies that have addressed naming abilities in children with lesions have emphasized the superiority of the left over the right hemisphere (Aram et al., 1985; Aram et al., 1986; Vargha-Khadem et al., 1985). However, these findings have been somewhat inconclusive in that an existent, but nonsignificant, disruption of naming abilities has also been suggested in right lesioned subjects (Aram et al., 1985; Aram et al., 1986; Kiessling et al., 1983; Vargha-Khadem et al., 1985). For example, in a recent case study of children with right hemisphere prefrontal cortical lesions, Eslinger, Biddle, and Gratton (1997) found fully intact lexical skills and normal verbal processing speed on the Rapid Automatized

Naming Test (RAN) and Rapid Automatized Switching Test (RAS; Wolf, 1986), but significant impairments in pragmatic linguistic abilities on narrative and discourse tasks or whenever complex demands in the assembly of language was involved. Eslinger and his colleagues concluded that these deficits were the "result of impaired interaction between executive and linguistic systems following right dorsolateral prefrontal cortical injury" (p. 330). Other, more specialized populations, such as children with hemispherectomy, children with TBI, and children with right hemisphere syndrome, have also contributed to an emerging picture of the right hemisphere's different, but critical, linguistic capacities (Dennis & Whitaker, 1976; Gross-Tsur et al., 1995).

What remains unclear, however, is whether naming problems in such populations represent: (a) the disruption of lexical processes (semantic and/or phonological); (b) more generalized underlying deficits—for example, deficits in arousal (Glosser, Kaplan, & LoVerme, 1982), higher order executive processes (Biddle et al., 1996), or timing mechanisms (Ojemann, 1983, 1990; Wolf, 1995); or (c) combinations of these dependent on lesion site, severity, and age. The further study of children with acquired brain lesions provides an opportunity for greater theoretical understanding of the development of the naming process, and can provide additional clarification of the nature of the naming abilities or problems these children exhibit.

Because of the limited available data regarding naming abilities in children with acquired brain lesions, 17 children, all diagnosed with brain tumors, were evaluated using an extensive battery of naming and naming-related measures. All subjects had documented normal neurological, genetic, developmental, and speech/language status prior to tumor diagnosis, and normal visual acuity at the time of evaluation. For all 17 subjects (see Table 8.1), brain tumor diagnosis had occurred after age 5, a criterion utilized in order to maximize the possibility that automaticity of basic language abilities had probably been established, and to minimize the effects of any ongoing tumor treatments on early brain development. Nonsymptomatic tumor development may have occurred in some cases prior to this age, but this would be impossible to control. All children had at least 2 years of tumor stability after diagnosis and treatment. Because tumor types vary and therefore could differentially affect the extent of injury to the brain, children with meningiomas, ependymomas, and multiple tumors were excluded from the study. Tumor types included were astrocytomas (6), medulloblastomas (2), neuroblastomas (1), gliomas (3), craniopharyngiomas (3), and germinomas (2).

The 17 children were divided into three groups according to the general location of their identified tumor. Subgroup 1 ($n = 5$) consisted of patients with cortical tumors. Of these, four were located in the left cerebral

TABLE 8.1
Demographic and General Characteristics of Children With and Without Brain Tumors

Variable	Measure	Cortical (N = 5)	Subcortical (N = 6)	Cerebellar (N = 6)	Tumors (N = 17)	Nontumor (N = 19)
Left-Handed	Percent	20%	0%	17%	12%	5%
Female	Percent	80%	50%	67%	65%	37%
Test Age (Months)	Mean	165	190	160	172	178
	Median	176	192	154	176	180
	Range	123–190	163–213	125–196	123–213	128–217
Diagnosis Age (Months)	Mean	108	161	114	129	—
	Median	114	164	118	118	—
	Range	111–201	80–131	67–164	67–201	—
Composite Stanford–Binet IQ	Median	112	109	88	104	—
	Range	79–114	79–133	81–115	79–133	—
	Deficit	20%	17%	50%	29%	—
Verbal Reasoning Score	Median	108	105	96	103	—
	Range	71–114	88–127	86–112	71–127	—
	Deficit	40%	0%	0%	13%	—

(Continued)

TABLE 8.1
(Continued)

Variable	Measure	Cortical (N = 5)	Subcortical (N = 6)	Cerebellar (N = 6)	Tumors (N = 17)	Nontumor (N = 19)
Abst. Vis. Reasoning Score	Median	101	107	98	102	—
	Range	87–115	76–136	81–109	76–136	—
	Deficit	0%	33%	17%	18%	—
Vineland Composite Score	Median	79	90	86	85	—
	Range	59–126	65–121	75–111	59–126	—
	Deficit	60%	50%	40%	50%	—
Vineland Communication Score	Median	83	98	86	90	—
	Range	56–127	79–110	66–118	56–127	—
	Deficit	60%	33%	20%	38%	—
Peabody PVT	Median	118	102	88	96	—
	Range	73–126	78–123	78–124	73–126	—
	Deficit	20%	17%	50%	29%	—
Verbal Cancellation Test	# Errs	0	0	0	0	1
	Err. Range	0–10	0–2	0–4	0–10	0–5
	Sec. Range	79–220	84–170	72–261	72–261	60–143
	Seconds	144	106	120	120	96
	Time Deficit	80%	33%	67%	59%	16%

Note: Percent Deficit—subjects with scores > 1 standard deviation below average

hemisphere and one in the right. Hearing and visual acuity of these children, as determined by neurological and audiological evaluations, was in the normal range. One child had seizures that were well controlled by Tegretol. This group obtained a Composite Score mean of 101, a Verbal Domain mean of 97, and a Visual Abstract Reasoning Domain mean of 106 on the Stanford–Binet Intelligence Scale (4th ed.).

Subgroup 2 ($n = 6$) consisted of patients with subcortical, thalamic, or upper brainstem tumors. One of the six subjects was found on audiological evaluation to have a drop at 6,000 Hz in the right ear (35 dB) and at 6,000 and 8,000 Hz in the left ear (60 and 30 dB, respectively). This hearing loss may have been related to the fact that this child was actively involved as a musician in a rock band. Hearing was determined by audiological evaluation to be adequate for conversational speech and listening. Subjects in this group obtained a Composite Score mean of 107, a Verbal Reasoning Domain mean of 105, and a Visual Abstract Reasoning Domain mean of 104 on the Stanford–Binet.

Subgroup 3 ($n = 6$) consisted of patients with primary cerebellar lesions. In this group, one child had a high frequency hearing loss (50 to 65 dB between 6,000 and 8,000 Hz bilaterally), following chemotherapy. However, this child readily responded to the limited auditory information in the structured testing situation so that speech reception and expression was judged to be adequate in this restricted condition. Subjects in this group received a Composite Score mean of 92, a Verbal Reasoning Composite mean of 98, and a Visual Abstract Reasoning Composite mean of 95 on the Stanford–Binet.

Because some nonstandardized test instruments were utilized in the study, a normal, randomly selected sample of children ($n = 19$), matched in age and other demographic characteristics with the brain tumor group, was given the battery of nonstandardized tests to obtain comparative data. Children utilized in this normative group were drawn from a sample of children between age 12 years, 7 months and 17 years, 9 months (Mean Age = 14 years, 8 months), who were enrolled in general public school classes. Eligibility criteria included normal hearing and vision, absence of learning problems, neurological deviations, or other developmental and/or genetic deviations. One of the 19 children was left handed.

GENERAL FUNCTIONING

The following tests of general abilities and functioning were given to all children with brain tumors: The Stanford–Binet Intelligence Scale (4th ed.; Thorndike, Hagen, & Sattler, 1986) was administered to assess general intellectual levels and abilities in the verbal reasoning and abstract/visual reasoning areas. The Vineland Adaptive Behavior Scales (Sparrow, Balla, & Cicchetti, 1985) was administered to determine general adaptive functioning and particularly adaptive functioning in the communication domain. The Peabody Picture Vocabulary Test (PPVT–R) (L. M. Dunn & L. M. Dunn, 1981) was administered to determine receptive vocabulary level. The Verbal Cancellation Test (Mesulam, 1985) was administered to assess visual-attentional and scanning abilities.

As can be seen from the scores from each of these general standardized tests (Table 8.1), the children with brain tumors in all subgroups typically scored in the average range. The t tests conducted between the tumor and comparison group (contrast sample or test standardization sample), and nonparametric analyses between the three tumor subgroups indicate that the children with tumors performed only slightly lower on the Vineland Composite ($t = -1.94, p = .07$) and Communication Domains ($t = -1.79$, $p = .09$), than did children in the standardization group. Children with cortical tumors identified fewer As on the Verbal Cancellation Test than did the children in the nontumor group ($t = 8.81, p < .001$). Children with cerebellar ($t = 9.01, p < .001$) or cortical ($t = 5.63, p < .01$) tumors took more time to complete the scanning task, but were more accurate than the children with no tumor, suggesting a speed/accuracy trade-off difference in some situations. Otherwise, there were no other significant differences between or among the subgroups on these measures of general functioning.

In summary, all groups of children with brain tumors functioned in the average range on the Stanford–Binet Intelligence Scale, and on a test of receptive vocabulary. Appropriate receptive vocabulary capabilities suggest that the expected vocabulary words are known and "stored" in inactive memory; Wolf and Obregón (1992) showed that failure to name "stored" words is indicative of retrieval difficulties, rather than a general deficit in vocabulary acquisition in children. The question in this study was whether children with brain tumors show a similar discrepancy between receptive word knowledge and retrieval.

On a visual attentional scanning task, children in the tumor group took significantly more time while making significantly less errors, suggesting a more cautious approach to the speed/accuracy trade-off requirements on such timed scanning tasks. On the other hand, children with brain tumors were rated by their parents as functioning slightly lower, although still within the average range, in general adaptive and communicative functioning domains than were children in the Vineland standardization sample. There was also a lower correlation between IQ and communication functioning in the children with brain tumors, which is in contrast to normal children for whom there is a strong correlation between overall IQ and Communicative abilities (Sparrow et al., 1985). One possible interpretation for these results is that children with brain tumors have subtle language difficulties that go undetected on common standardized testing and measures of vocabulary knowledge (see discussions of these issues in Curtis, 1987; Segal & Wolf, 1993), but problems are elicited in both qualitative testing and unstructured, decontextualized (i.e, ambiguous) situations in the real world. Thus, when parameters are restricted and clear, and the demands of the task are contextualized and redundant, such as in standardized structured tests, performance may appear fairly normal. On the other hand, when the task is less structured and decontextualized, with interference from increased possibilities heightened (as in day-to-day interactions), performance may be diminished.

NAMING AND NAMING-RELATED FUNCTIONING

Although naming is known to be affected by many factors such as stimulus-exposure time, quality, fluency demands, and so on (Wolf, 1982, 1991, 1995), naming has most typically been examined through confrontation naming tasks, in which a single stimulus word is targeted. This mode of elicitation, however, focuses only on an explicitly cued target word; thus, it does not test other critical factors, nor does it incorporate many of the higher level problem-solving strategies required in less structured, narrative language that requires naming (Biddle et al., 1996; German, 1992, 1993). To investigate the more conceptual underpinnings of the naming function, additional tasks were employed alongside confrontation-naming tasks, including fluency tasks, paired-associate learning tasks, and the elicitation of superordinate categories. Using fluency or productivity schema, naming was also studied in a spontaneous language situation where the stimulus context is less tightly controlled.

SINGLE WORD/FLUENCY MEASURES

The following measures were given to the children with brain tumors, and for tasks with no adequate age norms, were also given to control children for comparison purposes. The Boston Naming Test (Kaplan, Goodglass, & Weintraub, 1983) assessed naming ability to picture confrontation. The Rapid Automatized Naming Test (RAN; Denckla & Rudel, 1974) required rapid, serial naming of 50 random, visual presentations of five exemplars in three semantic categories: colors, use objects, and high frequency, uppercase letters. The three RAN tasks (Denckla & Rudel, 1974) were presented according to an invariant order of presentation (RAN Colors, RAN Letters, and RAN Objects) after one practice trial to insure correct naming of the exemplars in each category. The Verbal Associative Fluency Test

(FAS; Benton & Hamsher, 1983) required the generation of word lists (i.e., initiating with letter F, then letter A, and finally S), each within a 1-minute time limit. The Verbal Fluency Test (Categories) required that a subject provide as many items in a category as possible (animals, foods, clothing, vehicles), each within a 1-minute time limit. The Similarities Subtest (WISC–R) (Wechsler, 1949, 1974) is a test of verbal concept formation and requires the classification of basic auditorially presented words into a single superordinate category.

The Word-Finding Test (Wiegel-Crump & Dennis, 1984) assessed a child's ability to produce target words in three cuing or lexical access conditions: semantic, rhyming, and visual confrontation. It was standardized on normally developing children by Wiegel-Crump and Dennis (1986). The test is comprised of 45 words, 9 each in the categories of animals, food, clothing, household items, and actions. Target words across categories occur with equal frequency (Carroll, Davies, & Richman, 1971) and are equated for semantic characteristics of concreteness, imagery, categorizability, meaningfulness, familiarity, number of attributes, and pleasantness (Toglia & Battig, 1978). Each lexical access condition was audiotaped and scored for latency of response (using a digital stopwatch) and for errors (percent) from the audiotaped recording following the procedures outlined in the Word-Finding Test Manual (Wiegel-Crump, 1984). Qualitative error analyses were conducted as outlined by Wiegel-Crump and Dennis (1986).

The Basic and Subordinate Level Naming Test (Brownell, Bihrle, & Michelow, 1986) required the naming on visual confrontation of 16 high typicality stimuli (e.g., pictures of a kitchen chair, living room couch) and 16 corresponding low typicality stimuli (e.g., beach chair, antique couch). This test was designed to distinguish basic level naming (Rosch, Mervis, Gray, Johnson, & Boyes-Braem, 1976) from the more conceptual and abstract levels of naming. Each subject was presented first with the set of high typicality visual stimuli and then the low typicality stimuli. Subjects were asked for the "best, most common name" for the depicted object. Results were analyzed based on four error types described by Brownell et al. (1986). They included *basic names*, or the correct superordinate name for stimuli; and *subordinate names*, or the correct subordinate name for stimuli. These two response types together provide an overall measure of intact performance. *Basic plus elaborations* are comprised of a basic name followed by the full subordinate term (e.g., "car, racing car") or by an appropriate description (e.g., "car, one that goes fast"), which modifies the basic category. Presence of this response type is indicative of conceptual understanding, difficulty with subordinate naming, and intact basic naming. *Other* includes all unintelligible responses, neologisms, incorrect basic or subordinate labels including semantic paraphasias, and descriptions that do not provide correct identifications at the basic or subordinate level.

The Concrete-Abstract Paired-Associate Learning Task was developed to assess the ease with which noun–noun versus verb–verb pairs are recalled in a paired-associate learning task. The stimulus words for this task consist of 10 "concrete" nouns and 10 "abstract" verbs with frequency of 50 or more occurences per million, according to Thorndike and Lorge (1944). A paired-associate list was constructed from lists of random nouns and verbs, except for the restriction that pairs comprised of words beginning with the same letter, or with obvious meaningful associations (e.g., flower–garden), were not permitted. Words in noun and verb pairs were also matched for the number of syllables, with no word longer than two syllables. The concrete noun pairs were farmer–bank, river–daughter, chair–milk, heart–kitchen, and glass–face. The abstract verb pairs were eat–forget, start–reach, enjoy–marry, add–hurry, and grow–cry. There were three recall trials, wherein the child was provided the first word in the word pair and required to recall the second associated word. The stimulus and recall pairs were presented in a different, randomly determined, serial order on each recall trial.

Analyses of the naming and naming-related tests using t-test comparisons, failed to find significant differences between tumor and nontumor groups, or among tumor subgroups on the Boston Naming Test, Verbal Fluency Test, Verbal Associative Fluency Test, or Similarities Subtest of the WISC–R (Table 8.2). Significant differences were found on the following measures, which will be further detailed later (Table 8.2).

Rapid Automatized Naming Test

The mean latency for the tumor group on the RAN (Table 8.2) was significantly longer than for the nontumor group ($t = 3.24; p < .02$), but only for the color condition. Significant differences in latency of response occured between the cerebellar and nontumor group ($t = 6.01; p < .005$), with the cerebellar subgroup taking a longer time to name colors. Further analysis among subgroups indicated that the children in the subcortical tumor subgroup named colors significantly faster than children with cortical tumors ($p < .02$, 2-sample median test), but only slightly faster than the cerebellar ($p = .08$, 2-sample median test) subgroup. Despite a failure to find significance in the letter and object use conditions, more children with tumors had deficits (latencies exceeding the norms by at least 1 S.D., 41% and 71%, respectively) compared to the nontumor group (10% and 16%, respectively). The order of latencies across naming conditions was upheld across subgroups, with letters named most rapidly and use objects named least rapidly. Colors were named with latencies intermediate between let-

TABLE 8.2
Naming Tests

Variable	Measure	Cortical (N = 5)	Subcortical (N = 6)	Cerebellar (N = 6)	Tumors (N = 17)	Nontumor*
Boston Naming Test	Mean	44.6	49.5	42.0	45.0	ns
	Median	45	48.5	42	46	—
	Range	33–57	44–57	33–51	33–57	46–56
	Deficit	20%	0%	17%	12%	—
Rapid Automatized Naming-Color Condition	Mean	39.0[c]	27.8[cd]	40.2[bd]	35.5[a]	30.2[ab]
	Median	40	28.5	37	34	30
	Range	34–43	20–34	26–37	20–43	21–43
	Deficit	80%	0%	50%	41%	10%
Rapid Automatized Letter Naming-Condition	Mean	22.6	19.5	26.0	22.4	19.0
	Median	23	19	23	22	19
	Range	14–26	14–25	21–38	14–38	14–29
	Deficit	60%	17%	50%	41%	10%
Rapid Automatized Naming-Use Condition	Mean	50.8	43.7	47.5	47.1	36.8
	Median	50	44	46	46	36
	Range	44–60	33–54	42–58	33–60	27–52
	Deficit	100%	50%	67%	71%	16%

	.6	.3	.0	.3	.4
Rapid Automatized Naming–Error Scores, All Conditions					
Mean	0	0	0	0	0
Median					
Range	0–2	0–1	0–0	0–2	0–1
Deficit	40%	33%	0%	24%	0%
Verbal Fluency-FAS					
Mean	26.2	31.0[a]	22.8[a]	26.7	34.3
Median	26	29.5	22	26	34
Range	11–38	23–40	10–42	10–42	22–58
Deficit	20%	0%	33%	18%	10%
Verbal Fluency-Categories					
Mean	56.2	61.3	63.0	60.4	69.9
Median	59	62.5	57.5	59	67
Range	37–76	47–76	29–99	22–99	52–98
Deficit	40%	33%	33%	35%	21%
Analysis of Similarities Subtest from WISC–R					
Mean	12.6	12.2	9.0	11.2	—
Median	14	13	8.5	11	—
Range	7–18	6–15	6–13	6–18	—
Deficit	20%	13%	17%	17%	—

Note: A subject was labeled Deficit if the score fell one or more standard deviations below the national norm.

*Scores on nontumor group represent age-based standardization norms; subjects were not actually tested.

[a]Significance between tumor and nontumor groups at $p < .05$

[b]Significance between groups at $p < .01$

[c]Significance between groups at $p < .05$

[d]Significance between groups at $p < .10$

ters and use objects, and replicated the order of other developmental groups studied to date (Wolf, 1991; Wolf, Bally, & Morris, 1986). Naming errors occurred rarely in any of the groups.

Cued Word-Finding Test

In the rhyming and visual access conditions (Table 8.3), the tumor children produced a significantly greater percentage of errors than did children in the comparison group (rhyming: $t = -3.70, p < .005$; visual: $t = -3.22, p = .005$). Examining the latency of responses, it was observed that children with tumors responded significantly slower during the semantic and visual-lexical access conditions than did the nontumor comparison group on this task (Semantic Latency: $t = 3.21, p < .005$; Visual Latency: $t = -2.30; p < .05$). In the visual latency condition, the cortical tumor subgroup differed only slightly from the subcortical and cerebellar subgroups (both at $p = .08$, 2-sample median test). For each of the tumor subgroups, the rhyming condition prompted the highest error rate on the task that was responded to most quickly. The semantic condition was the next most difficult condition (error- and latency period-wise), whereas the visual

TABLE 8.3
Cued Word Finding Test

Variable	Measure	Cortical (N = 5)	Subcortical (N = 6)	Cerebellar (N = 6)	Tumors (N = 17)	Nontumor (N = 19)
Semantic Targets	Median	43	43	40	41	—
	Range	40–43	38–44	39–42	38–44	41.2–42.6
	Deficit	0%	17%	33%	17%	—
Semantic Latency	Median	1.1	1.3	1.2	1.2	—
	Range	1.1–2.8	1.0–2.9	.8–1.7	.8–2.9	.8–1.4
	Deficit	80%	67%	33%	59%	—
Rhyming Targets	Median	34	33.5	27	31	—
	Range	22–37	29–37	23–34	22–37	33.5–35.6
	Deficit	40%	50%	33%	41%	—
Rhyming Latency	Median	2.4	3.4	2.9	3.0	—
	Range	2.0–3.9	2.2–3.9	1.8–3.1	1.8–3.9	2.5–3.4
	Deficit	40%	67%	33%	47%	—
Visual Targets	Median	43	43	42	43	—
	Range	41–45	42–44	42–45	41–45	43.7–44.6
	Deficit	60%	33%	33%	41%	—
Visual Latency	Median	1.4	1.0	1.0	1.1	—
	Range	0.9–1.9	0.5–1.3	0.8–1.4	.5–1.9	.6–1.0
	Deficit	80%	50%	33%	53%	—

Note: A subject was labeled Deficit if the score fell one or more standard deviations below the national mean.

*Scores on nontumor group represent age-based standardization norms; subjects were not actually tested.

condition was responded to most rapidly and with the lowest error rate. The increased error rate relative to the decreased latency period on the rhyming condition again suggested a speed/accuracy trade-off.

Error analyses, in which the total number and percent of total errors for each error type were evaluated by tumor subgroup, and in comparison to age-related norms (Wiegel-Crump & Dennis, 1986), was also evaluated. Error frequency for the 17 children with tumors for each of the three naming conditions was significantly greater than for the 50 normal, nontumor children in the Wiegel-Crump and Dennis (1986) study. Comparison of the error rates between the children with tumors and the standardization children revealed greater similarity of error types in the semantic condition than the rhyming or visual conditions. The two groups were relatively similar in the semantic condition in that they both made more in-class errors than any other error type. However, category-only responses were offered less frequently and only by the children with tumors. One of the most distinctive differences between the children with tumors and those without them was that the children with tumors alone had difficulty (6%) recognizing the hierarchical nature of the superordinate–hyponym relations (i.e., errors of "level"), whereas the children without tumors made no hierarchical errors (0% "level" errors). Likewise, the children with tumors alone made unrelated (3%), syntactic (3%), and associative errors (1.5%), whereas the children without tumors made no errors of these types.

In the rhyming condition, error frequency for the 17 children with tumors (246 errors) was greater than for all of the 50 normal children (40 errors). Over one half of the errors (58%) of the children with tumors were failures to respond at all, whereas, in contrast, normal children failed to make a response only 15% of the time. Both groups produced a low percentage of unrelated responses for which no relation between the rhyming cue and response could be discerned. Overall, the normal children gave a larger proportion (78%) of related responses than did the children with tumors (41%). Children without tumors made approximately equal numbers of category only and rhyme only errors; these children made more category only than rhyming only errors. Finally, although the actual error frequency and proportion of hierarchical "level" errors was low for both groups, only the children with tumors made any errors (2 errors, 1%) of this type.

In the visual condition, children in the tumor group made more semantically related errors (58%) than the comparison group (38%). This error type generally indicates some knowledge of the target (Wolf & Obregón, 1992). In contrast, the normal comparison children made more visual errors (62%) than the children with tumors (30%). Only the children with tumors made errors based on failure to respond (12%). Neither subject group produced unrelated- or phonetically based errors; the latter errors are more typical of language- and reading-impaired populations (German, 1987; Wolf & Goodglass, 1986).

On the Word-Finding Test (Table 8.4) the children with tumors responded significantly slower during the semantic and visual lexical access conditions than did the nontumor comparison group. This relatively decreased latency period in the rhyming lexical access condition may have represented tumor children's responses to the increased difficulty of this task relative to the amount of naming ease encountered on the two other lexical access conditions, thereby increasing their tendency to respond more impulsively and quickly. In other words, the increase in naming speed may have been at the expense of accuracy. If they had been cautioned to give their "best" response, their latency period may have increased. Regardless of which factor (speed or accuracy) was more affected, the fact remains that the children with tumors encountered more difficulty on this task than did their peers without tumors. Task analysis of the rhyming access condition suggested that, unlike the semantic access condition, this task requires increased integration (i.e., of the conceptual and phonological aspects of language).

The three tumor subgroups were more similar than dissimilar to each other in their types of naming errors on the Cued Word-Finding Test. The majority of errors made in the semantic condition bore some relation to the target name, thus indicating comprehension of the task demands and cue information. All subgroups seemed to recognize the hierarchical nature of the superordinate–hyponym relation, although occasional production of a wrong-level response occurred for each subgroup. The children's errors generally honored the syntactic markers delineating the grammatical class of the target. Paradigmatic association errors were rarely made.

The greatest difference in the weighting of naming errors among tumor subgroups was seen in their responses on the rhyming condition. Children with cerebellar tumors gave fewer responses to these stimulus cues than did the children with subcortical tumors ($p < .05$, 2-sample median test). Furthermore, the latter subgroup tended to divide the related response errors less evenly than did children in the cortical and cerebellar tumor subgroups. Children in the subcortical tumor subgroup made errors more frequently by providing a word that corresponded on the semantic and categorical, but not rhyming, dimension of the cue. For example, these children might respond to the cue "I'm thinking of an animal and it rhymes with 'rammel' " with "lion," instead of the intended target "camel." In addition, children in the subcortical tumor subgroup made proportionately fewer errors that were nonword, but shared some element of the cue rhyme (onomatopoetic).

The error rate in the visual access condition was also rather evenly divided, although children in the cortical tumor subgroup tended to pro-

TABLE 8.4
Word-Finding Test

Variable	Measure	Cortical		Subcortical		Cerebellar		Tumors		Nontumor	
		N	%	N	%	N	%	N	%	N	%
Semantics	No Response	1	6.6	2	9.0	9	29.0	12	17.9	5	17.0
	Repetition	2	13.3	0	0.0	3	9.7	5	7.5	1	3.0
	Unrelated Response	1	6.6	1	5.0	0	0.0	2	3.0	0	0.0
	Related Response Syntagmatic	1	6.6	0	0.0	1	3.2	2	3.0	0	0.0
	Paradigmatic Phonetic	0	0.0	0	0.0	0	0.0	0	0.0	0	0.0
	Semantic Category Only	0	0.0	1	5.0	1	3.2	2	3.0	0	0.0
	Cat, 1 Features	2	13.3	2	9.0	5	16.1	9	13.4	7	24.0
	Cat, 2 Features	3	20.0	6	28.0	6	19.4	15	22.4	3	10.0
	Cat, 3 Features	5	33.3	7	33.0	3	9.7	15	22.4	13	45.0
	Associative	0	0.0	1	5.0	0	0.0	1	1.5	0	0.0
	Level	0	0.0	1	5.0	3	9.7	4	6.0	0	0.0
Rhyming	No Response	41	58.5	37	53.6	65	60.7	143	58.1	6	15.0
	Repetition	0	0.0	0	0.0	0	0.0	0	0.0	0	0.0
	Unrelated Response	0	0.0	0	0.0	2	1.9	2	1.0	3	8.0
	Related Response Onomatopoetic	9	12.8	1	1.4	12	11.2	22	8.9	5	13.0
	Category Only	10	14.3	29	42.0	20	18.7	59	24.0	12	30.0
	Rhyme Only	9	12.8	1	1.4	8	7.5	18	7.3	14	35.0
	Level	1	1.4	1	1.4	0	0.0	2	1.0	0	0.0
Visual	No Response	2	20.0	1	9.0	1	8.3	4	12.1	0	0.0
	Unrelated Response	0	0.0	0	0.0	0	0.0	0	0.0	0	0.0
	Related Response Visual	2	20.0	4	36.4	4	33.3	10	30.3	8	62.0
	Semantic	6	60.0	6	54.5	7	58.3	19	57.6	5	38.0
	Phonetic	0	0.0	0	0.0	0	0.0	0	0.0	0	0.0

Note: Data from 50 normal 14 year olds (Wiegel-Crump & Dennis, 1986).

vide proportionately more "no response" errors than did the other two tumor subgroups. A greater percentage of all the errors made across the groups were based on semantic associations (e.g., cup/glass). Errors based on visual misinterpretations were the next most highly represented error. No errors across any of the three tumor subgroups were based on unrelated responses or phonemic associations.

Basic and Subordinate Level Naming Test

When tumor and nontumor groups were compared on this test (Table 8.5), they differed in their use of responses containing incorrect basic or subordinate labels, including semantic paraphasias and incomplete descriptions. That is, the children with tumors produced more "other" type responses (e.g., circumlocutory responses, "plug in kind of knife" for "electric knife") than did the normal comparison group ($t = 2.55$; $p = <.05$). These "other" responses were correlated with children's subordinate level naming abilities ($r = .50, p < .04$), suggesting that naming errors occured frequently for less often used, subordinate names. Although not statistically significant, 24% of the children with tumors fell in the "deficit" range on the subordinate plus elaboration dimension, as compared to 0% of the normal children. On this task, they tended to revise and reformulate their thoughts through successive approximations until they were comfortable with their labeling of the presented picture. For instance, a child with a tumor stated "truck, one with cement in the middle" when attempting to label a "cement truck." This suggests that, compared individually,

TABLE 8.5
Basic and Subordinate Level Naming Test

Variable	Measure	Cortical (N = 5)	Subcortical (N = 6)	Cerebellar (N = 6)	Tumors (N = 17)	Nontumor (N = 19)
Basic	Median	17	12	16	14	18
	Range	10–21	8–18	14–29	8–29	4–30
	Deficit	20%	33%	50%	33%	10%
Subordinate	Median	10	19	11	14	14
	Range	8–22	14–21	1–17	1–22	2–27
	Deficit	40%	0%	7%	19%	16%
Elaborations	Median	0	0	0	0	0
	Range	0–1	0–2	0–1	0–2	0–0
	Deficit	20%	33%	17%	24%	0%
Others	Median	3	1	2	1	0
	Range	0–4	0–2	0–5	0–5	0–4
	Deficit	60%	17%	67%	48%	16%

Note: A subject was labeled Deficit if the score fell one or more standard deviations worse than the mean of the nontumor group.

children with tumors tended to more often resort to an elaborative form of expression when attempting to name simple pictures than did the children in the nontumor group.

Concrete-Abstract Paired-Associate Learning Task

Analysis (Table 8.6) showed that the effects of abstractness were significant only in the second recall condition for verbs. Children with no tumors recalled significantly more verbs ($t = 3.88, p < .01$) than did children in the tumor group. Further analysis revealed that children with subcortical tumors ($t = 17.65, p = .005$) recalled significantly fewer verbs than did the nontumor comparisons. Although not significantly different except in the second recall condition, a more regular learning slope was observed for the nontumor children, with the children with tumors' greatest difficulty in learning noted during the second verb recall condition. At no point did the children with tumor's learning exceed the nontumor children's learning. This is further highlighted by the tumor group's increased "deficit" percentage and the difference between total recall in the combined recall condition. More children with tumors (65%) were in the "deficit" range relative to the nontumor children (21%) in the total number of nouns and total number of verbs recalled over all learning trials.

Finally, the learning of verbs by children in the tumor group was less regular, with little increase in recall of verbs between the first and second learning trials. Plausible explanations for specific difficulty in the recall of

TABLE 8.6
Concrete-Abstract Paired-Associate Learning Test

Variable	Measure	Cortical (N = 5)	Subcortical (N = 6)	Cerebellar (N = 6)	Tumors (N = 17)	Nontumor (N = 19)
Trial 1	Median	0	0	0	0	1
# Nouns Recalled	Range	0–5	0–1	0–2	0–5	0–5
Trial 1	Median	0	0	0	0	0
# Verbs Recalled	Range	0–4	0–1	0–1	0–4	0–4
Trial 2	Median	1	1	2	1	3
# Nouns Recalled	Range	0–5	0–4	0–4	0–5	0–5
Trial 2	Median	0	0	1	0	2
# Verbs Recalled	Range	0–3	0–1	0–2	0–3	0–5
Trial 3	Median	2	2	3	2	5
# Nouns Recalled	Range	0–5	0–4	0–5	0–5	1–5
Trial 3	Median	1	1	1	1	3
# Verbs Recalled	Range	0–5	0–2	0–5	0–5	0–5
All Trials	Median	2	3	5	3	8
# Nouns Recalled	Range	0–15	0–7	0–10	0–15	1–15
All Trials	Median	1	2	2	1	4
# Verbs Recalled	Range	0–12	0–3	0–7	0–12	0–14

verbs include: (a) Children in the tumor group may have had more difficulty attaching meaning to the initially presented words. This would suggest an initial encoding weakness. (b) In addition, children in the tumor group may have also had more difficulty finding the connections necessary to mediate recall of the associates, particularly the pairs consisting of abstract verb stimuli. (c) Children in the tumor group may have found the necessary associations between the presented words, but still had difficulty with simple verb recall.

OVERVIEW OF NAMING RESULTS
AT THE SINGLE WORD LEVEL

In summary, there is some evidence in this study that children with brain tumors have more difficulty with the naming of single words than do children without brain tumors. They make more errors and take a longer time to name. Findings suggest that naming accuracy increases in situations that do not require integration of cues across modalities, such as semantic situations in which the information is presented auditorially alone, or in situations in which naming speed is not a factor. Naming speed appears to slow under all but the most automatic, less abstract conditions (serial, redundant object, and letter naming). Note, however, that this pattern is quite distinct from children with language and reading disabilities for whom letter naming and object naming are also significantly slower than control peers.

Contrary to expectations, untimed, single word naming did not differentiate the children in the three tumor subgroups. However, whereas simple naming failed to differentiate these children, significant differences were noted when speed of naming was evaluated. In the visual access condition, children with cortical tumors took longer to name pictures than the children in either the subcortical, cerebellar, or normal groups. In the semantic access condition, children in both the cortical and subcortical subgroups took longer to name than did the children in the cerebellar or normal comparison group. Overall, and consistent with predictions, children in the subcortical subgroup's naming speed fell at the extremes, with them taking a significantly longer time to name in the semantic access condition and a significantly shorter time to name in the visual access condition. Furthermore, the children with cerebellar tumors were not significantly different from the normal comparison group on the number of words recalled or the time to recall the words in the semantic or visual condition.

Examining responses by semantic category, children in the subcortical subgroup again distinguished themselves in that they took a shorter time to name colors (RAN) than did children in the cortical and cerebellar subgroups. Overall, their naming speed more closely approximated the naming speed of the children in the normal, nontumor comparison group. Children in the subcortical subgroup also gave more specific responses to the target words than did the children in the cerebellar group. For example, they differentiated a common couch into a modern versus an antique couch more often than did the children in the cerebellar group. This suggests they were able to both perceive and label the salient distinguishing variable, and at a rate higher than that of the other two groups.

On a paired-associate verbal learning task assessing the dimension of abstractness, children with subcortical and cerebellar tumors recalled fewer of the more abstract verbs on the second recall trial than did children in the normal comparison group. They showed no significant differences among themselves, however. Interestingly, the three subgroups displayed dissimilar learning curves for verbs. That is, children in the subcortical and cortical tumor subgroups recalled fewer verbs during the second recall trial but similar numbers on the third and final recall trial as children in the normal and cerebellar tumor subgroups. In contrast, children in the cerebellar and nontumor groups exhibited a progressive, stable learning curve for verbs. All subgroups displayed a stable learning curve for nouns, and only the cortical subgroup recalled as many verbs as nouns by the last recall.

CONNECTED LANGUAGE

A *language sample* was also acquired to ascertain productivity and word retrieval problems during spontaneous speech. Each subject was asked to describe "The Cookie Theft" picture from the Boston Diagnostic Aphasia Examination (Goodglass & Kaplan, 1972, 1983). Subjects were asked to tell a story about the cookie theft scene that would include each of the target words. As productivity was one of the variables of interest, subjects were permitted to control the length of their discourse. Utterances were taped and later transcribed for analysis according to guidelines on narrative speech set out by German (1987; see also German, 1992). These included:

1. *Total Verbalizations*—This category represented a frequency count of the total number of words including repetitions, starters, empty words, and reformulations.
2. *Modified Mean Length of Utterance*—This measurement is a modification of the traditional MLU procedure. It is calculated by dividing the total number of words by the total number of utterances.

3. *Total Word-Finding Categories*—This index is the sum of the frequency counts of the number of word-finding categories present in each entry.

4. *Mean Categories per Utterance*—This measurement is the mean number of categories per utterance. It is calculated by dividing the total word-finding category score by the number of utterances.

In order to determine if groups differed in their productivity and in the number of naming errors generated in spontaneous speech, analyses were conducted using length of stories, length of utterance, total number of word-finding categories, and total number of word-finding categories/utterance as the units of analysis (Table 8.7). The mean length of utterance for children without tumors was only slightly longer than that of the children in the tumor group ($t = 2.4, p = .08$). Although tumor subgroups did not differ significantly among themselves in other dimensions, children in the subcortical tumor subgroup produced a smaller modified mean length of utterance ($t = 9.30, p = .02$) than did the children in the nontumor group. The three tumor subgroups did not differ significantly among themselves on dimensions of total story length, modified mean length of utterance, number of word-finding categories, or the category/utterance ratio.

Contrary to expectations, children with tumors did not display a greater number of naming errors in their connected discourse, nor did they produce significantly shorter narrations than did children in the nontumor comparison group. Their sentences were slightly shorter than

TABLE 8.7
Spontaneous Language Results

Variable	Measure	Cortical (N = 5)	Subcortical (N = 6)	Cerebellar (N = 6)	Tumors (N = 17)	Nontumor (N = 19)
Total	Median	59	71	66	63	79
Verbalizations	Range	21–146	43–112	39–152	21–152	29–244
	Deficit	20%	0%	17%	12%	5%
Mean Length of	Median	15	18	13.7	16	21
Utterance	Range	10–22	16–22	8–23	8–23	10–42
	Deficit	40%	0%	50%	35%	5%
Total Word-	Median	2	2	2	2	3
Finding Cats	Range	1–12	1–9	0–10	0–12	0–16
	Deficit	20%	17%	17%	18%	16%
Category/	Median	.75	.75	.46	.50	1
Utterance	Range	.40–1.5	.14–1.5	0–1.4	0–1.5	0–1.8
Ratio	Deficit	0%	17%	17%	19%	16%

Note: A subject was labeled Deficit if the score fell one or more standard deviations below the mean of the nontumor group.

were the sentences of children in the normal comparison group, but these differences may not be clinically meaningful because both groups produced lengthy utterances. More in-depth analysis of their sentences, however, highlighted several areas of group differences. That is, 35% of the children in the tumor group produced mean length of utterances at least 1 *SD* below the nontumor group's mean length of utterance. In addition, the utterances for children with tumors' tended to be less complex (1.7 subordinate conjunctions/utterance) than their nontumor peers (2.6 subordinate conjunctions/utterance). Thus, the utterance length for children with tumors may reflect reduced proficiency in the face of the semantic prerequisites for complex sentence formation.

A reduction in the mean length of utterance would be consistent with German's (1987, 1993) findings that there are two distinct categories of naming problems in spontaneous language. According to her findings, the first profile consists of a reduction in oral language despite a lack of the other word-finding behaviors typically seen in children with word-finding problems. Reduction in clinically meaningful utterance length appears to apply only to a small portion of the children with tumors assessed in this study. However, a lack of semantic complexity on the whole, as evidenced in the fewer numbers of subordinate conjunctions used, may undercut this demonstrated sentence length reduction. In contrast to German's first pattern, a second profile is represented by a language sample unrestricted in productivity, but that includes more of the characteristics traditionally classified as naming problems. This second pattern was not found in the current study.

The sole variable that distinguished the subgroups on the language sample was the mean length of their utterances. On this variable, the sentences of the children in the subcortical tumor subgroup were significantly shorter, although not clinically so, than sentences generated by children in the nontumor comparison group. Because the children in the subcortical subgroup were often distinguished on a time-of-retrieval dimension, it may be that they tended to "rush" and thus abbreviate their thoughts, culminating in shorter, but still semantically and syntactically accurate, sentences. The shortened sentences may alternatively reflect their difficulty with underlying semantic connections.

Associations Among Naming and Naming-Related Measures

In order to investigate the redundancy among the various measures, correlations among them were calculated for the children with brain tumors. The strongest correlations were found among the cluster of general functioning tests. Specific naming tests were poorly correlated with the more standardized tests of general verbal or intellectual ability. The literature on children with language development indicates a modest but clearly significant relation between confrontation naming tests and tests of intellectual abilities. However, Bowers, Steffy, and Tate (1988) and Spring and Davis (1988) found no relation between IQ and naming speed.

Single word naming was also not well correlated across the different naming measures. The primary exceptions were the correlation of Semantic Targets Scores with Rhyming Targets Scores ($r = .57, p < .02$), and the rapidity of retrieval (RAN Use Latency and Visual Latency, $r = .78, p < .001$). Wolf (1982) reported similar conclusions among RAN tasks and between RAN tasks and Boston Naming Test, another confrontation naming test. Overall, level of naming errors on picture confrontation tasks was correlated with retrieval speed for naming in the semantic and rhyming access conditions (RAN Error Score with Semantic Latency: $r = .68, p < .005$; RAN Error Score with Rhyming Latency: $r = .51, p < .05$). Errors in naming were also correlated with subordinate naming ($r = .50, p < .04$).

Language fluency was correlated under specific conditions. These included Language Total Verbalizations and FAS Total Raw Score ($r = .67, p < .003$), and superordinate categories both with phonemic skills (WISC–R Similarities Subtest and Rhyming Targets: $r = .72, p < .001$), and semantic conceptualization (WISC–R Similarities Subtest and Semantic Targets: $r = .58, p < .015$). Use of subordinate labels was also correlated with Rhyming Targets ($r = .58, p < .014$). Finally, naming tasks involving phonemic skills alone were inversely correlated with each other (FAS and Rhyming Targets: $r = -.59, p < .013$).

Analysis of connected language components indicated that increased length of narrations was correlated with a greater frequency of word-finding errors (Word-Finding Categories and Total Verbalizations: $r = .62, p < .01$). The length of the narration and mean length of utterance, however, were not significantly correlated ($r = -.22, p = .40$). In addition, utterance length was inversely correlated with Rapid Automatized Naming color and letter stimuli (MLU and RAN Color: $r = -.49, p < .05$; MLU and RAN Letter: $r = -.50, p < .05$), but not object use stimuli (MLU and RAN Use: $r = -.16, p = .53$). That is, the slower the latency, the shorter the utterance length.

DISCUSSION

Overall, these results indicate that children with brain tumors make more naming errors and take a longer time to name, but they have no more difficulty with abstract learning and do not use shorter sentences than do children without tumors and without other forms of pathology. This study also provided preliminary indications that the type of naming error and the condition by which names are accessed are somewhat related to site of lesion. Whereas tumor subgroups were more alike than not, the subcortical tumor subgroup emerged as a distinct entity when compared to the cerebellar and cortical tumor subgroups. The results also suggested a strong relation between the semantic aspects of language and naming processes evaluated in this study.

Although children with tumors make more naming errors and take a longer time to name, their latency period prior to recall differentiates them from normals more greatly than does the occurrence of naming errors. Moreover, although abstract learning does occur for children with tumors, it appears to proceed less systematically. Finally, children with tumors slightly shorten their sentences, which may be related to underlying semantic difficulties or alternatively to nonlinguistic, higher order problems in executive planning. Findings suggest that naming proficiency is a function of the nature of the stimuli used in testing, the demands of the task, and the amount of complex integration required for processing.

Findings also suggest that naming pathways of children with tumors are more similar than dissimilar to naming pathways of children without brain tumors. That is, as a group, children with tumors demonstrate similar patterns of lexical access when compared to normal children. First, children with tumors demonstrated a greater ease of access/recall for concrete as compared to abstract words. Second, their pattern of speed on the RAN was in the same direction and consistent with the pattern of latency by children with uninjured brains (in order of difficulty: letters, colors, use objects). Third, it is important to note that children with oral and written language impairments evidence a much more profound set of latency deficits on the RAN (Bowers & Swanson, 1992; Wolf, 1991). Confrontation naming of pictures was less difficult than finding a name in response to a description for the same set of lexical items, which in turn was easier than naming to a rhyme. These findings are consistent with data from Wiegel-Crump and Dennis (1986) on normal children. Thus, the tumor groups' pattern of difficulty was consistent with normal children's pattern for error frequency and for latency period prior to retrieval. Again, it is important to note that the latter result is dissimilar from language- and reading-impaired populations. Obregón (1994), for example, in a very sophisticated computerized analysis of the speech stream during RAN naming speed tasks, has found that it is exactly this latency prior to retrieval that differentiates reading-impaired from average children.

Interesting, however, were the striking differences between children with and without brain tumors when their errors were analyzed qualitatively. Findings suggest that, regardless of the type of access condition, children with tumors have more difficulty with the semantic configuration underlying naming than do nontumor children. On the Word-Finding Test, only children with tumors made more semantic than visually based errors, were more limited in their semantic accuracy and made syntagmatic errors in the semantic access condition, made more categorical (semantic) errors in the rhyming access condition than rhyming errors, and displayed errors of level in the semantic and rhyming conditions. Thus, this population's problems with names does not seem to be interpretable solely in terms of an inability to gain access to existing lexical items. Limitations in naming appear related to underlying conceptual and organizational problems that leave children with brain lesions less sensitive to hierarchical relations of word class; to syntactic information limiting the grammatical class of the to-be-named item, although mildly so; and to the facility and speed in organizing a set of contextual features that cue a name. Findings further suggest that when the cues or stimuli are more divergent (e.g., encompassing features of both sound configuration and semantic conceptualization) or require a greater degree of abstraction, naming may become proportionately more impaired. Overall, findings emphasize the degree to which lexical retrieval is dependent on the type of stimuli involved, the demands of the task, and the strategy of problem solving utilized. Thus, these results provide strong parallels with conclusions drawn about language functions within the traumatic brain injury populations. This is, disturbances in basic linguistic functions are fairly limited. On most of these tasks children appear close to or within normal limits; however, significant differences begin to occur when complex demands in the assembly of language tasks are involved. Like in Eslinger, Biddle, and Gratton (1997), therefore, it may be concluded that the noted deficits (particularly in discourse) were more the result of an impaired interaction between executive and linguistic systems, rather than a discrete problem in language.

Another conclusion in this study regards the effect of lesion site on naming performance. Like Goodglass' conclusions regarding the adult aphasic populations, findings in this study are not strongly compatible with the hypothesis that site of lesion contributes to differences in naming ability. In general, subgroups were more similar to each other than dissimilar. Some results suggest that the subcortical tumor subgroup stand out as more of a distinct entity than the cortical and cerebellar subgroups in their naming performances. Children in the subcortical subgroup were more variable on tasks in which speed or latency of retrieval was a variable. In a number of these timed situations, the children in the subcortical subgroup responded at either extreme, slower or faster, than children in the other two groups or than children with no brain tumor. Whereas children in the cortical and cerebellar tumor subgroups took longer to identify A's on the Verbal Cancellation Test, the children in the subcortical subgroup responded only slightly slower than the children in the nontumor group. They also named colors significantly faster than children in either the cortical or cerebellar subgroups. This variability may be related to a fluctuation in arousal levels for the subcortical tumor subgroup, or alternatively, it may be related to the fact that this subgroup included some children with thalamic tumors. Ojemann (1990), Llinas (1993), and Wolf (1997) described the importance of timing in naming and reading functions and have hypothesized about the role of the thalamus in coordinating the rate of processing among various sensory and linguistic systems. Thus, if the subcortical group included children with and without thalamic tumors, then the significant variabilities that were found would be predicted.

Findings also suggested that the task demands may have had less effect on the speed of retrieval in the subcortical group than it did on the children in the cortical and cerebellar tumor subgroups. Conceptually based errors were also increased for the subcortical tumor subgroup, with their errors more semantically than phonologically based. In keeping with this semantic-phonological dichotomy, they also generated slightly more FAS words than did children in the cerebellar subgroups, recalled fewer verbs on the paired-associate learning task, and had a more restricted mean length of utterance on the language sample than did children in the nontumor group. Findings also support their difficulties with abstract conceptualization and variability of latency periods on timed tasks. In future studies, it would be of particular interest to have a sufficient number of children with thalamic level tumors to explore issues involved in timing processes in languages and other systems.

In summary, this study offers information about the subtle differences in naming between children with and without brain tumors. Moreover, it identifies the importance of a comprehensive assessment of naming and language functions under varying conditions. Verbal abilities, as assessed on general, standardized cognitive tests, provided little insight into the subtle naming problems that may impede the rapid processing and recall of information in children with brain tumors. This finding replicates a similar set of conclusions for children with traumatic brain injury in which both oral and graphic (reading and writing) discourse appear to be affected along with word recall in children with brain tumors. The problems in narratives and discourse abilities, in turn, may obscure the child's actual knowledge, and may be inappropriately diagnosed as due to poor memory or motivation.

Thus, assessment batteries with children with brain tumors must assess lexical and pragmatic aspects of language. The current study offers limited information about how site of lesion relates to naming dysfunction in children. This finding mirrors similar conclusions among adult aphasic patients. Children with subcortical tumors were in a few ways different as compared to other subgroups of children with brain tumors. These more global results may be related to the somewhat secondary, but diffuse, insults that children with brain tumors sustain due to their associated hydrocephalus, radiation treatments, and different rates of tumor growth, all of which would differentially affect CNS and language functioning (Dennis, 1992). Another hypothesis for these differences relates to the nature of thalamic involvement. The roles of subcortical arousal systems, hypothesized timing mechanisms (Ojemann, 1990; Llinas, 1993; Wolf, 1995), and their cortical connections to naming and executive functions in children demand careful investigation in future studies of naming.

ACKNOWLEDGMENTS

Funding for this research was provided by grants from the Childhood Brain Tumor Foundation, NCI Grant CA33097 to Dr. Donna Copeland, and to the Chancellor's Initiative Fund from the Vice President for Research at Georgia State University. These results are based on a study completed by L. Lazarus-Benbenisty as partial fulfillment of her doctoral dissertation requirements. Special thanks are also extended to all of the children and families who participated in this study.

REFERENCES

Aram, D. M., Ekelman, B. L., & Whitaker, H. A. (1986). Spoken syntax in left and right brain lesioned children. *Brain and Language, 27*, 75–100.

Aram, D. M., Ekelman, B. L., Rose, D. F., & Whitaker, H. A. (1985). Verbal and cognitive sequelae following unilateral lesions acquired in early childhood. *Journal of Clinical and Experimental Neuropsychology, 7*, 55–78.

Benton, A. L., & Hamsher, D. (1983). *Multilingual Aphasia Examination*. Iowa City: University of Iowa.

Biddle, K. R., McCabe, A., & Bliss, L. (1996). Narrative skills following traumatic brain injury in children and adults. *Journal of Communication Disorders, 29*, 447–469.

Bowers, P. G., Steffy, R., & Tate, E. (1988). Comparison of effects of IQ control methods on memory and naming speed predictors of reading disability. *Reading Research Quarterly, 23*, 304–309.

Bowers, P. G., & Swanson, L. B. (1991). Naming speed deficits in reading disability: Multiple measures of a singular process. *Journal of Experimental Child Psychology, 51*, 195–219.

Brownell, H. H., Bihrle, A. M., & Michelow, D. (1986). Basic and subordinate level naming by agrammatic and fluent aphasic patients. *Brain and Language, 28*, 42–52.

Caramazza, A., & Berndt, R. (1978). Semantic and syntactic processes in aphasia: A review of the literature. *Psychological Bulletin, 65*, 898–918.

Caroll, J. B., Davies, P., & Richman, B. (1971). *Word frequency book*. Boston: Houghton Mifflin.

Chapman, S., Culhane, K., Levin, H., Harward, H., Medelsohn, D., Ewing-Cobbs, L., Fletcher, J., & Bruce, O. (1992). Narrative discourse after closed head injury in children and adolescents. *Brain and Language, 43*, 42–65.

Curtis, M. E. (1987). Vocabulary testing and vocabulary instruction. In M. G. McKeown & M. E. Curtis (Eds.), *The nature of vocabulary acquisition* (pp. 37–51). Hillsdale, NJ: Lawrence Erlbaum Associates.

Denckla, M. B., & Rudel, R. G. (1974). "Rapid automatized naming" of pictured objects, colors, letters and numbers by normal children. *Cortex, 10*, 186–202.

Denckla, M. B., & Rudel, R. G. (1976). Rapid automatized naming (R.A.N.): Dyslexia differentiated from other learning disabilities. *Neuropsychologia, 14*, 471–479.

Dennis, M. B. (1992). Word finding in children and adolescents with a history of head injury. *Topics in Language Disorders, 13*(1), 66–82.

Dennis, M. B. (1980). Strokes in childhood: Communicative intent, expression, and comprehension after left hemisphere arteriopathy in a right-handed nine-year-old. In R. W. Rieber (Ed.), *Language development and aphasia in children* (pp. 112–138). New York: Academic Press.

Dennis, M. B., & Kohn, B. (1975). Comprehension of syntax in infantile hemiplegics after cerebral hemidecortication: Left-hemisphere superiority. *Brain and Language, 2*, 472–482.

Dennis, M., & Lovett, M. (1990). Discourse ability in children after brain damage. In Y. Joanette & H. H. Brownell (Eds.), *Discourse ability in children after brain damage: Theoretical and empirical perspectives* (pp. 199–223). New York: Springer-Verlag.

Dennis, M., & Whitaker, H. (1976). Language acquisition following hemidecortication: Linguistic superiority of the left over the right hemisphere. *Brain and Language, 3*, 404–433.

Dunn, L. M., & Dunn, L. M. (1981). *Peabody Picture Vocabulary Test–Revised*. Circle Pines, MN: American Guidance Service.

Eslinger, P. J., Biddle, K. R., & Grattan, L. M. (1997). Cognitive and social development in children with prefrontal cortex lesions. In N. A. Krasnegor, G. R. Lyon, & P. S. Goldman-Rakic (Eds.), *Development of the prefrontal cortex: Evolution, neurobiology and behavior* (pp. 295–335). Baltimore: Paul H. Brookes.

Gardner, H. (1974). Naming of objects and symbols by children and aphasic patients. *Journal of Psycholinguistic Research, 3*, 133–149.

German, D. J. (1992). Word-finding intervention for children and adolescents. *Topics in Language Disorders, 13*, 33–50.

German, D. J. (1993). *The Word Finding Intervention Program*. Houston, TX: Pro-Ed.

German, D. J. (1987). Spontaneous language profiles of children with word-finding problems. *Language, Speech, and Hearing Services in Schools, 18*, 217–230.

Glosser, G., & Deser, T. (1990). Patterns of discourse production among neurological patients with fluent language disorders. *Brain and Language, 40*, 67–88.

Glosser, D., Kaplan, E., & LoVerme, S. (1982). Longitudinal neuropsychological report of aphasia following left-subcortical hemorrhage. *Brain and Language, 15*, 95–116.

Goodglass, H. (1980). Disorders of naming following brain injury. *American Scientist, 68*, 647–665.

Goodglass, H., & Kaplan, E. (1983). *Boston Diagnostic Aphasia Examination*. Philadelphia: Lea & Febiger.

Goodglass, H., & Kaplan, E. (1972). *The assessment of aphasia and related disorders*. Philadelphia: Lea & Febiger.

Gross-Tsur, V., Shalev, R. S., Manor, O., & Amir, N. (1995). Developmental right-hemisphere syndrome: Clinical spectrum of the nonverbal learning disability. *Journal of Learning Disabilities, 28*(2), 80–86.

Jordan, F. M., Cannon, A., & Murdoch, B. E. (1992). Language abilities of mildly closed head injured children 10 years post injury. *Brain Injury, 6*, 39–44.

Kaplan, E., Goodglass, H., & Weintraub, S. (1983). *Boston Naming Test.* Philadelphia: Lea & Febiger.

Kiessling, L., Denckla, M., & Carlton, M. (1983). Evidence for differential hemispheric function in children with temioplegic cerebral palsy. *Developmental Medicine and Child Neurology, 25,* 727–734.

Lenneberg, E. (1967). *Biological foundations of language.* New York: Wiley.

Liederman, J., Kohn, S., Wolf, M., & Goodglass, H. (1983). Lexical creativity during instances of word-finding difficulty: Broca vs. Wernicke's aphasia. *Brain and Language, 20,* 21–32.

Llinas, R. (1993). Is dyslexia a dyschronia? In P. Tallal, A. Galaburda, R. Llinas, & C. von Euler (Eds.), Temporal information processing in the nervous system (pp. 48–62). *Annals of the New York Academy of Sciences, 682.*

McDonald, S. (1993). Pragmatic language skills after closed head injury: Ability to meet the informational needs of the listener. *Brain and Language, 44,* 28–46.

Mesulam, M. (1985). *Principles of behavioral neurology.* Philadelphia: F. A. Davis.

Obregón, M. (1994). *Exploring naming timing patterns by dyslexic and normal readers on the serial RAN task.* Unpublished master's thesis, Tufts University, Boston, MA.

Ojemann, G. A. (1983). Brain organization for language from the perspective of electrical stimulation mapping. *Behavioral Brain Science, 6,* 189–230.

Ojemann, G. A. (1990). Organization of language derived from investigations during neurosurgery. *Neuroscience, 2,* 297–305.

Rankin, J. M., Aram, D. M., & Horwitz, S. J. (1981). Language ability in right and left hemiplegic children. *Brain and Language, 12,* 292–306.

Rosch, E., Mervis, C. B., Gray, W., Johnson, D., & Boyes-Braem, P. (1976). Basic objects in natural categories. *Cognitive Psychology, 8,* 349–382.

Segal, D., & Wolf, M. (1993). Automaticity, word retrieval, and vocabulary development in children with reading disabilities. In L. Meltzer (Ed.), *Cognitive, linguistic, and developmental perspectives on learning disorders* (pp. 141–165). Boston: Little, Brown.

Sparrow, S., Balla, D., & Cicchetti, D. (1985). *Vineland Adaptive Behavior Scales.* Circle Pines, MN: American Guidance Service.

Spring, C., & Davis, J. (1988). Relations of digit naming speed with three components of reading. *Applied Psycholinguistics, 9,* 315–334.

Thorndike, E. L., & Lorge, I. (1944). *The teacher's word book of 30,000 words.* New York: Columbia University Press.

Thorndike, R., Hagen, E., & Sattler, J. (1986). *Stanford–Binet Intelligence Scale* (4th ed.). Chicago: Riverside.

Toglia, M. P., & Battig, W. F. (1978). *Handbook of semantic word norms.* Hillsdale, NJ: Lawrence Erlbaum Associates.

Vargha-Khadem, F., O'Gorman, A., & Watters, G. B. (1985). Aphasia in children with "prenatal" vs. postnatal left hemisphere lesions: A clinical and CT scan study. *Brain, 108,* 677–696.

Wechsler, D. (1974). *WISC–R manual. Wechsler Intelligence Scale for Children-Revised.* New York: Psychological Corporation.

Wechsler, D. (1949). *Wechsler Intelligence Scale for Children. Manual.* New York: Psychological Corporation.

Wiegel-Crump, C., & Dennis, M. (1984). *The Word-Finding Test.* (Experimental ed.). Unpublished test, Toronto, The Hospital for Sick Children.

Wiegel-Crump, C., & Dennis, M. (1986). Development of word finding. *Brain and Language, 27*(1), 1–23.

Wolf, M. (1982). The word-retrieval process and reading in children and aphasics. In K. Nelson (Ed.), *Children's language* (pp. 437–493). Hillsdale, NJ: Lawrence Erlbaum Associates.

Wolf, M. (1986). Rapid alternating stimulus naming in the developmental dyslexias. *Brain and Language*, 27, 360–379.

Wolf, M. (1991). Naming speed and reading: The contribution of the cognitive neurosciences. *Reading Research Quarterly*, 26, 123–141.

Wolf, M. (1995, March). *The "Double-Deficit Hypotheses" for the developmental dyslexias.* Paper presented at Society for Research in Child Development. Indianapolis, IN.

Wolf, M. (1997). A provisional, integrative account of phonological and naming-speed deficits in dyslexia: Implications for diagnosis and intervention. In B. Blachman (Ed.), *Cognitive and linguistic foundations of reading acquisition* (pp. 67–92). Mahwah, NJ: Lawrence Erlbaum Associates.

Wolf, M., Bally, H., & Morris, R. (1986). Automaticity, retrieval processes, and reading: A longitudinal study in average and impaired readers. *Child Development*, 57, 988–1000.

Wolf, M., & Goodglass, H. (1986). Dyslexia, dysnomia, and lexical retrieval. *Brain and Language*, 28, 154–168.

Wolf, M., & Obregón, M. (1992). Early naming deficits, developmental dyslexia and the specific retrieval-deficit hypothesis. *Brain and Language*, 24, 219–247.

Ylvisaker, M. (1993). Communication outcome in children and adolescents with traumatic brain injury. *Neuropsychological Rehabilitation*, 3, 367–387.

Ylvisaker, M., & Szekeres, S. F. (1989). Metacognitive and executive impairments in head-injured children and adults. *Topics in Language Disorders*, 9, 34–49.

## CHAPTER NINE

Patterns of Language Development Through Augmented Means in Youth With Mental Retardation

MaryAnn Romski
Rose A. Sevcik
Georgia State University

The emergence of communication and language skills is a hallmark of child development. Once these skills begin to appear at the end of the first year of life, most children follow a similar developmental path toward adult language skills, that is, from intentional communication and the production of single words to the generation of semantic relations and syntactic forms (Adamson, 1996; Berko-Gleason, 1996). When language and communication skills do not emerge during early childhood, as is the case for most children and youth with severe mental retardation, there are specific long-term effects on development that continue across the life span. Not only are children with severe mental retardation unable to communicate through conventional means, their intellectual and social-emotional development, as well as their educational achievements, are significantly compromised (Romski, Sevcik, & Adamson, 1997).

Over the past two decades, a great deal of attention has been focused on developing instructional approaches that compensate for the lack of speech and language development children with severe mental retardation evidence in an effort to reduce the impact the lack of speech exerts on their overall development. These specialized instructional approaches include manual signs, visual-graphic symbols, and computer-based speech output devices and replace or augment the children's existing receptive and expressive communication skills (see Mirenda, Iacono, & Williams, 1990; Romski & Sevcik, 1988, for reviews). Through the use of these approaches, children and youth have been able to develop conventional means by which to communicate.

This chapter focuses on one such instructional approach for learning language through augmented means and describes the paths youth with severe mental retardation and little or no functional speech adopt as they advance within the process of learning language. Continuing the theme of this book, that is, to examine variations in language development and learning, this chapter presents data from youth with severe mental retardation who encounter serious difficulty learning to speak. The first section provides a brief characterization of children and youth with moderate or severe mental retardation. The second section discusses findings from a longitudinal study of language acquisition and use employing the System for Augmenting Language (SAL). It describes the language and communication achievements of 13 youth with moderate or severe mental retardation who did not speak at the onset of the study, as well as some of their language-related outcomes. The final section discusses how these youth differ among themselves and also if and how they diverge from the typical path of development.

CHILDREN AND YOUTH WITH SEVERE
MENTAL RETARDATION

Children and youth with severe mental retardation, by definition, have significant intellectual impairments as evidenced by extremely low scores on standardized intelligence instruments (Snell, 1993). They exhibit a range of accompanying disabilities, which may include, although are not limited to, cerebral palsy, sensory impairments, seizure disorders, other medical conditions, or maladaptive behaviors (Guess & Horner, 1978; Snell, 1993). Children and youth with severe mental retardation typically require extensive ongoing support in major life activities, especially communication, in order to participate in their communities (American Association of Mental Retardation, AAMR, 1993). Some children and youth with severe mental retardation acquire oral communication skills, albeit slowly and often incompletely, and exhibit varying degrees of impairment in the comprehension and production of the semantics, syntax, pragmatics, and/or phonology of language (see Rosenberg & Abbeduto, 1993, for a review). The majority of children and youth with severe mental retardation, however, fail to develop functional spoken communication skills even after they have had extensive speech and language therapy directed toward that goal (e.g., Romski & Sevcik, 1996). These children and youth communicate in nonconventional ways often using idiosyncratic vocalizations, gestures, physical manipulation, and perhaps a few word approximations to get their messages across to others (Romski, Sevcik, Reumann, & Pate, 1989).

When children and youth lack productive language skills, their performance on standardized intelligence tests is likely to be limited. The ability to measure the underlying cognitive abilities of children and youth with severe mental retardation may be hindered because such tests typically rely heavily on a child's productive language skills. The group of children labeled with severe mental retardation, therefore, may actually encompass a more heterogeneous group in terms of intellectual abilities than the results of standardized testing reveal.

Youth with such profiles are of interest because they have not developed word production skills even though they have been exposed to spoken language since birth and have undergone extensive therapy aimed at teaching them to speak. First, and foremost, for children and youth with severe mental retardation who do not speak, creating a route by which they build initial language and communication production skills is a critical task for their subsequent success as communicators. Second, given their lack of productive language skills, findings about their language learning through augmented means can also provide a unique mechanism by which to view their overall development.

AUGMENTED LANGUAGE DEVELOPMENT: A LONGITUDINAL PERSPECTIVE

This section presents findings from a longitudinal study about augmented language development by youth with severe mental retardation using the System for Augmenting Language (SAL) (See Romski & Sevcik, 1996, for a detailed description). This study characterized how the use of the SAL influenced the youth's communicative use skills and vocabulary mastery. It also examined outcomes that were not directly taught as part of the SAL, specifically speech production skills and rudimentary reading skills.

Participants

The participants in this longitudinal study were 13 male school-age youth with moderate or severe mental retardation (mean CA = 12 years, 3 months; mean nonverbal MA = 3 years, 6 months). Each participant had a severe spoken language impairment, resided at home, and attended a special education program at their local public school. They all demonstrated intentional communication abilities (e.g., gestures, vocalizations), but no more than 10 intelligible word approximations at the study's onset. Each participant had varying amounts of speech-language therapy but still had not learned to speak. A general description of the participants' skills at the onset of the longitudinal study is provided in Table 9.1.

TABLE 9.1

Participants' Profiles at the Onset of the Longitudinal Study

P	CA (yrs:mos)	Medical Etiology	Level of Retardation[a]	PPVT-R[b] (yrs:mos)	Leiter[c] (yrs:mos)
BB	13:5	Cereb. palsy	Severe	< 1:6[d]	3:0
FG	20:1	Cereb. palsy	Severe	< 1:6[d]	< 2:0[d]
GJ	6:2	Unknown	Severe	< 1:6[d]	< 2:0[d]
KH	10:8	Unknown	Severe	< 1:6[d]	< 2:0[d]
DC	8:9	Unknown	Moderate	4:7	5:1
DE	11:11	Down syndrome	Severe	2:7	4:0
EC	16:7	Autism	Severe	3:1	5:0
JA	13:3	Unknown	Moderate	2:3	7:0
JL	20:5	Unknown	Severe	< 1:6[d]	< 2:0[d]
KW	13:2	Down syndrome	Severe	< 1:6[d]	4:2
MH	7:3	Autism	Moderate	< 1:6[d]	5:0
TE	11:9	Cereb. palsy	Severe	< 1:6[d]	3:3

Note: From Sevcik, R. A. & Romski, M. A. (1997). Comprehension and language acquisition: Evidence from youth with severe cognitive disabilities. In L. B. Adamson & M. A. Romski (Eds.), *Communication and language acquisition: Discoveries from atypical language development* (pp. 187–202). Baltimore: Paul H. Brookes Publishing Co. Reprinted by permission.

P = participant

[a]Level of retardation, as defined by Grossman (1983), was assigned as a result of psychological evaluations conducted by certified school psychologists prior to the onset of the study. These evaluations took into account both IQ, as measured by the Stanford–Binet Intelligence Scale (Terman & Merrill, 1960), and adaptive behavior, as measured by the AAMR Adaptive Behavior Scale (Lambert, Windmiller, Cole, & Figueroa, 1975). Moderate and severe mental retardation was defined as IQs of 50–70 and 20–40, respectively (Grossman, 1983)

[b]PPVT-R = the Peabody Picture Vocabulary Test–Revised (L. Dunn & L. Dunn, 1981)

[c]Leiter = the Arthur Adaptation of the Leiter International Performance Scale (Arthur, 1952)

[d]No basal was achieved and the participant's age equivalent score was estimated as being below the lowest age equivalent score available on the test.

The System for Augmenting Language (SAL)

The participants in this longitudinal study had no functional expressive communication system in place prior to the initiation of the study, thus they were required to learn language through instruction in an alternate modality. To provide such experience, an instructional approach was created using visual-graphic symbols coupled with speech-output communication devices to teach the participants to communicate symbolically.

The instructional approach is known as the System for Augmenting Language (SAL; Romski & Sevcik, 1996). The SAL consists of five integrated components, listed in Table 9.2, designed to supplement the

TABLE 9.2

Five Components of the System for Augmenting Language

- Electric computer-based speech-output communication devices are available for use in natural communicative environments
- Appropriate, initially limited, symbol vocabularies with the printed English word above each symbol are placed on the devices
- Participants are encouraged, though not required, to use the device during loosely structured naturalistic communicative exchanges
- Communicative partners are taught to use the device to augment their speech input to the participants with symbol input
- Ongoing resource and feedback mechanisms are provided to support the participants and their partners in their communication efforts

---

Note: From Romski, M. A. & Sevcik, R. A. (1996). *Breaking the speech barrier: Language development through augmented means.* Baltimore: Paul H. Brookes Publishing Co. Reprinted by permission.

youth's natural, albeit severely limited, language abilities with a symbol-embossed computerized keyboard that produced synthesized speech.

Speech-Output Communication Device.   The first component of the SAL was a speech-output communication device. Initially, the study employed a Words+ Portable Voice II (Words+, Inc., 1985) augmentative communication device consisting of a specially modified Epson HX-20 Notebook computer and an adapted Votrax Personal Speech System. A touch-sensitive Unicorn Expanded Keyboard was used to access the Words+ system. Because the participants were unable to read, spell, or write and could not access a computer keyboard in a conventional manner, this system permitted them to communicate by touching a visual-graphic symbol on a computer-based display. The computer produced a synthetic spoken word that corresponded to the symbol that was touched. To optimize portability in the home and school settings, the entire system was transported on a modified luggage cart. It facilitated use of the SAL in a variety of environments, including initially home or school, and subsequently within a range of community settings.

The Words+ system was later replaced with a WOLF (Adamlab, 1988). This device functioned like the Words+ system but was considerably smaller and significantly reduced in size and weight. The participants readily transferred their symbol use skills from the Words+ system to the WOLF (Romski & Sevcik, 1996).

Symbol Vocabulary.   The second component consisted of the symbol vocabulary. Lexigrams (Rumbaugh, 1977), arbitrary visual-graphic symbols, were chosen because they ensured that none of the participants were familiar with the symbols and there was an arbitrary relation between the symbol and its meaning. The symbols were placed on the display panel with the corresponding English word or phrase placed above each symbol to facilitate interpretation by literate unfamiliar partners. A lexigram was activated by touching it on the display and resulted in the production of a synthesized equivalent of the spoken word for that symbol.

Vocabulary was chosen individually for each participant by parents and teacher in conjunction with the investigators. Initial vocabulary included referential (e.g., basketball, Diet Coke, radio) and subsequently social-regulative words (e.g., I want, thank you, help). Vocabulary was expanded during the course of the study and updated and increased as needed thereafter.

Naturalistic Teaching Strategies. The third component of the SAL was the naturalistic teaching strategy. Communicative use of the device was not taught in the traditional sense. The use of the device was integrated into each youth's ongoing daily activities within the structure of the home and school settings. Partners were asked to use the device as part of their own spoken communications to the participant. The use of this approach permitted each individual to feel comfortable with the device and to facilitate its use in communicative exchanges as they occurred in everyday activities. The participant, himself, was always encouraged, but never required, to use the device whenever communicative opportunities arose.

Role of Communicative Partners. The fourth component was the role communicative partners (i.e., parents and teachers) play. They were taught to use the device to augment their speech input to the participants with symbol input (e.g., "MORE COOKIE PLEASE." "Let's go to the STORE.") where the words were spoken and symbols were touched in sequence. The parents and teachers themselves had participated in a series of instructional sessions in which the communicative use of the SAL was emphasized. Included was an orientation to the operation of the computer-linked device and to its use as a communicative tool through video-taped examples and role playing.

Resource and Feedback Mechanism. The fifth and final component of the SAL was the provision of an ongoing resource and feedback mechanism to support the youth and their partners' use of the SAL at home and school. This component consisted of obtaining regular and systematic feedback through the use of a questionnaire (QUEST) from the participant's primary partner about the participant's use of the device. It permitted the investigators to monitor communicative use and deal with any challenges (e.g., computer breakdown) that arose.

Use During Years 1 and 2

The longitudinal study encompassed a 2-year time period. During Year 1, participants were assigned to either a home group or a school group and took part in daily communicative interactions with adult partners (i.e., parents or teachers) employing the SAL within the setting. During Year 2, use of the SAL was expanded to include home and school for all participants. Across the 2 years of the study, participants also had opportunities to communicate with peers and siblings at school and at home, respectively, as well as a wide range of partners within the community.

Measurement Tools

Two primary measures were developed for assessing language and communication outcomes across the 2 years of the study. The first measure, Communicative Use Probes (CUPs), provided data about the youth's use of the SAL during daily communicative exchanges. Vocabulary Assessment Measures (VAMs), the second measure, provided data about the participant's comprehension and production of symbols outside of the setting of use.

CUPs were systematic nonverbal and verbal communicative samples collected by a nonparticipant observer in the setting of use. The sample consisted of applying an event-based coding scheme, the Communication Coding Scheme (CCS), and making an audiotape of the interaction. The CCS provided information about with whom the youth was communicating, how the youth was communicating (i.e., modes), what functions the communications were serving, the successfulness of the communications, and the discourse skills (e.g., turn taking, topic maintenance) employed (see Romski & Sevcik, 1996, for a complete description). After data were collected in the field, the information was compiled using the computer software program SALT (Systematic Analysis of Language Transcripts; Chapman & Miller, 1985) and resulted in a language transcript that incorporated both the youth's and their partners' communications for subsequent analyses. A sample excerpt from a transcript is shown in Table 9.3.

The VAMs consisted of a series of 10 structured tasks administered by the investigators on a monthly basis outside of the settings of communicative use. These tasks included measures of symbol comprehension as well as production using a nonidentity match to sample task format. In addition to providing a profile of the youth's vocabulary learning over the course of the study, VAMs measured skills that have been reported to emerge during augmented language instruction, such as the recognition of printed English words and production of intelligible speech.

TABLE 9.3
Sample of SALT (Chapman & Miller, 1985) Transcript

M	And I/'m go/ing to use a [L] {KNIFE} to spread it with.
M	J, what would you like for a drink?
M	Tell me what drink you would like.
J	[3L3S] {JUICE}.
M	You would?
M	I kinda thought so.
M	Look what I have at the table.
M	Look here.
=	M holds up the container of orange juice.
M	I already had some [L] {JUICE}.
M	I think I'll shake it.
J	[1V4S] XX.

Note: From Romski, M. A., & Sevcik, R. A. (1992). Developing augmented language in children with severe mental retardation. In S. F. Warren & J. Reichle (Eds.), *Causes and effects in communication and language intervention* (pp. 113–130). Baltimore: Paul H. Brookes Publishing Co. Reprinted by permission.

M = mother; J = youth; L = lexigram; { } = lexigram meaning; [3L3S] = CCS code for successful lexigram request response to an adult; [1V4S] = successful vocalization label initiation to an adult; XX = unintelligible vocalization.

Language and Communication Outcomes

Regardless of whether instruction took place at home or at school, the immersion and use of the SAL within the youths' daily lives offered them a viable learning environment (Romski & Sevcik, 1996; Romski, Sevcik, Robinson, & Bakeman, 1994; Romski, Sevcik, & Wilkinson, 1994). All of the youth acquired and used symbols during communicative exchanges. This section briefly summarizes achievements in three areas of language skill development: communicative use, vocabulary mastery, and additional language-related outcomes (see Romski & Sevcik, 1996, for a detailed discussion of these findings).

Communicative Use. Rather than relying on the new device as their only form of communication, all 13 youth used the SAL to communicate in conjunction with their already extant natural vocal and gestural communicative repertoires. Approximately one third of their total sampled utterances included symbol usages. For example, during the evening meal at home, one young man vocalized unintelligibly and simultaneously used a symbol to indicate his need for a fork. Their reliance on natural, unintelligible vocalizations did not change after the introduction of the communication device as the vocal mode accounted for nearly 50% of their utterances and was often used to gain the attention of their partners. Symbols were employed to encode a variety of messages, such as to request items and information and to answer questions directed to them. This integration of symbols with vocalizations and gestures resulted in a rich multimodal form of communication.

They used the SAL both successfully and effectively to communicate with adults (Romski, Sevcik, Robinson, & Bakeman, 1994) and on a more limited basis with peers (Romski, Sevcik, & Wilkinson, 1994). The overwhelming majority of their communications (96%), however, were directed to adults. Only 4% were directed to peers (Romski & Sevcik, 1996).

Vocabulary Mastery. Participants' initial vocabularies included both referential and social-regulative symbols (Adamson, Romski, Deffebach, & Sevcik, 1992). By the end of the study's first year, participants had access to from 12 to 18 referential symbols and 13 social-regulative symbols on their communication displays for a total of from 25 to 31 symbols. At the end of the second year, participants had access to a mean of 40.6 (range = 35–44) symbols on their display panels (Romski & Sevcik, 1996).

Performance on the VAMs revealed that referential symbols were correctly identified and maintained by the youth across the 2 years of the study. Comprehension performance was consistently better than production performance (Romski & Sevcik, 1996). Although referential symbol knowledge was generally better than social-regulative symbol knowledge, social-regulative symbols served to broaden the focus of conversations (Adamson et al., 1992). They also served as a foundation for the emergence of symbol combinations.

Language-Related Outcomes. Some of the youth also demonstrated language achievements beyond the acquisition of a single symbol vocabulary. They developed combinatorial symbol skills (Wilkinson, Romski, & Sevcik, 1994), as well as intelligible speech production skills (Romski, Sevcik, Wilkinson, & Robinson, 1990) and rudimentary reading skills (Sevcik, Romski, & Robinson, 1991).

The emergence of combinatorial symbol use skills was an important achievement (Wilkinson et al., 1994). Seven participants (DC, DE, JA, KH, MH, and TE) produced symbol combinations during the study. The majority of these combinations conformed to Braine's (1976) relational category scheme, suggesting they were producing semantic relations similar to those of typically developing children. Five participants also employed consistent symbol ordering rules, suggesting that at least some of the participants were capable of producing rule-governed combinations.

A second notable achievement associated with SAL experience was the emergence of intelligible spoken word productions in approximately half of the participants (54%). Using the VAMs as a database, increases were found in vocalization intelligibility and changes in phonetic structure of the vocalizations. Each of these youth more closely approximated the conventional spoken word that corresponded to the symbol after SAL experience than before (Romski et al., 1990). This change may be the result of a number of factors related to the synthetic speech signal (e.g., rate, consistency).

Another important language-related outcome was related to rudimentary reading skills. The printed words were placed above the symbols on the display to facilitate partner's recognition of the arbitrary symbols. The youths themselves were not expected to learn the printed words because many had not been successful in school-based reading programs. Six youth recognized an increased proportion of the printed English words that appeared above the symbols when presented in the VAMs independent of the symbol. In comparison to chance level performance at baseline measurement, across the course of the study they recognized, at minimum, 50% of the printed words displayed on their SALs. The printed words recognized were those that corresponded to the symbols with which the participant has demonstrated appropriate communicative use and for which understanding had been confirmed via the VAMs. Most importantly, the youth had not received any known explicit instruction concerning the relations between the symbols and their printed word equivalents. This finding suggests that the youth's experience with print paired with visual-graphic symbols may be one step in the development of at least a sight word vocabulary (Romski & Sevcik, 1996; Sevcik et al., 1991).

Overall Summary of Language and Communication Achievements

These findings strongly suggest that youth with moderate or severe mental retardation who are nonspeaking can learn to communicate via the SAL. This instructional approach provided experiences that resulted in a rich multimodal system of functional communication that served as a foundation on which additional language-related skills may emerge in youth with moderate or severe mental retardation.

PATHS OF LANGUAGE DEVELOPMENT THROUGH AUGMENTED MEANS

This final section discusses two issues related to the paths these youth took as they learned language through augmented means. First, what kind of variation existed within the group of youth who learned language through augmented means? And, second, in general how did their paths vary from the path typical children pursue?

Variations Among the Youth with Severe Mental Retardation

Although at the initiation of the study participants shared a similar language production profile, less than 10 spoken words, their performance has suggested that perhaps they did not form a single homogeneous group. Because participants' performances were studied in a variety of language-related domains across the 2-year period, it was possible to examine how individual participants performed across domains and if any similarities or differences emerged (Romski & Sevcik, 1996).

As reported in Romski and Sevcik (1996), domains were selected from the longitudinal study in which to examine performance. These nine domains were: communicates with adults (Romski, Sevcik, Robinson, & Bakeman, 1994), communicates with peers (Romski, Sevcik, & Wilkinson, 1994), produces symbol combinations (Wilkinson et al., 1994), comprehends initial symbol vocabulary (Romski & Sevcik, 1996), produces initial symbol vocabulary (Romski & Sevcik, 1996), maintains vocabulary from Year 1 to 2 (Romski & Sevcik, 1996), has a vocabulary greater than 35 symbols at 2 years (Romski & Sevcik, 1996), improves speech intelligibility (Romski et al., 1990), and recognizes printed English words (Sevcik et al., 1991). A dichotomous coding scheme (yes or no) was employed and each participant's documented achievement in every domain was coded based on performance within the domain. Table 9.4 presents the results of this coding for each participant in each domain. A review of the individual performance patterns in this table suggests that two distinct patterns of performance emerged.

Nine participants demonstrated achievement in at least seven of the nine domains. DC, JA, MH, and TE evidenced skill in every domain and DE, EC, JL, KW, and TF achieved skill in at least seven of the nine domains. They encountered difficulty with only a few domains: maintaining their vocabularies across years (DE, JL, and TF), generating symbol combinations (EC, TF, and KW), increasing speech intelligibility (DE, JL, and EC), or recognizing printed English words (KW).

The achievements of the remaining four participants—BB, KH, FG and GJ—however, were much more constrained. All four of them communicated with adults and comprehended their initial symbol vocabularies. By the end of Year 2, BB showed some minimal recognition of printed English words and KH produced a few ordered symbol combinations.

DC, DE, EC, JA, JL, KW, MH, TE, and TF evidenced then, what has been described as an advanced achievement pattern, composed of the rather swift acquisition of symbols followed by the emergence of symbol combinations and other language-related skills (e.g., printed word recognition). This pattern has been described as advanced because it permitted these

TABLE 9.4
Patterns of Achievement

Domain	Participants												
	BB	DC	DE	JL	KH	TF	EC	FG	GJ	JA	KW	MH	TE
Communicates with adults	Y	Y	Y	Y	Y	Y	Y	Y	Y	Y	Y	Y	Y
Communicates with peers	N	Y	Y	Y	N	Y	Y	N	N	Y	Y	Y	Y
Produces combinations	N	Y	Y	Y	Y	N	N	N	N	Y	N	Y	Y
Comprehends initial vocab.	Y	Y	Y	Y	Y	Y	Y	Y	Y	Y	Y	Y	Y
Produces initial vocab.	N	Y	Y	Y	N	Y	Y	N	N	Y	Y	Y	Y
Maintains vocab. from YR1 to YR2	N	Y	N	N	N	N	Y	N	N	Y	Y	Y	Y
Two-year vocabulary > 35 symbols	N	Y	Y	Y	N	Y	Y	N	N	Y	Y	Y	Y
Speech intelligibility improves	N	Y	N	N	N	Y	N	N	N	Y	Y	Y	Y
Recognizes printed English words	Y	Y	Y	Y	N	Y	Y*	N	N	Y*	N	Y*	Y

Note: From Romski, M. A., & Sevcik, R. A. (1996). *Breaking the speech barrier: Language development through augmented means.* Baltimore: Paul H. Brookes Publishing Co. Reprinted by permission.

Y = yes, N = no, * = recognized printed English words at the onset of the study.

nine participants to use basic skills as a solid foundation on which to develop skills in other language-related domains.

The four remaining participants (BB, FG, GJ, KH), on the other hand, evidenced a second distinct pattern referred to as a beginning achievement pattern. This pattern consisted of the slow acquisition of a small set (< 35) of single visual-graphic symbols in comprehension and production. This pattern was labeled "beginning" because it suggested that the participants had developed a set of rudimentary skills from which they could build additional communication skills. Although they had not, as yet, generalized their skills to other domains, two were showing signs of new skill development.

Understanding Achievement Patterns

What factors may have contributed to these distinct, nonoverlapping patterns achieved by these participants as they developed language through augmented means? When youth learn language through augmented means, two broad domains may exert influence on their learning patterns (Romski et al., 1997). First, the conditions under which language is acquired are altered by the introduction of the augmentation (i.e., mode, instruction). These conditions modify the communicative exchanges in a range of ways, and they are referred to as *extrinsic factors*. For example, it would be difficult to judge syntactic achievements because the symbols did not include grammatical markers. Second, although all the youth did not speak, they still presented with diverse biological and behavioral profiles. These may be described as *intrinsic factors*.

Extrinsic Factors. At least one extrinsic factor related to the investigation varied across participants with respect to the different achievement patterns that must be considered—the initial SAL instructional group (home or school) in which the participants were placed. It did not appear, however, to contribute to the two different achievement patterns because the four beginning achievers were equally distributed across both instructional groups.

Intrinsic Factors. Although all participants were matched on productive language skills at the outset of the study, that is, they each had less than 10 intelligible spoken words, there were a number of intrinsic factors that varied across participants that may have contributed to the path taken by each participant. This section discusses how general intellectual skills and cognitive abilities, as well as speech comprehension skills, may have influenced patterns of achievement.

First, the participants' general level of intellectual functioning was probably not a determining factor in SAL achievement. Participants evidencing severe mental retardation were represented in both achievement patterns. Although all the beginning achievers had a diagnosis of severe mental retardation, the advanced achievers had mixed diagnoses (both moderate and severe; see Table 9.1). The participants' performance on the battery of formal and informal cognitive measures, administered prior to their participation in the study, however, may help to uncover those factors that distinguish the two patterns of achievement. These measures included standardized instruments (i.e., The Leiter International Performance Scale; Arthur, 1952), as well as informal assessments of matching/sorting (for objects/colors) skills and representational matching (identity and nonidentity) skills. An examination of these data revealed that no specific cognitive skills differentiated the four beginning participants from the other participants. It is important to note, however, GJ's matching/sorting skills fell below those of all the other participants. A description of the participants' representational abilities clearly indicated that FG and GJ's abilities to grasp representational relations fell consistently below the remaining participants (See Romski & Sevcik, 1996, for a detailed review).

A second factor that may influence achievement is speech comprehension (Sevcik & Romski, 1997). Restricted formal and informal speech comprehension skills was a common characteristic of the four beginning achievers. The four participants with a beginning pattern did not obtain a basal score on the Peabody Picture Vocabulary Test–Revised (L. Dunn & L. Dunn, 1981) and had fairly low vocabulary scores on the Assessing Children's Language Comprehension (Foster, Giddan, & Stark, 1983). In addition, whereas all participants understood, in a very general sense, that spoken words represented real-world items, the four beginning achievers had not established specific word-referent relations when single word comprehension was systematically assessed through nonstandardized means.

These findings, although certainly preliminary given the small sample size, suggest that dimensions of speech comprehension may have influenced these two achievement patterns. Two additional investigations provide support for these findings. Romski, Sevcik, and Pate (1988) studied older adolescents and young adults with severe mental retardation who had been explicitly taught symbol production skills. They described distinct symbol acquisition and generalization patterns that were linked to the participants' extant speech comprehension skills. Franklin, Mirenda, and Phillips (1996) reported that learners with severe mental retardation who comprehended spoken words were better able to perform on visual matching tasks than learners who did not comprehend spoken words.

Both studies, in concert with these findings, suggest that extant speech comprehension skills may provide a foundation on which to build augmented language skills.

Variations from the Typical Path of Language Development

A developing child's first words typically emerge almost effortlessly (e.g., Bates, 1979; Bruner, 1983). They build on comprehension (Benedict, 1979) and learn through carefully orchestrated experiences. Children's vocabularies quickly expand to include upwards of 50 words (Nelson, 1973); then they begin to combine words and develop swiftly into competent multiword communicators (e.g., Brown, 1973).

Even given the variations across the 13 youth in this study, the advanced achievers in this study progressed through the language development process in a fashion similar to that of typical language learners who speak. They began the process by using a single symbol within the context of how they comprehended the symbol. They then developed a single symbol vocabulary that expanded to include more than 50 symbols. From there, the advanced achievers went on to develop symbol combinations. They even went on to fast map the meanings of novel symbols (Romski, Sevcik, Robinson, Mervis, & Bertrand, 1996). Their development, then, shared some commonalities with the process through which all children proceed as they learn to speak (Cicchetti & Pogge-Hesse, 1982; Lewis, 1987).

CONCLUSIONS

In conclusion, the System for Augmenting Language permitted the youth to reveal their capacities for language and communication development within social interaction and their previously unrealized conceptualizations of the world. These findings emphasize a learning process that couples extant skills and a unique configuration of technology combined with naturalistic augmented language learning opportunities to account for the youth's ability to learn augmented language. The findings suggest that there also is variation in the path these youth may take to learn language through augmented means. These two paths may be influenced by the extant speech comprehension skills the youth bring to the task. The advanced achievers also followed a path of language development that, in general, was similar to that of typical children. Precise examination of the augmented language learning process strengthens our understanding of some of the intricacies and variations of very early language development.

ACKNOWLEDGMENTS

The preparation of this chapter and the research described within was funded by NICHD-06016 and a Research Program Enhancement Grant from Georgia State University.

REFERENCES

Adamlab. (1988). *Wolf manual.* Wayne, MI: Author.

Adamson, L. B. (1996). *Communication development during infancy.* Boulder, CO: Westview.

Adamson, L. B., Romski, M. A., Deffebach, K. P., & Sevcik, R. A. (1992). Symbol vocabulary and the focus of conversations: Augmenting language development for youth with mental retardation. *Journal of Speech and Hearing Research, 35,* 1333–1344.

American Association on Mental Retardation (1993). *Mental retardation: Definition, classification, and systems of supports* (9th ed.). Washington, DC: Author.

Arthur, G. (1952). *The Arthur Adaptation of the Leiter International Performance Scale.* Chicago: C. H. Steolting.

Bates, E. (1979). *The emergence of symbols: Cognition and communication in infancy.* New York: Academic Press.

Benedict, H. (1979). Early lexical development: Comprehension and production. *Journal of Child Language, 6,* 183–200.

Berko-Gleason, J. (1996). *Language development.* Columbus, OH: Merrill.

Braine, M. (1976). Children's first word combinations. *Monographs of the Society for Research in Child Development, 41.*

Brown, R. (1973). *A first language.* Cambridge, MA: Harvard University Press.

Bruner, J. (1983). *Child's talk: Learning to use language.* New York: Norton.

Chapman, R., & Miller, J. (1985). *Systematic analysis of language transcripts.* Madison, WI: University of Wisconsin Press.

Cicchetti, D., & Pogge-Hesse, P. (1982). Possible contributions of the study of organically retarded persons to developmental theory. In E. Zigler & D. Balla (Eds.), *Mental retardation: The developmental-difference controversy* (pp. 277–318). Hillsdale, NJ: Lawrence Erlbaum Associates.

Dunn, L., & Dunn, L. (1981). *The Peabody Picture Vocabulary Test–Revised.* Circle Pines, MN: American Guidance Service.

Foster, R., Giddan, J. J., & Stark, J. (1983). *Assessment of Children's Language Comprehension.* Palo Alto, CA: Consulting Psychologist's Press.

Franklin, K., Mirenda, P., & Phillips, G. (1996). Comparison of five symbol assessment protocols with nondisabled preschoolers and learners with severe intellectual disabilities. *Augmentative and Alternative Communication, 12,* 63–77.

Grossman, H. (1983). *Classification in mental retardation.* Washington, DC: American Association on Mental Retardation.

Guess, D., & Horner, R. (1978). The severely and profoundly handicapped. In E. L. Meyen (Ed.), *Exceptional children and youth: An introduction* (pp. 218–268). Denver: Love Publishing.

Lambert, N. M., Windmiller, M., Cole, L., & Figueroa, R. A. (1975). Standardization of a public school version of the AAMD Adaptive Behavior Scale. *Mental Retardation, 13,* 3–7.

Lewis, V. (1987). *Development and handicap*. New York: Basil Blackwell.

Mirenda, P., Iacono, T., & Williams, R. (1990). Communication options for persons with severe and profound disabilities: State of the art and future directions. *Journal of the Association for Persons with Severe Handicaps, 15,* 3–21.

Nelson, K. (1973). Structure and strategy in learning to talk. *Monographs of the Society for Research in Child Development, 38*(1–2, Serial No. 139).

Romski, M. A., & Sevcik, R. A. (1988). Augmentative and alternative communication: Considerations for individuals with severe intellectual disabilities. *Augmentative and Alternative Communication, 4,* 83–93.

Romski, M. A., & Sevcik, R. A. (1992). Developing augmented language in children with severe mental retardation. In S. F. Warren & J. Reichle (Eds.), *Causes and effects in communication and language intervention* (pp. 113–130). Baltimore: Paul H. Brookes.

Romski, M. A., & Sevcik, R. A. (1996). *Breaking the speech barrier: Language development through augmented means*. Baltimore: Paul H. Brookes.

Romski, M. A., Sevcik, R. A., & Adamson, L. B. (1997). A framework for studying how children with developmental disabilities develop language through augmented means. *Augmentative and Alternative Communication, 13,* 172–178.

Romski, M. A., Sevcik, R. A., & Pate, J. L. (1988). The establishment of symbolic communication in persons with severe retardation. *Journal of Speech and Hearing Disorders, 53,* 94–107.

Romski, M. A., Sevcik, R. A., Reumann, R., & Pate, J. L. (1989). Youngsters with moderate or severe retardation and severe spoken language impairments: I. Extant communicative patterns. *Journal of Speech and Hearing Disorders, 54,* 366–373.

Romski, M. A., Sevcik, R. A., Robinson, B., & Bakeman, R. (1994). Adult-directed communications of youth with mental retardation using the System for Augmenting Language. *Journal of Speech and Hearing Research, 37,* 617–628.

Romski, M. A., Sevcik, R. A., Robinson, B. F., Mervis, C. B., & Bertrand, J. (1996). Mapping the meanings of novel visual symbols by youth with moderate or severe mental retardation. *American Journal of Mental Retardation, 100,* 391–402.

Romski, M. A., Sevcik, R. A., Robinson, B. F., & Wilkinson, K. M. (1990, November). *Intelligibility and form changes in the vocalizations of augmented language learners*. Paper presented at the annual meeting of the American Speech-Language-Hearing Association, Seattle, WA.

Romski, M. A., Sevcik, R. A., & Wilkinson, K. M. (1994). Peer-directed communicative interactions of augmented language learners with mental retardation. *American Journal on Mental Retardation 98,* 527–538.

Rosenberg, S., & Abbeduto, L. (1993). *Language and communication in mental retardation: Development, processes, and intervention*. Hillsdale, NJ: Lawrence Erlbaum Associates.

Rumbaugh, D. M. (Ed.). (1977). *Language learning by a chimpanzee: The LANA project*. New York: Academic Press.

Sevcik, R. A., & Romski, M. A. (1997). Comprehension and language acquisition: Evidence from youth with severe cognitive disabilities. In L. B. Adamson & M. A. Romski (Eds.), *Communication and language acquisition: Discoveries from atypical language development* (pp. 184–201). Baltimore: Paul H. Brookes.

Sevcik, R. A., Romski, M. A., & Robinson, B. R. (1991, November). *Printed english word recognition by nonspeaking children with mental retardation*. Poster presented at the annual convention of the American Speech-Language-Hearing Association, Atlanta, GA.

Snell, M. (1993). *Instruction of students with severe disabilities*. Columbus, OH: Merrill/Macmillian.

Terman, L. M., & Merrill, M. A. (1960). *Stanford–Binet Intelligence Scale*. Boston: Houghton Mifflin.

Wilkinson, K. M., Romski, M. A., & Sevcik, R. A. (1994). Emergence of visual-graphic symbol combinations by youth with moderate or severe mental retardation. *Journal of Speech and Hearing Research, 37*, 883–895.

Words +, Inc. (1985). *Words + Portable Voice II User's Manual*. Sunnyvale, CA: Author.

## CHAPTER TEN

Modeling Developmental and Individual Variability in Reading and Writing Acquisition: A Developmental Neuropsychological Perspective

Virginia W. Berninger
Robert D. Abbott
University of Washington

This chapter reviews and critiques traditional approaches to investigation of the development of reading and writing and of individual differences in reading and writing acquisition. It then examines alternative approaches to the investigation of development and individual differences in reading and writing. It presents evidence from a research program on reading and writing acquisition to support the claim that the alternative approaches more accurately reflect the variability that exists within and among individuals in the process of learning to read and write. This research program is grounded in the developmental neuropsychological perspective (Berninger, 1994a; Berninger & Hart, 1992), which focuses on the development of skill in a functional system rather than on the loss of skill later in development through injury or disease. However, the overall goal here is to provide an overview of the variety of approaches investigators might use to model variability among individuals at a given time in development or across development. Advantages and disadvantages of each approach are discussed. Although the approaches are illustrated with examples from research on normal and disabled reading and writing, these approaches may be applied to the investigation of variability in other domains of learning and development as well.

TRADITIONAL APPROACHES TO MODELING DEVELOPMENT

Traditional *stage models* assume skill development proceeds through discrete phases that are qualitatively different from each other and are ordered temporally in linear fashion. Individuals may vary in the rate at which they pass through the ordered stages but all individuals follow the same sequence in achieving the developmental outcome. Mastering a prior stage is a prerequisite for mastering the next stage.

Chall's Model of Stages of Reading Development

Chall (1979) proposed a macroscopic model of reading development that has been very influential in the field of reading research. Briefly, its claims are as follows.

Stage 0: Prereading Stage (Preschool–Kindergarten, Birth–Age 6). During this stage children learn the spoken language and are exposed to printed language at home and/or preschool (see Adams, 1990). In the process, they acquire skills needed for beginning reading, such as segmentation of sounds in spoken words and discrimination and identification of alphabet letters.

Stage 1: Initial Reading or Decoding Stage (Grades 1–2, Ages 6–7). During this stage, children abstract the correspondences between written words and spoken words, that is, the principles by which the spelling system of a language represents its phonology. Depending on a child's instructional program, these insights may be acquired *incidentally* through repeated exposure to written words (sight word method) or *explicitly* through patterns of rules the teacher brings to the child's attention (phonics method) or a combination of both incidental and explicit learning (eclectic method). Biemiller (1970) analyzed oral reading errors of children taught by the sight word method and identified three substages of Stage 1: (a) focus on semantic and syntactic aspects of text, (b) focus on graphic properties of words, and (c) focus on graphic and semantic properties of text. However, Barr (1972) showed that phonics instruction directs children's attention more to graphic features of text than does the sight word method. Thus, the nature of the instructional program may modify the developmental sequence of substages of decoding.

Stage 2: Confirmation, Fluency, Ungluing from Print (Grades 2–3, Ages 7–8). During this stage, children become more fluent and faster as they practice and consolidate skills acquired in Stage 1. According to Chall, Stage 2 readers do not read to gain new information but rather to confirm what they already know. During Stage 2, the gap widens between children from homes that provide books, magazines, trips to the libraries, and other activities to foster literacy, and children from homes that do not provide the same kind of opportunities.

Stage 3: Reading for Learning the New—From One Viewpoint (Grades 4–8, Ages 9–13). During this stage, children and youth who have already learned to read begin to read to learn, that is, to master ideas acquired through print. The difference between this stage and the subsequent one is that they read for information that is new from only one viewpoint. At the beginning, but not the end of Stage 3, children may learn more efficiently from listening and watching than from reading.

Stage 4: Multiple Viewpoints (High School, Ages 14–18). During this stage, youth learn to read texts from multiple points of view.

Stage 5: A World View (College, Ages 18 and Above). During this stage, adults learn to read texts selectively to achieve their own purposes, to integrate their knowledge with that of others, and to create new knowledge. A college education may be needed to achieve this stage but does not guarantee that this stage will be achieved.

In Chall's view, children with reading or learning disabilities are most likely to have difficulty with Stage 1 (decoding) and Stage 2 (fluency). Although Chall's stage model captures life-span developmental changes in the nature of reading observed by many teachers and clinicians, it does have some limitations, which should not be obscured by its contribution. To begin with, it assumes that the order of skill development, although not the rate, is invariant across individuals. It characterizes reading development as a uniform process and does not allow for the possibility that there may be alternative routes for achieving the same developmental outcome. Moreover, it implies that comprehension, the sense of gaining information from text, does not begin to develop (Stage 3) until word decoding (Stage 1) and fluent oral reading (Stage 2) are mastered. Alternatives to these assumptions are discussed later.

Frith's Model of Word Recognition Development

Frith (1985) proposed a microscopic model of the development of word recognition skills that has also been influential. According to this model, word recognition skill is acquired in the following three stages.

Logographic. In this stage, the child recognizes a few words on the basis of paired associations between written and spoken words. This stage probably begins during lap reading, as an adult points to written words in a text read so many times that the child has memorized it and the child begins to link the written and oral forms of the words (Morris, 1992).

Alphabet.   In this stage, letter–sound correspondences are acquired and form the basis of both nonlexical (grapheme-to-phoneme correspondences) and lexical routes.

Orthographic.   In this stage, automatic, direct, sound-free recognition of spelling units larger than the single letter is achieved.

The criticisms leveled against this stage model mostly involve its claims for a particular stage. Ehri (1992) refuted the claim that the orthographic stage is sound-free and noted research showing that even complex spelling regularities depend on sound. Vellutino (1992) argued that Goswami's work on analogies casts doubt that children go through a rigid sequence of development from the logographic stage to alphabetic stage to orthographic stage. Goswami (1988) showed that first-grade children can learn to recognize new written words through analogies to written words containing the same orthographic units—larger than a single letter but smaller than a whole word. Gough, Juel, and Griffith (1992) questioned whether the logographic stage is aptly named because, in their research, 4- and 5-year-old children recognized words on the basis of one salient, unique, or partial cue rather than on the basis of the written word as a *whole unit* as the term logograph implies. Like Chall's model, Frith's model assumes a uniform, invariant process of development and does not allow for alternative routes to the same developmental outcomes. Also, it is not known whether the instructional program may modify Frith's developmental sequence. Alternative views of the development of the word recognition process are considered later.

Stage Models of Spelling

Henderson's Model.   Henderson (1980) proposed the following stages of spelling development based on analysis of errors children make in spelling:

1. *Prereading stage:* Letters do not reflect any sound–symbol relations.
2. *Letter–name stage:* Spelling uses the phonemic features in a letter's name.
3. *Vowel transition stage:* Long vowels are spelled with a silent *e*.
4. *Mature stage.* Syntactic, semantic, and derivational aspects of words play a role in spelling.

Ehri's Model.   Ehri (1992) noted the difficulty in describing developmental stages based on a maturational time table independent of an instructional time table. She offered an alternative to Henderson's model, which is tied to the correspondence between orthographic and phonological/morphemic units reflected in children's invented spellings. This model included four stages.

1. *Precommunicative stage:* The spelling is unreadable because it has no relation to sound. The written symbols may be true alphabet letters or invented graphic symbols.

2. *Semi-phonetic stage:* The spelling reflects sounds but is phonetically incomplete. Sounds may be linked to letter names.

3. *Phonetic stage:* The spelling represents most of the sounds with letters. During this stage, spelling progresses from phonetic to phonemic level representation.

4. *Morphemic stage:* The spelling uses units larger than single letters. At this level, spelling is morphophonemic, that is, it preserves links to meaning in the word's root stem and links to sound (see Venezky, 1970). Results of Treiman's (1993) longitudinal study of first-graders' spelling are consistent with the claim that the phonetic stage precedes the morphemic stage. Although first-graders in her study were aware of the phonological basis of the spelling system, they were not yet aware of the morphological basis of the spelling system.

Gentry's Model. Gentry's (1982, 1984) model is very similar to Ehri's. The first three stages are the same, followed by transitional and correct stages described here:

4. *Transitional stage:* Alphabetic and phonetic strategies are replaced with some knowledge of orthographic rules, for example, inclusion of vowels in every syllable, and morphonological relations, for example, adding *-ed* to form the past tense.

5. *Correct stage:* Children master orthographic rules and morphological relations and adopt visual checking strategies.

Varnhagen (1995) observed that the stage approach to spelling development is incomplete at best. Progression from stage to stage may not be invariant for two reasons. First, sequence of development may be different for different words. Second, children seem to have a variety of strategies available to them from the very beginning of the spelling acquisition process. For example, Treiman (1993) found that children acquire orthographic strategies before they complete the phonetic stage. Varnhagen reviewed the phonological strategies, orthographic strategies, morphemic, and mnemonic (word-specific) strategies that developing spellers may apply.

Stage Models of Written Communication

A comprehensive stage model of written communication does not exist, but the following summary integrates developmental sequences reported in the literature for various phases of the process, from a *product* perspective. According to Henderson (1992), written communication originates at about 18 months when children develop an interest in scribbling and continues to develop as children begin to draw pictures and then letterlike scribbles and figures. Likewise, Gibson and Levin (1975) observed that written communication begins with the "fundamental graphic act" when a youngster discovers that scribbling with a crayon or pencil leaves a graphic trace and follows a predictable, ordered developmental pattern: random scribbling; zig-zag lines; variation in elements without segmentation into units; linear, wordlike arrangement of elements; true letters; words; sequences of related words; and finally sentences. Nonreading 3-year-olds' graphic productions resemble writing that can be differentiated from pictures (Lavine, 1972). Contemporary handwriting research confirms this observation and has investigated the development of motoric processes underlying handwriting (see Graham & Winetraub, 1996).

In a similar vein to Gibson and Levin (1975), Traweek and Berninger (1997) observed the following developmental sequence in the writing samples of kindergartners and first-graders: pictures without text; production of letterlike, nonletters; random or copied sequences of true letters; single words; phrases less than a clause in length; clause and sentence-length productions. Although all these categories of productions were found among the kindergartners, all the first-graders produced text—single words, phrases, clauses, or sentences—and not pictures without text or nonletters. However, first-graders often illustrated the written text with pictures.

Another approach to stages of written communication is to focus on the *cognitive processes* underlying writing rather than on the written product. Scardamalia and Bereiter (1987) compared the "knowledge-telling" process used by younger and less skilled writers and the "knowledge-transforming process" used by older and more skilled writers. In knowledge-telling, the writer searches memory for content relevant to a topic and writes down whatever comes to mind. In knowledge-transforming, goals are incorporated into the planning process and only content relevant to both the topic and the goals is written down. Hayes and Flower (1980) developed the most influential model of the cognitive processes underlying adult, skilled writing based on think-aloud protocols. Briefly, these processes—planning, translating, and reviewing/revising—are recursive rather than sequential and draw on the task environment and text produced so far. Berninger (1994a) and Berninger and Swanson (1994) reasoned that beginning and developing writing are not simply scaled-down versions of skilled writing. For example, in the model of adult, skilled writing translation is an empty box, but in the modified model that accounts for beginning and developing writing (Berninger, Abbott, Whitaker, Sylvester, & Nolen, 1995) translation has two components—text generation and transcription. Text generation is the transformation of ideas into language representations in working memory. Text generation occurs at the level of the word, sentence, paragraph, and discourse structure (Berninger, Mizokawa, Bragg, Cartwright, & Yates, 1994; Whitaker, Berninger, Johnston, & Swanson, 1994). Transcription involves the translation of those representations into written symbols. Also, distinctions were made in the modified model between advanced planning prior to translation and online planning during translation and between online revising and posttranslation revising.

Based on cross-sectional studies, component and subcomponent processes seemed to emerge at different phases of writing development. The goal of these studies was not to describe a rigid stage model, but rather to pinpoint when in development the multiple processes involved in writing seem to emerge. In the primary grades (see Berninger & Swanson, 1994, Fig. 1), translating emerged first, with transcription emerging relatively earlier than text generation, and generation of words emerging before generation of sentences (clauses), which were followed by generation of paragraphs (multiple clauses). Online planning was evident in children's construction of topic-comment units (Berninger, Fuller, & Whitaker, 1996). Only occasionally did online revising occur of a word (transcription) or of a sentence (text generation). In the intermediate grades (see Berninger & Swanson, 1994, Fig. 2), transcription became automatized, text generation expanded to include more mature discourse structures for narrative and expository literary genre, and posttranslation reviewing/revising and advanced preplanning emerged. In the junior high grades (see Berninger & Swanson, 1994, Fig. 3), these processes continued to develop and were increasingly constrained by working memory span and influenced by metacognition about writing.

A limitation of these stage models of development of written communication is that they are based on cross-sectional data or longitudinal data over relatively short (year or two) time windows. Individual children have not been followed from the preschool years through the middle school years to describe the variability that might exist in the developmental trajectories of individuals for developing written communication skills, from either a product or process perspective.

TRADITIONAL APPROACHES TO MODELING INDIVIDUAL DIFFERENCES

Five methods are often used to study individual differences in learning to read and write: bivariate correlation, multiple regression, comparison of good and poor readers or writers, reading-level matched design, and case study. Each has advantages and disadvantages. The first four methods primarily yield information about interindividual differences. The last method focuses on intraindividual differences within a single subject, but comparison across multiple case studies may shed light on interindividual differences.

Bivariate Correlation and Regression

In this approach, the degree of relation between two variables is computed and statistical significance is evaluated. An advantage of bivariate correlations is that they can evaluate relations taking into account the entire continuum of each measured variable (Lunneborg & Abbott, 1983).

Another advantage is that the relation (i.e., the shared variance) between component reading or writing skills and measures thought to be related to reading or writing can be evaluated to assess if the measures are indeed tapping reading or writing-related processes at different developmental stages. Often tasks in experimental studies only appear to have face validity for reading and writing and lack empirical evidence that performance on the experimental tasks predicts level of reading or writing skill. Such correlational analyses can be important supplements to experimental studies. For example, the correlations between measures in a multivariate data set and component reading and writing skills have been examined in grades 1 to 6. Berninger and Abbott (1994a) found that each of three orthographic codes (for whole words, letters, letter clusters) and each of three phonological codes (for whole words, phonemes, syllables) were significantly correlated with reading real words, reading pseudowords, and spelling words in a primary grade sample ($N = 300$). Berninger et al. (1992) found that all the orthographic codes, fine motor planning, the sensory-motor integration summary score, and the alphabet task (rate and accuracy of retrieval and production of alphabet letters from memory) were correlated with handwriting fluency (speed and accuracy of copying sentences) and compositional fluency (number of words of clauses produced in 5 minutes) in the primary grade sample. Berninger, Cartwright, Yates, Swanson, and Abbott (1994) found that, in an intermediate grade sample ($N = 300$), four orthographic measures and five phonological measures were correlated with reading real words and pseudowords and reading comprehension, and working memory was correlated with comprehension. In the intermediate grade sample, only orthographic coding measures were correlated with the handwriting copying task, but both orthographic and phonological coding measures and Verbal IQ were correlated with spelling from dictation, and orthographic coding and working memory span were correlated with compositional fluency. Taken together, these results showed that lower order processes (e.g., phonological, orthographic, fine motor) are correlated with writing skills in the primary and intermediate grades.

One disadvantage of bivariate correlations is that only two variables in a multivariate data set are considered at a time. Another disadvantage is that significant correlations do not necessarily imply causal relations between the variables. Berninger (1994a) argued that, at best, significant correlations between reading-related process variables and component reading skills or between writing-related process variables and component writing skills indicate that the process variables are constraints in the reading or writing system that limit degrees of freedom in skill acquisition but may not cause change independent of instructional variables and the constructive processes of the learner.

Violations of assumptions, such as bivariate normality and linearity of relation, must also be evaluated for their effects on the magnitude of the correlation. Additionally, characteristics of each measured variable, such as its degrees of reliability, need to be considered when considering the correlation among measured variables.

Multiple Regression and Correlation

Multiple regression and correlation have the advantage of examining the relation between a set of predictor variables and a criterion variable to determine the best set of variables for predicting the criterion, how much variance that set of variables accounts for in the criterion, and whether individual predictor variables account for unique increments of variance. Thus, this approach takes into account shared and unique variance in a multivariate data set and allows one to reduce a complex set of variables to a smaller set of the most predicting variables. Theory should carefully guide these analyses because only using empirical methods for examining predictors can lead to sample-specific results that do not cross-validate.

Examples of the use of multiple regression and correlation are found in the same studies cited under bivariate correlations. These theory-based multiple regressions were used to evaluate the set of best predictors of a component reading or writing skill, that is, the set in which each predictor accounted for a unique increment of variance. For the primary grade sample, the best predictors of reading real words included all three orthographic codes and all three phonological codes; the best predictor of reading pseudowords included all orthographic codes except letter coding and all three phonological codes; and the best predictor of spelling dictated words included all orthographic codes except whole word and all three phonological codes (Berninger & Abbott, 1994b). For the primary grade sample, the best combination of predictors of handwriting was the alphabet task, letter cluster coding, and the fine motor planning task; and the best combination of predictors of compositional fluency was the alphabet task, letter cluster coding, and fine motor planning (Berninger et al., 1992). For the intermediate grade sample, the best combination of predictors of reading real words was three orthographic coding and three phonological coding measures and Verbal IQ; the best combination of predictors for reading pseudowords included two orthographic coding and three phonological coding measures but not Verbal IQ; the best combination of predictors for reading comprehension included phoneme coding, orthographic coding, working memory, and Verbal IQ (Berninger et al., 1994). For the intermediate grade sample, the best combination of predictors for handwriting included three orthographic coding measures; the best combination for spelling from dictation included three orthographic measures, one phonological measure, and Verbal IQ. The best combination for predicting compositional fluency included two orthographic measures, one fine motor planning measure, and a working memory span measure (Berninger et al., 1994).

One disadvantage of multiple regression and correlation is that analysis is based on measured variables. Such measures have limited reliability (error of measurement can significantly affect results) and limited construct validity (it is rare that a single measure captures all facets of a theoretical construct). Latent variable structural equation models can reduce the effects of these limitations. Another disadvantage is that statements of cause and effect must be cautiously made. In the context of comparing competing theories (within which causal statements might be made) correlational studies can examine whether the relations present in the correlational data are more consistent with one theory versus another (Bentler, 1980) and thus provide evidence relative to the causal mechanisms hypothesized in one theory as compared to other theories postulating different causal mechanisms.

Comparison of Good and Poor Readers or Writers

A very popular design in reading and writing research compares those who fall at the upper or lower end of the distribution of reading or writing skill (e.g., Kim [Yoon] & Goetz, 1994; Vellutino, Scanlon, & Tanzman, 1995). One advantage of this design is that differences between those who excel and those who do not in a particular skill may be pinpointed. One disadvantage of this design is that it uses data only at the extremes of the distribution and not along the entire continuum of reading or writing skill. Another disadvantage is that all individuals at a certain level of achievement are treated as if they are a homogeneous group, when in fact the grouping may mask considerable heterogeneity. Individual differences may occur among poor readers and also among good readers (Berninger & Abbott, 1992) for several reasons. First, both reading and writing achievement are based on component skills. Children within a group may be matched on one component (e.g., word recognition), but may vary on another component (e.g., comprehension). Second, children within a group may differ in the development of processes (e.g., phonological or orthographic awareness) related to reading or writing that underlie skill acquisition. Third, children may have followed different routes to achieving comparable achievement levels (Berninger, 1994a).

Reading-Level Matched Design

In this design, a group of older disabled readers is compared to that of a younger nondisabled group; both groups are equated on reading level (e.g., Siegel, Geva, & Share, 1995). One advantage of this design is that it controls for variation due to amount of reading experience. Disabled readers often avoid reading and probably do not have as much reading experience as age-mates who are not disabled in reading. If disabled readers were compared to age-mates, differences could be related to differences in practice of reading skills as well as differences in processes skills related to reading. This design also has a number of disadvantages. Jackson and Butterfield (1989) discussed the serious methodological problems with it. One problem is that just because students are matched on one variable (e.g., reading achievement level), it does not mean they are comparable on all other reading-related variables. Often the groups differ significantly in IQ. In addition, Vellutino, Scanlon, and Chen (1995) noted conceptual problems with the design, namely, it does not allow for normal changes in the reading process across development. Moreover, the design is essentially correlational—associating processing differences with the groups—and permits limited causal inference. Treatment studies that manipulate instructional variables are needed in order to make stronger causal inferences about reading or writing acquisition.

Case Studies

A major advantage of the case study is its in-depth examination of the intraindividual differences within the individual learner. Case studies of students referred for school problems in the laboratory and clinic over the past 15 years—some of whom were found to have reading and/or writing disabilities, some of whom were not—suggest that students are like snowflakes: No two are alike. This variability is often at odds with the results of research on reading and writing disabilities or reading and writing acquisition, which claims there is a single causal mechanism such as phonological awareness. For example, children with reading disabilities vary as to whether they have problems in orthographic coding, phonological coding, or both orthographic coding and phonological coding (Berninger &

Abbott, 1994a), or rapid automatized naming or none of these problems (Berninger et al., 1997) or other problems. Likewise, there is considerable variation in the process deficits associated with writing disabilities (Berninger, Abbott, Whitaker, Sylvester, & Nolen, 1995).

A disadvantage of the case study is that it does not yield results that can be generalized across individuals. However, comparison across multiple case studies may provide clues about interindividual differences. For example, two nonreading children with highly similar pretreatment assessment protocols (deficits in both orthographic and phonological processing) were followed over time to compare their response to intervention (Berninger et al., 1997). One was a treatment responder and learned to read and write at the expected level. The other was a treatment nonresponder who to date has not responded positively to any of the interventions tried. Comparison of these two case studies demonstrated that processing skills alone are not the sole causal mechanisms in learning to read. Individual differences in the constructive processes of the learner for using instructional cues in varying ways and the nature of the instructional program also need to be considered (Berninger & Abbott, 1992).

ALTERNATIVE APPROACHES TO MODELING DEVELOPMENT

Multiple Developmental Domains and Working Brain Systems

One of the problems of stage models is that they assume the multiple domains of development mature in sequential, nonoverlapping time periods. An alternative view is that the multiple domains develop in parallel but each domain is on its own developmental trajectory. Functional reading and writing systems are not modules that are preformed in the infant brain and will be elicited at a certain time in maturation by a specific kind of environmental stimulation. Rather, like oral language that is constructed from and draws on nonlinguistic systems such as attentional, perceptual, and cognitive systems (Bates, 1993), the reading and writing systems are constructed from and draw on other systems (Berninger, 1994a; Berninger et al., 1994; Ellis, 1985, 1987; Wolf, 1991). Elsewhere these developmental domains have been referred to as working brain systems (Berninger et al., 1997) and nine developmental domains most important to the acquisition of reading and writing have been described: attention, memory, fine motor function, oral language, orthographic coding and imaging, executive functions, social/emotional, motivation and cognition (Berninger & Abbott, 1994b, Table 1).

Likewise, reading draws on subsystems and writing draws on subsystems, each on their own developmental trajectory. Little research has focused on how the various subsystems are orchestrated differently, depending on the task at hand and the developmental level of readers and writers. Abbott and Berninger (1995) used structural equation modeling to show that orthographic and phonological factors are orchestrated differently for beginning word recognition and beginning spelling. Berninger, Abbott, Thomson, and Raskind (2001) applied structural equation modeling to demonstrate that the same set of language processes (orthographic, phonological, and rapid automatic naming) are orchestrated differently, depending on the component reading or writing skill in a functional system and developmental level of individuals with learning disabilities. For children, the orthographic and phonological factors had direct paths to reading accuracy, spelling, and composition; the orthographic and rapid naming factors had direct paths to reading rate; the Verbal IQ and phonological factors had direct paths to reading comprehension; and only the orthographic factor had a direct path to handwriting. For the adults, however, the orthographic factor and Verbal IQ had direct paths to reading accuracy, spelling, and composition; the orthographic and rapid naming factors had direct paths to reading rate; only Verbal IQ had a direct path to comprehension; and only the orthographic factor had a direct path to handwriting. Only reading rate and handwriting orchestrated the language processes in exactly the same way in children and adults with learning disability. This flexible orchestration would be missed with a traditional stage model of development.

To illustrate the notion of multiple developmental domains (or working brain systems) for development, modifications of Chall's and Frith's models are offered. These modifications contrast with the stage models in that each of the stages is reconceptualized as a developmental domain on its own trajectory.

Modification of Chall's Model. In Chall's sequential model, comprehension does not become important until Stage 3 when children begin to read to learn. In our modified version, working brain systems for word recognition and comprehension are developing from the beginning of the reading acquisition process, but each is on its own developmental trajectory. This model is consistent with claims of the simple view of reading (Hooven & Tunmer, 1993): Reading consists of word recognition and comprehension, both of which are necessary, neither being sufficient by itself. Over the course of development the relative weighting of these components may change, but both are important throughout development (Gough & Walsh, 1991). Although immaturity of word recognition may constrain reading comprehension initially, comprehension is still possible to some degree and is developing. For example, see the case study of the boy with deep dyslexia reported by Berninger and Hart (1992). In this unusual case, the comprehension system seemed to be developing at a faster rate than the word recognition system.

This view of reading developing along multiple pathways is consistent with other research findings. O'Flaven (1989) documented that second-grade children, who would not yet have reached Stage 3 in Chall's model, can discuss the meaning of stories they read with sophisticated insight with respect to developing comprehension. Meaning-oriented whole language approaches to reading may have advantages in kindergarten, although not in the later grades (Stahl, McKenna, & Pagnicco, 1994). Thus meaning, which is not mentioned in Chall's model until Stage 3 (grades 4–8), seems to play a role from the earliest stages of reading acquisition. Just like word recognition, which seems to follow a developmental trajectory from accuracy (Stage 1) to fluency (Stage 2), comprehension probably follows a developmental trajectory. Further research is needed to describe this trajectory, but perhaps it proceeds from computation of propositions sstated in text, to understanding the unstated presuppositional and implicational structure underlying but going beyond the stated propositions, to understanding larger discourse structures such as the narrative scheme, to high-level interpretation of the author's intent and perspective.

Modifications of Frith's Model.   In Frith's sequential model, logographic word recognition precedes alphabet word recognition, which precedes sound-free orthographic word recognition utilizing automatic recognition of multiletter units. A modification of Frith's model consists of two changes. First, the alternative modes of word recognition do not emerge in discrete stages where only one mode is used. Rather, each of these alternative modes of word recognition is on its own developmental trajectory and may emerge at different times in individual learners; yet, most beginning readers acquire a repertoire of word recognition strategies that include all three modes. Second, each of these modes involves the integration of orthographic and phonological codes of corresponding unit size (see Berninger, 1994a, Table 4.1); none is sound-free or purely orthographic. The logographic mode involves integration of whole written word units (not configuration but all the letters in the word) and whole spoken word units (name codes or lexical units). In the earliest phases of development of the logographic mode, salient features of the written word unit rather than a precise representation of all letters may be involved (see Gough et al., 1992). The alphabetic mode involves integration of single letters or multiletter units and corresponding phonemes. The orthographic mode involves integration of multiletter units and syllable or subsyllabic units (e.g., rime) of spoken words. Moreover, the orthographic and phonological codes may develop along their own trajectories affecting when in development connections are formed between codes of corresponding unit size (see Berninger, 1987). In addition, morphological awareness is also developing along its own trajectory (e.g., Nagy, Osborn, Winsor, & O'Flahaven, 1994). The logographic stage probably involves free morphemes that stand alone and are unanalyzed, whereas the orthographic stage probably involves analysis of bound morphemes that attach to these stems, such as inflectional suffixes marking tense and number, prefixes, and derivational suffixes. A complete understanding of the development of word recognition requires knowledge of the orthographic, phonological, and morphological trajectories and their interconnections. Within a connectionist architecture (e.g., Harm & Seidenberg, 1999), connections form between orthography and phonology, between orthography and morphology, and between morphology and phonology—all of which contribute to the functioning of the word recognition system.

Alternative Pathways

Stage models with rigid forward progressions cannot account for the discontinuities in development, which may occur as waves of a tide that flows forward and recedes periodically over time. Developmental psychologists have recognized the continuity–discontinuity problem for a long time. For example, Werner (1957) proposed that the perception of continuous growth is an artifact of statistical procedures that average development or achievement scores of individuals to describe a composite curve for the group. Individual development may be characterized by quantitative and qualitative discontinuous process changes, but analysis of data at the group rather than the individual level masks this discontinuity. Werner recognized both the unilinearity and multilinearity of development—that is, that development can be studied in terms of universal sequences and also in terms of individual variations in that sequence. He rejected the extremes of viewing all developmental sequences as identical and of denying any comparability among individual developmental sequences. Rather, he viewed the polarity between the uniformity of a general regulative principle and the multiformity of specific developmental changes as the driving force in the study of development.

Unfortunately, much of contemporary developmental psychology and developmental neuropsychology places more emphasis on the universal patterns that emerge across individuals and little emphasis on the developmental paths individuals follow. Stage models might be considered an example of a developmental science focused on the unilinear and uniform processes in development. More attention should be given to Werner's

(1937, 1957) insight that the same achievement outcome can be reached in qualitatively different ways. This notion of alternative pathways or routes to the same developmental outcome is an important alternative to the Stage model. A complete developmental science will be based on both universal sequences abstracted from individual trajectories to describe universal developmental sequences and on individual developmental sequences to describe variations in those universal sequences.

This notion of alternative pathways is illustrated with examples from research programs.

Longitudinal Study of Beginning Reading in the Classroom. Berninger and Abbott (1992) applied four approaches to the analysis of the same set of data in a longitudinal study of first-grade reading. The first approach was the same as that used in research designs that compare groups of good and poor readers. A top, middle, and low group was identified on the basis of standardized tests of reading achievement. Children were drawn from different classrooms and did not experience a common instructional environment. Variation among children within achievement-level groups was treated as error, as is typically done in studies in which the group is the unit of analysis for individual difference variables. On the reading-related process variables (measures of lexical decision, naming, and written reproduction for phonically regular real words, phonically irregular real words, and phonically regular pronounceable pseudowords), performance of the low group at the end of first grade was comparable to that of the middle group at the middle of first grade, and performance of the middle group at the end of first grade was comparable to that of the high group at the middle of first grade. These results were consistent with the conclusion—also reached by Bruck (1988) and Stanovich, Nathan, and Zolman (1988)—that there is one process of learning, but individuals vary in the rate of mastering that process. In the second, third, and fourth approaches, a teacher's intact instructional groups for the high, middle, and low achieving children from the same data set were used. Thus, variability could be examined when instructional program was kept as constant as possible in a classroom.

In the second approach, like the first, variation among children within an instructional group was treated as error and the results were the same. Thus, whether achievement groups were defined on the basis of standardized tests or teacher-created instructional groups, there appeared to be one process in learning to read and variation only in the rate of mastering that process.

In the third approach, variation among children in an instructional group was treated as systematic variance rather than error. Data were aggregated over individual stimulus items rather than over individual subjects; individual response over stimulus trials was used to estimate error. The main effect for individuals and all interactions involving individuals were statistically significant. These results were not consistent with the notion of only one process in learning to read. Individual differences in process variables related to reading acquisition became apparent only when they were considered an explanatory variable in their own right.

In the fourth approach, which was justified on the basis of the significant main effect for individuals in the third analysis, a separate analysis of variance was performed on the stimulus trials for each subject at the beginning, middle, and end of first grade. Children within the same instructional group varied considerably as to which main effects or interactions were significant. Sometimes individual children differed from the pattern of significant main effects or interactions for their instructional group. These results were consistent with the notion of alternative pathways to the same developmental outcome, even when the instructional environment is reasonably constant. As noted by Werner (1957), alternative pathways were not evident until the data were analyzed at the individual unit of analysis. Berninger and Abbott attributed these alternative pathways to the constructive processes of individual learners who use the same instructional cues in varying ways.

Year-Long Tutoring Study. Sixteen children with reading problems were identified at the end of first grade and tutored, using standardized instructional protocols, the summer before second grade and throughout second grade (see Berninger et al., 1997). Hierarchical linear modeling (HLM; Bryk & Raudenbush, 1987) was used to analyze growth curves (Rogosa, Brandt, & Zimowski, 1992) from beginning to end of the year-long tutoring. HLM has the advantage of explicitly analyzing data at the individual subject level and at the group level. Thus, conclusions can be drawn about the effectiveness of an intervention for the group as a whole and for each individual.

Growth curves were computed for four achievement outcome measures: Word Identification, Word Attack, and Passage Comprehension on the Woodcock Reading Mastery Test–Revised (WRMT–R; Woodcock, 1987) and Spelling on the Wide Range Achievement Test–Revised (WRAT–R; J. Jastak, Bijou, & S. Jastak, 1978). At the group level, both the slopes and intercepts were statistically significant at $p < .001$ for all four outcome measures, indicating that as a group the children had shown significant improvement in reading and spelling. At the individual level, only two children were not treatment responders on Word Identification, that is, they did not have slopes significantly different from zero. All children were treatment responders, that is, had slopes significantly different from zero, on Word Attack, Passage Comprehension, and Spelling.

But did children follow comparable developmental paths to achieve these outcomes? A standard battery of process measures was administered prior to, during, and at the end of treatment. Children varied considerably in their processing profiles prior to treatment. Seven of the children did not have any problems in orthographic coding of letters and one did not have any problem in orthographic coding of whole word units. Four did not have any problems in phoneme deletion and four (only one the same as for phoneme deletion) did not have any problems in phoneme localization across word contexts. Children varied as to whether they had single, double, or triple deficits in orthographic coding, phonological coding, or rapid automatized naming that requires orthographic-phonological integration (see Berninger et al., 1997).

Growth curves were also computed on these process measures. At the group level, both intercepts and slopes were statistically significant at .007 or better. However, at the individual level, considerable variability existed in whether individual children were treatment responders on these process variables, all of which have been shown to be related to reading and spelling acquisition in numerous studies. Excluding children who had no problems at pretest, 12 were treatment responders on rapid automatized naming of letters, 6 were not; 7 were treatment responders on rapid automatized naming of letters and numbers, 9 were not; 11 were treatment responders on phoneme segmentation, 1 was not; 8 were treatment responders on phoneme localization, 4 were not. Thus, in keeping with Werner's (1937, 1957) notion of alternative pathways to the same achievement outcome, individuals reached that outcome via a variety of developmental routes that varied in the quality of different orthographic, phonological, and orthographic-phonological integration processes available to them.

Comparison of Beginning Reading Programs. Traweek and Berninger (1997) compared achievement outcomes of children in comparable at risk urban schools whose instructional programs in beginning reading contrasted sharply. The Integrated Reading-Writing (IR-W) program encouraged children to tell stories and write stories. They were taught "What I can think, I can say. What I can say, I can write." Teachers modeled how one could think stories, compose spoken sentences, say the words in the sentences slowly, and then write the letters for the sounds they heard. In spelling the words children referred to Sunshine Cards, which displayed alphabet letters paired with a picture of a word beginning with the associated sound. Children were also taught "What I can write, I can read." During reading time, children read each others' written stories as well as literature available in the classroom. The teacher also read to the children from Big Books as they followed along in little books. Distar, on the other hand, explicitly teaches letter–sound relations or decoding using direct instruction techniques in which children repeat verbatim the teachers' verbalizations. Distar emphasizes word decoding in isolation and does not emphasize the functional communicative context for literacy activities.

Not surprisingly, children in both programs learned to read. There were no significant differences in reading achievement (word reading) on the Stanford Diagnostic Reading Test at the end of first grade. There is more than one developmental pathway to the same learning outcome. However, the two groups did seem to differ in the processes followed to reach that outcome. Children in the IR-W program, who had lots of opportunities to write and read whole words, showed evidence of orthographic-phonological connections at the whole word level as well as subword level, whereas children in Distar, who had extensive opportunities to segment spoken and written words into their component parts, showed evidence of orthographic-phonological connections mainly at the subword level.

Optimal Orthographic/Phonological Units. Olson and Wise conducted a number of studies (e.g., Olson & Wise, 1992; Wise et al., 1989) using a "talking computer" to give disabled readers oral feedback about words they target as unknown. They have systematically manipulated the unit size into which the word is segmented during feedback—whole word, syllables, letter-phoneme, or onset-rime. The outcome of these various studies is that unit size per se does not matter. Children learned from a variety of unit sizes in the feedback.

Research by Levy and Lysynchuk (1995a, 1995b) leads to a similar conclusion. They compared a control group given regular classroom instruction only (whole language) and four instructional conditions in addition to regular classroom instruction:

Instructional Condition 1: Emphasis on similarity of word beginnings (onset + vowel).

Instructional Condition 2: Emphasis on similarity of word endings (rimes—all of the syllable remaining after onset sound deleted).

Instructional Condition 3: Phoneme segmentation and blending.

Instructional Condition 4: Simple repetition of whole words.

Children in Study 1 were beginning readers in first grade or senior kindergarten. Children in Study 2 were delayed readers in Grade 2. Although reliable differences were found among the conditions, all instructional conditions resulted in better performance than the control condition and led to rapid acquisition, good retention, and good generalization.

The results of the Olson and Wise studies and the Levy and Lysynchuk studies are consistent with the findings of early intervention studies for at-risk beginning readers (Berninger, Abbott, Brooksher et al., 2000) and at risk beginning spellers (Berninger et al., 1998). Children in both studies were given, following explicit modeling of alphabet principle, ortho-graphic-phonological feedback at the level of the whole word, 1- or 2-letter spelling unit, or onset-rime unit or each combination of two or three kinds of feedback for a set of taught words that varied in spelling-sound predictability. In both studies, compared to contact controls, the children learned to read or spell the taught words better, but the specific kinds of feedback did not differ significantly among themselves. However, when transfer to untrained words was considered, three kinds of feedback were superior to the control and the other kinds of feedback for reading: whole written and whole spoken word, 1- and 2-letter spelling units and pho-nemes, and combined whole word and letter(s)-phoneme. One kind of feedback was superior to the control and other kinds of feedback for spell-ing on transfer words: combined whole word and onset-rime.

Metanalysis of Basic Skills Versus Whole Language (Meaning) In-structional Programs. By the end of the 20th century, the earlier Great Debate deteriorated into a Great War over whether reading instruc-tion should be based on low-level word recognition skills or high-level meaning. It is difficult to find sufficient studies that meet rigorous meth-odological criteria for the traditional requirements for meta-analysis. Nev-ertheless, recent reviews of studies comparing the two instructional ap-proaches for both beginning reading and writing instruction support the same conclusion: whole language and basal approaches to instruction ap-pear to produce similar effects on reading achievement (Stahl et al., 1994) and writing achievement (Graham & Harris, 1994). This finding is consis-tent with the notion of alternative pathways in learning to read. There is more than one way to learn to read and write. Children in instructional programs that tend to be inductive and meaning based may abstract the connections between print and sound from repeated exposure to the same words. Children in instructional programs that tend to be skills-based may learn the connections between print and sound by applying ex-plicit rules. Children who have deficits in orthographic and phonological awareness may have difficulty in both programs. If experiencing whole language instruction, they may have difficulty abstracting orthographic-phonological connections. If experiencing basic skills instruction, they may have trouble applying explicit rules of orthographic-phonological correspondence. Indeed, Traweek et al. (1997) found that orthographic and phonological skills, not teaching method, were significant predictors of reading achievement at the end of first grade. However, a more recent metaanalysis (National Institute of Child Health and Human Development, 2000) concluded that the evidence supported the superiority of explicit code instruction in optimizing reading achievement. Thus, although children can learn in more than one way, they all benefit from systematic instruction in how to translate written words into spoken words.

However, recent computer simulations based on connectionist modeling (Harm & Seidenberg, 1999) offer the most illumination on this issue of matching individual differences in learners' processing abilities and instructional programs. In their simulations, the network learned with minimal explicit instruction on orthographic-phonological connections when the phonological attractor was enabled and functioned optimally. However, the network required considerable explicit instruction on orthographic-phonological connections when the phonological attractor was disabled. There was a relation between the degree of impairment in the phonological attractor and the amount of explicit instruction required beyond repeated exposure to written words. Likewise, children vary along a continuum of phonological processing ability and may vary in the degree of explicit instruction required to compute orthographic-phonological connections.

Critical Developmental Periods

Stage models imply that individuals progress through successive stages at their own rate, but this progression can occur at any age. In reality, reading and writing may have critical developmental periods in which they are most easily acquired, but after which it is less probable, but not impossible, for them to be acquired with a reasonable degree of proficiency (see Berninger, 1994a). In a large-scale study (N = 10,000) cited in Keeney and Keeney (1968, p. 92), 82% of those diagnosed in grades 1 or 2, 46% of those diagnosed in grade 3, 42% of those diagnosed in grade 4, and from 10% to 15% of those diagnosed in grades 5–7 were brought up to grade level. Kraus (1973) reported that students who by Grade 3 scored significantly below the norms on achievement tests and did not receive special help continued to fail throughout their schooling. Muehl and Forell (1973) found that early diagnosis, regardless of how much subsequent remediation a student receives, is associated with better reading performance 5 years later. Satz, Taylor, Friel, and Fletcher (1978) found that children with reading or writing problems are often not referred for evaluation or special services until the intermediate grades after years of failure.

Critical developmental periods may be related to two factors other than biological ones. One factor is the emotional sequelae. Early intervention may be more effective, because emotional factors interfere with learning later in development after chronic failure. Another factor is that there may be an interaction between development and the instructional program. For example, genetic influences in reading may be more constraining in the primary grades when instruction in word recognition draws on orthographic and phonological coding skills, which may be delayed for age. Yet, later in development, when orthographic and phonological skills have matured, the instructional program in the intermediate grades may have changed to focus on comprehension skills. Thus not enough instruction in word recognition is provided when the student is developmentally ready to benefit from such instruction (see Berninger, 1994a). Abbott and Berninger (1999) found that older students in grades 4 to 7 were developmentally ready to benefit from explicit instruction in word recognition embedded in lessons aimed at all levels of language in a functional reading system.

Even if reading is acquired more easily earlier in development, it is not impossible to learn to read later in development (Fink, 1998). In the past, most research on adult reading was based on college students who generally have above average reading skills. Through the National Centers of Adult Literacy, research on adult reading has expanded to include the lower end of the adult reading distribution. These adults exhibit considerable individual differences in processing skills that are monitored during instructional intervention programs (Sabatini & Venezky, 1995). Longitudinal investigation of adults still struggling to acquire literary skills is an important supplement to longitudinal studies of literacy acquisition early in development. Combining results of the literacy studies of adults, whose maturation of the nervous system is complete, and literacy studies of children, whose maturation is still evolving, may shed light on the issue of critical developmental periods (Sabatini, personal communication, April 21, 1995).

ALTERNATIVE APPROACHES TO MODELING INDIVIDUAL DIFFERENCES

Developmental Dissociations

The potential for developmental dissociations arises because the multiple brain systems related to reading and writing are on their own trajectory and each trajectory develops at its own rate (discussed earlier). At any given moment in maturation, the various working brain systems may be developed to different levels, and sometimes the levels are different enough that learning to read or write may be difficult. For example,

Berninger and Hart (1992) analyzed a large multivariate data set containing measures of component reading and writing skills and reading- and writing-related processes in a primary grade sample (N = 300). They found that 8% of the first-graders, 8% of the second-graders, and 18% of the third-graders had extreme development dissociations in that they scored in the bottom 5% of the normal distribution on at least one measure and in the top 5% of the normal distribution on at least one measure. Thus, the incidence of developmental dissociations, which are the origin of intraindividual differences, increased rather than decreased over the course of development. However, longitudinal studies are needed to determine if these dissociations continue over development.

Intraindividual Differences

Research on individual differences in reading and writing acquisition has given more attention to differences among than within individuals. One aim of the studies conducted over the past decade has been to examine potential intraindividual differences.

Reading Acquisition. Carr and Pollatsek (1985) reviewed the research literature on word recognition and identified two separate mechanisms of word recognition—word-specific and rule-governed, which are roughly analogous to what educators call the sight word and phonics (or word attack) methods. Individual children may vary in the rate at which word-specific and rule-governed mechanisms for word recognition develop (Berninger, Yates, & Lester, 1991). Berninger and Abbott (1994a) developed and validated measures of multiple orthographic and phonological codes that underlie the word-specific and rule-governed mechanisms. Individual children may vary in the rate at which these codes develop and thus whether orthographic-phonological codes of corresponding unit size form (Berninger & Abbott, 1994a). Thus, the word-specific and rule-governed mechanisms and the codes underlying them may dissociate. Word recognition and reading comprehension may also dissociate (Berninger, 1994b). In a sample of 300 unreferred primary grade children, 15% had a dissociation in which age-corrected word recognition scores were 1 standard deviation or more greater than age-corrected reading comprehension scores. No dissociations were found in which reading comprehension was developed to 1 standard deviation or more beyond word recognition in the primary grade sample. In a sample of 300 intermediate grade children, 10.7% had a dissociation in which word recognition exceeded reading comprehension by at least one standard deviation and 4% had a dissociation in which reading comprehension exceeded word identification by 1 standard deviation or greater.

Berninger and Hart (1993) analyzed dissociations in the primary grade sample for those whose reading achievement fell in the bottom 5% of the normal distribution (absolute criterion) or was significantly discrepant from Verbal IQ (relative criterion) on at least one component reading skill. Dissociations (one skill meets disability criterion, another skill does not) between the word-specific and rule-governed mechanisms did not occur when absolute criteria were used but did when relative criteria were used. Dissociations between word recognition and reading comprehension occurred in from 6% to 14% of the cases, depending on criteria. These results (Berninger, 1994b; Berninger & Hart, 1993) are consistent with the claim that the developmental trajectory for comprehension has a smaller slope than word recognition and is constrained by the trajectory for word recognition, but word recognition and comprehension are separate developmental domains from the beginning of reading acquisition.

Dissociations between word recognition and reading comprehension were also found in a sample of children who had been tutored during first grade and were followed during second grade (Berninger, Abbott, & Stage, 1999). Half were only monitored during second grade because they had improved to grade level or better after the first-grade tutorial. Consistently at the beginning and end of second grade, 29% of these children had higher word recognition than comprehension skills (mean difference of 14.2 standard score points), and 46% had higher reading comprehension than word recognition skills (mean difference 11.5 standard score points). The other half who were still below grade level in reading received continuing tutoring during second grade. Consistently at the beginning and end of second grade, they showed a different pattern of dissociation than the monitoring only group: 60% had higher word recognition than comprehension (mean difference 19.6 standard score points) and 13% had higher comprehension than word recognition (mean difference 27.3 standard score points). Thus, those children who responded fastest to early intervention may have a tendency to have better text level comprehension skills than single word recognition skills, whereas those who respond but respond more slowly to early intervention may have a tendency to have better single word recognitions than text level comprehension skills.

Analysis of dissociations of reading or writing skills for individual children reveals the variation in the level to which component skills are developed at different phases of the development of a functional reading or functional writing system. This developmental variability, which may have instructional applications, would be masked by an approach that simply evaluated whether correlations between component skills were significant for a sample as a whole.

Writing Acquisition. Developmental dissociations also occur in the levels of language involved in written composing. Berninger, Mizokawa, Bragg, Cartwright, and Yates (1994) reported the results of two experiments (one involving a production task and one involving a metalinguistic judgment task) that pointed to the same conclusion in intermediate grade students: Performance at the word level does not predict performance at the sentence or paragraph levels and performance at the sentence level does not predict performance at the paragraph level. Whitaker et al. (1994) replicated this finding on the translating and revising tasks in another experiment. They also found intraindividual differences in the advanced planning and online planning tasks.

Using Children as Their Own Controls

Group designs, with treatment and control groups, are usually used to evaluate the effectiveness of instructional interventions. However, even if there is a significant effect at the group level, it does not mean that every individual in the treatment group benefitted from the intervention.

An alternative approach to evaluating effectiveness of interventions exists—at the individual level—if psychometric instruments with age-corrected standard scores are used to measure achievement before, during, and after treatment. Psychometric instruments report the standard error of measurement, which can be used to establish the 95% confidence interval. The size of a gain that is likely to represent a true gain, over and beyond that expected purely on the basis of age-related maturation, can be computed. Based on this approach, Berninger and Traweek (1991) showed that 70% of the individuals showed improvement in reading real words and 90% showed improvement in reading pseudowords from the beginning to the end of an intervention that taught multiple orthographic-phonological connections. Of course, this alternative approach at the individual level can be used in conjunction with the traditional approach at the group level (as Berninger and Traweek did).

Latent Variable Structural Equation Modeling

Latent variable structural equation modeling combines the advantages of factor analysis and multiple regression (Biddle & Marlin, 1987). It can model latent variable factors based on the covariance of the measured variables as factor analysis can. It can describe the degree of structural relation among predictor latent factors and between predictor latent factors and criterion latent factors, as multiple regression can for single variables (Lunneborg & Abbott, 1983). It can take into account intraindividual differences in terms of the covariance among the predictor latent factors and interindividual differences in terms of an individual's relative standing on each of the indicators on which a latent factor is based (Willett & Sayer, 1994).

Berninger, Abbott, and Shurtleff (1990) applied structural equation modeling to the investigation of two reading tasks and one spelling task at the beginning and end of first grade. Results showed that the orthographic coding (visible language) and oral language systems became increasingly differentiated as children gained in reading skill. That is, intraindividual differences increased as children improved in reading.

Abbott and Berninger (1995) used multiple group structural modeling to model the structural relations among a predictor orthographic latent factor, a predictor phonological factor, and a criterion word recognition factor at the first-, second-, and third-grade levels. In first grade, the path from the orthographic coding factor was stronger than the path from the phonological coding factor to the criterion reading factor, but in the second and third grades the path from the phonological coding factor was stronger.

Abbott and Berninger (1993) used multiple group structural model to model the structural relations among the same predictor latent factors and a different criterion factor—spelling—at the same grade levels. The structural relations changed when the criterion was changed, at least in the second and third grades. At the first-grade level, the path from the orthographic coding factor to spelling was stronger than the path from the phonological coding factor, as had been the case for reading, but at the second and third grade the strongest path to spelling was from the orthographic coding factor, rather than from the phonological coding factor, as had been the case for reading. Regardless of whether the criterion was reading or spelling, there was shared covariance between the predictor latent factors. Taken together, these results show that both intraindividual and interindividual differences contribute to word reading and spelling in the primary grades, but the patterns of interrelationships change over the course of development.

Abbott and Berninger (1993) also applied multigroup structural equation modeling to handwriting and composition as criterion factors. For handwriting, both fine motor skills and orthographic coding contributed to the model fit, but only the path from orthographic coding was significant in grades 1, 2, and 3. For compositional quality, both reading and oral language contributed in the primary grades, but the relative contribution changed with each grade. Initially, in grade 1, the oral language and reading factors contributed; in grades 2 and 3, only the reading factor made a significant incremental contribution.

Two-level structural modeling allows one to describe the same data set at multiple levels. For example, Lundberg and Rosen (1995) reanalyzed the data from the International Educational Achievement (IEA) Study of Reading Literacy at both the country level (comparison across countries) and the classroom level (comparison across classes within countries). They found that factor structure varied at different levels of analysis.

Hierarchical Linear Modeling

Hierarchical linear modeling (HLM; Bryk & Raudenbush, 1987) has the advantage of combining group and individual level analysis. In Level 1, the individual's observed growth trajectory is described in terms of individual parameters (e.g., intercept and slope). At Level 2, the individual parameters are used as outcome measures to be explained by the group variable to test hypotheses at the group level of analysis. HLM was used to analyze the results of treatment studies in reading and writing at both the group and individual level (e.g., Abbott & Berninger, 1995; Berninger, Abbott, Greep et al., 1997). At the group level, the analysis examined whether the treatment group outperformed the control group (e.g., Berninger, Abbott, Whitaker et al., 1995) or one treatment group outperformed the other treatment group. At the individual level, the analysis evaluated whether each individual in a treatment group was a treatment responder, that is, had a slope significantly different from zero. HLM was applied to data collected at multiple time points so conclusions could be drawn about rate of growth. Taken together, these analyses documented a large amount of variation in treatment responding over time at the individual level for children given the same instructional protocols.

Comparison of Growth Groups. Individual growth curves from HLM analyses were used to form four growth groups in a sample of first-graders ($n = 128$) and of third-graders ($n = 96$) tutored in reading: significant growth in both real-word and pseudoword reading, significant growth in real-word reading only, significant growth in pseudoword reading only, and no significant growth. Significant growth is defined as a slope significantly different from chance. At both developmental levels, the children who improved at a faster rate in both real-word and pseudoword reading reached higher achievement outcomes for reading accuracy than did those who improved in only one or neither of these reading skills. Third-graders who grew at a faster rate in both reading skills also had significantly higher automaticity of word recognition than the other groups (unpublished data). These findings support the claims of Multiple Connections Theory (e.g., Berninger & Abbott, 1994b); not only can children form connections between written and spoken words at more than one unit size, but also there is an advantage for developing and coordinating multiple orthographic-phonological connections.

Advantages and Disadvantages. Individual growth curves derived from HLM analyses have some advantages over individual growth curves based on ordinary least squares regression. HLM growth curves have shown to be more reliable estimates of slopes because the estimates are based on the growth of the sample as a whole and not just one individual. Also, HLM growth curves are able to handle missing data better.

However, HLM has some limitations with which users should be aware because it is a relatively recent innovation in data analysis (also see Abbott & Berninger, 1995). First, it models quantitative change when some changes may be qualitative in terms of stages or categories. However, special procedures such as Latent Transition Analysis are being developed to analyze qualitative change. Second, it assumes that the construct being modeled is stable, when in fact some constructs may change in meaning over time. Third, it assumes that a measurement scale without floor or ceiling effects is used throughout the study, when in fact such effects may occur. Fourth, it assumes that measurements are reliable at each of multiple time points. Fifth, the form of change or developmental function must be specified (e.g., linear, nonlinear). Sixth, spacing of the time points must be considered and specified—unequal intervals may be better than equal intervals for some functions. Seventh, issues of power are still being explored. Eighth, it is not yet well specified how sensitive the technique is to violations of assumptions. Ninth, interpretation of the parameters of the model in terms of psychological processes may be problematic. A function may fit the data but not be easily interpreted.

CONCLUSIONS WITHIN A DEVELOPMENTAL
NEUROPSYCHOLOGICAL FRAMEWORK

Developmentalists have given little attention to the valuable insight offered by Werner (1937, 1957): The same developmental outcome or achievement outcome can be reached by different routes and qualitatively different processes. Contemporary developmental psychology tends to focus on the uniformity and unilinearity of development, as exemplified by stage models. It tends not to consider the multiformity and multilinear developmental trajectories of the individual subject. A mature developmental science would combine both approaches in order to be able to describe the broad strokes of development abstracted from many individual cases and the precise developmental trajectories of individuals.

The latter sections proposed conceptual frameworks and data analytic techniques investigators might apply to studying developmental change at the individual level to document the variability that does exist in reaching the same developmental outcome. Research used these alternative techniques, some of which focus on the individual as well as the group level of analysis and some of which focus on intraindividual as well as interindividual differences.

Results have been consistent with the developmental neuropsychological perspective described by Berninger (1994a). Reading and writing acquisition are characterized by normal variation, that is, diversity not related to pathology. Normal variation occurs along the continuum of single developmental domains of processes related to the acquisition of component reading or writing skills. Normal variation also occurs across the multiple developmental domains. Intraindividual differences emerge as the different developmental domains develop at different rates in the same individual. Reading and writing acquisition may follow alternative pathways to the same outcome. There is more than one way to learn to read and write. There is more than one way to teach reading and writing that will result in effective learning. Individual differences in teachers and teaching methods are as great as individual differences in learners. Yet most children learn to read and write. Variability is the hallmark of the normal reading and writing acquisition process, not an exception, and also occurs among individuals with reading and writing disabilities.

ACKNOWLEDGMENT

Preparation of this chapter was supported by grants R01 25858-06 and P50 HD 33812-04 from the National Institute of Child Health and Human Development.

REFERENCES

Abbott, R., & Berninger, V. (1993). Structural equation modeling of relationships among developmental skills and writing skills in primary- and intermediate-grade writers. *Journal of Educational Psychology, 85*, 478–508.

Abbott, R., & Berninger, V. (1995). Structural equation modeling and hierarchical linear modeling: Tools for studying the construct validity of orthographic processes in reading and writing development. In V. W. Berninger (Ed.), *The varieties of orthographic knowledge: II. Relationships to phonology reading and writing* (pp. 321–353). Dordrecht, The Netherlands: Kluwer Academic.

Abbott, S., & Berninger, V. (1999). It's never too late to remediate: A developmental approach to teaching word recognition. *Annals of Dyslexia, 49*, 223–250.

Adams, M. (1990). *Beginning to read: Thinking and learning about print*. Cambridge, MA: MIT Press.

Barr, R. (1972). The influence of instructional conditions on word recognition errors. *Reading Research Quarterly, 7*, 509–529.

Bentler, P. M. (1980). Multivariate analysis with latent variables: Causal modeling. *Annual Review of Psychology, 31*, 419–456.

Bentler, P., & Wu, E. (1996). *EQS program manual*. Los Angeles, CA: Multivariate Software.

Berninger, V. (1987). Global, component, and serial procedures for printed words in beginning reading. *Journal of Experimental Child Psychology, 43*, 387–418.

Berninger, V. (1994a). *Reading and writing acquisition: A developmental neuropsychological perspective*. Madison, WI: W. C. Brown & Benchmark.

Berninger, V. (1994b). Intraindividual differences in levels of language in comprehension of written sentences. *Learning and Individual Differences, 6*, 433–457.

Berninger, V., & Abbott, R. (1992). The unit of analysis and constructive processes of the learner: Key concepts for educational neuropsychology. *Educational Psychologist, 27*, 223–242.

Berninger, V., & Abbott, R. (1994a). Redefining learning disabilities: Moving beyond aptitude-achievement discrepancies to failure to respond to validated treatment protocols. In G. R. Lyon (Ed.), *Frames of reference for assessment of learning disabilities: New views on measurement issues* (pp. 163–202). Baltimore: Paul H. Brookes.

Berninger, V., & Abbott, R. (1994b). Multiple orthographic and phonological codes in literacy acquisition: An evolving research program. In V. Berninger (Ed.), *The varieties of orthographic knowledge: I. Theoretical and developmental issues* (pp. 277–317). Dordrecht, The Netherlands: Kluwer Academic.

Berninger, V., Abbott, R., Brooksher, R., Lemos, Z., Ogier, S., Zook, D., & Mostafapour, E. (2000). A connectionist approach to making the predictability of English orthography explicit to at-risk beginning readers: Evidence for alternative, effective strategies. *Developmental Neuropsychology, 17*, 241–271.

Berninger, V., Abbott, R., & Shurtleff, H. (1990). Developmental changes in interrelationships of visible language codes, oral language codes, and reading or spelling. *Learning and Individual Differences, 2*, 45–67.

Berninger, V., Abbott, R., & Stage, S. (1999, April). *Educational and biological factors in preventing and treating dyslexia*. Presentation at the Society for Research in Child Development, Alburquerque, NM.

Berninger, V., Abbott, R., Thomson, J., & Raskind, W. (2001). Language phenotype for reading and writing disability: A family approach. *Scientific Studies in Reading, 5*, 59–105.

Berninger, V., Abbott, R., Whitaker, D., Sylvester, L., & Nolen, S. (1995). Integrating low-level and high-level skills in instructional protocols for writing disabilities. *Learning Disability Quarterly, 18*, 293–309.

Berninger, V., Abbott, S., Greep, K., Reed, E., Sylvester, L., Hooven, C., Clinton, A., Taylor, J., & Abbott, R. (1997). Directed reading and writing activities: Aiming instruction to working brain systems. In S. M. Clancy Dollinger & L. F. DiLalla (Eds.), *Prevention and intervention issues across the life span* (pp. 123–158). Hillsdale, NJ: Lawrence Erlbaum Associates.

Berninger, V., Cartwright, A., Yates, C., Swanson, H. L., & Abbott, R. (1994). Developmental skills related to writing and reading acquisition in the intermediate grades. *Reading and Writing: An Interdisciplinary Journal, 6*, 161–196.

Berninger, V., Fuller, F., & Whitaker, D. (1996). A process approach to writing development across the life span. *Educational Psychology Review, 8*, 193–218.

Berninger, V., & Hart, T. (1992). A developmental neuropsychological perspective for reading and writing acquisition. *Educational Psychologist, 27*(4), 415–434.

Berninger, V., & Hart, T. (1993). From research to clinical assessment of reading and writing disorders: The unit of analysis problem. In R. M. Joshi & C. K. Leong (Eds.), *Reading disabilities: Diagnosis and component processes* (pp. 33–61). The Netherlands: Kluwer Academic.

Berninger, V., Mizokawa, D., Bragg, R., Cartwright, A., & Yates, C. (1994). Intraindividual differences in levels of written language. *Reading and Writing Quarterly, 10,* 259–275.

Berninger, V., & Swanson, H. L. (1994). Modifying Hayes and Flower's model of skilled writing to explain beginning and developing writing. In E. Butterfield (Ed.), *Children's writing: Toward a process theory of development of skilled writing* (pp. 57–81). Greenwich, CT: JAI Press.

Berninger, V., & Traweek, D. (1991). Effects of a two-phase reading intervention on three orthographic-phonological code connections. *Learning and Individual Differences, 3,* 323–338.

Berninger, V., Vaughan, K., Abbott, R., Brooks, A., Abbott, S., Reed, E., Rogan, L., & Graham, S. (1998). Early intervention for spelling problems: Teaching spelling units of varying size within a multiple connections framework. *Journal of Educational Psychology, 90,* 587–605.

Berninger, V., Yates, C., Cartwright, A., Rutberg, J., Remy, E., & Abbott, R. (1992). Lower-level developmental skills in beginning writing. *Reading and Writing: An Interdisciplinary Journal, 4,* 257–280.

Berninger, V., Yates, C., & Lester, K. (1991). Multiple orthographic codes in reading and writing acquisition. *Reading and Writing: An Interdisciplinary Journal, 3,* 115–149.

Biddle, B., & Marlin, M. (1987). Causality, confirmation, credulity, and structural equation modeling. *Child Development, 58,* 4–17.

Biemiller, A. (1970). The development of the use of graphic and contextual information as children learn to read. *Reading Research Quarterly, 6,* 75–96.

Bruck, M. (1988). The word recognition and spelling of dyslexic children. *Reading Research Quarterly, 23,* 51–69.

Bryk, A., & Raudenbush, S. (1987). Application of hierarchical linear models to assessing change. *Psychological Bulletin, 101,* 147–158.

Carr, T., & Pollatsek, A. (1985). Recognizing printed words: A look at current models. In *Reading Research: Advances in theory and practice* (Vol. 5, pp. 1–82). New York: Academic Press.

Chall, J. (1979). The great debate: Ten years later, with a modest proposal for reading stages. In L. Resnick & P. Weaver (Eds.), *Theory and practice of early reading* (Vol. 1, pp. 22–55). Hillsdale, NJ: Lawrence Erlbaum Associates.

Ehri, L. (1992). Review and commentary: Stages of spelling development. In S. Templeton & D. Bear (Eds.), *Development of orthographic knowledge and the foundations of literacy* (pp. 307–332). Hillsdale, NJ: Lawrence Erlbaum Associates.

Ellis, A. (1985). The cognitive neuropsychology of developmental (and acquired) dyslexia: A critical survey. *Cognitive Neuropsychology, 2,* 169–205.

Ellis, A. (1987). Review of problems in developing cognitively transmitted cognitive modules. *Mind & Language, 2,* 242–251.

Fink, R. (1998). Literacy development in successful men and women with dyslexia. *Annals of Dyslexia, 48,* 313–346.

Frith, U. (1985). Beneath the surface of developmental dyslexia. In K. Patterson, J. Marshall, & M. Coltheart (Eds.), *Surface dyslexia* (pp. 301–330). London: Lawrence Erlbaum Associates.

Gentry, J. R. (1982). An analysis of developmental spelling in GNYS at WRK. *Reading Teacher, 36,* 192–200.

Gentry, J. R. (1984). Developmental aspects of learning to spell. *Academic Therapy, 20*(1), 11–19.

Gibson, E., & Levin, H. (1975). *The psychology of reading.* Cambridge, MA: MIT Press.

Goswami, U. (1988). Orthographic analogies and reading development. *Quarterly Journal of Experimental Psychology, 40A,* 239–268.

Gough, P., Juel, C., & Griffith, P. (1992). Reading, spelling, and the orthographic cipher. In P. Gough, L. Ehri, & R. Treiman (Eds.), *Reading acquisition* (pp. 35–48). Hillsdale, NJ: Lawrence Erlbaum Associates.

Gough, P., & Walsh, M. (1991). Chinese, Phoenicians, and the orthographic cipher of English. In S. A. Brady & D. P. Shankweiler (Eds.), *Phonological processes in literacy: A tribute to Isabelle Y. Liberman* (pp. 199–210). Hillsdale, NJ: Lawrence Erlbaum Associates.

Graham, S., & Harris, K. (1996). The effects of whole language on children's writing: A review of literature. *Educational Psychologist, 19*(4), 187–192.

Graham, S., & Weintraub, N. (1996). Review of handwriting research: Progress and prospect from 1980 to 1994. *Educational Psychology Review, 8*(1), 7–87.

Harm, M., & Seidenberg, M. (1999). Phonology, reading acquisition, and dyslexia: Insights from connectionist models. *Psychological Review, 106,* 491–528.

Hayes, J., & Flower, L. (1980). Identifying the organization of the writing process. In L. W. Gregg & E. R. Steinberg (Eds.), *Cognitive processes in writing* (pp. 3–30). Hillsdale, NJ: Lawrence Erlbaum Associates.

Henderson, E. H. (1980). Developmental concept of word. In E. H. Henderson & J. W. Beers (Eds.), *Developmental and cognitive aspects of learning to spell: A reflection of word knowledge* (pp. 1–14). Newark, DE: International Reading Association.

Henderson, E. H. (1992). The interface of lexical competence and knowledge of written words. In S. Templeton & D. Bear (Eds.), *Development of orthographic knowledge and foundations of literacy* (pp. 1–30). Hillsdale, NJ: Lawrence Erlbaum Associates.

Hooven, W., & Tunmer, W. (1993). The components of reading. In G. Thompson, W. Tunmer, & T. Nicholson (Eds.), *Reading acquisition processes* (pp. 1–19). Clevedon, UK: Multilingual Matters LTD.

Jackson, N., & Butterfield, E. (1989). Reading-level matched designs: Myths and realities. *Journal of Reading Behavior, 21,* 387–412.

Jastak, J., Bijou, S., & Jastak, S. (1978). *Wide Range Achievement Test.* Wilmington, DE: Jastak Associates.

Karlson, B., Madden, R., & Gardner, E. (1976). *Stanford Diagnostic Reading Test Red Level: Manual for administering and interpreting.* New York: Harcourt, Brace, & Jovanovich.

Keeney, A., & Keeney, V. (1968). *Dyslexia. Diagnosis and treatment of reading disorders* (p. 92). St. Louis: Mosby Co.

Kim (Yoon), Y. H., & Goetz, E. T. (1994). Context effects on word recognition and reading comprehension of poor and good readers: A test of the interactivecompensatory hypothesis. *Reading Research Quarterly, 29,* 178–188.

Kraus, P. (1973). *Yesterday's children: A longitudinal study of children from kindergarten into the adult years.* New York: Wiley.

Lavine, L. O. (1972). *The development of perception of writing in pre-reading children: A cross-cultural study.* Unpublished doctoral dissertation, Department of Human Development, Cornell University.

Levy, B., & Lysynchuk, L. (1995a, April). *Segmentation versus whole word repetition: Optimal training methods for beginning and delayed readers.* Paper presented at the annual meeting of the Society for the Scientific Study of Reading, San Francisco.

Levy, B., & Lysynchuk, L. (1995b). Beginning word recognition: Benefits of training by segmentation and whole word methods. *Scientific Studies of Reading, 1*(4), 359–387.

Lundberg, I., & Rosen, M. (1995, April). *Two-level structural modeling of reading achievement as a basis for evaluating teaching effects.* Paper presented at the annual meeting of the American Educational Research Association, San Francisco.

Lunneborg, C., & Abbott, R. (1983). *Elementary multivariate analysis for the behavioral sciences*. Amsterdam: North Holland.

Morris, D. (1992). Concept of word: A pivotal understanding in learning-to-read process. In S. Templeton & D. Bear (Eds.), *Development of orthographic knowledge and foundations of literacy* (pp. 53–77). Hillsdale, NJ: Lawrence Erlbaum Associates.

Muehl, S., & Forell, E. (1973). A follow-up study of disabled readers: Variables related to high school reading performance. *Reading Research Quarterly, 9*, 110–123.

Nagy, W., Osborn, J., Winsor, P., & O'Flahaven, J. (1994). Structural analysis: Some guidelines for instruction. In F. Lehr & J. Osborn (Eds.), *Reading, Language, & Literacy* (pp. 45–58). Hillsdale, NJ: Lawrence Erlbaum Associates.

National Institute of Child Health and Human Development. (2000). *Report of the national reading panel: An evidence-based assessment of the scientific research literature on reading and its implications for reading instruction*. Bethesda, MD: NICHD Clearinghouse.

O'Flahaven, J. O. (1989). *Second graders' social intellectual, and affective development in varied group discussions about narrative texts: An exploration of participation structures*. Unpublished doctoral dissertation, University of Illinois at Urbana-Champaign.

Olson, R., & Wise, B. (1992). Reading on the computer with orthographic and speech feedback. *Reading and Writing: An Interdisciplinary Journal, 4*, 107–144.

Rogosa, D., Brandt, D., & Zimowski, M. (1992). A growth curve approach to the measurement of change. *Psychological Bulletin, 92*, 726–748.

Sabatini, J., & Venezky, R. (1995, April). *Visual and phonological skills in adult reading acquisition*. Paper presented at the annual meeting of the American Educational Research Association, San Francisco.

Satz, P., Taylor, H. G., Friel, J., & Fletcher, J. (1978). Some developmental and predictive precursors of reading disabilities: A six year follow-up. In A. Benton & D. Pearl (Eds.), *Dyslexia: An appraisal of current knowledge* (pp. 313–347). New York: Oxford University Press.

Scardamalia, M., & Bereiter, C. (1987). *The psychology of written compositions*. Hillsdale, NJ: Lawrence Erlbaum Associates.

Siegel, L., Geva, E., & Share, D. (1995). The development of orthographic skills in normal and disabled readers. *Psychological Science, 6*, 250–254.

Stahl, S., McKenna, M., & Pagnucco, J. (1994). The effects of whole language instruction: An update and a reappraisal. *Educational Psychologist, 29*(4), 175–185.

Stanovich, K., Nathan, R., & Zolman, J. (1988). The developmental lag hypothesis in reading: Longitudinal and matched reading-level comparisons. *Child Development, 59*, 71–86.

Traweek, D., & Berninger, V. (1997). Comparison of beginning literacy programs: Alternative paths to the same learning outcome. *Learning Disability Quarterly, 20*, 160–168.

Treiman, R. (1993). *Beginning to spell*. New York: Oxford University Press.

Varnhagen, C. K. (1995). Children's spelling strategies. In V. W. Berninger (Ed.), *The varieties of orthographic knowledge: II. Relationships to phonology reading and writing* (pp. 251–290). Dordrecht, The Netherlands: Kluwer Academic.

Vellutino, F. (1992). Afterword. In S. Templeton & D. Bear (Eds.), *Development of orthographic knowledge and the foundations of literacy* (pp. 353–357). Hillsdale, NJ: Lawrence Erlbaum Associates.

Vellutino, F., Scanlon, D., & Chen, R. (1995). The increasingly inextricable relationship between orthographic and phonological coding in learning to read: Some reservations about current methods of operationalizing orthographic coding. In V. W. Berninger (Ed.), *The varieties of orthographic knowledge: II. Relationships to phonology reading and writing* (pp. 47–111). Dordrecht, The Netherlands: Kluwer Academic.

Vellutino, F., Scanlon, D., & Spearing, D. (in press). Semantic and phonological coding in poor and normal readers. *Journal of Experimental Child Psychology*.

Venezky, R. (1970). *The structure of English orthography*. The Hague: Mouton.

Werner, H. (1937). Process and achievement. A basic problem of education and developmental psychology. *Harvard Educational Review, 7,* 353–368.

Werner, H. (1957). The concept of development from a comparative and organismic point of view. In D. B. Harris (Ed.), *The concept of development: An issue in the study of human behavior* (pp. 125–148). Minneapolis: University of Minnesota Press.

Whitaker, D., Berninger, V., Johnston, J., & Swanson, H. (1994). Intraindividual differences in levels of written language in intermediate grade writers: Implications for the translation process. *Learning and Individual Differences, 6,* 107–130.

Willett, J. B., & Sayer, A. G. (1994). Using covariance structure analysis to detect correlates and predictors of individual change over time. *Psychological Bulletin, 116,* 363–381.

Wise, B., Olson, R., Anstatt, M., Andrews, L., Terjak, M., Schneider, V., Kostuch, J., & Krtho, L. (1989). Implementing a long-term computerized remedial reading program with synthetic speech feedback: Hardware, software, and real-world issues. *Behavior Research Methods Instruments and Computers, 21,* 173–180.

Wolf, M. (1991). Naming-speed and reading: The contribution of the cognitive neurosciences. *Reading Research, 26,* 123–141.

Woodcock, R. (1987). *Woodcock Reading Mastery Test–Revised*. Circle Pines, MN: American Guidance Service.

## CHAPTER ELEVEN

The Search for Individual and Subtype Differences in Reading Disabled Children's Response to Remediation

Maureen W. Lovett
*The Hospital for Sick Children
and University of Toronto*

Roderick W. Barron
University of Guelph

Since the 1980s, much progress has been made in identifying the primary nonreading skills that predict reading acquisition success. Recently, increasing attention has been paid to the role that these skills may play as diagnostic markers of developmental reading disorders and mediators of individual children's response to remediation. The present chapter provides a brief review of longitudinal and individual differences research on the nonreading skills that predict success in reading acquisition and on the role these skills play in identifying reading disabled children or children at risk for such a diagnosis. The primary focus of the chapter, however, is to examine evidence for the contribution of these skills as individual differences predictors of reading disabled children's response to remediation. Among the issues considered is evidence for the existence of optimal "developmental windows" for benefiting from some types of remediation and the role of minimum "threshold" levels of critical nonreading skills in predicting remedial gains.

CRITICAL NONREADING SKILLS FOR ACQUIRING LITERACY

Research on the skills that predict successful reading acquisition often involve an attempt to link a primary component of the reading process to a set of basic nonreading cognitive skills that play a causal role in the reading process and its acquisition. The fact that reading begins with visual pattern recognition, requires visual–motor coordination, integrates visuospatial with auditory-temporal information, involves phonological awareness, utilizes name retrieval, places demands on working memory, draws on attentional resources, and is essentially a language-based skill suggests a number of potential nonreading skills that might predict later reading skill. Neuropsychological perspectives on reading disability have suggested links to other nonreading skills, including a range of hemispheric specialization functions (e.g., Bakker, Bouma, & Gardien, 1990), neurological soft signs such as finger agnosia (e.g., Benton, 1975), and aspects of auditory (Tallal, 1980) and visual (Lovegrove & Williams, 1993) temporal processing speed.

Wagner, Torgesen, and their colleagues developed a comprehensive research program to identify those nonreading skills that are causally linked to reading acquisition. These investigators confined their analyses to phonological processing tasks because of the very large body of evidence indicating that a core of phonological processing skills underlie success in acquiring literacy skill (Bradley & Bryant, 1983; Goswami & Bryant, 1990; Share, 1995; Stanovich, 1986; Wagner & Torgesen, 1987).

Drawing on earlier research (Wagner, Torgesen, Laughon, Simmons, & Rashotte, 1993; Wagner et al., 1987), Wagner, Torgesen, and Rashotte (1994) conducted a longitudinal study involving 244 children who were followed over a 3-year period beginning in kindergarten. The children performed 17 nonreading tasks that were found to measure five distinct, yet correlated, latent phonological processing variables: phonological awareness: analysis (phoneme elision, categorization, and segmentation tasks); phonological awareness: synthesis (tasks involving the blending of phonemes and onset-rime units); phonological coding in working memory (digit span and working memory tasks); serial naming (digits, letters, digits + letters speeded naming tasks); and isolated naming (digits, letters, digits + letters response time tasks). These latent variables appeared to be stable across kindergarten, grade 1, and grade 2, and were highly correlated with a print decoding latent variable. In addition, each of the nonreading latent variables measured in kindergarten was causally related to decoding in grade 1 when decoding performance in kindergarten, the primary predictor of grade 1 decoding performance, was removed as an autoregressive effect. A similar pattern was obtained between each of the latent variables measured in grade 1 and decoding performance in grade 2.

In a subsequent longitudinal study involving most of the same children ($N = 216$), Wagner et al. (1997) examined the relative causal influences of a reduced set of latent phonological processing variables over 5 years (kindergarten–grade 4). Analysis and synthesis were combined in this data set to produce a single latent variable of phonological awareness and the naming variable consisted solely of serial naming. Phonological awareness, memory, and naming were very consistent across all 5 years in their ability to predict word reading when each variable was considered separately. When each variable was considered simultaneously, however, only phonological awareness emerged as a unique predictor of word reading performance at every time interval across the 5 years (the autoregressive effect of word reading in earlier grades was removed). Serial naming was also a unique predictor of word reading from kindergarten to grade 3 and a measure of vocabulary knowledge (Stanford–Binet Vocabulary subtest) was a unique predictor for grades 1 through 3. Phonological memory failed to have any unique causal effect across the 5 years.

Scarborough (1997) reviewed several longitudinal studies predicting successful reading development and her findings are consistent with those of Wagner et al. (1994, 1997). Both phonological awareness and serial naming in kindergarten (or earlier) emerge as strong predictors of reading skill in grades 1 to 3, but early print knowledge involving letter–name and letter–sound association was also a very strong predictor (Barron, 1994, 1998; Barron et al., 1992). In addition, memory measures involving sentences and stories, measures of general language ability, vocabulary, receptive syntax, and Verbal IQ were also reasonably strong predictors. Consistent with earlier research (e.g., Vellutino, 1979), visual and visual-motor measures have little predictive power. Stringer (1997) showed that auditory and visual temporal processing are not strong predictors.

Taken together, these results suggest that, although there is a fairly large number of possible nonreading variables that might mediate individual differences in dyslexic children's response to remediation, the most influential variables appear to be related to underlying phonological processing skill; these variables all involve language-based tasks that rely on phonological representations to support their execution. It is possible, however, that only a subset of the phonological processing variables (e.g., phonological awareness, serial naming) is sufficiently stable and independent to predict gains in word identification accuracy beyond that predicted by the autoregressive effects of earlier reading performance (e.g., Wagner et al., 1997). In addition, many of these phonological processing variables may be of limited value in predicting individual differences in the remedial responses of reading disabled children because most of the supporting research reviewed involves normally developing children (not identified as developmentally dyslexic or at risk for such a classification) who are acquiring reading skill in normal classroom settings.

These concerns are mitigated by a great deal of research indicating that deficits in core phonological skills are linked to reading failure for children who are reading below expectations for their age and/or IQ level (e.g., Bradley & Bryant, 1978; Felton & Brown, 1990; Lovett, 1997; Manis, Seidenbert, Doi, McBride-Change, & Peterson, 1996; Shankweiler et al., 1995), for children whose low level of reading performance might be expected based on their lower IQ level ("garden variety" poor readers; Fletcher et al., 1994; Francis, S. E. Shaywitz, Steubing, B. A. Shaywitz, & Fletcher, 1996; Stanovich & Siegel, 1994), and for subtypes of reading disabled children identified across levels of intelligence (Morris et al., 1998). Although Castles and Coltheart (1993) identified one group of dyslexic readers with a deficit in phonological processing (developmental phonological dyslexia) and another with a deficit in orthographic processing (developmental surface dyslexia), more recent evidence from Manis et al. (1996) and Stanovich, Siegel, and Gottardo (1997) indicates that only phonological dyslexia qualifies as a distinct and stable type of dyslexia when reading age controls are employed. Morris et al. (1998) showed that whereas subtypes of developmentally dyslexic readers can be identified that vary in cognitive skills, all of the subtypes are characterized by impairments in phonological processing skills. Furthermore, the phonological processing deficits of developmental dyslexics persist into adulthood, even when some literacy skills have been attained (Bruck, 1992; Pennington, van Orden, Smith, Green, & Haith, 1990), underlying the life-span significance of this diagnostic marker. Finally, there is recent evidence from behavioral genetics suggesting a genetic linkage between phonological awareness and adjacent markers on chromosome six (Grigorenko et al., 1997).

The critical question for the present discussion, however, is whether or not any of these phonological core, nonreading variables, either singly or in combination, provide information about individual differences in dyslexic children's response to remediation—beyond that which might be predicted by the child's level of reading ability/disability at diagnosis. It is possible that phonological processing variables differ in their predictive potency across development (i.e., there may be a developmental window effect) and minimal levels of performance on the tasks that index these variables may be necessary for remediation to be effective (i.e., there may be a threshold skill level effect). Finally, the relative success of these variables as predictors is likely to depend on the interaction between the specific content of the instructional program and the profile of strengths and weaknesses in each child's phonological processing skills (see Scanlon & Vellutino, 1997; Vellutino et al., 1996). These issues are not discussed until later in the chapter, however, because the early research on subtype and individual differences in dyslexic readers' response to remediation is considered first.

DO DIFFERENT TYPES OF DISABLED READERS
RESPOND DIFFERENTIALLY TO TREATMENT?

Early studies in this area were not motivated by a phonological core deficit model of dyslexia; instead, dyslexic readers tended to be subgrouped by perceptual-motor, general oral language, and/or neuropsychological variables that were not tightly linked to phonological processing constructs. The studies involved a wide variety of instructional methods, materials, and outcome measures (e.g., nonreading performance and comprehension as well as word recognition) and they did not provide much evidence that reading disability could be successfully remediated or offer much insight into the role of individual differences (see Gittleman, 1983; Hewison, 1982; and Lovett, 1992, for reviews). A few investigators grouped dyslexic readers according to their actual reading performance as well as their performance on nonreading tasks, and some of these studies did include phonological processing variables (e.g., Fiedorowicz, 1986; Lovett, Ransby, & Barron, 1988; Prior, Frye, & Fletcher, 1987). In addition, some of these studies employed instructional procedures, materials, and measures that focused on improving word recognition per se.

One representative study was conducted by Lovett et al. (1988), who investigated two different instructional methods for remediating the reading skills of two different groups of dyslexic readers ($N = 112$) at different stages of reading development. All aspects of word recognition skill in their accuracy-disabled readers were below age- and grade-level expectations, and their rate-disabled readers were age- and grade-appropriate in context-free word recognition accuracy but deficient in reading speed and contextual reading accuracy (Lovett, 1984, 1987). Both groups of disabled readers were characterized by visual naming speed deficits. The children were randomly assigned to one of two remedial reading programs or to a control treatment for 40 hours of intervention on a one-to-two ratio. The first remedial program offered training in word identification, spelling, letter–sound correspondences and decoding skills (Decoding Skills, DS, program); and the second program provided instruction in oral and written language using connected text and higher order language skills (Oral and Written Language Stimulation, or OWLS). The Classroom Survival Skills program (CSS) was an alternative treatment control procedure that provided instruction in social skills and academic study strategies, but no direct instruction in oral or written language skills. Both the DS and OWLS programs produced improvement that was significantly greater than that achieved by the CSS control group. Many of these effects were of equal magnitude for accuracy- and rate-disabled readers. Improvements in word recognition skill, however, were achieved by the accuracy disabled children following the DS program only, whereas rate-disabled children demonstrated word identification gains following both the DS and the OWLS programs.

Lovett, Ransby, Hardwick, Johns, and Donaldson (1989) described an intervention study in which 178 disabled readers, with varying levels and specificity of reading deficit, were randomly assigned to one of the DS, OWLS, or CSS programs. This extended sample included the 112 subjects from the Lovett et al. (1988) study. Forty hours of remediation in DS or OWLS yielded improvement on selected tests significantly greater than that observed following the CSS control treatment. DS instructed children were significantly improved in their identification of both regular and exception words, and demonstrated gains on two of three standardized word identification measures. OWLS instructed children were improved on experimental measures of text reading and oral language skill, but the effects did not generalize to standardized measures in the same skill domain.

Although the DS trained children demonstrated greater generalization of treatment effects, successful DS graduates failed to abstract from trained vocabulary letter–sound knowledge that could guide their identification of new words—even when letter–sound invariants and pronunciation patterns were explicitly taught. These results focused attention on dyslexic subjects' tendency toward item-specific learning and their difficulty generalizing some dimensions of new language learning beyond what had been specifically taught. This interest in transfer-of-learning, particularly as it impacts on the word identification learning failures of severely dyslexic children, has fueled most recent intervention research, some of which is described later.

ARE THERE INDIVIDUAL DIFFERENCES DIMENSIONS THAT CAN PREDICT DIFFERENCES IN THE REMEDIAL OUTCOMES OF DYSLEXIC CHILDREN?

A multiple regression methodology was developed by Lovett, Benson, and Olds (1990) to address individual differences in response to the DS, OWLS, and CSS programs in Lovett et al. (1989). Because no consensus existed on an appropriate subtyping scheme for the dyslexic population, emphasis was placed on the dimensions of cognitive and academic functioning on which the dyslexic subjects reliably varied in order to determine which of these was predictive of remedial outcome. As part of their pre- and posttest battery, a set of standardized reading achievement, sound–symbol processing, and speech and language measures had been administered to the 178 children in Lovett et al. (1989). A factor analysis was conducted on standardized age-corrected scores at pretest, with an additional factor analysis on the same measures at posttest replicating the pretest factor solution. The pretest analysis revealed four main factors that characterized subjects' profiles at entry.

The first factor, which accounted for 42% of the total variance, involved the skill dimension that led to these children's clinical referral and included measures of word identification, contextual decoding, reading comprehension, and spelling skill. This factor was critical both to defining the subjects' disability and to accounting for substantial individual variation within the treatment sample. Because of its significance, this factor constituted the standard against which the treatments were evaluated in this individual differences study.

The remaining three factors represented empirically and theoretically meaningful individual differences dimensions in the context of the reading disability literature and the review on preceding pages. Factor 2 consisted of subjects' performance speeds on the four serial naming tasks and was labeled "rapid automatized naming" (RAN; Denckla & Rudel, 1974, 1976); it accounted for 10.5% of the variance at pretest. Factor 3 was labeled "phonological processing and nonword reading/spelling"; it included subtests from the GFW Sound-Symbol Test (Goldman, Fristoe, & Woodcock, 1974) and accounted for 5.3% variance. Factor 4 was labeled "oral language" and included measures of word knowledge, syntax, and inference comprehension; it accounted for 4% of the pretest variance. Together, the four factor solution accounted for 61.8% of the pretest variance. Composite scores were calculated for the pre- and posttest data sets according to the pretest factor solution for use in the multiple regression model described later.

The multiple regression model allowed prediction of posttest performance on the reading/spelling factor (Factor 1), a composite measure of the specific skill deficits that prompted referral of these children. The question of primary interest was whether or not any of the nonreading skill dimensions represented in the other factors predicted differential response to the DS, OWLS, and CSS treatment programs. An equation was constructed in which the criterion (predicted) variable was posttest reading/spelling and the predictor variables included pretest reading/spelling, treatment group, an independent pretest variable (Factors 2, 3, 4, WISC Verbal IQ, Performance IQ, or age), and interaction terms for pretest reading/spelling × treatment group and for the pretest independent variable × treatment group.

The phonological processing factor, Factor 3, reliably predicted the subjects' posttest reading achievement. This factor was the pretest factor (with the exception of Factor 1 at pretest) that was most highly correlated with the posttest reading/spelling factor ($r = .605$). Factor 3 did not interact with treatment assignment in the multiple regression analysis, however, indicating that disabled readers with better developed phonological processing skill before treatment achieved better reading and spelling performance after treatment regardless of the actual treatment program they received. It is notable that this individual differences dimension did not predict DS treatment response because the DS program attempted to train phonological reading skills in its approach to training words with regular orthography. This aspect of the DS program was not particularly effective, however, because subsequent program evaluation data indicated that DS treatment gains appeared based on the acquisition of specific lexical knowledge rather than on the successful learning of letter–sound patterns (Lovett, 1991; Lovett et al., 1989). It was only in later studies that significant letter–sound knowledge gains in severely dyslexic readers was demonstrated; these gains were obtained with programs that are generally more effective than the DS program used in this design (Lovett, Borden et al., 1994; Lovett & Steinbach, 1997). The second factor, rapid automatized naming, was not predictive of these disabled readers' reading and spelling achievement after training, nor did it predict differential response to the three treatment programs.

The individual differences dimensions that did predict differential response to the three treatments were oral language ability (Factor 4), and both verbal and nonverbal estimates of intellectual ability (Wechsler Intelligence Scale for Children, WISC–R). Disabled readers with relatively higher levels of oral language skill and intellectual ability at entry demonstrated the greatest gains in reading/spelling performance following the DS program. At first glance, these data would appear to suggest that a certain threshold level of language and intellectual ability may be necessary for disabled readers to benefit optimally from a DS oriented word recognition and spelling training program.

These data can only be interpreted conservatively, however, because subjects' level of reading achievement/disability at entry was the single most powerful predictor of reading performance after remediation regardless of actual treatment assignment: Pretest reading/spelling performance accounted for 89% of the variance in posttest reading/spelling skill. Each of the significant interactions, in contrast, accounted for no more than 1% of the variance, respectively! Until interactions are reported that account for a far greater proportion of posttest performance variance, these individual differences results reported by Lovett, Benson, and Olds (1990) may be more interesting for the model developed to accommodate a three-program comparison than for any actual evidence supporting diagnosis × treatment effects.

HOW DO CORE SKILL DEFICITS AFFECT READING
DEVELOPMENT IN DISABLED READERS?

The experience of Lovett and her colleagues in developing, using, and evaluating the DS and OWLS programs led to recognition that transfer-of-learning difficulties characterize disabled readers and their response to training. Other investigators have also recognized the significant problem of generalization failures after intervention for dyslexia (Olson, Wise, Ring, & Johnson, 1997; Snowling, 1996).

A compelling demonstration of this problem was provided in a subsequent remedial outcome study (Lovett, 1991; Lovett, Warren-Chaplin, Ransby, & Borden, 1990). This study focused on the question of whether disabled readers could profit better from letter–sound training if the amount of attention allocated each training word was increased to approximate that routinely allocated sight words. Two word recognition and spelling training programs were compared: One trained constituent letter–sound mappings in orthographically regular words, and the other taught regular and exception words by a whole word approach. Two sets of training words (two lists of regular words and two lists of exception words) were prepared and matched for word frequency, letter length, proportion of multisyllabic words, and an index of orthographic familiarity (single letter positional frequency). Each set of words constituted the training content for half the sample in each training program, with the other set allowing careful measurement of transfer of training gains on uninstructed content matched for difficulty and familiarity. The efficacy of the two programs was evaluated relative to that of the same control treatment described earlier, the Classroom Survival Skills program.

The subjects in this study were all accuracy-disabled readers and were experiencing pervasive problems with word identification learning: On average, they were performing below the seventh percentile for age on several standardized measures of reading achievement. After 35 hours of remediation, these children more than doubled the number of regular and exception words they could identify following the two word recognition training programs—from the taught-to training words. These groups failed to show significant gains relative to the control subjects, however, on the uninstructed regular and exception word lists or in their ability to decode nonwords. The two programs were equivalent in their effects, suggesting that these children did not benefit differentially from the instructional condition that included training on constituent letter–sound mappings in the training words, even under the format of increased lexical attention. The sizable gains in reading vocabulary by the trained subjects appeared to reflect the acquisition of specific lexical knowledge, with no accompanying abstraction of letter–sound invariant patterns (even when explicitly taught). The children acquired a number of trained words, therefore, but they failed to acquire general knowledge that could transfer and facilitate identification of new words and nonwords.

The transfer failures of these children were quite dramatic: Disabled readers who acquired and retained the training words *rake* and *fall*, for instance, were not reliably better in their ability to identify *fake* and *tall*. This was even true of those who practiced *bake, shake, take*, and *ball, wall*, and *mall*: Children in the letter–sound training condition practiced reading rhyming words during their lessons. These transfer-of-learning problems were attributed to difficulties dyslexic children experience in parsing syllables into subsyllabic units. These parsing difficulties appear to prevent the acquisition of word identification skill by limiting the child's extraction of spelling-to-sound patterns at both the level of larger subsyllabic units (i.e., the rime—the vowel and what comes after: e.g., the *ain* in *rain*) and smaller units (letter-phoneme and letter-cluster-phoneme mappings) (Lovett, 1991). This subsyllabic learning difficulty can be attributable to, and is another manifestation of, the core deficits in phonological processing associated with reading disability.

Other more general difficulties in the metacognitive domain may also be implicated in this pattern of transfer failures. For a beginning reader to be able to identify new unfamiliar words, age-appropriate phonological processing skills and adequate letter–sound knowledge should be accompanied by effective and flexible decoding strategies and the ability to maintain some metacognitive control over word identification attempts. Many children with reading problems, however, have been described as deficient and inefficient in their application of decoding, reading comprehension, and other cognitive and academic strategies (Borkowski, Estrada, Milstead, & Hale, 1989; Gaskins & Elliott, 1991; Kavale, 1980, Meltzer, 1991; Paris & Oka, 1989). Reading disabled children have been characterized as not reliably using whatever they do know about print to help them figure out what they do not know (Gaskins et al., 1988). Strategy use and metacognitive knowledge, although critical to transfer-of-learning issues in many learning domains, has not been extensively studied with respect to the word identification learning failures of reading disabled children.

ARE CORE DEFICITS IN WORD IDENTIFICATION LEARNING AMENABLE TO TREATMENT?

Interest in transfer-of-learning issues has motivated some recent research on the treatment of severe developmental reading disabilities. In intervention studies by Lovett, Borden et al. (1994) and Lovett and Steinbach (1997), children with severe reading disabilities were randomly assigned to one of two word identification training programs or to the Classroom

Survival Skills program, the control treatment. Both of the word identification programs address and promote transfer and generalization of training gains, but they do so through somewhat different training approaches and at different levels of linguistic analysis.

One program is known as the Phonological Analysis and Blending/Direct Instruction Program (PHAB/DI). This program uses direct instructional materials developed by Engelmann and his colleagues at the University of Oregon and trains phonological analysis, phonological blending, and letter–sound association skills in the context of word recognition and decoding instruction (Engelmann & Bruner, 1988; Engelmann, Carnine, & Johnson, 1988; Engelmann, Johnson et al., 1988). The emphasis is one of addressing phonemic awareness and subsyllabic segmentation deficits through direct and very intensive phonological training and direct instruction of letter–sound correspondences. The second program, Word Identification Strategy Training (WIST), has a strong metacognitive focus and teaches the children how to use and monitor four metacognitive decoding strategies. The WIST program was developed in laboratory classrooms at the Hospital for Sick Children, and is based in part on the Benchmark School Word Identification/Vocabulary Development Program (I. W. Gaskins, Downer, & R. W. Gaskins, 1986).

PHAB/DI and WIST address subsyllabic segmentation with units of different size: PHAB/DI trains the smallest spelling-to-sound units (grapheme-phoneme) and WIST emphasizes larger spelling-to-sound units, particularly the rime. Both programs attempt to facilitate transfer in different ways— PHAB/DI by intensive remediation of sound analysis and blending deficits, WIST by teaching a set of flexible word identification strategies and a set of specific skills and content needed for their successful implementation.

Both intervention programs proved more effective than previous interventions and were associated with significant improvement on several standardized and experimental measures: Following PHAB/DI or WIST, severely disabled readers achieved transfer on a set of word and nonword reading measures that included transfer probes varying in their distance from instructed target words. These results demonstrate that the transfer-of-learning deficits undermining dyslexics' word identification learning can be addressed with systematic interventions designed to remediate core learning deficits. Before training, severely disabled readers were incorrectly identifying one-syllable words like *way*, *left*, and *put*: After training in PHAB/DI or WIST, many of these children were able to decode accurately (although slowly) multisyllabic words like *unintelligible*, *mistakenly*, and *disengaged*. After 35 hours of intervention, they typically were not yet reading at grade level, but they demonstrated significantly improved letter–sound knowledge, increased decoding abilities, and better word identification skill following treatment.

The two most encouraging findings from this work to date have been the demonstration of transfer to uninstructed words, and the demonstration that the phonological analysis, sound blending, and letter–sound learning abilities of severely disabled readers could be improved with focused intensive remediation of this type. Although the phonological and letter–sound learning deficits of these children were not completely ameliorated after these short-term interventions, both print- and speech-based phonological skills were significantly improved and closer to age-appropriate levels. Although both the PHAB/DI and WIST approaches were associated with large positive effects, different patterns of transfer were observed following the two programs, confirming the existence of treatment-specific effects. The phonological program, PHAB/DI, resulted in broader-based and deeper transfer within the phonological domain, and WIST, with its metacognitive focus, resulted in broader-based transfer for real English words (i.e., regular and exception word identification was improved for WIST-trained Ss).

The efficacy of PHAB/DI and WIST in remediating the word identification deficits of dyslexic children was equivalent on many measures and different on others. The relative success of both interventions, however, suggests that the effective remediation of reading disability can occur through more than one route of subsyllabic segmentation. The letter–sound approach of PHAB/DI and the letter cluster–sound approach of WIST both resulted in improvements in word identification accuracy and decoding skill. What is important is that some level of subsyllabic segmentation be achieved to allow transfer from a just-learned word to a similarly spelled word. Although some reading vocabulary can be acquired through whole-word techniques (Lovett, Warren-Chaplin et al., 1990), disabled readers do not transfer new word learning unless subsyllabic segmentation is explicitly trained and practiced in interventions that effectively target core learning problems. Lovett, Borden et al. (1994) suggested that only systematic deficit-directed remediation will allow severely reading disabled children to overcome transfer-of-learning failures during word recognition learning. It appears that effective remediation of reading disabilities must address the transfer-of-learning issue directly and provide intensive focused training of the core processing deficits contributing to reading acquisition failure (Lovett, 1997).

DO CORE SKILL DEFICITS PREDICT RESPONSE TO SPECIFIC REMEDIAL READING APPROACHES?

Because a treatment focus on core processing deficits appears critical to improved outcomes, the severity and number of processing deficits may prove to be reliable predictors of remedial response beyond that predicted by reading skill at entry. Earlier in this chapter, evidence was reviewed indicating that nonreading correlates of reading development consist of a core of phonological processing variables. Based on the evidence to date, phonological awareness and serial naming speed have emerged as stable and independent predictors of early reading development in longitudinal studies and of reading disability (Scarborough, 1997; Wagner et al., 1994, 1997).

Deficient phonological awareness appears to play a role by impairing subsyllabic segmentation during word identification learning and thus preventing the acquisition of spelling-to-sound correspondences by severely reading disabled children. Deficits in visual naming speed disrupt reading development by preventing the effective development of connections between phonemic and orthographic representations at both word and subword levels of representation during word identification learning and by reducing the quality of orthographic codes in the disabled reader's memory (Bowers & Wolf, 1993; Wolf & Bowers, 1999). Evidence on the role that individual differences in phonological awareness plays in dyslexic readers' response to remediation will be reviewed first as it is the most widely researched potential predictor. This is followed by a consideration of the role of individual differences in visual naming speed, particularly within the context of the "double deficit" hypothesis (Bowers & Wolf, 1993; Wolf, 1991, 1997; Wolf, Pfeil, Lotz, & Biddle, 1994).

The role of individual differences in phonological awareness skill was examined by Olson and Wise (1992) in response to their finding that subsyllabic segmentation feedback was not more effective than whole word feedback in remediation training for disabled readers. Olson, Wise, and their colleagues (e.g., Olson, Foltz & Wise, 1986; Wise et al., 1989) developed a computer speech-based training system employing high-level computer-synthesized speech generated by DECtalk. Children in their studies were required to read a passage of text displayed on a computer monitor and then, using a mouse or light pen pointing device, target words they did not know. An unknown word (e.g., *steam*) was highlighted in reverse video and DECtalk generated the pronunciation of the word under whole word or segmented feedback conditions consisting of syllables or of subsyllabic units corresponding to onsets (*st* = /st/) and rimes (*eam* = /im/; see Treiman, 1992) or graphemes and phonemes (*s* = /s/, *t* = /t/, *ea* = /i/, *m* = /m/). Following 6 to 8 hours of computer reading time per subject, disabled readers produced greater gains in word and nonword reading than an untreated control group. Contrary to expectations, however, both the segmentation and whole word feedback conditions were equally effective in producing gains on the two outcome measures. In fact, grapheme-phoneme segmentation produced the smallest gains compared to the other conditions in a short-term (2-day) study (Wise, 1992; see also similar results by van Daal & Reitsma, 1990, and Spaai, Ellerman, & Reitsma, 1991, in Dutch).

Olson and Wise (1992) found that phonological awareness (pig latin and phoneme deletion task performance) was moderately correlated with both word and nonword gain scores, particularly for the onset-rime feedback condition. When their subjects were divided into high and low phonological awareness groups, however, the critical subgroup × type-of-online feedback interaction was not consistently significant across the word and nonword gain scores. Although these results are not very strong, they suggest the possibility that children with more severe phonological awareness deficits may be less likely to benefit from remediation training involving subsyllabic segmentation (see also Lyon, 1985a,b). The decision to seek feedback about an unknown word in the Olson and Wise (1992) study was largely at the discretion of the child as the online reading was not consistently monitored. Furthermore, segmental feedback about unknown words was not augmented by intensive training associating the subsyllabic segments (phonemes, onsets, rimes) with their corresponding graphemes and blending those segments into a syllable. Effective remediation of blending difficulties appears critical to the success of interventions with this population and a feature on which many phonologically based remedial reading programs vary.

In contrast, Lovett, Barron, Forbes, Cuksts, and Steinbach (1994; see also Barron, Lovett, & McCabe, 1998) used a DECtalk-based training procedure that involved longer (24 45-minute sessions) and more intensive training on onset-rime and phoneme units with both neurologically impaired and developmentally dyslexic readers. In this DECtalk study, the groups receiving grapheme-phoneme, onset-rime, and whole word feedback all performed at a significantly higher level on measures of word identification and spelling than a control group instructed in mathematics. The onset-rime and grapheme-phoneme groups made the greatest word identification gains on those words that could be trained with segmented speech feedback (i.e., orthographically regular words). The grapheme-phoneme group was significantly higher than the other two experimental groups on a measure of word recognition transfer following training.

Although the Olson and Wise (1992) results are consistent with other evidence, indicating that children with severe phonological processing deficits are less likely to benefit from remediation involving subsyllabic segmentation (e.g., Lyon, 1985a,b), the Lovett, Barron et al. (1994) results suggest that longer and more intensive instructional programs that specifically target the identification and blending of subsyllabic units may offset such threshold effects. Hatcher, Hulme, and Ellis (1994), for example, provided 130 disabled readers with training on subsyllabic units that was similar in duration and intensity (40 30-minute sessions) to that offered by Lovett, Barron et al. (1994) and Lovett, Borden et al. (1994). Three different conditions were compared by Hatcher and his colleagues: (a) phonological awareness training without any reading (phonology-alone group); (b) reading training emphasizing the meaning and the sentence context of words but without any reference to their sounds (reading-alone group); (c) training that specifically linked phonology and reading (reading-with-phonology group). The reading-with-phonology group was significantly better than the untreated control group on four different word reading measures, and the other two groups did not differ from the control. The reading-with-phonology group's superior performance was maintained at retesting 9 months later, indicating that establishing an explicit connection between the subsyllabic units of print and sound is important for improving the word recognition skills of disabled readers.

Hatcher et al. (1994) also found that a composite phonological processing measure was the best predictor of reading performance in the reading-alone and reading-with-phonology groups ($r = .72$ and $.54$, respectively), whereas reading ability was the best predictor for the phonology-alone group ($r = .54$). These individual difference findings suggest that strong phonological skills are an important prerequisite for children to benefit from training that involves teaching reading skills without any phonological content (reading-alone group). In contrast, a lower threshold for phonological skill may be possible when the training involves both reading and phonology.

Hatcher et al. (1994) and Snowling (1996) pointed out, however, that children with very severe phonological processing deficits may have great difficulty acquiring word recognition skills even when the instruction is intensive and is designed to make the connection between phonological segments and print explicit (e.g., Hulme & Snowling, 1992a,b; Snowling & Hulme, 1989; Stackhouse & Snowling, 1992). Finally, Hatcher et al.'s (1994) results also indicate that children with higher pretest levels of reading skill are more likely to benefit from pure phonological awareness training and they provide further evidence for a reciprocal relation between phonological awareness and reading (e.g., Morais, Cary, Alegria, & Bertelson, 1979; but see Wagner et al., 1997).

Foorman et al. (1997) examined the relative effectiveness of different programs of instruction for grade 2 and 3 disabled readers ($N = 114$). Like Lovett, Borden et al. (1994), Lovett, Barron et al. (1994), and Olson and Wise (1992), these investigators compared intervention programs that varied in the unit of instruction: analytic phonics (onset and rime units), synthetic phonics (phoneme units), and sight word approaches (whole word units) (1 hour of instruction daily). Synthetic phonics emerged as the most effective instructional intervention even when the variables of SES, gender, Verbal IQ, and ethnicity were considered, but this result occurred only when measures of phonological awareness constituted the outcome variable; the same results were not obtained when word identification skill was the outcome measure. Children with better phonological awareness skill at entry showed more rapid growth in word identification skill across the school year than those with lower pretest levels, even when pretest levels of orthographic skill were controlled. This individual differences effect in phonological awareness skill on the growth of word identification skill was the same for all three interventions, however, and did not differentially interact with a specific instructional condition. This latter result is similar to that reported by Lovett, Benson, and Olds (1990) that pretest levels of phonological processing predicted posttest reading achievement equally regardless of program assignment.

The evidence presented suggests that children with relatively higher levels of phonological awareness are more responsive to efforts to remediate their reading disability. Vellutino et al. (1996) also addressed this issue in an early intervention study in which 76 reading-impaired grade 1 children were chosen from a large sample of children (1,200+) tested initially in kindergarten on a variety of cognitive, language, and reading measures. These at-risk readers were given one semester of reading instruction that involved both phonics and sight word instruction, as well as practice in reading connected text. After instruction, 67% of these children scored within or above the average range on word and nonword reading performance; these findings were used to suggest that a large proportion of children who may appear learning disabled in first grade may, in fact, move into the normal range of reading performance following early and intensive intervention. Vellutino and his colleagues also found, however, that children who were relatively difficult to remediate tended to have phonological processing skills deficits (phonemic awareness, letter and number identification and naming, memory, visual-verbal learning, language processing with substantial memory components) that were more severe than those of the easier-to-remediate at risk readers; in contrast, group differences were not obtained on measures of visual, semantic, or syntactic skills. The Vellutino et al. (1996) results provide further evidence that children who have particularly low levels of core phonological processing skills may be the most difficult to remediate.

Olson, Wise, Ring, and Johnson (1997) and Torgesen, Wagner, and Rashotte (1997) developed programs of instruction that specifically target the phonological skills of reading disabled children. Olson et al. (1997) combined features of the C. Lindamood and P. Lindamood (1974) oral-motor program for training phonological awareness with computer-based training procedures for segmenting and blending letter–sound associations, spelling, and nonword recognition (Wise & Olson, 1995; Wise,

Ring, Sessions, & Olson, 1997). Another group of disabled readers received instruction in comprehension strategies in a reciprocal teaching program (Palinscar & Brown, 1984). Both groups also spent time reading computer-displayed stories in which unknown words were highlighted by the child and the computer provided a whole word pronunciation online (Olson & Wise, 1992); total training time was approximately 25 hours. The children receiving phonological training were superior to the comprehension-trained group after training and 1 year later on nonword decoding and phoneme awareness measures but, like Foorman et al. (1997), they were not superior on measures of word recognition.

Torgesen et al. (1997) reported a similar finding following 88 hours of intensive, one-to-one instruction delivered as part of a longitudinal training study. Beginning in kindergarten, children at risk for reading disability were given oral-motor instruction patterned very closely after C. Lindamood and P. Lindamood (1974). At the end of the second grade, the oral-motor group was superior to children given phonics instruction using word and sentence contexts and to children given regular classroom support: This superiority was demonstrated on measures of phonological awareness, nonword reading, and spelling. The groups did not differ, however, on measures of word identification skill.

When considered together, the studies reviewed in this section suggest, although not very strongly, that individual differences in phonological awareness influence disabled readers' response to remediation that is specifically targeted at acquiring phonology-based reading skills (i.e., Foorman et al., 1997; Hatcher et al., 1994; Olson & Wise, 1992). In addition, Vellutino et al. (1996) showed that there may be a small group of disabled readers (approximately 3% of their total population of children) who have such severe phonological deficits that they appear to fall below a threshold for eliciting a positive response to phonics-based remediation. Although it can be argued that one semester of instruction is not sufficient to remediate these below-threshold disabled readers, long-term training procedures that employ oral-motor instruction to teach phonological skills (e.g., Olson et al., 1997; Torgesen et al., 1997) do not offer any evidence that this form of intensive instruction produces transfer-of-training to word recognition skills. It is possible, however, that Torgesen et al.'s (1997) longitudinal study will yield such transfer data when their subjects are assessed at 1- and 2-year follow-up, after they have had more opportunity to apply their newly acquired phonological skills and obtain more experience with print (e.g., Share, 1995). It should be noted that Lovett, Borden et al. (1994) and Lovett and Steinbach (1997) showed that remediation procedures that involve intensive phonology-based instruction do yield transfer to real words, although transfer to both regular and exception words appears to require metacognitive-based phonics training.

A study of individual differences in treatment response (Lovett, Benson, & Olds, 1990) found that a phonological processing factor (at pretest) significantly predicted posttest reading/spelling achievement, regardless of the program assigned. In contrast, visual naming speed did not predict differential response to treatment in the DS, OWLS, and CSS design, nor was it generally predictive of posttest reading and spelling achievement when the predictive contribution of initial level of reading ability/disability was removed. With the development and adaptation of improved interventions for teaching word identification skills to severely impaired readers (i.e., WIST, PHAB/DI), it is of interest to ask whether premediation levels of phonological awareness and visual naming speed reliably and meaningfully predict a child's response to active intervention in the PHAB and WIST design. An attempt to address this question has been undertaken recently using remedial outcome data from the first 166 subjects to complete 35 hours of training in PHAB/DI, WIST, or CSS (Lovett, Steinbach, & Frijters, 2000). The approach is different to the individual differences regression model outlined in Lovett, Benson, and Olds (1990). This analysis attempted to subgroup reading disabled children using a metric based on the double deficit hypothesis. The double deficit hypothesis (Bowers & Wolf, 1993; Wolf & Bowers, 1999; Wolf, 1997) contends that deficits in phonological awareness and deficits in visual naming speed represent two independent causal impediments to reading acquisition for reading disabled individuals.

Based on pre-intervention diagnostic testing, three subgroups were defined according to these two deficit dimensions. Disabled readers were characterized as having a phonological deficit, a visual naming speed deficit, or both types of deficits. A total of 84% of subjects from the sample were classified, with 54% exhibiting a double deficit, 22% a phonological-only deficit (PHON-only), and 24% a visual naming speed deficit only (VNS-only). Examination of the subgroups' diagnostic profiles emphasized the impact of both deficits in combination in depressing all aspects of written language learning: The double deficit subgroup was more globally impaired than the other two groups. In contrast, the children with VNS deficits only were the highest achieving and most selectively impaired of these reading disabled subjects. All three subgroups were significantly impaired on all measures of reading, spelling, and reading comprehension skill and in basic letter–sound knowledge. The VNS-only subjects did not resemble the rate-disabled subjects reported in earlier work (Lovett, 1987; Lovett, Ransby, & Barron, 1988): The VNS-only group are accuracy- and rate-disabled, and far more impaired than the earlier described rate-disabled children. The level of disability characterizing the intervention sample in general is severe: More than one half of the most recent treatment samples have been below the first percentile for age on multiple standardized reading achievement tests at entry. The severity of the sample's reading disabilities is reflected in the fact that the majority of subtyped subjects in this study demonstrated a double deficit.

When the remedial outcomes of the three deficit subgroups were assessed following 35 hours of PHAB/DI, WIST, and CSS, more similarities than differences in outcome were observed. All three subgroups were significantly improved in word identification skill and letter–sound knowledge following the two remedial reading programs, and all three groups achieved transfer to uninstructed reading vocabulary. This result is particularly significant given the severity of impairments in the double deficit group. On only one of the four transfer measures was the double deficit subgroup noted to make fewer gains than the other two groups following WIST or PHAB. This pattern of lesser gain with treatment was not replicated on other outcome measures.

Children with phonological-only deficits were intermediate to the other two subgroups both with respect to the level and the extent of their impairment on several tests. Although as impaired as the double deficit group on speech-based phonological measures and nonword reading, the PHON-only subjects were relatively less disabled that the double deficit group on some standardized word identification and reading comprehension measures and in their identification of high frequency spelling patterns in the English language (keywords). The PHON-only subgroup was revealed to make the greatest nonword reading gains following treatment.

With a few exceptions, these results do not indicate that subgroups of disabled readers defined according to a double deficit model respond differently to the PHAB/DI and WIST intervention models. These data do demonstrate the amenability of severe phonological and word identification learning deficits to focused and intensive remediation, and reveal that word identification accuracy and speed can be improved with intervention programs that target core areas of processing deficit. The PHAB and WIST programs do not specifically remediate visual naming speed impairments: Programs that address the VNS impairment directly and its impact on reading acquisition are in development (Wolf, 1997) and will prove important to evaluate from this perspective. In the present work, treatment-related change occurred in the domains of word identification learning and phonological processing and treatments did not target the speed/fluency components of developmental dyslexia. The ultimate utility of the double deficit subgroups in predicting treatment response perhaps cannot be properly evaluated until both phonological- and VNS-deficit directed treatment programs can be compared in one design.

One recent report does address the construct of reading fluency and word identification speed in a training study using a sample of underachieving grade 4 readers. Levy, Abello, and Lysynchuk (1997) trained their subjects to read a set of single words and to repeatedly read stories that contained the trained words and stories that did not contain trained words. Gains in the speed with which subjects could identify single words resulted in significantly improved reading speeds when these words occurred in connected text. Word recognition training gains generalized to story reading formats although faster word recognition speeds were not associated with improved reading comprehension performance until naming times were decreased to less than 1 second during training. Of significance to the present discussion, children who were slow or fast in visual naming speed (assessed on the RAN) did not differ in their response to the training. These investigators note that the fluency gains with training were unrelated to rapid automatized naming speed per se contrary to earlier predictions by Bowers (1993).

CONCLUSIONS

The preceding pages have reviewed a sizable literature on early reading development and reading acquisition failure in reading disabled children. The evidence from developmental longitudinal studies has been overwhelming in highlighting the significance of phonemic awareness and phonological processing skills as stable, reliable, and unique predictors of later reading achievement in the early elementary grades. In the reading disabilities literature, core phonological processing variables have been demonstrated to be signature nonreading symptoms of a developmental reading disorder characterized by failure to acquire context-free word identification skills. Evidence is accumulating to identify visual naming speed as a second unique predictor of reading acquisition success, and a diagnostic marker of reading disorder across languages and throughout the life span. This continuity of constructs and convergence of evidence from the cognitive development literature and the clinical research literature on reading disabilities is important and should allow better informed study designs and remedial interventions to be developed and evaluated.

At the conclusion of the search for predictors of individual variation in treatment response, what is left is a limited set of answers and a more refined set of research questions. The studies reviewed in this chapter have been valuable for what they teach of the nature of the word identification learning deficits of disabled readers, how they can be effectively addressed in intervention programs, and how intervention programs can be better designed to facilitate generalization. There is growing consensus in some segments of the clinical research community that better outcomes are observed from remedial programs that include a phonological training component (Foorman et al., 1997; Torgesen et al., 1997), that target and remediate core processing deficits (rather than promote compensatory strategies to circumvent the deficits) (Lovett et al., 1994; Lovett & Steinbach, 1997; Lovett, Steinbach, & Frijters, 2000), that facilitate the development of subsyllabic segmentation skills and letter–sound knowledge (Levy & Lysynchuk, 1997; Lovett, Barron et al., 1994; Lovett, Borden et al., 1994), and that directly teach word identification, text comprehension, spelling, and basic literacy skills (Vellutino et al., 1996). Evidence is beginning to be reported that outlines conditions under which gains in context-free word identification accuracy and speed reliably generalize to text reading and reading comprehension (Levy et al., 1997).

Although the problem of developmental reading disabilities has been recognized for the past century, it is only within the past decade that reliable evidence from controlled evaluations has been reported on its remediation. In the mid-1980s, there was almost no scientifically credible evidence to indicate that reading disabilities were amenable to treatment or that any one treatment approach was better than any other (Gittelman, 1983; Hewison, 1982). Very few studies were undertaken that attempted to evaluate the efficacy of interventions in a controlled design with alternative treatment approaches systematically compared. Failures to include a control group and to compare two or more interventions rendered reported evidence as little more than anecdotal in import. Unless alternative approaches are evaluated in controlled designs, there is no opportunity to separate treatment-specific effects from general treatment effects (e.g., halo effects due to inclusion in a special program, individualized attention, access to a teacher or therapist with specialized reading disabilities expertise) and change due to maturation and experience.

For decades, the intervention literature has been characterized by measurement and methodological problems. There has been little recognition of the fact that outcome is necessarily a multidimensional and multivariate construct, which is complex to measure. Even today, measurement issues plague otherwise successful intervention protocols yielding positive and specific intervention effects: It is notoriously difficult, for example, to adequately measure reading comprehension abilities in a child with word identification problems, and to assess whether word identification gains have produced improved text reading and comprehension performance (Berninger & Abbott, 1994; Levy et al., 1997). The efficacy of an intervention must be assessed with respect to transfer, generalization, and maintenance effects, yet basic questions remain regarding their reliable and valid measurement (Lyon, 1996; Lyon & Moats, 1997; Shanahan & Barr, 1995).

Finally, the outcome measures that have been used in many studies have varied enormously in their power and sensitivity to treatment-related change. Many standardized measures with steep item gradients, for example, allow relatively few chances for an improving disabled reader to demonstrate newly acquired skills before item difficulty levels rise and ceilings are quickly reached (Lovett, Hinchley, & Benson, in preparation). As can be expected, experimental measures with more trials per level of difficulty result in more visible gains and better opportunities to demonstrate treatment-related change over the short term. At present, many questions remain unanswered regarding the best measurement models for evaluating the success or failure of a given intervention (Lyon & Moats, 1997). The lack of power inherent to traditional measurement choices has perhaps masked the effects of some potentially promising treatment approaches.

Although better designed studies are beginning to yield positive results and valuable insight into some of the parameters of effective treatment for reading disability, the review offered in the preceding pages offers limited insight into the individual differences dimensions that mediate optimal treatment response and predict who will be a responder and who a nonresponder to specific treatment approaches. The paucity of individual differences results, however, is perhaps also a consequence of measurement and design limitations in the intervention literature. The traditional use of pre- and posttest designs in intervention studies has not produced optimal data for examining change with treatment and individual differences in that process.

Within the past decade, attention has been focused on the advantages afforded by a different type of model for analyzing change and assessing intervention effects. The analysis of individual growth curves (Rogosa & Willitt, 1985) provides an alternative to pre- and posttest designs and a more powerful model for analyzing change in individuals and groups (Francis, S. E. Shaywitz, Steubing et al., 1994; Lyon & Moats, 1997; B. A. Shaywitz & S. E. Shaywitz, 1994). Growth curve modeling provides an avenue for estimating what proportion of change can be attributed to the intervention itself and what to nonintervention factors like maturation and a range of environmental influences (B. A. Shaywitz & S. E. Shaywitz, 1994). Of greater importance to the present discussion, growth curve modeling focuses attention on rate of change: The focus of measurement moves from static achievement and performance levels to an analysis of the rate and shape of a growth function reflecting a process of learning over time and requiring repeated measurement for its estimation.

Growth curve models allow investigators to address variability within a sample in a more productive manner: Individual differences questions can be addressed with a sophistication that far exceeds that furnished by traditional median split or simple linear regression approaches. A wide range of environmental, treatment, demographic, developmental, and diagnostic characteristics of children in intervention samples can be used to assess what characteristics and conditions mediate/predict/determine the rate and shape of the growth curve representing change over time—before, during, and after the intervention. These methodologies for the measurement of change over time are beginning to be applied to issues of definition and treatment in the field of developmental reading disabilities with promising early results (Foorman et al., 1997; Francis, Shaywitz, Steubing et al., 1996; Torgesen et al., 1997).

New conceptualizations of developmental reading disabilities, the core underlying learning impairments, and their effective remediation place researchers in a better position to undertake rigorous and productive research on the disorder, its optimal remediation, and long-term outcome. Recent developments that will allow researchers to refine their methodologies for the measurement of change, its evaluation and analysis, now place them in a position to study individual and developmental variation within a richer and more coherent theoretical context and with improved clinical research tools. The questions of what mediates and predicts change for children with developmental reading disorders and what treatment or treatment combinations will best serve them can now be addressed with a increased likelihood of yielding answers.

ACKNOWLEDGMENTS

The first author's research described in this chapter has been supported by operating grants from the Ontario Mental Health Foundation, the Vellman Foundation, the Medical Research Council of Canada, and the Social Sciences and Humanities Research Council of Canada. The second author's research has been supported by the Social Sciences and Humanities Research Council of Canada. Joint research has been supported by the Social Sciences and Humanities Research Council of Canada and the Ontario Mental Health Foundation. Chapter preparation was supported by NICHD Award R01 HD30970-01A2 to the first author with Robin Morris and Maryanne Wolf.

REFERENCES

Bakker, D. J., Bouma, A., & Gardien, C. J. (1990). Hemisphere-specific treatment of dyslexia subtypes: A field experiment. *Journal of Learning Disabilities, 23*(7), 433–438.

Barron, R. W. (1994). The sound-to-spelling connection: Orthographic activation in auditory word recognition and its implications for the acquisition of phonological awareness and literacy skills. In V. W. Berninger (Ed.), *The varieties of orthographic knowledge: I. Theoretical and developmental issues* (pp. 219–242). Dordrecht, The Netherlands: Kluwer Academic.

Barron, R. W. (1998). Proto-literate knowledge: Antecedents and influences on phonological awareness and literacy. In C. Hulme & R. M. Joshi (Eds.), *Reading and spelling: Development and disorder* (pp. 153–173). Hillsdale, NJ: Lawrence Erlbaum Associates.

Barron, R. W., Golden, J. O., Seldon, D. M., Tait, C. F., Marmurek, H. H. C., & Haines, L. P. (1992). Teaching prereading skills with a talking computer: Letter–sound knowledge and print feedback facilitate nonreaders' phonological awareness training. *Reading and Writing: An Interdisciplinary Journal, 4,* 179–204.

Barron, R. W., Lovett, M. W., & McCabe, R. (1998). Using talking computers to remediate reading and spelling disabilities: The critical role of the print-to-sound unit. *Behavior Research Methods, Instruments, and Computers, 30*(4), 610–616.

Benton, A. L. (1975). Developmental dyslexia: Neurological aspects. In W. J. Friedlander (Ed.), *Advances in neurology* (Vol. 7, pp.). New York: Raven.

Berninger, V. W., & Abbott, R. D. (1994). Redefining learning disabilities: Moving beyond aptitude-achievement discrepancies to failure to respond to validated treatment protocols. In G. R. Lyon (Ed.), *Frames of reference for the assessment of learning disabilities: New views on measurement issues* (pp. 163–183). Baltimore: Paul H. Brookes.

Borkowski, J. G., Estrada, M. T., Milstead, M., & Hale, C. A. (1989). General problem-solving skills: Relations between metacognition and strategic processing. *Learning Disability Quarterly, 12,* 57–70.

Bowers, P. G. (1993). Text reading and rereading: Determinants of fluency beyond word recognition. *Journal of Reading Behavior, 25,* 133–153.

Bowers, P. G., & Wolf, M. (1993). Theoretical links between naming speed, precise mechanisms, and orthographic skill in dyslexia. *Reading and Writing: An Interdisciplinary Journal, 5,* 69–85.

Bradley, L., & Bryant, P. E. (1978). Difficulties in auditory organization as a possible cause of reading backwardness. *Nature, 271*(5647), 746–747.

Bradley, L., & Bryant, P. E. (1983). Categorizing sounds and learning to read—a causal connection. *Nature, 301,* 419–421.

Bruck, M. (1992). Persistence of dyslexics' phonological awareness deficits. *Developmental Psychology, 28,* 874–886.

Castles, A., & Coltheart, M. (1993). Varieties of developmental dyslexia. *Cognition, 47,* 149–180.

Denckla, M. B., & Rudel, R. G. (1974). Rapid "automatized" naming of pictured objects, colors, letters, and numbers by normal children. *Cortex, 10,* 186–202.

Denckla, M. B., & Rudel, R. G. (1976). Rapid "automatized" naming (RAN): Dyslexia differentiated from other learning disabilities. *Neuropsychologia, 14,* 471–479.

Engelmann, S., & Bruner, E. C. (1988). *Reading mastery I/II fast cycle: Teacher's guide.* Chicago: Science Research Associates.

Engelmann, S., Carnine, L., & Johnson, G. (1988). *Corrective reading, word attack basics, decoding A.* Chicago: Science Research Associates.

Engelmann, S., Johnson, G., Carnine, L., Meyer, L., Becker, W., & Eisele, J. (1988). *Corrective reading: Decoding strategies, decoding B1.* Chicago: Science Research Associates.

Felton, R. H., & Brown, I. S. (1990). Phonological processes as predictors of specific reading skills in children at risk for reading failure. *Reading and Writing: An Interdisciplinary Journal, 2,* 39–59.

Fiedorowicz, C. A. M. (1986). Training of component reading skills. *Annals of Dyslexia, 36,* 318–334.

Fletcher, J. M., Shaywitz, S. E., Shankweiler, D. P., Katz, L., Liberman, I. Y., Stuebing, K. K., Francis, D. J., Fowler, A. E., & Shaywitz, B. A. (1994). Cognitive profiles of reading disability: Comparisons of discrepancy and low achievement definitions. *Journal of Educational Psychology, 86*(1), 6–23.

Foorman, B. R., Francis, D. J., Winikates, D., Mehta, P., Schatschneider, C., & Fletcher, J. M. (1997). Early interventions for children with reading disabilities. In J. P. Williams (Ed.), *Scientific studies of reading* (pp. 255–276). Hillsdale, NJ: Lawrence Erlbaum Associates.

Francis, D. J., Shaywitz, S. E., Steubing, K., Shaywitz, B. A., & Fletcher, J. M. (1994). Measurement of change: Assessing behavior over time and within a developmental context. In G. R. Lyon (Ed.), *Frames of reference for the assessment of learning disabilities: New views on measurement issues* (pp. 29–58). Baltimore: Paul H. Brookes.

Francis, D. J., Shaywitz, S. E., Stuebing, K. K., Shaywitz, B. A., & Fletcher, J. M. (1996). Developmental lag versus deficit models of reading disability: A longitudinal, individual growth curves analysis. *Journal of Educational Psychology, 88*(1), 3–17.

Gaskins, I. W., Downer, M. A., Anderson, R. C., Cunningham, P. M., Gaskins, R. W., Schommer, M., & School, Teachers of the Benchmark School. (1988). A metacognitive approach to phonics: Using what you know to decode what you don't know. *Remedial and Special Education, 9*, 36–41, 66.

Gaskins, I. W., Downer, M. A., & Gaskins, R. W. (1986). *Introduction to the Benchmark School Word Identification/Vocabulary Development Program*. Media, PA: Benchmark School.

Gaskins, I. W., & Elliot, T. T. (1991). *Implementing cognitive strategy training across the school: The Benchmark manual for teachers*. Cambridge, MA: Brookline Books.

Gittleman, R. (1983). Treatment of reading disorders. In M. Rutter (Ed.), *Developmental neuropsychiatry* (pp. 520–541). New York: Guilford.

Goldman, R., Fristoe, M., & Woodcock, R. (1974). *G-F-W Sound-Symbol Tests*. Circle Pines, MN: American Guidance Service.

Goswami, U., & Bryant, P. E. (1990). *Phonological skills and learning to read*. Hillsdale, NJ: Lawrence Erlbaum Associates.

Grigorenko, E. L., Wood, F. B., Meyer, M. S., Hart, L. A., Speed, W. C., Shuster, A., & Pauls, D. L. (1997). Susceptibility loci for distinct components of developmental dyslexia on chromosomes 6 and 15. *American Journal of Human Genetics, 60*, 27–39.

Hatcher, P. J., Hulme, C., & Ellis, A. W. (1994). Ameliorating early reading failure by integrating the teaching of reading and phonological skills: The phonological linkage hypothesis. *Child Development, 65*, 41–57.

Hewison, J. (1982). The current status of remedial intervention for children with reading problems. *Developmental Medicine and Child Neurology, 24*, 183–186.

Hulme, C., & Snowling, M. J. (1992a). Deficits in output phonology: A cause of reading failure? *Cognitive Neuropsychology, 9*, 47–72.

Hulme, C., & Snowling, M. J. (1992b). Phonological deficits in dyslexia: A "sound" reappraisal of the verbal deficit hypothesis? In N. N. Singh & I. L. Beale (Eds.), *Learning disabilities: Nature, theory, and treatment* (pp. 270–301). New York: .

Kavale, K. A. (1980). The reasoning abilities of normal and learning disabled readers on measures of reading comprehension. *Learning Disability Quarterly, 3*, 34–45.

Levy, B. A., Abello, B., & Lysynchuk, L. (1997). Transfer from word training to reading in context: Gains in reading fluency and comprehension. *Learning Disability Quarterly, 20*(3), 173–188.

Levy, B. A., & Lysynchuk, L. (1997). Beginning word recognition: Benefits of training by segmentation and whole word methods. In J. P. Williams (Ed.), *Scientific studies of reading* (pp. 359–387). Hillsdale, NJ: Lawrence Erlbaum Associates.

Lindamood, C., & Lindamood, P. (1974). *Auditory discrimination in depth*. Columbus, OH: Science Research Associates.

Lovegrove, W. J., & Williams, M. C. (1993). Visual temporal processing deficits in specific reading disability. In D. M. Willows, R. S. Kruk, & E. Corcos (Eds.), *Visual processes in reading and reading disability* (pp. 311–329). Hillsdale, NJ: Lawrence Erlbaum Associates.

Lovett, M. W. (1984). A developmental perspective on reading dysfunction: Accuracy and rate criteria in the subtyping of dyslexic children. *Brain and Language, 22*, 67–91.

Lovett, M. W. (1987). A developmental approach to reading disability: Accuracy and speed criteria of normal and deficient reading skill. *Child Development, 58*, 234–260.

Lovett, M. W. (1991). Reading, writing, and remediation: Perspectives on the dyslexic learning disability from remedial outcome data. *Learning and Individual Differences, 3*, 295–305.

Lovett, M. W. (1992). Developmental dyslexia. In I. Rapin & S. J. Segalowitz (Eds.), *Handbook of neuropsychology: Vol. 7. Child neuropsychology* (pp. 163–185). Amsterdam: Elsevier Science.

Lovett, M. W. (1997). Developmental reading disorders. In T. E. Feinberg & M. J. Farah (Eds.), *Behavioral neurology and neuropsychology* (pp. 773–787). New York: McGraw-Hill.

Lovett, M. W., Barron, R. W., Forbes, J. E., Cuksts, B., & Steinbach, K. A. (1994). Computer speech-based training of literacy skills in neurologically-impaired children: A controlled evaluation. *Brain and Language, 47*, 117–154.

Lovett, M. W., Benson, N. J., & Olds, J. (1990). Individual difference predictors of treatment outcome in the remediation of developmental dyslexia. *Learning and Individual Differences, 2*(3), 284–314.

Lovett, M. W., Borden, S. L., DeLuca, T., Lacerenza, L., Benson, N. J., & Brackstone, D. (1994). Treating the core deficits of developmental dyslexia: Evidence of transfer-of-learning following phonologically- and strategy-based reading training programs. *Developmental Psychology, 30*(6), 805–822.

Lovett, M. W., Hinchley, J., & Benson, N. J. (in preparation). Assessing the remedial gains of disabled learners: Conceptual, measurement, and statistical considerations in the evaluation of remedial outcome.

Lovett, M. W., Ransby, M. J., & Barron, R. W. (1988). Treatment, subtype, and word type effects in dyslexic children's response to remediation. *Brain and Language, 34*, 328–349.

Lovett, M. W., Ransby, M. J., Hardwick, N., Johns, M. S., & Donaldson, S. A. (1989). Can dyslexia be treated? Treatment-specific and generalized treatment effects in dyslexic children's response to remediation. *Brain and Language, 37*, 90–121.

Lovett, M. W., & Steinbach, K. A. (1997). The effectiveness of remediation for reading disabled children of different ages: Is there decreased benefit for older children? *Learning Disability Quarterly, 20*(3), 189–210.

Lovett, M. W., Steinbach, K. A., & Frijters, J. C. (2000). Remediating the core deficits of developmental reading disability: A double deficit perspective. *Journal of Learning Disabilities, 33*(4), 334–358.

Lovett, M. W., Warren-Chaplin, P. M., Ransby, M. J., & Borden, S. L. (1990). Training the word recognition skills of reading disabled children: Treatment and transfer effects. *Journal of Educational Psychology, 82*, 769–780.

Lyon, G. R. (1985a). Educational validation studies of learning disability subtypes. In B. P. Rourke (Ed.), *Neuropsychology of learning disabilities: Essentials of subtype analysis* (pp. 228–253). New York: Guilford.

Lyon, G. R. (1985b). Identification and remediation of learning disability subtypes: Preliminary findings. *Learning Disability Focus, 1*(1), 21–35.

Lyon, G. R. (1996). Learning disabilities. In E. Marsh & R. Barkley (Eds.), *Childhood psychopathology* (pp. 390–435). New York: Guilford.

Lyon, G. R., & Moats, L. C. (1997). Critical conceptual and methodological considerations in reading intervention research. *Journal of Learning Disabilities, 30*(6), 578–588.

Manis, F. R., Seidenbert, M. S., Doi, L. M., McBride-Chang, C., & Peterson, A. (1996). On the basis of two subtypes of developmental dyslexia. *Cognition, 58*, 157–195.

Meltzer, L. J. (1991). Problem-solving strategies and academic performance in learning-disabled students: Do subtypes exist? In L. V. Feagans, E. J. Short, & L. J. Meltzer (Eds.),

Subtypes of learning disabilities: Theoretical perspectives and research (pp. 163–188). Hillsdale, NJ: Lawrence Erlbaum Associates.

Morais, J., Cary, L., Alegria, J., & Bertelson, P. (1979). Does awareness of speech as a series of phones arise spontaneously? *Cognition, 7*, 323–331.

Morris, R. D., Stuebing, K. K., Fletcher, J. M., Shaywitz, S. E., Lyon, G. R., Shankweiler, D., Katz, L., Francis, D. J., & Shaywitz, B. A. (1998). Subtypes of reading disability: Variability around a phonological core. *Journal of Educational Psychology, 90*(3), 1–27.

Olson, R. K., Foltz, G., & Wise, B. (1986). Reading instruction and remediation with the aid of computer speech. *Behavior Research Methods, Instruments, and Computers, 18*, 93–99.

Olson, R. K., & Wise, B. W. (1992). Reading on the computer with orthographic and speech feedback. *Reading and Writing: An Interdisciplinary Journal, 4*, 107–144.

Olson, R. K., Wise, B. W., Ring, J., & Johnson, M. (1997). Computer-based remedial training in phoneme awareness and phonological decoding: Effects on the posttraining development of word recognition. *Scientific Studies of Reading, 1*(3), 235–253.

Palincsar, A. S., & Brown, A. L. (1984). The reciprocal teaching of comprehension-fostering and comprehension-monitoring activities. *Cognition and Instruction, 1*, 117–175.

Paris, S. G., & Oka, E. R. (1989). Strategies for comprehending text and coping with reading difficulties. *Learning Disability Quarterly, 12*, 32–42.

Pennington, B. F., van Orden, G. C., Smith, S. D., Green, P. A., & Haith, M. M. (1990). Phonological processing skills and deficits in adult dyslexics. *Child Development, 61*, 1753–1778.

Prior, M., Frye, S., & Fletcher, C. (1987). Remediation for subgroups of retarded readers using a modified oral spelling procedure. *Developmental Medicine and Child Neurology, 29*, 64–71.

Rogosa, D. R., & Willitt, J. B. (1985). Understanding correlates of change by modelling individual differences in growth. *Psychometrika, 50*, 203–228.

Scanlon, D. M., & Vellutino, F. R. (1997). A comparison of the instructional backgrounds and cognitive profiles of poor, average, and good readers who were initially identified as at risk for reading failure. In J. P. Williams (Ed.), *Scientific studies of reading* (Vol. 1, pp. 191–216). Hillsdale, NJ: Lawrence Erlbaum Associates.

Scarborough, H. S. (1997, April). *Predicting the predictors of reading: Early precursors to phonological awareness, naming, letter knowledge in kindergarten.* Paper presented to the biennial meetings of the Society for Research in Child Development, Washington, DC.

Shanahan, T., & Barr, R. (1995). Reading recovery: An independent evaluation of the effects of an early instructional intervention for at-risk learners. *Reading Research Quarterly, 30*, 958–996.

Shankweiler, D., Crain, S., Katz, L., Fowler, A., Liberman, A., Brady, S., Thornton, R., Lundquist, E., Dreyer, L., Fletcher, J., Stuebing, K., Shaywitz, S., & Shaywitz, B. (1995). Cognitive profiles of reading disabled children: Comparison of language skills in phonology, morphology and syntax. *Psychological Science, 6*, 149–156.

Share, D. L. (1995). Phonological recoding and self-teaching. Sine qua non of reading acquisition. *Cognition, 55*, 151–218.

Shaywitz, B. A., & Shaywitz, S. E. (1994). Measuring and analyzing change. In G. R. Lyon (Ed.), *Frames of reference for the assessment of learning disabilities: New views on measurement issues* (pp. 59–68). Baltimore: Paul H. Brookes.

Snowling, M. J. (1996). Annotation contemporary approaches to the teaching of reading. *Journal of Child Psychology and Psychiatry, 37*, 139–148.

Snowling, M. J., & Hulme, C. (1989). A longitudinal case study of developmental phonological dyslexia. *Cognitive Neuropsychology, 6*, 379–401.

Spaai, G. W. G., Ellermann, H. H., & Reitsma, P. (1991). Effects of segmented and whole-word sound feedback on learning to read single words. *Journal of Educational Research, 84*, 204–213.

Stackhouse, J., & Snowling, M. J. (1992). Barriers to literacy development in two cases of developmental verbal dyspraxia. *Cognitive Neuropsychology, 9,* 273–300.

Stanovich, K. E. (1986). Matthew effects in reading: Some consequences of individual differences in the acquisition of literacy. *Reading Research Quarterly, 21,* 360–407.

Stanovich, K. E., & Siegel, L. S. (1994). Phenotypic performance profile of children with reading disabilities: A regression-based test of the phonological-core variable-difference model. *Journal of Educational Psychology, 86*(1), 24–53.

Stanovich, K. E., Siegel, L. S., & Gottardo, A. (1997). Converging evidence for phonological and surface subtypes of reading disability. *Journal of Educational Psychology, 89*(1), 114–127.

Stringer, R. (1997). *Adult reading disability and temporal processing deficits.* Unpublished doctoral dissertation, University of Toronto.

Tallal, P. (1980). Auditory temporal perception, phonics, and reading disabilities in children. *Brain and Language, 9,* 182–198.

Torgesen, J. K., Wagner, R. K., & Rashotte, C. A. (1997). Prevention and remediation of severe reading disabilities: Keeping the end in mind. In J. P. Williams (Ed.), *Scientific studies of reading* (Vol. 1, pp. 217–234). Hillsdale, NJ: Lawrence Erlbaum Associates.

Torgesen, J. K., Wagner, R. K., Rashotte, C. A., Alexander, A. W., & Conway, T. (1997). Preventive and remedial interventions for children with severe reading disabilities. *Learning Disabilities: A Multidisciplinary Journal, 8,* 51–62.

Treiman, R. (1992). The role of intrasyllabic units in learning to read and spell. In P. B. Gough, L. C. Ehri, & R. Treiman (Eds.), *Reading acquisition* (pp. 65–106). Hillsdale, NJ: Lawrence Erlbaum Associates.

van Daal, V. H. P., & Reitsma, P. (1990). Effects of independent word practice with segmented and whole-word sound feedback in disabled readers. *Journal of Research in Reading, 13,* 133–148.

Vellutino, F. R. (1979). *Dyslexia: Theory and research.* Cambridge, MA: MIT Press.

Vellutino, F. R., Scanlon, D. M., Sipay, E. R., Small, S. G., Pratt, A., Chen, R., & Denckla, M. B. (1996). Cognitive profiles of difficult-to-remediate and readily remediated poor readers: Early intervention as a vehicle for distinguishing between cognitive and experiential deficits as basic causes of specific reading disability. *Journal of Educational Psychology, 88*(4), 601–638.

Wagner, R. K., & Torgesen, J. K. (1987). The nature of phonological processing and its causal role in the acquisition of reading skills. *Psychological Bulletin, 101,* 192–212.

Wagner, R. K., Torgesen, J. K., Laughon, P., Simmons, K., & Rashotte, C. A. (1993). Development of young readers' phonological processing abilities. *Journal of Educational Psychology, 85*(1), 83–103.

Wagner, R. K., Torgesen, J. K., & Rashotte, C. A. (1994). Development of reading-related phonological processing abilities: New evidence of bidirectional causality from a latent variable longitudinal study. *Developmental Psychology, 30*(1), 73–87.

Wagner, R. K., Torgesen, J. K., Rashotte, C. A., Hecht, S. A., Barker, T. A., Burgess, S. R., Donahue, J., & Garon, T. (1997). Changing relations between phonological processing abilities and word-level reading as children develop from beginning to skilled readers: A five year longitudinal study. *Developmental Psychology, 33*(3), 468–479.

Wise, B., & Olson, R. K. (1995). Computer-based phonological awareness and reading instruction. *Annals of Dyslexia, 45,* 99–122.

Wise, B. W. (1992). Whole words and decoding for short-term learning: Comparisons on a "talking-computer" system. *Journal of Experimental Child Psychology, 54*(2), 147–167.

Wise, B. W., Olson, R., Anstett, M., Andrews, L., Terjak, M., Schneider, V., Kostuch, J., & Kriho, L. (1989). Implementing a long-term computerized remedial reading program with synthetic speech feedback: Hardware, software, and real world issues. *Behavior Research Methods, Instruments, and Computers, 21,* 173–180.

Wise, B. W., Ring, J., Sessions, L., & Olson, R. K. (1997). Phonological awareness with and without articulation: A preliminary study. *Learning Disability Quarterly, 20*(3), 211–225.

Wolf, M. (1997). A provisional integrative account of phonological and naming speed deficits in dyslexia: Implications for diagnosis and intervention. In B. Blachman (Ed.), *Foundations of reading acquisition and dyslexia: Implications for early intervention* (pp. 67–92). Mahwah, NJ: Lawrence Erlbaum Associates, Inc.

Wolf, M. (1997). *RAVE-O: A curriculum for the development of skills in retrieval-rate, accuracy, vocabulary elaboration, and orthography.* Instructional manual, Tufts University, Medford, MA.

Wolf, M. (1991). Naming speed and reading: The contribution of the cognitive neurosciences. *Reading Research Quarterly, 26,* 123–141.

Wolf, M., & Bowers, P. (1999). The "double-deficit hypothesis" for the developmental dyslexias. *Journal of Educational Psychology, 91*(3), 415–438.

Wolf, M., Pfeil, C., Lotz, R., & Biddle, K. (1994). Towards a more universal understanding of the developmental dyslexias: The contribution of orthographic factors. In V. W. Berninger (Ed.), *The varieties of orthographic knowledge* (Vol. 1, pp. 137–171). Dordrecht: Kluwer Academic.

Author Index

A

AAMR, 258, 272
Abbeduto, L., 258, 273
Abbott, R., 280, 282, 283, 284, 285,
    286, 287, 290, 291, 292, 294,
    296, 297, 298, 299, 300, 301,
    302, 304, 305, 307, 329, 332
Abbott, S., 286, 291, 292, 294, 301,
    303, 304, 305
Abello, B., 327, 329, 333
Adamlab, 261, 272
Adams, A., 155, 156, 176, 179
Adams, M., 276, 304
Adamson, L., 257, 265, 269, 272, 273
Adler, A., 2, 21
Adolfsson, R., 60, 78
Agronin, M., 28, 31, 34, 35, 36, 47, 50
Ahearn, M., 47, 51
Akhtar, N., 85, 103, 109
Aldenderfer, M., 132, 133
Alegria, J., 323, 335
Alexander, A., 325, 328, 331, 336
Allen, D., 69, 79
Allen, T., 162, 182
Als, H., 209, 220
Albert, J., 158, 180
Aman, C., 167, 176

Amir, N., 226, 228, 253
Anderson, J., 49, 51
Anderson, J. R., 72, 77
Anderson, P., 152, 153, 176
Anderson, R., 318, 333
Anderson, V., 152, 153, 176
Andrews, L., 293, 321, 308, 336
Anstatt, M., 293, 321, 308, 336
Antalffy, B., 66, 77
Antonak, R., 5, 20
Anthony, B., 47, 51
Anvret, M., 66, 78
APA, 68, 77
Appel, K., 121, 135
Aram, D., 226, 227, 252, 254
Arcus, D., 72, 79
Armstrong, D., 66, 77
Arthur, G., 260, 270, 272
Ashbaker, M., 166, 183
Atkins, M., 23, 50, 168, 184
Auld, P., 124, 127, 136
Avenovoli, S., 64, 79
Aylward, E., 65, 77
Azuma, H., 86, 109

B

Baddeley, A., 153, 154, 176
Baer, R., 114, 134, 148, 151, 177

Baillargeon, R., 122, 125, 126, 133
Bakeman, R., 83, 264, 265, 267, 109,
    273
Baker, S., 154, 156, 179
Bakker, D., 310, 331
Baldwin, C., 85, 111
Balla, D., 232, 250
Ballard, J., 87, 109
Bally, H., 227, 238, 254
Balow, B., 5, 22, 47
Barkeley, R., 47, 50, 117, 133, 163,
    167, 168, 176
Barker, T., 310, 311, 321, 323, 333
Barkovich, A., 129, 133
Barnard, K., 4, 18, 83, 20, 109
Barocas, R., 18, 22
Baron-Cohen, S., 160, 176
Barr, R., 276, 304, 335
Barron, R., 311, 314, 322, 323, 326,
    329, 331, 332, 334
Barta, P., 65, 77
Barthelemy, C., 164, 185
Bartolucci, G., 164, 184
Bartsch, K., 121, 124, 137
Bates, E., 271, 272
Batshaw, M., 65, 78
Battig, W., 234, 254
Bauman, M., 70, 77, 78
Bayley, N., 89, 109, 203, 209, 220
Bayles, J., 159, 181
Bayles, K., 159, 181
Beaver, S., 119, 135
Beck, B., 18, 22
Beck, E., 191, 192, 193, 221, 223
Beck, F., 5, 20
Becker, M., 149, 152, 176
Becker, W., 319, 332
Beckwith, L., 188, 221
Bee, H., 4, 18, 20, 83, 109
Bell, J., 160, 176
Bell, M., 122, 125, 128, 129, 130, 131,
    132, 133
Bellugi, U., 67, 68, 78, 79
Belichenko, P., 66, 78
Benedict, H., 271, 272
Benersky, M., 88, 109
Bennett, W., 197, 221

Bennetto, L., 117, 136, 141, 143, 144,
    147, 165, 166, 167, 176, 182
Benson, D., 142, 143, 183
Benson, N., 314, 316, 318, 320, 323,
    324, 326, 329, 330, 334
Bentler, P., 19, 20, 284, 304
Bento, S., 187, 223
Benton, A., 133, 140, 141, 147, 151,
    152, 153, 176, 180, 234, 252,
    310. 332
Bereiter, C., 280, 307
Berko Gleason, J., 257, 272252
Berndt, R., 225
Berninger, V., 275, 280, 281, 282, 283,
    284, 285, 286, 287, 288, 289,
    290, 291, 292, 294, 295, 296,
    297, 298, 299, 300, 301, 302,
    303, 304, 305, 307, 308,.329,
    332
Bernstein, A., 6, 21
Berry, H., 167, 182
Bertelson, P., 323, 335
Bertolino-Kusnerik, L., 120, 130, 136
Bertrand, J., 271, 273
Best, C., 168, 180
Betz, J., 190, 222
Bhanttacharyya, A., 168, 176
Biddle, B., 253, 299, 305
Biddle, K., 114, 115, 134, 228, 227,
    233, 250, 252, 266, 283, 305,
    321, 337
Biemiller, A., 276, 305
Bihrle, A., 234, 252
Bijou, S., 291, 306
Belichenko, P., 66, 78
Birbaumer, N., 190, 223
Bjorklund, D., 59, 74, 78, 145, 150,
    160, 161, 176, 179
Black, J., 122, 125, 126, 133
Blashfield, R., 132, 133, 136
Bliss, L., 252, 228, 233, 266
Blumenstein, E., 120, 137
Blum, L., 49, 51
Bocian, K., 50, 51
Bockes, T., 158, 162, 166, 172
Bohan, T., 119, 135
Bolter, J., 147, 148, 176
Bonjean, C., 9, 20

Boone, K., 144, 176
Borden, S., 316, 317, 318, 320, 323, 325, 329, 334
Borkowski, J., 116, 134, 318, 332
Bornstein, M., 86, 105, 109
Borys, S., 152, 176
Boucher, J., 163, 176
Boucugnani, L., 167, 176
Bouma, A., 310, 331
Bowers, P., 248, 249, 252, 321, 326, 328, 332, 337
Boyd, R., 58, 79
Boyes-Braem, P., 234, 254
Bracken, B., 18, 20
Brackstone, D., 316, 318, 320, 323, 325, 329, 334
Bradley, L., 310, 312, 332
Bradley, R., 9, 20
Brady, S., 312, 335
Bragg, R., 281, 284, 286, 305
Braine, M., 265, 272
Brandt, D., 291, 307
Brandt, T., 119, 135
Brazelton, T., 209, 220, 221
Brennan, M., 175, 184
Breslau, N., 2, 21
Bringle, R., 4, 22
Broekhoven, L., 3, 21
Brooks, A., 294, 305
Brooksher, R., 294, 304
Brookshire, B., 119, 135
Broverman, D., 189, 224
Brown, A., 325, 335
Brown, I., 312, 332
Brown, JE., 163, 179
Brown, JV., 83, 109
Brown, R., 271, 272
Brownell, H., 234, 252
Bruce, D., 120, 130, 136, 140, 180
Bruce, O., 226, 253
Bruck, M., 290, 312, 332
Bruhn, P., 162, 180
Bruner, E., 319, 332
Bruner, J., 82, 90, 110, 111, 271, 273
Bryant, P., 310, 312, 332, 333
Bryk, A., 102, 110, 119, 134, 281, 301, 305
Buck, R., 63, 77

Buhrke, R., 208, 222
Bullugi, U., 67, 78
Burgemeister, B., 49, 51
Burger-Judisch, L., 208, 222
Burgess, P., 143, 183
Burgess, S., 310, 311, 321, 323, 336
Burgoyne, K., 83, 110
Burke, J., 116, 134
Burstein, R., 87, 111
Burstein, V., 87, 111
Busk, J., 193, 197, 198, 221
Butler, B., 198, 199, 203, 221
Butterfield, E., 285, 306
Butterworth, G., 91, 110

C

Cairns, N., 65, 70, 78
Caldwell, B., 9, 20
Callender, G., 127, 134, 158, 162, 166, 174, 178
Callaway, C., 190, 221
Callaway, E ., 193, 195, 197, 198, 205, 223
Campbell, T., 156, 179
Cannon, A., 226, 253
Caramazza, A., 225, 252
Carlton, M., 226, 227, 254
Carnine, L., 319, 332
Caroll, J., 234, 252
Carpenter, P., 153, 157, 176
Carr, R., 167, 184
Carr, T., 297, 305
Carrel, T., 191, 206, 221
Cartwright, A., 282, 286, 304, 305
Carullo, J., 156, 178
Carvajal, H., 5, 20
Cary, L., 323, 335
Case, R., 141, 145, 148, 153, 154, 155, 156, 164, 166, 176
Castles, A., 312, 332
Ceci, S., 6, 17, 18, 21
Chajcsyk, D., 167, 184
Chalke, F., 193, 194, 196, 203, 205, 221
Chall, J., 276, 287, 305
Chamove, A., 162, 176
Chan, M., 65, 77
Chance, G., 187, 223

Chandler, M., 16, 22
Changeux, J., 144, 145, 176
Chapieksi, M., 83, 84, 85, 94, 110
Chapman, R., 263, 264, 272
Chapman, S., 180, 226, 253
Chapman, S.B., 120, 130, 136, 140
Charraro, A., 180, 259
Chase, G., 163, 179
Chattopadhyay, P., 168, 176
Chelune, G., 114, 134, 148, 151, 167, 176
Chen, R., 284, 285, 307, 312, 324, 325, 329, 336
Chou, C., 19, 20
Chueh, D., 65, 78
Chugani, H., 129, 134, 148, 171, 176
Cicchetti, D., 232, 254, 271, 272
Cicerello, A., 175, 184
Clark, B., 4, 18, 20
Clark, H., 61, 62, 63, 72, 77
Clark, W., 119, 137
Clinton, A., 286, 291, 292, 301, 304
Cloninger, C., 60, 78
Cochran, K., 166, 183
Cohen, D., 162, 183
Cohen, J., 140, 144, 145, 176
Cohen, S., 3, 16, 21, 188, 221
Cohen, H., 207, 208, 223
Cole, L., 260, 272
Collins, K., 156, 178
Collins, P., 60, 78
Coltheart, M., 312, 332
Connell, F., 65, 79
Conway, A., 145, 176
Conway, T., 325, 328, 331, 336
Cookson, N., 175, 180
Cooley, E., 47, 51
Cooper, F., 207, 221
Copeland, D., 82, 108, 111
Corter, C., 84, 110
Costa, P., 157, 176
Cote, F., 167, 178
Cournoyer, M., 159, 176
Cox, C., 163, 179
Crain, S., 312, 335
Crammond, J., 154, 176
Crawford, J., 83, 110

Crisafi, M., 2, 21
Critchey, M., 119, 134
Crnic, K., 83, 110
Crockenberg, S., 81, 110
Crook, C., 103, 110
Cross, D., 121, 124, 137
Cross, P., 160, 176
Crowson, M., 160, 176
Cuksts, B., 322, 323, 329, 334
Culbertson, W., 144, 176
Culhane, K., 114, 117, 120, 130, 136, 140, 175, 180, 226, 253
Cuneo, K., 159, 160, 171, 175, 176, 184
Cunningham, P., 318, 333
Curtis, M., 233, 253
Curtis, S., 219, 221

D

Dabholkar, A., 129, 136
Damasio, A., 114, 134
Damasio, H., 114, 134
Daneman, M., 157, 176
Das, J., 168, 176
Davidson, K., 118, 119, 135
Davies, P., 234, 252
Davis, D., 167, 178
Davis J., 248, 254
Davison, R., 157, 135
Dawson, G., 148, 178
Day, L., 158, 180
de Jong, L., 163, 164, 183
Deffebach, K., 265, 272
Dehaene, S., 144, 145, 176
Delis, D., 120, 137
DeLuca, T., 316, 318, 320, 323, 325, 329, 334
Dembure, P., 162, 180
Dempster, F., 158, 176
Denckla, M., 140, 163, 166, 167, 176, 178, 179, 182, 226, 227, 253, 254, 312, 315, 324, 325, 329, 332, 336
Dennis, M., 226, 227, 228, 234, 252, 253, 254
Denson, S., 84, 88, 110
Depue, R., 60, 78

Deser, T., 226, 253
DeVos, J., 122, 125, 126, 133
Diamond, A., 121, 123, 125, 126, 127,
    128, 129, 131, 134, 140, 144,
    147, 158, 159, 162, 166, 167,
    171, 174, 176, 179
Diaz, S., 154, 178
Dickey, T., 167, 176
DiLalla, L., 4, 21
Doar, B., 123, 125, 126, 129, 134
Dodge, K., 81, 110
Doi, L., 312, 334
Donahue, J., 310, 311, 321, 323, 336
Donaldson, S., 314, 315, 316, 334
Dorans, B., 152, 162, 165, 167, 176
Douglas, V., 165, 178, 183
Downer, M., 318, 319, 333
Downes, J., 141, 181
Doyle, A., 155, 184
Dreyer, L., 312, 335
Drillien, C., 83, 110
Driscoll, J., 2, 21
Driver, M., 87, 109
Drudge, O., 4, 21
Druin, D., 127, 134, 158, 162, 166,
    174, 178
Dubes, R., 1, 21
Duncan, C., 47, 51
Dunham, F., 85, 103, 109
Dunham, P., 85, 103, 109
Dunn, K., 66, 77
Dunn, L., 209, 232, 253, 260, 270, 272,
    221
Dunn, L. M., 209, 232, 253, 260, 270,
    272, 221
Dunn, M., 69, 79
DuPaul, G., 163, 168, 176
Dustman, R., 191, 192, 193, 221, 223

E

Edgell, D., 142, 168, 183
Edwards, R., 4, 5, 21
Ehri, L., 278, 305
Eimas, P., 206, 208, 221
Eisele, J., 319, 332
Eisenberg, H., 120, 130, 136, 140, 151,
    152, 153, 180

Ekelman, B., 226, 227, 252
Ekman, P., 60, 78
Elbert, T., 190, 223
Eliez, S., 67, 79
Ellermann, H., 322, 335
Ellingson, R., 189, 221, 224
Elliott, T., 318, 333
Ellis, A. E., 124, 127, 128, 131, 136,
    286
Ellis, A. W., 305, 322, 323, 325, 333
Elsas, L., 162, 180
Embretson, S., 117, 134
Engel, R., 191, 192, 193, 198, 199, 203,
    205, 206, 221
Engelmann, S., 319, 322
Engle, R. W., 145, 176, 178
Ertl, J., 190, 191, 193, 194, 196, 203,
    205, 221
Escobar, M., 29, 43, 48, 52, 119, 137
Eslinger, P., 114, 115, 116, 134, 227,
    250, 253
Espy, K., 119, 123, 126, 130, 134
Estrada, M., 318, 332
Evankovich, K., 114, 117, 136
Evans, B., 187, 223
Evans, W., 121, 135
Everett, J., 167, 178
Ewers, C., 166, 183
Ewing Cobbs, L., 114, 117, 120, 136,
    226, 253
Eyres, S., 4, 18, 20

F

Fang-Fircher, S., 65, 70, 78
Farah, M., 140, 144, 145, 180
Farrar, J., 85, 103, 110
Faust, D., 164, 178
Fay, W., 198, 199, 203, 205, 206, 221
Fedorov, A., 66, 78
Fein, D., 68, 69, 70, 79
Feinstein, C., 69, 70, 79
Felton, R., 312, 332
Ferguson, J., 75, 78
Ferguson, W., 167, 176
Ferris, G., 5, 22
Fiducia, D., 150, 153, 178
Fiedorowicz, C., 313, 332

Figueroa, R., 260, 272
Fiks, K., 2, 21
Fink, R., 296, 305
Finlayson, M., 164, 184
Fischer, K., 148, 178
Fischer, M., 4, 21
Fiske, A., 59, 78
Flavell, J., 141, 178
Fletcher, C., 313, 335
Fletcher, J., 51, 52, 88, 23, 29, 43, 47,
        48, 110, 114, 115, 117, 118,
        119, 120, 130, 131, 132, 135,
        136, 137, 140, 180, 226, 253,
        295, 307, 312, 323, 325, 328,
        330, 331, 332, 333, 335
Flick, G., 5, 22
Flower, L., 280, 306
Flynn, J., 6, 21
Foltz, G., 321, 335
Foorman, B., 323, 325, 328, 331, 332
Forbes, J., 322, 323, 329, 334
Foreman, N., 154, 156, 178
Forell, E., 295, 307
Foster, R., 270, 272
Fowler, A., 312, 332, 335
Fowler, D., 4, 18, 21
Fox, N., 122, 125, 128, 129, 130, 131,
        132, 133, 312, 334
Francis, D., 23, 51, 118, 119, 134, 135,
        312, 330, 331, 323, 325, 328,
        331, 332, 333, 335
Franklin, K., 270, 272
Freeman, R., 222
Friedes, D., 162, 180
Friedman, S., 175, 183
Friel, J., 295, 307
Frijters, J., 326, 329, 334
Fristoe, M., 315, 333
Frith, U., 163, 179, 277, 287, 288, 305
Fruth, M., 161, 179
Frye, S., 313, 335
Fuerst, D., 82, 110
Fuller, F., 281, 304
Fuster, J., 135, 179

G

Galbraith, G., 193, 197, 198, 221

Galbraith, R., 3, 21
Gallaburda, A., 67, 68, 78
Gardien, C., 310, 331
Gardner, E., 293, 306
Gardner, H., 225, 253
Garner, P., 82, 85, 90, 94, 108, 110,
        111
Garon, T., 310, 311, 321, 323, 336
Garreau, B., 164, 185
Gartner, G., 84, 110
Gaskins, I., 318, 319, 333
Gaskins, R., 318, 319, 333
Gathercole, S., 155, 156, 176, 179
Geary, D., 59, 74, 78
Gelfer, M., 208, 221
Gentry, J., 279, 305
German, D., 225, 233, 240, 245, 247,
        253
Gerstadt, C., 159, 179
Geva, E., 285, 307
Gholson, B., 160, 179
Giannuli, M., 5, 21
Gibson, E., 280, 306
Giddan, J., 270, 272
Gifford, E., 117, 135
Gill, L., 201, 222
Girnius-Brown, O., 86, 105, 110
Gittleman, R., 313, 329, 333
Glassman, M., 2, 21
Gliddon, J., 193, 197, 198, 221
Glisky, M., 123, 126, 130, 134
Glosser, D., 228, 253
Glosser, G., 226, 253
Gnys, J., 140, 179
Goel, V., 140, 141, 175, 179
Goetz, E., 284, 306
Goffman, E., 61, 62, 72, 78
Goldberg, S., 84, 105, 110, 111
Golden, C., 114, 135
Golden, J., 311, 332
Goldman, P., 121, 132, 135
Goldman, R., 315, 333
Goldman-Rakic, P., 129, 134, 135, 140,
        175, 179, 180
Goldstein, H., 119, 131, 135
Gonzalez, J., 144, 176
Goodglass, H., 225, 233, 240, 245,
        253, 254, 255

Gopnik, A., 60, 78
Gorenstein, E., 165, 167, 179
Gorsuch, R., 144, 176
Goswami, U., 278, 306, 310, 333
Gottardo, A., 312, 336
Gough, P., 278, 287, 288, 306
Gould, J., 68, 79
Graber, M., 122, 125, 126, 133
Grafman, J., 140, 141, 175, 179
Graham, P., 52
Graham, S., 117, 135, 280, 294, 305, 306
Grant, E., 187, 224
Gratch, G., 121, 135
Grattan, L., 114, 115, 134, 227, 250, 253
Gray, C., 4, 18, 20
Gray, J., 60, 78
Gray, W., 234, 254
Green, L., 70, 79
Green, P., 312, 335
Greenberg, M., 83, 110
Greene, C., 163, 181
Greenspan, S., 18, 22
Greep, K., 286, 291, 292, 301, 304
Gresham, F., 50, 51
Griffith, P., 278, 288, 306
Grigorenko, E., 312, 333
Grodzinsky, G., 140, 163, 167, 168, 176, 179
Groisser, D., 114, 117, 132, 137, 148, 150, 151, 152, 153, 158, 163, 171, 174, 182, 184
Gross Tsur, V., 226, 228, 253
Grossman, F., 4, 18, 21
Grossman, H., 260, 272
Grotjohn, D., 161, 179
Grover, W., 158, 162, 166, 178
Gualin, C., 156, 179
Gualtieri, C., 156, 179
Guess, D., 258, 272

H

Hack, M., 2, 21
Hagberg, B., 66, 78
Hagen, E., 9, 22, 231, 254

Hager, L., 140, 144, 146, 147, 174, 182
Haier, R., 65, 78
Haines, L., 311, 331
Haith, M., 312, 335
Halberstadt, A., 161, 179
Hale, C., 318, 332
Hall, S., 83, 84, 94, 110
Halliday, S., 154, 155, 156, 179
Halminski, M., 162, 180
Hamburger, S., 163, 167, 182, 183
Hammond, M., 4, 18, 20, 83, 109
Hamsher, D., 234, 252
Hans, L., 208, 222
Hardwick, N., 314, 315, 316, 334
Harlow, J., 114, 135
Harm, M., 289, 295, 306
Harnishfeger, K., 145, 150, 160, 161, 176, 179
Harris, E., 140, 163, 167, 179, 182
Harris, K., 117, 135, 294, 306
Harris, P., 121, 135
Harris, Y., 160, 181
Hart, L., 312, 333
Hart, T., 275, 288, 297, 298, 304, 305
Harward, H., 114, 117, 120, 130, 136, 140, 180, 226, 253
Hatcher, P., 322, 323, 325, 333
Hartmann, J., 114, 117, 136
Hayes, A., 65, 78
Hayes, J., 280, 306
Hayes, S., 117, 135
Hearn, E., 75, 78
Heaton, R., 114, 131, 135
Hecht, S., 310, 311, 321, 323, 336
Helwig, S., 16, 21
Henderson, E., 278, 280, 306
Henderson, N., 191, 192, 193, 198, 199, 204, 205, 221
Henriksen, L., 162, 180
Hermelin, B., 163, 179
Heron, C., 140, 144, 146, 147, 174, 182
Hertzog, C., 120, 135
Hess, T., 207, 208, 222
Hewison, J., 313, 329, 333
Hicks, R., 162, 179
Hill, R., 9, 20

Hinchley, J., 330, 334
Hitch, G., 153, 154, 155, 156, 166,
    176, 179, 184
Hoffman, W., 167, 182
Hofstadter, M., 124, 126, 128, 131, 135
Holahan, J., 23, 28, 29, 30, 31, 34, 35,
    36, 47, 50, 51
Holcomb, L., 16, 21
Hollingshead, A., 87, 110
Honeycutt, N., 65, 77
Hong, Y., 159, 179
Hooper, S., 147, 184
Hooven, C., 286, 291, 292, 301, 304
Hooven, W., 287, 306
Horn, J., 193, 195, 196, 197, 203, 205,
    223
Horner, R., 258, 272
Horowitz, S., 254
Howe, M., 121, 136
Hughes, C., 167, 179
Huisman, ., 163, 164, 183
Hulme, C., 153, 156, 157, 166, 322,
    323, 325, 333, 335
Humes, G., 175, 179, 180
Hunt, M., 167, 182
Hurwitz, W., 158, 162, 166, 176
Huttenlocher, P., 129, 148, 180
Hutton, J., 1, 21
Hynd, G., 149, 150, 152, 176, 181

I

Iacono, T., 257, 173
Insel, T., 60, 62, 65, 70, 71, 75, 78
Isaac, W., 149, 150, 152, 176, 181

J

Jackson, N., 285, 306
Janowsky, J., 131, 136
Jaspser, H., 190, 221
Jastak, J., 291, 306
Jastak, S., 291, 306
Jensen, J., 163, 164, 167, 168, 181
Jerram, M., 65, 77
Johns, M., 314, 315, 316, 334
Johnson, C., 161, 179, 180
Johnson, D., 234, 254

Johnson, G., 319, 332
Johnson, H., 2, 21
Johnson, K., 4, 18, 21
Johnson, M., 30, 317, 324, 325, 335
Johnson, M. B., 30, 52
Johnston, J., 281, 299, 308
Jones, R., 167, 176
Jones, W., 67, 79
Jordan, F., 226, 253
Jorm, A., 48, 49, 51
Juel, C., 278, 288, 306
Jusczyk, P., 206, 208,
Just, M., 153, 176

K

Kagan, J., 72, 78, 79, 158, 180
Kaler, S., 89, 110
Kalverboer, A., 163, 164, 183
Kaplan, E., 228, 233, 245, 253, 254
Karchmar, E., 3, 21
Karlson, B., 293, 306
Karnes, F., 4, 5, 21
Katada, A., 168, 184
Katz, K., 187, 224
Katz, L., 23, 51, 312, 332, 335
Kaufman, J., 6, 22
Kaufmann, P., 120, 121, 123, 126, 130,
    131, 134, 136
Kavale, K., 318, 333
Keeney, A., 295, 306
Keeney, V., 295, 306
Kellam, S., 47, 51
Kelly, M., 168, 180
Kemper, T., 70, 77, 78
Keogh, B., 23, 50, 51
Kepler, M., 152, 153, 161, 180
Keppel, G., 118, 136
Kiessling, L., 226, 227, 254
Kim (Yoon), Y., 284, 306
Kimberg, D., 140, 144, 145, 180
Kinchla, R., 47, 51
King, S., 5, 20
Kirk, U., 168, 180
Kitao, S., 168, 184
Klahr, D., 152, 180
Klausmeier, K., 5, 21

Kochanska, G., 86, 92, 105, 110
Koch, D., 191, 206, 221
Koegel, L., 73, 78
Koegel, R., 73, 78
Kohn, B., 226, 253
Kohn, S., 225, 254
Kolb, B., 141, 158, 180
Koon, R., 167, 176
Kopp, C., 89, 91, 159, 108, 110, 180, 184
Koslow, S., 190, 221
Kostuch, J., 293, 321, 308, 336
Kovar, C., 163, 181
Krakow, J., 159, 184
Kramer, J., 157, 181
Krasnegor, N., 113, 116, 131, 136, 140, 180
Kraus, N., 191, 206, 221
Kraus, P., 295, 306
Krause, W., 162, 180
Kreder, S., 162, 183
Kritho, L., 293, 321, 308, 336
Kuczynski, L., 86, 92, 105, 110
Kusnerick, L., 130, 140, 180

L

Labudova, O., 65, 70, 78
Lacerenza, L., 316, 318, 320, 323, 325, 329, 334
Lai, Z., 67, 79
Lajoie, G., 152, 153, 176
Lalonde, C., 171, 178
Lambert, N., 260, 272
Landry, S., 82, 83, 84, 85, 86, 88, 92, 94, 95, 98, 103, 108, 110, 111
Laughon, P., 310, 336
Laure-Kamionowska, M., 65, 79
Lavine, L., 280, 306
Leckman, J., 71, 78, 121, 130, 131, 136
LeCompte, G., 121, 135
Lecours, A., 148, 185
Lee, E., 158, 162, 166, 176
Leech, G., 61, 63, 78
Leicht, D., 208, 223
Lelord, G., 164, 185
Lemos, Z., 294, 305
Lenneberg, E ., 189, 209, 226, 221, 254

Lenzenwager, M., 72, 79
Leontovich, T., 66, 78
Leslie, N., 167, 182
Lester, B., 209, 220
Lester, K., 297, 305
Leung, E., 92, 111
Levesque, J., 167, 178
Levin, H., 70, 79, 114, 117, 118, 120, 130, 135, 136, 140, 151, 152, 153, 180, 226, 252, 280, 306
Levine, D., 145, 180
Levine, M., 160, 179
Levy, B., 293, 294, 306, 327, 329, 333
Lewis, M., 88, 105, 109, 111
Lewis, V., 271, 273
Li, Q., 65, 77
Liberman, A., 48, 51, 207, 221, 312, 335
Liberman, I., 23, 48, 51, 312, 332
Libon, D., 164, 178
Liederman, J., 225, 254
Lilly, M., 120, 130, 136, 140, 180
Lindamood, C ., 324, 325, 333
Lindamood, P., 324, 325, 333
Lindsey, J., 5, 20
Linnville, S., 208, 222
Littman, B., 209, 222
Livesey, P., 160, 176, 180
Llinas, R., 251, 252, 254
Loew, D., 4, 21
Logan, G., 167, 168, 183, 184
Logan, C., 167, 183
Lojkasek, M., 84, 110
Long, C., 147, 148, 176
Logue, A., 159, 180
Lord, C., 73, 78
Lorge, I., 49, 51, 235, 254
Lott, I., 65, 78
Lotz, R., 321, 337
Lou, H., 162, 180
Lovegrove, W., 310, 333
Loveland, K., 167, 182
LoVerme, S., 228, 253
Lovett, M., 226, 253, 312, 313, 314, 315, 316, 317, 318, 320, 322, 323, 324, 325, 326, 329, 330, 332, 333, 334
Low, J ., 3, 21

Lowy, J., 5, 20
Lubec, G., 65, 70, 78
Luciana, M., 140, 151, 152, 155, 174, 180
Ludemann, P., 86, 109
Lundberg, I., 301, 306
Lundquist, E., 312, 335
Lunnenborg, C., 282, 299, 306, 307
Luria, A., 116, 136, 141, 142, 180
Lutzenberger, W., 190, 223
Luu, P., 64, 78
Lyon, G., 113, 116, 131, 136, 140, 180,
    322, 329, 330, 334, 335
Lysynchuck, L., 293, 294, 306, 327,
    329, 333

M

Macar, F., 190, 223
Maccoby, E., 82, 85, 111
MacDonald, K., 105, 111
Mackenzie, S., 153, 156, 157, 166, 179
Maclean, R., 48, 49, 51
Madden, R., 293, 306
MacMillian, D., 50, 51
Mahoney, A., 168, 184
Maker, J., 5, 21
Makuch, R., 29, 51, 119, 137
Mammato, C., 165, 167, 179
Manis, F., 312, 334
Manor, O., 226, 228, 253
Marchione, K., 23, 51
Marfo, K., 105, 111
Marlin, M., 299, 305
Marmurek, H., 311, 332
Marriott, M., 167, 183
Martin, J., 82, 111, 162, 183
Matthews, A., 124, 127, 128, 131, 136
Matthews, R., 48, 49, 51
Mattson, A., 114, 117, 136
Matzuk, M., 75, 78
Maurice, C., 73, 78
Mazzocco, M., 163, 181
McAleer, O., 117, 136, 141, 143, 144,
    147, 182
McArdle, J., 131, 136
McAuley, E., 166, 179
McBride Chang, C., 312, 334

McCabe, A ., 228, 233, 252, 266
McCabe, E., 140, 152, 162, 163, 166,
    167, 182, 184
McCabe, R., 322, 332
McCall, R., 158, 181
McCallum, S., 4, 5, 21
McCarthy, D., 18, 21, 209, 222
McCrae, R., 157, 176
McDiarmid, M., 123, 126, 130, 134
McDonald, S., 226, 254
McDonald, L., 162, 180
McEvoy, R., 124, 127, 164, 167, 181
McGee, R., 47, 49, 51, 52, 188, 221, 224
McGee, T., 191, 206, 224
McIntyre, C., 167, 178
McKenna, M., 288, 294, 307
McKnab, P., 5, 20
McLemore, S., 9, 20
McMahon, W., 164, 167, 181
Mearn, E., 75
Mehta, P., 323, 325, 328, 331, 332
Meisels, S., 85, 111
Meltzer, L., 318, 334
Meltzoff, A., 60, 78
Mendelsohn, D., 120, 130, 136, 140,
    180, 226, 253   ·
Menkes, J., 118, 136
Menna, R., 154, 181
Mensink, D., 168, 176
Merrill, M., 203, 224, 273
Mervis, C., 234, 254, 271, 273
Mesulam, M., 232, 254
Meyer, L., 319, 332
Meyer, M., 312, 333
Michaud, D., 167, 176
Michelow, D., 234, 252
Milich, R., 157, 181
Miller, B., 144, 176
Miller, J., 263, 264, 272
Miller, P., 160, 181
Miller-Loncar, C., 82, 85, 86, 95, 98, 111
Milner, B., 140, 141, 181
Milstead, M., 318, 332
Mims, S., 167, 178
Minarcik, C., 158, 162, 166, 178
Miner, M., 120, 135, 136
Mirenda, P., 257, 270, 273

Mirsky, A., 47, 51
Mischel, W., 159, 181
Mishra, R., 168, 176
Mishra, S., 5, 21
Mizokawa, D., 281, 284, 286, 297, 305
Moats, L., 329, 330, 334
Modahl, C., 68, 70, 79
Moenkemann, H., 65, 70, 78
Mohr., 163, 179
Moizo, C., 155, 181
Molfese, D., 187, 190, 198, 200, 201,
        202, 205, 206, 207, 208, 209,
        210, 211, 212, 213, 214, 215,
        215, 219, 220, , 222, 223, 224
Molfese, V., 3, 4, 16, 190, 198, 200,
        201, 205, 206, 207, 208, 209,
        212, 213, 214, 215, 219, 223
Molinario, T., 162, 176
Morgan, G., 160, 180
Morias, J., 323, 335
Morine Dershimer, G., 50, 51
Morra, S., 155, 181
Morris, D., 277, 307
Morris, M., 70, 79
Morris, R., 47, 51, 69, 119, 132, 137,
        227, 238, 225, 335
Mostafapour, E., 294, 304
Muehl, S., 295, 307
Muir, D., 3, 21
Muir, S., 1, 21
Mukhina, J., 66, 78
Munson, R., 190, 223
Murdoch, B., 226, 253
Murray, M., 167, 178
Murray, P., 154, 156, 178
Mutter, B., 154, 160, 171, 181

N

Nagy, W., 289, 307
Nass, T., 124, 127, 136
Nathan, R., 290, 307
Neale, M., 49, 51
Nelson, C., 124, 127, 128, 131, 136,
        140, 151, 152, 155, 174, 180,
        190, 223
Nelson, K., 271, 273
NICHHD, 295, 307

Nicol, T., 191, 206, 221
Nolen, S., 280, 286, 301, 304
Nord, A., 163, 181
Norman, D., 143, 181
Norton, A., 167, 182
Novak, K., 87, 109

O

Oades, R., 162, 181
Obregon, M., 225, 232, 239, 249, 254
O'Brien, D., 71, 78
Oconnor, M., 3, 21
O'Connor, N., 163, 179
O'Flahven, J., 288, 289, 307
Ogier, S., 294, 304
O'Gorman, A., 226, 227, 254
Ojemann, G., 228, 251, 252, 254
Oka, E., 318, 335
Olds, J., 314, 316, 324, 326, 334
OLeary, D., 150 153, 178
Olson, R., 293, 307, 308, 317, 321, 322,
        323, 324, 325, 335, 336, 337
Olson, S., 159, 181
Ort, S., 121, 130, 131, 136,
Osborn, J., 289, 307
Owen, A., 141, 181
Ozonoff, S., 140, 152, 162, 163, 164,
        167, 168, 181, 182, 184

P

Pagnucco, J., 288, 294, 307
Palermo, D., 222
Palincsar, A., 325, 335
Palmer, J., 83, 84, 94, 110
Papile, L., 87, 111
Paris, S., 318, 335
Parmelee, A., 3, 16, 21, 188, 179, 209,
        218, 221, 222
Parpal, M., 85, 111
Passler, M., 149, 150, 152, 181
Pate, J., 258, 270, 273
Patterson, C. J., 159, 181
Patterson, C. M., 120, 137
Pauls, D., 312, 333
Pearlson, G., 65, 77
Pearson, D., 167, 182

Pecheux, M., 86, 109
Pederson, D., 187, 223
Pelham, W., 23, 50
Pennington, B., 82, 108, 114, 116, 117,
    124, 127, 132, 133, 136, 137,
    139, 140, 141, 142, 143, 144,
    147, 148, 150, 151, 152, 153,
    158, 161, 162, 163, 164, 165,
    166, 167, 168, 171, 174, 176,
    181, 182, 184, 312, 335
Perecman, E., 140, 182
Perret, E., 141, 182
Peterson, A., 312, 334
Peterson, S., 47, 51
Pfeil, C., 321, 337
Phelps, M., 129, 134
Phillips, G., 270, 272
Phillips, S., 160, 179
Phillips, W., 158, 180
Piaget, J., 121, 125, 126, 136
Pinion, D., 132, 137
Pirie, D., 82, 90, 111
Plotkin, H., 72, 79
Plunkett, J., 85, 110
Pogge Hesse, P., 271, 272
Polkey, D., 141, 181
Pollatsek, A., 297, 305
Pontoon, M., 144, 176
Porter, T., 155, 184
Posner, M., 47, 51
Pratt, A., 312, 324, 325, 329, 336
Prevor, M., 127, 134, 158, 162, 166,
    174, 178
Prewett, P., 4, 5, 18, 21
Prior, M. M., 313, 335
Prior, M. R., 167, 182
Prueitt, P., 145, 180
Pueschel, S., 164, 178
Pulsifer, M., 65, 66, 77, 79

Q

Quiatt, D., 72, 79

R

Radke Yarrow, M., 86, 105, 110
Rahbar, M., 6, 21

Rahn, C., 86, 109
Rankin, J., 254
Ransby, M., 313, 314, 315, 316, 317,
    320, 326, 334
Rapoport, J., 162, 185
Rashotte, C., 310, 311, 321, 323, 324,
    325, 328, 331, 336
Raskind, W., 287, 304
Raudenbush, S., 102, 110, 119, 134,
    301, 305
Reader, M., 140, 163, 167, 179, 182
Reed, E., 286, 291, 292, 294, 301, 304,
    305
Reilly, T., 4, 21
Reiss, A., 67, 79
Reitsma, P., 322, 335, 336, 337
Remy, E., 282, 283, 305
Remy, P., 164, 185
Retzlaff, P., 175, 180
Reumann, R., 258, 273
Rey, H., 2, 21
Reynolds, V., 72, 79
Reznick, J., 124, 126, 128, 131, 132,
    135, 137
Rheingold, H., 92, 111
Rhodes, L., 191, 192, 193, 223
Richardson, M., 83, 84, 94, 110
Richerson, P., 58, 79
Richman, B., 234, 252
Richman, N., 52
Riese, M., 119, 134
Ring, J., 317, 324, 325, 335, 337
Ringholtz, G., 114, 117, 134
Ris, M., 167, 182
Risser, A., 142, 168 , 183
Robbins, P., 167, 182
Robbins, T., 141, 167, 181, 192
Roberts, R., 117, 136, 141, 140, 143,
    144, 146, 147, 167, 174, 176,
    182
Robertson, M., 160, 176
Robinson, B., 264, 265, 266, 267, 271,
    273
Robinson, S., 82, 108, 11
Rocissano, L., 85, 110
Rockstroh, B., 190, 223
Rogan, L., 294, 305

Rogers, S., 124, 127, 136, 162, 164,
     165, 166, 167, 176, 181
Rogosa, D., 291, 307
Rogosa, D. R., 330, 335
Romski, M., 257, 258, 259, 260, 261,
     264, 265, 266, 267, 268, 270,
     271, 272, 273, 274
Rosch, E., 234, 254
Rose, D., 226, 252
Rosen, J., 4, 21
Rosen, M., 301, 306
Rosen, T., 2, 21
Rosenberg, S., 258, 273
Rosenthal, R., 162, 182
Rosman, B., 158, 180
Ross, G., 124, 127, 136
Rosvold, H., 121, 135
Rothlisberg, B., 5, 22
Rourke, P., 82, 110
Rouse, B., 140, 152, 162, 163, 167, 184
Rubin, R., 5, 22
Ruchkin, D., 190, 223
Ruckstuhl, L., 117, 135
Rudel, R., 227, 233, 253, 315, 332
Ruff, H., 95, 110
Rumbaugh, D., 261, 273
Rumsey, J., 163, 167, 182, 183
Russell, J., 167, 179
Rutberg, J., 282, 283, 305
Rutter, M., 49, 51, 118, 136
Ryan, E., 165, 183

S

Sabatini, J., 296, 307
Sahakian, B., 141, 181
Salapatek, P., 190, 223
Salvo, R., 162, 180
Sameroff, A., 16, 18, 22
Samson, Y., 164, 185
Sandy J., 165, 167, 179
Satterlee Cartmell, T., 140, 175, 185
Sattler, J., 9, 22, 231, 254
Satz, P., 119, 132, 136, 137, 295, 307
Sayer, A., 300, 308
Scaafstal, A., 154, 155, 156, 179
Scaife, M., 90, 110

Scanlon, D., 284, 285, 307, 312, 324,
     325, 329, 335, 336
Scarborough, H., 311, 321, 335
Scardamalia, M., 280, 307
Scarr, S., 65, 73, 79
Schachar, R., 167, 168, 183
Schafer, E., 190, 191, 193, 205, 221
Schaffer, H., 81, 103, 110
Schaimberg, L., 18, 22
Schatschneider, C., 120, 323, 325, 328,
     331, 332
Schmidt, A., 208, 223
Schmitt, J., 67, 79
Schneider, V., 293, 308, 321, 336
Scholnick, E., 175, 183
Schommer, M., 318, 333
Schraagen, J., 154, 155, 156, 179
Schucard, D., 193, 195, 196, 197, 203,
     205, 223
Schuerholz, L., 140, 163, 167, 179, 182
Schwartz, S., 159, 184
Scopesi, A., 155, 181
Scottish Council for Research
     Education., 49, 51
Searock, K., 198, 200, 205, 210, 223
Segal, D., 233, 254
Segalowitz, S., 207, 208, 223
Sahakian, B., 141, 181
Seidenbert, M., 312, 334
Seifer, R., 18, 22
Seldon, D., 311, 332
Sellmann, A., 5, 22
Servan Schreiber, D., 145, 176
Sessions, L., 325, 337
Sevcik, R., 257, 258, 259, 260, 261,
     264, 265, 266, 267, 268, 269,
     270, 271, 272, 273, 284
Shalev, R., 226, 228, 253
Shallice, T., 143, 181 183
Shanahan, T., 329, 335
Shankweiler, D., 48, 51, 207, 221, 312,
     332, 335
Share, D., 48, 49, 51, 285, 310, 325, 335
Shatz, M., 85, 110
Shaywitz, B., 23, 28, 29, 30, 31, 34, 35,
     36, 43, 47, 48, 50, 51, 52,
     119, 131, 135, 137, 162, 183,
     312, 330, 332, 333, 335

Shaywitz, S., 23, 24, 28, 29, 30, 31, 34, 35, 36, 43, 47, 48, 50, 51, 52, 119, 131, 135, 137, 162, 183, 312, 330, 332, 333, 335
Sheinberg, L., 64, 79
Shepherd, G., 79
Shneider, A., 23, 51
Shue, K., 165, 183
Shurtleff, H., 300, 304
Shuster, A., 312, 333
Siedenberg, M., 289, 295, 306
Siegel, L., 2, 3, 4, 8, 16, 18, 22, 165, 183, 187, 223, 285, 307, 312, 336
Siegler, R., 141, 183
Sigueland, E., 206, 208, 221
Sigman, M., 188, 221
Silva, P., 47, 49, 51, 52 188, 224
Simmons, K., 310, 336
Simon, H., 115, 131, 137
Simos, P., 201, 208, 222, 224
Singer, H., 163, 179
Sipay, E., 312, 324, 325, 329, 336
Sleator, E., 23, 52
Slijper, F., 163, 164, 183
Small, S., 312, 324, 325, 329, 335, 336
Smith, A., 5, 22
Smith, C., 50, 51
Smith, K., 82, 85, 86, 95, 98, 111
Smith, P., 65, 77
Smith, R., 52
Smith, S., 312, 335
Smith, Y., 187, 224
Snell, M., 258, 273
Snidman, N., 72, 79
Snowling, M., 317, 323, 333, 335, 336
Snyder, C., 4, 18, 20
Soltis, J., 58, 79
Sostek, A., 187, 224
Spaai, G., 322, 335
Sparrow, S., 232, 254
Spearing, D., 307
Speed, W., 312, 333
Sperber, D., 61, 62, 72, 79
Spietz, A., 4, 18, 20
Spitz, H., 152, 176

Sprague, R., 23, 52
Spreen, O., 142, 168, 183
Spring, C., 248, 254
Spruill, J., 18
Spurlock, D., 5, 20
Stack, D., 160, 185
Stackhouse, J., 323, 336
Stage, S., 156, 183, 298, 304
Stahl, S., 288, 294, 307
Stamm, J., 162, 183
Stanovich, K., 48, 52, 290, 307, 310, 312, 336
Stark, J., 270, 272
Steffy, R., 248, 252
Steinbach, K., 316, 318, 322, 323, 325, 326, 329, 224
Stemerdink, N., 163, 164, 183
Sternberg, R., 6, 22
Steubing, K., 23, 51, 118, 312, 330, 332, 333, 335
Steubing, S., 119, 131, 135
Stevenson, J., 52
Stine, M., 140, 175, 185
Stoff, D., 168, 184
Straus, E., 67, 79
Strayer, D., 164, 167, 168, 181
Strich, S., 120, 137
Stringer, R., 311, 336
Strumpf, H., 126, 137
Studdert-Kennedy, M., 207, 221
Stuss, D., 142, 143, 183
Sueko, T., 86, 109
Sutton, S.K., 190, 223
Sutton, S., 157, 183
Svanunm, S., 4, 22
Svrakic, N., 60, 78
Swallow, J., 219, 224
Swank, P., 82, 84, 85, 86, 90, 95, 98, 110, 111
Swanson, H., 166, 183, 184, 280, 281, 282, 286, 299, 304, 305, 308
Swanson, L., 249, 252
Sylvester, L., 280, 286, 291, 292, 301, 304
Syrota, A., 164, 185
Szekeres, S., 226, 255
Szamari, P., 164, 184

T

Tait, C., 311, 332
Tal, J., 86, 109
Tallal, P., 310, 335
Tamis-LeMonda, C., 86, 105, 109
Tan, A., 201, 222
Tannock, R., 167, 183
Tate, E., 248, 252
Taylor, H., 115, 117, 120, 135, 137, 295, 304
Taylor, J., 286, 291, 292, 301
Terjak, M., 293, 308, 321, 336
Terman, L., 203, 223, 274
Tesman, J., 124, 127, 136
Teuber, H., 141, 184
Thatcher, R., 132, 137
Thomas, J., 167, 178
Thompson, L., 151, 176, 178
Thompson, N., 118, 119, 135
Thomson, A., 83, 110
Thomson, J., 287, 304
Thorndike, E., 235, 254
Thorndike, R., 9, 22, 231, 254
Thornton, R., 312, 335
Tipper, S., 168, 184
Tizard, J., 49, 51
Toglia, M., 234, 254
Tomasello, M., 85, 103, 110
Torgesen, J., 310, 311, 321, 323, 325, 328, 331, 336
Touchette, P., 65, 78
Trahan, M., 166, 184
Tramontana, M., 147, 184
Trannel, D., 114, 134
Travis, L., 209, 224
Traweek, D., 280, 292, 294, 299, 305, 307
Treiman, R., 279, 321, 307, 336
Tronick, E., 209, 220
Trudel, M., 159, 176
Tucker, D., 64, 78
Tueting, P., 190, 221
Tuff, L., 164, 184
Tunmer, W., 287, 306
Turkeimer, E., 58, 79

U

Ullman, R., 23, 52
Umetani, T., 168, 184

V

Vacc, N., 4, 22
Van Daal., 332, 336
van der Meere, J., 163, 164, 183
van der Molen, M., 163, 164, 183
van Doorninck, W., 163, 166, 167, 181, 182
van Orden, G., 312, 335
van Spronsen, F., 163, 164, 183
Vardi, D., 86, 109
Vargha Khadem, F., 226, 227, 254
Varnhagen, C., 279, 307
Vaughan, K., 294, 305
Vaughn, B., 159, 184, 279, 307
Vellutino, F., 278, 284, 285, 307, 311, 312, 324, 325, 329, 335, 336
Venezky, R., 279, 296, 307, 308
Verderk, P., 163, 164, 183
Vigorito, J., 206, 208, 221
Vitiello, B., 168, 184
Vogel, W., 188, 189, 224
Volpe, J., 86, 110
Vygotsky, L., 81, 110

W

Wagner, R., 156, 183, 310, 311, 321, 323, 324, 325, 328, 331, 336
Wahlstroem, J., 66, 78
Walker, P., 155, 184
Wallner Allen, K., 175, 183
Walsh, M., 287, 306
Wang, S., 208, 222
Warren, A., 65, 77
Warren Chaplin, P., 317, 320, 334
Warry, R., 154, 156, 178
Waterhouse, L., 68, 69, 70, 79
Waters, G., 226, 227, 254
Weaver, K., 5, 20
Wechsler, D., 6, 9, 22, 30, 49, 52, 216, 224, 234, 254

Weinberg, H., 194, 197, 224
Weintraub, N., 280, 306
Weintraub, S., 233, 254
Wellman, H., 121, 124, 137
Welsch, M., 82, 108, 110, 114, 117,
    137, 139, 140, 142, 148, 150,
    151, 152, 153, 158, 159, 160,
    162, 163, 165, 167, 171, 174,
    175, 176, 180, 182, 184, 185
Wen, G., 65, 79
Werker, J., 171, 178
Werner, E., 52
Werner, H., 289, 291, 292, 302, 308
Wertsch, J., 83, 110
Wetzel, W., 208, 223
Whishaw, I., 141, 158, 180
Whitaker, D., 280, 281, 286, 299, 301,
    304, 308
Whitaker, H., 226, 227, 228, 252
Winsor, P., 289, 307
Whorton, J., 5, 22
Wiegel Crump, C., 227, 234, 239, 241,
    249, 254
Wilkinson, G., 216, 224
Wilkinson, J., 3, 21
Wilkinson, K., 264, 265, 266, 267, 273
Willats, P., 171, 185
Willett, J., 300, 308
Williams, M., 310, 333
Williams, R., 257, 273
Williams, S., 47, 49, 51, 52, 167, 182,
    188, 224
Willis, G., 140, 179
Willitt, J., 330, 335
Wilson, D., 61, 62, 72, 79
Wilson, R., 3, 22
Windmiller, M., 260, 272
Wing, L., 68, 72
Winikates, D., 323, 325, 328, 331, 322
Winslow, J., 75, 78
Wise, B., 293, 302, 308, 317, 321, 322,
    323, 324, 325, 335, 336, 337

Wisniewski, K., 65, 79
Witelson, S., 219, 224
Whitmore, K., 49, 51
Wolf, C., 321
Wolf, M., 228, 225, 227, 228, 232, 233,
    238, 239, 240, 248, 251, 252,
    254, 255, 286, 308, 321, 326,
    332, 337
Wood, F., 312, 333
Woodcock, R., 30, 52, 291, 308, 315,
    333
Woodin, M., 154, 156, 179
Woodward, S., 72, 79
Word + inc., 261, 274
Wright, N., 121, 135
Wu, E., 284, 304

Y

Yafee, L., 167, 182
Yakolev, P., 148, 185
Yatchmink, Y., 85, 110
Yates, C., 282, 286, 304, 305
Yeates, K., 120, 137
Yehigiazaryan, K., 65, 70, 78
Ylvisaker, M., 226, 251
Young, L., 75, 78 183
Young, J., 162, 136
Yule, W., 118, 136

Z

Zelazo, P., 132, 137, 160, 170, 185
Zametkin, A., 162, 185
Zax, M., 18, 22
Zecker, S., 191, 206, 221
Zelazo, P., 160
Zibovicius, M., 164
Zillmer, E., 144
Zimowski, M., 291
Zolman, J., 290
Zook, D., 294

Subject Index

A

Achievement Tests, 1
AB, 125, 126, 127, 128, 129, 130
AB Performance, 125
AB/DR, 130, 132
Academic, 24, 31, 35 42, 44, 47
Academic Attention, 34
Academic Difficulties, 24
Academic Performance, 24, 25
Academic Status, 24
Achievement, 42, 269, 270, 285, 291, 292, 293, 294, 295, 298, 214, 295, 314, 315, 316, 327, 328, 329
Achievement Scores, 4, 5, 6, 7, 10, 15, 16, 18, 19, 20
Achievement Tests, 2, 5, 6, 7, 8, 9, 16, 17, 18
Activity, 24, 31, 35, 40, 47, 49
Activity Category, 29
Activity/Impulsivity, 31, 34, 47
ADHD, 29, 30, 44, 45, 47, 49, 144, 163, 164, 165, 166, 167, 168, 172, 173
Adolescent MIT (ADMIT), 29, 30, 31, 34, 35, 36, 40, 42, 43, 44, 47, 48, 49, 50
Affective Significance, 68

A-not-B (AB) Tasks, 121
Asociality, 68
Attention, 24, 29, 31, 36, 40, 42, 47, 49, 113, 143, 286
Attention Deficit Hyperactivity Disorder (ADHD), 24, 162
Attention Scale, 28
Attentional Status, 24
Autism, 68, 70, 71, 72, 77, 162, 163, 164, 165, 167, 168, 172, 173
Autistic, 67, 73, 77, 127, 164

B

Behavior, 31, 34, 36, 40, 47, 49
Behavior Scale, 33
Behavior Scales, 28
Behavioral, 47
Behavioral Broadband Scale, 47
Behavioral Scale, 28
Behavioral Status, 24, 28
Biomedical, 2
Biomedical Risk, 2, 3, 5, 8, 17, 18
Biomedical Risks, 4, 6, 16, 70
Brain Deficit, 70
Brain Deficits, 57, 64, 71, 77
Brain Disorders, 189
Brain Structures, 57

Brain Tumors, 228, 231, 232, 233, 244, 248
Brain Wave, 220
Brain Wave Activity, 188, 189, 193, 205
Brain-Behavior Relation, 116
Brain-Behavior Relations, 114, 115, 132

C

Canalesthesia, 68
Canalization, 76
Canalized, 70
Central Nervous System (CNS), 57, 133
Chall's Model of Stages of Reading Development, 276, 287, 288
Chronological Age, 2, 7, 15, 17
Classroom Survival Skills Program (CSS), 313, 314, 315, 317, 326, 327
CLS, 43
CNS, 252
Cognitive Broadband Scale, 47
Cognitive Scale, 28
Communication, 232, 257, 258, 259, 263, 264
Communication Coding Scheme (CCS), 263
Communicative Use Probes (CUPS), 263
Comprehension, 282, 285, 287, 288, 297, 298, 318, 326, 329
Connecticut Longitudinal Study (CLS), 24, 29
Conversation, 61, 62, 63, 64
Crystallized Intelligence, 196
CSS, 327

D

Decoding Skills, (DS), 313
Delayed Response, 121
Developmental Disabilities, 116, 133
Developmental Disorders, 64, 65, 69
Developmental Neuropsychology, 113, 289, 303
Dexterity, 33, 35, 36
Disabilities, 18
Down Syndrome, 57, 65, 66, 69, 70, 71, 72, 73, 76, 77, 166

Downs, 197
DR, 125, 126, 127, 128, 129, 130
DS, 314, 315, 317, 326
DS Program, 316
Dyslexia, 118, 288, 312, 313, 317, 327
Dyslexic, 217, 311, 314, 316, 318, 320, 321
Dyslexic Children, 216, 217
Dyslexic's, 319

E

Ecological Domain, 59
Ecological Domains, 75
Ehri's Model, 278
Electroencephalogram (EEG), 188, 189
Environmental Factors, 6
Environmental Influences, 329
Event-Related Potential (ERP), 192, 196, 198, 206, 207, 208, 209, 210, 211, 212, 213, 214, 215, 217, 218, 219, 220
Executive Function, 113, 115, 116, 120, 130, 131, 142, 143, 144, 145, 148, 149, 151, 161, 162, 163, 164, 165, 166, 169, 171, 172, 173, 174
Executive Functions, 114, 115, 117, 133, 139, 140, 141, 146, 147, 152, 153, 286
Executive Skill, 132
Executive Skills, 113, 114, 117, 120
Extended Selective Attention, 68

F

False Negative, 187
Family Environment, 58
Flexibility, 141, 143, 144, 151, 158, 161, 163, 164, 166, 167
Flexible, 148, 152
Fluid Intelligence, 196
Flynn effect, 6
Focal Cerebral lesions, 226
Focal Damage, 225
Frith's Model of Word Recognition Development, 277, 287, 288
Frontal Cortex, 115, 141, 143, 147, 157

Frontal Lobe, 66, 114, 116, 128, 141,
      143, 147, 148, 149, 150, 151,
      162, 164, 173, 226
Frontal Lobes, 65, 68, 189
Frontal Metaphor, 133, 143

G

Gc, 197
Gender, 28, 35, 36, 47, 49, 209, 324
Gene, 60
General Ability, 196
Genes, 57, 58
Genetic, 65, 73, 133,162, 218, 219,
      296, 312
Gentry's Model, 279
Gf, 197

H

Hemidecorticate, 226
Henderson's Model, 278
Hippocampus, 65, 66, 68, 76
Home Observation for Measurement of
      the Environment, HOME, 2,
      3, 4, 6, 7, 9, 10, 15, 16, 18
Horn, 197

I

Individual Difference, 323
Individual Differences, 113, 118, 119,
      126, 129, 130, 132, 146, 275,
      309, 311, 312, 313, 315, 316,
      321, 325, 326
Individual Patterns, 113
Inhibition, 141, 142, 143, 144, 145,
      146, 147, 148, 150, 151, 152,
      155, 157, 158, 160, 161, 163,
      164, 165, 166, 167, 168, 169,
      172, 173, 174
Inhibitory Process, 171
Instructional Methods, 313
Intellectual, 196, 316
Intellectual Intelligence, 193
Intelligence, 2, 15, 16, 17, 18, 19, 20,
      118, 188, 189, 190, 193, 196,
      198, 204, 205, 218, 231, 232,
      258, 259, 312
Intelligence Scores, 4, 5, 6, 10, 15, 16,
      18, 20
Intelligence Tests, 1, 2, 3, 4, 5, 7, 8, 9,
      16, 17, 18
Intentional Communication, 259
Intraindividual, 297
Intraindividual Differences, 299, 303

L

Language, 24, 33, 35, 47, 142, 143,
      187, 188, 190, 193, 203, 204,
      206, 208, 209, 210, 211, 212,
      214, 215, 219, 220, 226, 233,
      248, 251, 252, 257, 258, 259,
      260, 263, 266, 269, 271, 276,
      313, 314, 316, 324, 326
Language Development, 258
Language Disorders, 226
Language II, 42
Language Sample, 245
Learn to Read, 296
Learned To Read, 277
Learning Disabilities, 1
Learning To Read, 290, 291
Left Brain Lesions, 227
Left Hemisphere Lesions, 226
Left Lesions, 227

M

Mean Categories Per Utterance, 246
Mean Length of Utterances, 247
Medical Risk, 7
Memory, 113, 114, 115, 143, 282, 286,
      311, 324
Mental Retardation, 257, 258, 259, 266
Mimic, 65, 66
Mimicry, 60, 61, 64, 74, 75
Multigrade Inventory for Teachers
      (MIT), 24, 25, 28, 29, 30, 34,
      35, 40, 42, 43, 47, 48, 49, 50
MIT Language, 31
Models of Spelling, 278
Models of Written Communication, 279
Modified Mean Length of Utterance, 245

Monitoring, 143

N

Naming, 225, 251, 290, 310, 311, 313, 321, 324, 326, 328
Naming Errors, 227, 240, 242, 246, 248, 249
Naming Problems, 228
Narrative, 226, 288
Neuroimaging Technologies, 148
Neurotransmitter, 75
Neurotransmitters, 71
Non Speech Sounds, 211
Nonreading Skill, 315
Nonreading Skills, 310
Nonword Reading, 315

O

Occipital Lobe, 67
Occipital Lobes, 67
Oppositional-Defiant Disorder (ODD), 29, 31, 34, 47, 49
Oral Written Language Stimulation (OWLS), 313, 314, 315, 317, 326
Orthographic, 278, 282, 284, 285, 287, 288, 289, 292, 294, 296, 297, 300
Orthography, 316

P

Parietal Lobe, 68
Parietal Lobes, 189
Perception, 143
PHAB/DI, 319, 320, 326, 327
Phenylketonuria (PKU), 162, 163, 164, 165, 166, 168, 172, 173, 197
Phineas Gage, 114
Phonemic Awareness, 319
Phonics Method, 276
Phonological, 282, 283, 284, 285, 287, 288, 289, 292, 294, 296, 297, 300

Phonological Awareness, 310, 311, 322, 323, 324, 325
Phonological Processing, 312, 315, 316, 318, 321, 327, 328
Place of Articulation (POA), 206, 207, 208
Planning, 140, 141, 142, 143, 144, 150, 151, 163, 164, 171, 280
Posterior Lesions, 225
Prefrontal, 162
Prefrontal Cortex6, 66, 114, 115, 128, 129, 141, 142, 149, 157, 162, 165

R

Read To Learn, 277, 287
Reading, 282, 283, 284, 285, 286, 288, 294, 295, 296, 298, 300, 301, 309, 310, 317, 323, 326
Reading Acquisition, 310
Reading Comprehension, 315
Reading Disabilities, 168, 285, 328, 329
Reading Disability, 42, 43, 48, 49, 50, 163, 310, 313, 315, 318
Reading Disabled, 166, 309, 312, 326
Reading Skill, 310, 311
Reading Skills, 216, 218, 316
Remediated, 313
Remediation, 311, 312, 321, 322, 329
Rett Syndrome, 57, 65, 66, 69, 70, 71, 72, 75, 76, 77
Right Brain Lesions, 226, 277
Right Hemisphere, 64, 129, 210, 211, 213, 215, 217
Right Hemisphere Lesions, 226
Right Lesions, 227

S

SAL, 258, 259, 260, 262, 263, 264, 265, 266, 269, 270
SES, 2, 3, 4, 5, 6, 7, 10, 15, 16, 18
Sex Differences, 126, 189
Sight Work Method, 276
Social Cohesion, 59, 60, 64

Social Domain, 59, 75
Social Interaction, 60, 61, 63, 64, 66, 67, 68, 70, 72, 73, 74, 77
Social Interaction Skills, 57
Social-Environment Scores, 18
Social-Environmental Measures, 9
Social-Environmental Variables, 16
Speech Disorders, 226
Speech Perception, 206, 207
Speech Skills, 218
Speech Sound Discrimination, 206, 208
Speech Sounds, 205, 206, 209, 211, 212, 216
Stage Model, 277, 281
Stage Models, 275, 286, 289, 295
Structural Equation Modeling, 131
Structure-Function Relation, 119
Structure-Functions Relations, 132
System For Augmenting Language, 271

T

TBI, 228
Temporal, 66
Temporal Lobe, 68
Temporal Lobes, 189
Text Generation, 280, 281
Time In School, 2, 6, 7, 10, 17
Tower of Hanoi (TOH), 131, 140, 141, 151, 152, 162, 163, 164, 165, 169, 171
Tower of London (TOL), 141, 151, 152, 171
Total Verbalizations, 245
Total Word-Finding Categories, 246
Transcription, 280
Traumatic Brain Injury (TBI), 226, 250, 251

True Positive, 187
Tumor Subgroup, 246, 250, 251
Tumor Subgroups, 235, 238, 239, 240, 242, 244, 249
Tumors, 228

V

Verbal Abilities, 17, 18
Verbal Scores, 2, 20, 203
Verbal Scores, 20, 203
Verbal Skills, 213, 214
Visual Event-Related Potential (VERP), 190, 192, 193, 196, 197, 198, 203, 204, 206
Vocabulary Assessment Measures (VAMs), 263, 265
Voice Onset Time (VOT), 206, 207, 208

W

Williams Syndrome, 57, 65, 67, 68, 69, 70, 71, 76, 77
Wisconsin Card Sorting Test (WCST), 141, 148, 151, 158, 167
Word Identification Strategy Training (WIST), 319, 320, 326, 327
Word Recognition Skill, 277
Working Memory, 121, 140, 141, 142, 144, 145, 146, 147, 148, 150, 151, 152 153, 154, 155, 156, 157, 158, 161, 163, 164, 165, 166, 168, 169, 171, 172, 173, 174, 282, 184, 310
Writing, 280, 281, 282, 283, 285, 286, 294, 295, 298, 299
Written Communication, 280

www.ingramcontent.com/pod-product-compliance
Ingram Content Group UK Ltd.
Pitfield, Milton Keynes, MK11 3LW, UK
UKHW020434010325
455677UK00029B/1152